Critical Political Theory and Radical Practice

Series Editor
Stephen Eric Bronner, Department of Political Science, Rutgers
University, New Brunswick, NJ, USA

D1610886

The series introduces new authors, unorthodox themes, critical interpretations of the classics and salient works by older and more established thinkers. A new generation of academics is becoming engaged with immanent critique, interdisciplinary work, actual political problems, and more broadly the link between theory and practice. Each in this series will, after his or her fashion, explore the ways in which political theory can enrich our understanding of the arts and social sciences. Criminal justice, psychology, sociology, theater and a host of other disciplines come into play for a critical political theory. The series also opens new avenues by engaging alternative traditions, animal rights, Islamic politics, mass movements, sovereignty, and the institutional problems of power. Critical Political Theory and Radical Practice thus fills an important niche. Innovatively blending tradition and experimentation, this intellectual enterprise with a political intent hopes to help reinvigorate what is fast becoming a petrified field of study and to perhaps provide a bit of inspiration for future scholars and activists.

More information about this series at
http://www.palgrave.com/gp/series/14938

Sabby Sagall

MUSIC and CAPITALISM

Melody, Harmony and Rhythm in the Modern
World

Sabby Sagall
London, UK

Critical Political Theory and Radical Practice
ISBN 978-1-349-70526-9   ISBN 978-1-137-52095-1   (eBook)
https://doi.org/10.1057/978-1-137-52095-1

Cover image: © Ekely/Getty Images

This Palgrave Macmillan imprint is published by the registered company Springer Nature America, Inc.
The registered company address is: 1 New York Plaza, New York, NY 10004, U.S.A.

For Hilary

ACKNOWLEDGEMENTS

A number of colleagues, comrades and friends read different parts of the manuscript and provided interesting and valuable comments or directed me to important sources and texts. I would like to thank Aidan Kelly, Professor Alison Sealey, Professor Barry Cooper, Professor Bob Carter, Daniel Snowman, Professor Frank Millward, James Conway, Jeremy Peyton-Jones, Jocelyn Pook, John Rees, Dr. John Rose, Jonathan Kenny, Luca Salice, Lucie Skeaping, Dr. Mark Abel, Mateusz Rettner, Mel Norris, Professor Michael Rustin, Rodula Gaitanou, Professor Roy Foster. I would also like to thank my jazz piano teacher Paul Abrahams. Steve Wald provided important technical support.

I greatly appreciate the encouragement and patience on the part of Palgrave series editor Stephen Bronner, my current editor Rebecca Roberts, but also former editors Brian O'Connor, John Stegner, Elaine Fan, Chris Robinson and Michelle Chen. I would also like to thank Dr. Kurt Jacobsen for suggesting that I write the book.

I would also like to thank my friends, Dr. George Paizis, Gerry Norris, Ken Muller, Michael Rosen, Mike Milotte for their interest and encouragement.

Any errors of fact or judgement remain my responsibility. I have tried to write this book in as jargon-free a style as possible. But given the complex development of modern European 'art-music', it is impossible to avoid all technical terminology. I have, therefore, compiled a glossary defining such terms and have italicised them in the text.

My partner Hilary Westlake edited the entire manuscript and compiled the index: her comments and suggestions, at times critical but always constructive, helped to sustain me in a long and at times difficult writing process.

Introduction

'... the effect of music is so very much more powerful and penetrating than is that of the other arts, for these speak only of the shadow, but music of the essence'. A. Schopenhauer.

Music is 'something which has made life worth living...'

'Without music, life would be a mistake'. Friedrich Nietszche.

"Poets, not otherwise than philosophers, painters, sculptors and musicians, are, in one sense, the creators, and, in another, the creations, of their age."
Percy Bysshe Shelley

Everyone loves music—if not every kind of music, then some kind or kinds. Nearly everyone in the modern world has experienced, mostly enjoyably, some public performance of some kind of music, whether it be a classical concert, an opera, a Broadway musical, or a pop concert, either live or on television or radio. Moreover, cinema is a central part of modern culture, and virtually all feature films and many, if not most, documentaries, carry a sound track with music.

Can we go further, however? Can we say that all human beings in all societies, including pre-modern and non-European communities, have created some kind of music, some specific style or form. There is no doubt that musical expression, whether public and collective or private and individual, is a universal experience. All human beings have experienced some form of public, collective musical performance. This is true whether we are ardent music lovers or feel we can take it or leave it. Nor should we forget informal, social music—school choirs, teenage parties, weddings, music from other drivers' car radios, buskers, 'musak'—the list is endless.

Thirdly, I want to argue that music, in common with the other arts, does not simply happen to be a universal phenomenon. Enjoyment of music, participation in music, either as practitioner or listener, is not a contingent matter, but a necessary one. We may not feel music is particularly important to us in our daily lives. We may rarely attend a public music performance. Nevertheless, the love of and need for music exists in all of us as a universal potential feature. It is an aspect of human nature, as is the need for the other arts.

But can we go further still? Can we apply this to our earliest development? Can we conclude that music is not simply a potential, an optional add-on, a luxury in the education of middle-class children, rather like a foreign language, but an essential subject for the training of all our children? Most politicians and educators relegate music to this minor league of subjects, assuming that music is an ephemeral pleasure, not something essential to the development of all children as human beings in a social world. It is for this reason that music is always the first subject to be cut when governments trim educational budgets. Their assumption is that music may be enjoyable, uplifting even, but it is an indulgence rather than a necessity, an extra that should remain within the private preserve of the family, not a discipline that warrants demands on the public purse, especially in a period of financial retrenchment. So, let us enjoy music, they say, but let us not go overboard in our estimation of its meaning and potential role, especially in a period of pandemic and economic crisis. In an education system that has become increasingly utilitarian, we prepare children to fulfil necessary jobs in the economy so that, as adults, they can work to bolster our country's position in the world. In such an atmosphere, music acquires a backseat, banished from the schools, or, if it features at all, it is confined to the sidelines, the Cinderella of the disciplines.

I want to argue, on the contrary, that the need for music and the ability to produce and enjoy it, is an essential element in our nature, that every human society known to our history has produced some characteristic style of musical production. Moreover, the confinement of classical musical education to the children of the elite and the middle class, and the termination of musical education or the apparent reduced ability to enjoy many kinds of 'art-music' on the part of many under-privileged children, is an expression of profound deprivation, one rooted in the social system of capitalism with its alienation and its various forms of exploitation and oppression.

In the first chapter of this book, I shall develop the argument about the universality of the potential for musical expression and enjoyment, and its objective basis in the human psyche. I shall go on to argue that the historical development of music, the changes in style and the divisions within it—for example, classical, pop, jazz, etc.—again are not arbitrary as they express but also help to shape the wider social structures and processes of our society. I shall argue that the development and changes in capitalist society, in its social structure, since the decline of European feudalism contextualises the emergence of 'modern' art music. The rise of capitalist social relations reveals the ways human beings have used their capacity to create and enjoy music as these have developed since roughly the end of the seventeenth and beginning of the eighteenth centuries. I shall be confining myself to western classical music since, sadly, there won't be the space, nor do I have the time or the expertise to develop a wider historical analysis embracing non-European and pre-modern styles or popular musical styles—though there has been much cross-fertilisation.

I also want to argue that music, like any art, is not merely a mirror of the world, its more or less accurate reflection, but a practical intervention in it. Of course, music, like the other arts, tells us truths about the world through its impact on our emotional life. As Trotsky put it—art helps us orient ourselves in the world. But does it do more than that? Does music help to shape that world? I shall discuss this debate in Chapter 1.

Chapters 2 to 5 will attempt to analyse the development of western music from the rise of the modern, capitalist world in the seventeenth and eighteenth centuries through the period of bourgeois revolution, economic growth and consolidation in the late eighteenth and nineteenth centuries to the onset of crisis and intensifying capitalist rivalry in the late nineteenth and twentieth centuries. I will take each period and attempt to relate four characteristic musical styles to the social, economic and political contexts in which they arose and outside of which they cannot be understood: late Baroque, Classical, Romantic and Modernist.

Of course, each of these historical societies, and the musical styles that predominated within them, are the product of human social action. They were created by human beings interacting with each other through different various forms of cooperation and conflict. This is true whether

we are looking at the German princes and Lutheran bishops of seventeenth and eighteenth-century Germany, the mercantile bourgeoisie or
the capitalist farmers of the seventeenth and eighteenth centuries in
England, France and the American colonies, or the industrial bourgeoisie
of nineteenth-century Europe. For example, if the late Baroque and Classical styles of the early and late eighteenth-century express the confidence
of the German Protestant church and the rising bourgeoisie of Europe, so
twentieth-century Modernism expresses the crisis of the bourgeois world.
In sum, this book will attempt to analyse the different styles as a means
of establishing the relationship of music to its social world.

This book is aimed not at musicologists or professional musicians but at
ordinary music lovers who want to know a bit more about music's social
origins. Some might ask, does one need to read a book, for example,
about sex in order to enhance one's enjoyment? I hope readers would
agree that any work that enhances our ordinary understanding and enjoyment of a positive human activity is worth reading. My readers will judge
whether or not I have been successful.

CONTENTS

CHAPTER 1

The Necessity of Music

The universality of music is a fact we are all aware of, especially in a global world which the huge increase in low-cost travel has made increasingly familiar since the 1960s. Whether we have visited a country in Europe or North America, Latin America, Africa, Asia or Australia, we have experienced some particular musical style, whether a European or non-European classical style or music performed in a local popular or folk style. We are also increasingly aware of different local, traditional instruments. Moreover, with so many channels on our media playing music from different countries, we don't necessarily need to travel to become aware of these different styles. We can often readily identify music that is Indian, Chinese, Brazilian, Russian, Middle Eastern and so on. We have become familiar with existing traditional forms of non-European music such as the Ihu music of the Amazon Indians or the different musical styles of pre-colonial Africa, for example, the Benga music of Kenya recalling the melodies of the Kenyan eight-string Nyatiti lyre.

What about the earliest human communities? Whereas we do have knowledge of Paleolithic forms of visual art (2.5–2 million years ago up to around 10,000 in Europe and the Middle East)—for example, cave paintings—no record of prehistoric music survives since no form of musical notation had yet been created. Evidence of the existence of music in those times does exist, however, with the discovery of early instruments such as flutes made out of bone (Storr 1997, p. 1). And according to

© The Author(s) 2021
S. Sagall, *MUSIC and CAPITALISM*,
Critical Political Theory and Radical Practice,
https://doi.org/10.1057/978-1-137-52095-1_1

Goodall, the oldest list of musical instruments—that is, objects made as instruments, not simply found and used as such—was discovered on a clay tablet in Mesopotamia (modern Iraq) and dated 2600 BC. One instrument mentioned is the 'kinnor', the hand-held harp-like instrument also known in its ancient Greek version as a lyre. A slightly younger Babylonian clay tablet, dating from 2000–1700 BC, provides basic details of how to learn and tune a four-stringed fretted lute, including instructions on which notes to play. This is the oldest surviving readable notation, though sadly none of the lutes have survived (Goodall 2013, p. 9).

What are the reasons for this universality? Does it have roots in the human psyche and body? Blacking argues that 'many, if not all, of music's essential processes can be found in the constitution of the human body and in patterns of interaction of bodies in society' (Blacking 1974, pp. x–xi).

Research has shown that listening to music stimulates both emotional and physiological changes. Investigations by psychologist Roger Brown revealed the existence of widespread consensus between listeners about the emotional content of different pieces of music even when the listeners don't recognise them or cannot identify them (Brown 1981, quoted in Storr 1997, p. 30).

However, to conclude that the emotions expressed in the music—joy, sadness, fear—are necessarily those aroused in the listener is to oversimplify. As Storr points out, Othello's suicide is profoundly moving but it doesn't make us suicidal, unless one were already in a suicidal state, one might add. What moves us is the way Shakespeare and Verdi make sense out of tragedy by integrating it into an artistic whole (Storr 1997, p. 30). So there isn't a simple deterministic relationship between emotional meaning and emotional effect.

In general, we know how music arouses the majority of us who respond to it, creating an enhanced mood of awareness, interest and even excitement. Many of these changes reveal themselves physiologically and can be measured on an electro-encephalogram, for example, dilution of the eye pupil, a rise or fall of the respiratory rate, a rise in blood pressure. In addition, an electro-myograph reveals increases in electrical activity in the leg muscles while listening to music. Some people are driven to beat time with their feet or drum with their fingers, even in a concert hall. A study of tracings recorded the increase in Herbert von Karajan's pulse-rate while conducting Beethoven's Leonora No. 3 overture. His pulse-rate showed the greatest increase during those passages which moved him emotionally rather than those that required the greatest physical effort. Also note-worthy is the fact that his pulse-rate revealed much slower fluctuations when he was piloting and landing a jet aircraft (Storr 1997, pp. 25–26).

In addition, there is the apparently closer relation between hearing and emotional arousal than between seeing and arousal. In the days of silent films, a pianist was always present to sharpen the emotional impact of the various scenes—love, fear, awe. A friend of Storr's, on visiting the Grand Canyon for the first time, was surprised at his lack of response. He then realised that he had seen it on the screen many times but always with music. The sight of it in reality without music created a weaker response than seeing it in the cinema. Moreover, seeing a wounded person or animal who is silent may provoke little emotional response in someone. But if they scream, the observer will generally be strongly aroused. 'At an emotional level, there is something 'deeper' about hearing than seeing; and something about hearing other people which fosters human relationships even more than seeing them' (Storr 1997, p. 26).

The human capacity to create and enjoy music is rooted in our physi-ological make-up, with our musical ability located in a distinct part of the brain, separate from that which governs speech. Language is predom-inantly processed in the brain's left hemisphere while our capacity to scan and appreciate music occurs in the right hemisphere. However, the division of functions is not primarily that between words and music but between logic and emotion. When words arouse or give voice to emotions, as in poetry and song, the experience corresponds to activity in the right hemisphere. When conceptual thought occurs, the phys-ical correlate is in the left hemisphere. The musician portrayed in Oliver Sacks's 'The Man Who Mistook His Wife for a Hat' suffered from a brain lesion which meant he could not recognise the nature of objects. But his musical capacity was undamaged, so that he could only eat, dress or wash if he sang. Music became the only means by which he could relate to and organise the world around him. Indeed, the effects of music on patients suffering from neurological disorders can be astonishing.

How does music impact our repetitive physical actions? Of music's three predominant aspects—melody, harmony, rhythm,—the latter is clearly the most important factor in music's effect on our repetitive actions. The roots of rhythm lie in our physical make-up in a way that isn't so directly the case with melody or harmony (Storr 1997, p. 33).

The capacity of music to evoke similar emotional and physical responses in different people means it is able to bring individuals and groups together. Music is a supreme unifier, despite the fact that different individuals will respond to a piece of music in different ways, for example, a musician and a listener unversed in music. For example, a dirge or funeral march will be experienced differently by different people who will nevertheless share aspects of the musical experience, seeing it within the context of the total event and sharing the emotions it arouses.

ORIGINS AND FUNCTIONS OF MUSIC

Music is also a method of communication between people. But what does it communicate? It isn't generally a representational art, providing us with images of the external world, with some notable exceptions—Beethoven's 'Pastoral' symphony, Schubert's 'Trout' quintet, Delius's 'On Hearing the First Cuckoo in Spring'. Nor does it offer us theories or information about the world in the way language does.

There are two approaches to the question of the significance of music: one is to examine its origins—how did it begin? How did it become so complex and varied? Is it an aspect of human nature? There is no universal agreement about this. The second question is to ask whether the different styles are related to social processes? And what has music's functions in different historical societies been?

The sounds which constitute music, generally referred to as tones, are not the same as those which emanate from nature such as the sounds of animals, the various forms of running water or trees in a breeze. Each musical tone is made up of soundwaves at a specific pitch, high or low, and the assembling of different tones that make-up a piece of music is a human creation. 'Nature's sounds, with the exception of birdsong and some other calls between animals, are irregular noises rather than the sustained notes of definable pitch which go to form music... "tones"... are separable units with constant auditory waveforms which can be repeated and reproduced' (Storr 1997, p. 3).

Moreover, science can analyse the differences between musical tones in terms of *pitch*, loudness, *timbre* or soundwaves, but it cannot convey that specific combination of tones which constitutes music. There continues to be much disagreement about the origins, purpose and meaning of music but general agreement that it bears only a distant link with the sounds and rhythms of nature. Music is, in fact, the most abstract of the arts, normally lacking any formal, concrete external references. However, given its central, universal use as a vital means of expressing human emotions and attitudes, it is much more than a disembodied set of relationships between sounds. Music penetrates to the core of our being, it can move us emotionally like nothing else. Yet the precise nature of its links to our lives and emotions is hard to pin down.

Is music related to sounds emitted by other species, for example, bird-song? Birds emit both noises and tones in their 'singing', with a high proportion of tones, leading some observers to argue that their sound does constitute music. According to Charles Hartshorne, 'bird songs resemble human music both in the sound patterns and in the behaviour setting' (Hartshorne 1973, p. 56, in Storr 1997, p. 4). Birds sing in order to indicate a certain territory as desirable, and male birds sing more vigorously when searching for a mate and also to repel rivals. Hartshorne believes that birds sing much more than is required for communication, concluding that they sing as an expression of 'joie de vivre' (Hartshorne 1973, p. 56, in Storr 1997, p. 5). However, other analysts argue that bird singing is too physically demanding for it to be undertaken except as a means of fulfilling some necessary function.

So the issue is whether human music originated as an imitation of birdsong. Storr rejects this notion on two grounds: firstly, if human music did begin as birdsong, we should be able to point to examples of music in pre-literate communities resembling it. However, what we find instead are complex, rhythmic patterns in no way resembling avian sounds. Secondly, birdsong is complex and cannot easily be imitated. There are, of course, famous pieces of music that suggest the sound of birdsong—Liszt's 'Legende No. 1, St. Francois d'Assise', for piano solo, suggesting the twittering of birds around St. Francis, Dvorak's 'American' Quartet' with its imitation of the scarlet tanager, 'Hens and Roosters' from Saint-Saens' 'Carnival of the Animals', Vaughan Williams' 'The Lark Ascending', Respighi's 'The Birds' and the master of 'musical ornithology' Olivier Messiaen with his 'La Merle Noir'—'The Blackbird'.

However, these examples occur relatively late in the development of music and there is no evidence that early humans were interested in birdsong since it would have been of little relevance to their immediate practical needs.

We move up the evolutionary scale—from birds to subhuman primates—gelada monkeys who emit a wide variety of sounds of different pitches, rhythms and accents which accompany all their social interactions. The specific sound which a gelada monkey emits indicates his or her emotional state at the time, and, over the longer term, facilitates the development of lasting bonds between individuals. If tensions arise, these can on occasion be resolved through coordinating vocal expressions. The result is, as Richman puts it: 'a culturally agreed-upon pattern of rhythm and melody, i.e. a song, that is sung together, provides a shared form of emotion that... carries along the participants so that they experience their bodies responding emotionally in very similar ways. This is the source of the feeling of solidarity and good will that comes with choral singing...' (Richman, Bruce, April 1987, in Storr 1997, p. 7).

Another theory of the origins of music suggests that it emerged from the babbling of infants, sounds which can sometimes be described as tones. Infant babbling seems to express both tones and incipient words. However, Harvard psychologist Howard Gardner disputes this, arguing that children's early melodic fragments have no strong musical identity. Not until they reach a year and a half do children develop the ability to produce discrete pitches. During the following year, children often use discrete pitches—seconds, *minor* and *major* thirds—and by the age of two or two and a half start to notice and learn songs sung by others. According to Geza Revesz, babies' lallation in their second year are shaped by songs picked up from music they have been exposed to. If so, then one can't argue that music itself developed from infant lalling (Revesz 1953, p. 229 in Storr 1997, p. 8).

So the question whether or not music is specific to the human species, having seemed somewhat straightforward to begin with, now appears rather more complicated, with the lines of separation between humans and monkeys emerging as somewhat blurred. Perhaps the issue is incapable of definitive resolution.

In ancient Greek society, the cradle of European civilisation, music had an important place. Although advanced instrumental skills were confined to professionals, as in modern European society, the Greeks believed that playing the lyre and singing should be part of every freeman's education. Music was widely played at domestic celebrations and feasts, and in religious rituals. Music competitions and athletic contests were held alongside each other.

Moreover, music and poetry were inseparable: Homer's poetry, for example, was recited with lyre accompaniment. Poet and composer were often the same person: indeed, the Greek word 'melos' signified both music and poetry. It is the root of our word 'melody'. Hence, whereas modern Western verse is mainly linguistic, consisting of words which may or may not be set to music, the language in ancient Greek verse contained within itself a musical rhythm (Storr 1997, pp. 14–15).

However, the musical element gradually shrank, replaced by a system of accents bearing little relation to the original rhythm and which were not intoned at different pitches as music would be. In other words, poetry was now determined by linguistic patterns where verse rhythms are determined by stress rather than pitch. Musicians and poets were now separate people, and it became possible to set both prose and poetry to music in ways with which we are familiar. This also meant that music and language could be reunited when it was so desired, as, for example, in the Christian liturgy.

Jean-Jacques Rousseau, revolutionary social thinker and accomplished composer, also delved into this issue. For him, in the earliest human societies, there was no distinction between speech and song: their languages were melodic rather than prosaic and were chanted rather than spoken. In other words, it was their passions rather than their practical needs which prompted their first utterances (Cranston 1983, pp. 289–290 in Storr 1997, p. 12). Moreover, according to psychoanalyst and musician Anton Ehrenzweig, '… speech and music have descended from a common origin in a primitive language which was neither speaking nor singing, but something of both' (Ehrenzweig 1975, pp. 164–165, in Storr 1997, p. 16). Hence, music and language share a common precursor.

We can surmise that as song and speech moved apart, the differences in their functions became more emphasised. As society developed, so the forms of language changed, especially with the emergence of rational thought and science. Prose became more impersonal, more objective, less metaphorical and was used in conveying information and expressing ideas, whereas poetic forms of speech and music were now the means of expressing religious and other rituals.

So, debate about the origins of music is not new: it also exercised the minds of the Victorians. According to Herbert Spencer, when we use speech to express emotions, the sounds we emit span a greater tonal range and thus approximate to music. Darwin drew the opposite conclusion: he believed that music preceded speech and arose as an expression of mating calls. He observed that male animals with a vocal apparatus emit voice sounds most frequently when experiencing sexual arousal. And a sound originally used to attract a potential mate could be elaborated into speech (Spencer, London, 1857, Darwin, The Descent of Man, and 'Selection in Relation to Sex', 1871, in Gearney, Edmund, 'The Power of Sound', London, Smith, Elder, 1880, p. 119, in Storr 1997, p. 11).

Geza Revesz produced an additional theory derived from Carl Stumpf. Observing that the singing voice has greater power than the speaking voice, Revesz surmised that early humans, when needing to communicate with their fellows, found that they could do so more effectively by singing rather than speaking. He argued that emitting loud, resounding signals is pleasurable, and concluded that such calls can easily pass over into song. In other words, he attempted to derive all music from the yodel.

Now, musical sounds are indeed used by pre-literate people for distance communication. Wind instruments have also been invented for this purpose. Moreover, signalling by means of drums and horns is widespread in Africa and elsewhere. And the Mura Native Americans of the Amazon communicate across great rivers in a special musical language played on a three-holed flageolet. However, as Storr points out, communication using musical sounds does not in itself constitute music. Nor is there evidence that such signals became transformed into music. Revesz's theory fails to account for the rhythmic element in music: neither he nor Darwin nor Spencer seem able to tell us why music appealed to early humans and their descendants, why it came to play such an important role in our lives (McLaughlin 1970, p. 14, in Storr 1997, p. 12).

Deryck Cooke tried to demonstrate that there was a consensus among composers in the Western tradition as to which musical devices represent specific emotions. For example, the interval of a *major* third generally expresses joy, while the *minor* third is usually associated with grief. The augmented fourth, labelled *diabolus in musica* by medieval theorists due to its 'flawed' sound, is often used to depict demons or other horrors (Cooke 1959/1962, pp. 88–89).

Music, and the enormous variety of musical styles—'art-music', pop, jazz, folk—are created by human beings, not in the abstract but within specific contexts of culture and social relations. Every musical work, indeed every work of art, can be located within a specific aesthetic system, a system of rules and conventions, which is what the word 'style' refers to. As Leichtentritt puts it: 'Even the most revolutionary art has its conventional traits—one may go so far as to define style as a sum of conventional features—for without certain well-established conventions, no great art of any kind can exist' (Leichtentritt 1954, p. 151). Moreover, no musical work can be appreciated to the full unless the listener has a degree of familiarity with that style. And as will become evident in subsequent chapters, no composer, no artist, can resist the power of the dominant ideas of their age.

Henry Raynor develops the argument further, that '…music is not written and does not exist in a vacuum. The composer, whether or not he likes to recognise the fact, lives in some relationship to his age and a community, for even the most inaccessible of ivory towers is only a negative relationship to his age and his community' (Raynor 1972, p. 5). It is, of course, the principal theme of this book that the changing musical styles of successive historical eras, express the socio-economic and political contexts within which they were developed.

In other words, these styles are not the mechanical product of those external contexts but are shaped and influenced by them. Humans create music in order to make sense of their social environment, to enable them to cope with the challenges they face collectively and individually, and as part of the process of shaping and re-shaping their relationships and the social and natural world they inhabit. As John Blacking put it: 'Music is a synthesis of cognitive processes which are present in culture and in the human body: the forms it takes, and the effects it has on people, are generated by the social experiences of human bodies in different cultural environments. Because music is humanly organised sound, it expresses aspects of the experience of individuals in society' (Blacking 1974, p. 89). As Trotsky put it: 'Art is one of the ways in which man finds his bearings in the world' (Trotsky 1963, p. 12). Specifically, the leading composers of the different eras expressed in music the aspirations of the dominant or aspiring social classes.

Hence, the theoretical assumption underlying the analysis in this book is that there is some kind of homology or structural correspondence between society and music. For example, the competitiveness of the rising bourgeoisie in the late seventeenth and eighteenth-century Europe is perhaps mirrored in Bach's version of 'luxuriant *counterpoint*', the interpenetration of harmony and *counterpoint*, where the dividing lines between melody, bass line and harmony are blurred, creating a quasi-competitive situation between treble and bass lines (see Chapter 2); or where the Classical bass line becomes the treble line's equal partner in melodic development so that the principles of Liberty, Equality and Fraternity, seem to liberate the bass from its role of service to the upper instruments (see Chapter 3).

In sum, the music of Bach and Handel cannot be understood in isolation from the social practice and understanding of the world of the eighteenth-century bourgeoisie. Moreover, the aesthetic theories of that age comprised 'a complicated doctrine of emotional expression, going back to certain primitive correlations of rhythm and melodic line with the various emotions...' (Leichtentritt 1954, p. 143). The new spirit—scientific, rationalist, philosophical—is a powerful component of music around 1720. Bach and Handel are the composers who introduced it into music with a superior artistic instinct. Naturally, no composer sat down to analyse the socio-political character and ethos of their time and consciously fit their style to these features. Art is largely unconscious, as Trotsky attested.

I am not arguing that classical music was determined by these social changes, but they did create a new framework that helped to shape the new style. Composers internalised, as we all do, the social institutions around them, albeit unconsciously. Society was not directly reflected in music but mediated though the composers' activity.

Moreover, no Chinese Wall separates 'art-music' from popular music. Often, features of the former are derived from conventions in the latter. We shall see this particularly in Romantic music—Chopin, Verdi, Tchaikovsky, Dvorak—but also in Classical and Modernist music: Haydn and Beethoven used folk songs, as, of course, did composers such as Bartok who drew heavily on Hungarian peasant songs. The Classical emphasis on melody was also indebted to the folk songs and dance tunes of the ordinary people; 'it was indeed of the same type, but a little more finished, shaped by an artist's hand, fitted for use in a composition of larger dimensions' (Leichtentritt 1954, p. 164).

A second, subsidiary theme running through this book, as suggested in the Introduction, is that changes in musical style not only reflect, but in turn also help to shape changes in society and social movements. 'Art is not a mirror held up to reality but a hammer with which to shape it'. This statement has been attributed to both Brecht and Mayakovsky. Trotsky says something almost identical in 'Literature and Revolution' (Trotsky 1960, p. 137). And as Ernst Fischer argued, 'art is... never merely a clinical description of reality. Its function is always... to enable the 'I' to identify itself with another's life... Art is necessary in order that man should be able to recognise and change the world'. Rouget de Lisle, an officer in the French revolutionary army, composed *La Marseillaise* in 1792. He may well have heard 'Mozart's Piano Concerto No.

25' (1786), whose *allegro* maestoso contains a remarkably similar *theme*. Arguably, Beethoven's music did not merely reflect revolutionary Europe and North America in the late eighteenth and early nineteenth centuries, but helped to create that world. The Russian writer Gorki relates how Lenin described Beethoven: 'I know of nothing better than the Appassionata and could listen to it every day. What astonishing, superhuman music! It always makes me proud, perhaps naively so, to think that people can work such miracles!' [Gorki, *V.I. Lenin*, 1896–1899]. Could Beethoven have helped inspire Lenin to develop his vision of a socialist world?

Later examples are the nationalisms expressed in the operas of Verdi and Wagner, and in Chopin's Romanticism: all these gave significant encouragement to the Italian, German and Polish nationalist political movements of the mid-nineteenth century. We see it, too, in Mozart's 'The Marriage of Figaro'.

Music's role as resistance and its unconscious character were also underlined by Trotsky: 'Generally speaking, art is an expression of man's need for a harmonious and complete life... his need for those major benefits of which a society of classes has deprived him. That is why a protest against reality, either conscious or unconscious, active or passive, optimistic or pessimistic, always forms part of a really creative piece of work. Every new tendency in art has begun with rebellion' (Trotsky 1950, p. 61).

In modern times, there are powerful examples drawn from popular music—jazz as the music of the American black community, the popular songs of the 1960s, expressing the revolt of the youth, or today, the music of the Palestinian people.

In 1999, Palestinian scholar Edward Said and Israeli musician Daniel Barenboim founded the West Eastern Divan Orchestra bringing together young musicians from the Middle East, including Palestine and Israel. It surely counts as an expression of cultural resistance despite its drawbacks (the Israeli musicians have to do military service) since, as an artistic union, it flies directly in the face of the ethnic exclusiveness of the Israeli state.

In Barenboim's book 'Everything is Connected: The Power of Music', there is a chapter, 'A Tale of Two Palestinians', in which he describes how the lives of two young Palestinians were transformed by music. As a music student in France, Ramzi Aburedwan 'enriched the musical life of the conservatory with Middle Eastern harmonies' (Barenboim 2009, p. 96).

He also created an association to collect money for the musical education of Palestinian children and organised a day of benefit concerts of 'musicians for Palestine'. Saleem Abboud Ashkar complained that the only Arab literature included in his Israeli education was either Egyptian or pre-Islamic: contemporary Palestinian literature would be too politicised and would present the difficult issue of Palestinian identity (Barenboim 2009, pp. 98 and 102).

Palestinian writer Nadine Sayegh describes the recent development of music in the Palestinian territories. 'Many of the musicians emerging in the early noughties did so as an act of resistance against the Israeli occupation… With lyrics attacking the occupiers, the occupying forces—and even the Palestinian Authority—it stirs the imagination of the audience to a possible alternative to their current station in life' (Sayegh, online article, 2018).

Theodor Adorno's philosophy of music also attempts to relate music to society. 'Music's processes, the result of human labour, are invariably always already socially anchored… they carry social meanings, though indirectly' (Leppert 2002, p. 98). For Adorno, 'musical truth' is ascertained by the way composers situate themselves within musical history, firstly, how they deal with the forms and materials they inherit, secondly with the way 'the composer reflects the existing social conditions via the formal structure of the composition… For music to be truthful, it must express in structural form the reality of social life, a reality that is obscured by the cliches inherent in the commodified art that dominates culture under late capitalism' (Behrman 2009, p. 122). However, Adorno here neglects the extent to which the late Baroque and Classical styles evoke the aspirations of the radical bourgeoisie, their demands for freedom, their determination to sweep away the old feudal order and build a new society. Also, Adorno's elitism leads him to over-emphasise the composer's relationship to musical history, ignoring the impact on them of political struggles. He believed in music's potential to uphold the strength of 'subjectivity'—artistic and political agency—in the face of an 'objectivity'—the existing social and musical world seeking to constrain it. But he saw virtually all twentieth-century music and the culture industry as having stifled the possibility of radical change (Abel 2020, p. 14).

A brief look, finally, at the work of French scholar Jacques Attali and American feminist musicologist Susan McClary. Attali seems to use the term 'noise' to describe the condition of the planet, of nature and human society: all are characterised by violence and destructiveness, of rivalry and death. So, noise is violence, but '*music is a channelization of noise*, a simulacrum of the sacrifice... thus a sublimation...' (Attali 1985, p. 26). It controls and conquers 'noise' by creating a harmonious order in the realm of sound. In so doing, it upholds and legitimises the social order in general. The result was the creation of hierarchy and social stability. It has thus from the outset been a key tool of the ruling class of every society (Johanning 1998, p. 2). Music seems here to be the equivalent of Hobbes' Leviathan state, whereby social cohesion is achieved through a strong, undivided government.

Attali argues that at any moment in any society, a struggle is taking place between the 'official' music, which reflects the existing order and functions to channel people's aggression into harmony with that order, and a subversive counter-music which expresses the anger of those excluded from power and struggling to determine a new form of society. Attali offers an analysis of the development of western music from its origins in ritual up to modern recording. He argues that music has gone through four cultural stages in its history.

(a) 'Sacrificing' describes music's pre-history—the period of the oral tradition (prior to 1500 CE)—before notation, when music exists in people's memory in the form of songs and folk stories. Music is contrasted to the 'noise' of nature—of death, chaos and destruction. Music's function is to preserve and transmit that cultural heritage through strengthening our collective memory. Attali calls the chapter 'Sacrificing' since in this era music and the rituals surrounding it sublimates the violence of nature.

(b) 'Representing' refers to the era of printed music -roughly 1500–1900. For the first time, music becomes linked to a physical medium, a commodity for sale on the market. It becomes a 'spectacle attended at specific places: concert halls... a confinement made necessary by the collection of entrance fees' (Attali 1985, p. 32).

(c) 'Repetition' appears at the end of the nineteenth century with the arrival of recording. This technology created a new 'organisational network for the economy of music... The consumption of music is individualised... the network is no longer... an opportunity for spectators to meet and communicate, but rather a tool making the individualised stockpiling of music possible...' (Attali 1985, p. 32).

(d) 'Composition' is the final stage, beyond exchange, in which music could potentially be performed for the musician's own enjoyment, for communing with oneself, a solitary, non-commercial act'.

Attali also claims that the changes which occur in music predict the shape of future societies. Changes in music foreshadow changes in society (Johanning 1998, p. 1). At first sight, this is putting the cart before the horse and smacks of idealist philosophy whereby ideas or cultural artefacts shape social formations. We are arguing, on the contrary, that music reflects and expresses the major social and political processes, events and structures, of the composer's epoch. However, there are examples which validate Attali's claim. Mozart's operas 'The Marriage of Figaro' (1786) and 'Don Giovanni' (1787) are harbingers of the French revolution. But they also reflect the rise of bourgeois social and economic power, as does 'The Magic Flute' (1791).

Attali's work analyses the relationship of music to its consumers and creators, noting the changes as determined by changes in technology. It doesn't relate the changes in musical style to social and political changes— the relationship of late Baroque to early capitalism, of the Classical style to bourgeois political revolution, of Romantic style to the disillusion at the failure of political revolution, of Modernism to the crisis of the capitalist order. It lumps together in a single category these different styles of *tonal* and *atonal* music.

Three specific criticisms can be made of Attali's analysis.

Firstly, is music the sublimation of ritualised human sacrifice, and more broadly, of social violence? Attali is not an anthropologist and, therefore, lacks the knowledge to adduce counter-examples such as the social solidarity both within and between various tribal communities.

Secondly, Attali claims to provide a materialist analysis of music. However, the book encompasses far too broad a historical sweep of music since the middle ages, lumping together very different periods and social formations, therefore obscuring important differences in musical style. The entire 'modern' period from 1500 to 1900 is subsumed within the single category of 'repetition' simply on the grounds of technology—the fact of printed music. He fails to differentiate between the various phases of Baroque, and the Classical, Romantic and Modernist styles.

Thirdly, Attali's dependence on Adorno results in his failure to provide sufficient insight into the liberationist features of modern music—late Baroque as expressing the aspiration of the rising European bourgeoisie,

Classical style as the political expression of that emerging class, Romanticism as the lament over the failure of the promises of the French revolution, Modernism as expressing the crisis of capitalist society.

Attali also argues that 'it is deceptive to conceptualise a succession of musical codes corresponding to a succession of economic and political relations... because time traverses music and music gives meaning to time'. By this, he presumably means that time is above history and society, and that music structures time outside of our economic and political relations. However, as Mark Abel argues, 'the meaning of time, and possibly even time itself, is socially and historically constructed, and, therefore, a study of changes in the organisation of time in music is one way of tracing its history' (Abel 2015, p. 7). We shall see how changes in rhythmic patterns, varying approaches to accents and beats, are influenced by social and historical factors.

In 1991, Susan McClary put forward a feminist critique of classical music which shocked and unsettled conservative musicologists. She refers to the musical term 'feminine ending'—formerly used to describe a weak phrase or movement ending on an unstressed beat or weak *cadence*; a 'masculine' *cadence* occurs if the final chord of a section occurs on a strong beat (Harvard 1970, in McClary 1991, p. 9). The book analyses musical constructions of sexuality and the gendered aspects of traditional music theory and sonata form.

According to McClary, the rise of opera in the seventeenth century sees composers working to develop a musical 'semiotics' (study of signs or symbols) of gender—'a set of conventions for constructing 'masculinity' or 'femininity' in music' (McClary 1991, p. 7). The codes indicating gender difference in music are shaped by the prevailing attitudes of their time. But they in turn help to shape social formations insofar as individuals are partly socialised into gendered beings through their interactions with cultural discourses such as music. Music does not just passively reflect society; it also serves as a public forum within which various models of gender organisation... are... adopted...' (McClary 1991, pp. 7–8).

Similarly, among the narrative paradigms that emerged during the history of *tonality* are gendered features such as the custom of describing the opening *theme* of a *sonata* as 'masculine' and the second *theme* 'feminine'. 'The second theme... serves as contrast to the first, energetic statement, though dependent on and determined by it. It is of a more tender nature, flexibly rather than emphatically constructed... the feminine as opposed to the preceding masculine' (A.B. Marx [1845] in

McClary 1991, p. 13). The primary key represents 'masculine protagonist' 'while satisfactory resolution… demands the containment of whatever is… structurally marked as "feminine", whether a second theme or
simply a non-tonic key area' (McClary 1991, p. 15).

McClary's analysis is valuable in shedding light on gendered aspects
of European art music. It highlights the way traditional sexist attitudes
and values informed every social and cultural institution, even the most
rarefied art such as music.

An additional important consideration is that artists need a sense of
community, to identify with the wider society, or at least sections of
it. Their stylistic choices are not made in the abstract but flow in part
from the artists' own social needs and ideas, and their political aspirations
(Locke 1986, p. 121).

Bibliography

Abel, Mark. 2015. *Groove-An Aesthetic of Measured Time*. Chicago: Haymarket
Books.

Abel, Mark. 2020. *The Politics of the Subject-Object Dialectic in Adorno's Musical
Aesthetics*. University of Brighton, research output.

Adorno, Theodor W. 2002. *Why Is the New Art so Hard to Understand?* In
Essays on Music, ed. Richard Leppert. University of California Press.

Attali, Jacques. 1985. *Noise: The Political Economy of Music*. University of
Minnesota.

Barenboim, Daniel. 2009. *Everything Is Connected: The Power of Music*. Weidenfeld & Nicolson.

Behrman, Simon. 2009. *From Revolution to Irrelevance: How Classical Music Lost
Its Relevance*. International Socialism Journal 121 (January).

Blacking, John. 1974. *How Musical Is Man?* Seattle and London: University of
Wasington Press.

Bloom, Peter. 1974. *Letter*. Journal of the American Musicological Society 27
(1).

Boyd, Malcolm. 1993. *Rome: The Power of Patronage*, ed. G. J. Buelow.
Macmillan Press Ltd.

Cooke, Deryck. 1959/1962. *The Language of Music*. Oxford University Press.

Cranston, Maurice. 1983. *Jean-Jacques*. London: Allen Lane.

Ehrenzweig, Anton. 1975. *The Psychoanalysis of Artistic Vision and Hearing*, 3rd
ed. London: Sheldon Press.

Gearney, Edmund. 1880. *The Power of Sound*. London: Smith, Elder.

Goodall, Howard. 2013. *The Story of Music*. London: Vintage Books.

Harman, Chris. 1999. *A People's History of the World*. London: Bookmarks.

Hartshorne, Charles. 1973. *Born to Sing*. Bloomington: Indiana University Press.
Johanning, Jon, online review of Attali, 1998.
Leichtentritt, Hugo. 1954. *Music, History and Ideas*. Cambridge, MA: Harvard University Press.
Locke, Ralph, P. 1986. *Music, Musicians and the Saint-Simonians*. University of Chicago Press.
McClary, Susan. 1987. *The Blasphemy of Talking Politics During Bach Year*, in *Music and Society: The Politics of Composition, Performance and Reception*, ed. R. Leppert & S. McClary. Cambridge University Press.
McClary, Susan. 1991. *Feminine Endings*. University of Minnesota.
McLaughlin, Terence. 1970. *Music and Communication*. London: Faber & Faber.
Raynor, Henry. 1972. *A Social History of Music: From the Middle Ages to Beethoven*. London: Barrie & Jenkins.
Revesz, Geza. 1953. *Introduction to the Psychology of Music*, trans. G.I.C. de Courcy. London: Longman.
Richman, Bruce. 1987. *Rhythm and Melody in Gelada Vocal Exchanges*, in *Primates* 28, (April): 199–223.
Sayegh, Nadine. 2018. www.trtworld.com/opinion/music-as-a-form-of-resistance-in-Palestine.
Stauffer, George B. 1993. *Leipzig: A Cosmopolitan Trade Center*, in *The Late Baroque Era: From the 1680s to 1740*, ed. G. J. Buelow. Macmillan Press.
Storr, Anthony. 1997. *Music and the Mind*. London: HarperCollins.
Trotsky, Leon. 1950. *Art and Politics in Our Epoch*, in Partisan Review 11, no. 2, March–April: 61–64.
Trotsky, Leon. 1960. *Literature and Revolution*. Ann Arbor Paperback, University of Michigan Press.
Trotsky, Leon. 1963. *Culture and Socialism*. London: New Park Publications.

CHAPTER 2

The Late Baroque Style

Part I: Musical Background

The earliest harmony we know of, developed by the Greeks, used only octaves, that is, the same two notes, one at a higher pitch. The earliest recorded attempts at harmony in ninth-century Europe added only a third note to the octave. This type of harmony was called organum and it moved in parallel fourths and fifths (i.e. chords later described as consisting of the *tonic*, and the *subdominant*, or else the *tonic* and the *dominant*) (Cooke 1959/1962, p. 42). Around the eighth century, the medieval church attempted to introduce order into 'plainchant' music by borrowing from the Greek idea of 'tonoi' or tones. It did so by taking over the outdated Greek regional names and applying them to new 'modes' or 'families of notes' (Goodall 2013, p. 46): so we have the *Lydian mode* (F to F on the white notes of the piano, the *Dorian mode* (D to D on the white notes), the *Myxolydian mode* (*G to G on the white notes*), and the *Phrygian mode* (E to E on the white notes).

The system of modes persisted as a means of organising notes into families well beyond the medieval era, only giving way to the new system of 'keys' in the late seventeenth century. The *modal* system in Western sacred music was far more ambiguous than the modern key system. For example, the sense of 'home' in plainchant music was not especially pronounced. The introduction of harmony played a crucial role in undermining the modal system: the ancient Greek modes and those of the

© The Author(s) 2021
S. Sagall, *MUSIC and CAPITALISM*,
Critical Political Theory and Radical Practice,
https://doi.org/10.1057/978-1-137-52095-1_2

Byzantine and Roman churches had been primarily designed for solo, unaccompanied melodies, whereas the new harmony introduced notes into a piece from outside the key or 'family group' (Goodall 2013, p. 47).

The medieval church had allowed only 'plainchant' (non-metrical music of the medieval church, for example, a Gregorian chant). 'Plainchant' developed gradually and independently throughout Christian Europe—Italy, France, Spain, Britain—during the first millennium AD, before a universal system of notation was created. What the different versions had in common was *monophony*, music played as a single, unaccompanied vocal melody, 'one, memorised, meandering tune with no accompaniment and no harmonising, the Greek term for which is monophonic: one voice'. 'Plainchant' was memorised and passed on aurally for centuries prior to the creation of a system of notation. It has often been described as the 'Gregorian chant', after the sixth-century Pope Gregory. Goodall describes it as 'beautiful, ancient, mysterious' but nothing to do with Pope Gregory (Goodall 2013, p. 18).

'Plainchant' style was, therefore, quite different from the rhythms of secular music, particularly dance music which based itself on the *tonic-dominant* relationship. The early masters of *polyphony* came from the Netherlands and England, where the peasants had liberated themselves during the thirteenth and fourteenth centuries. And as their political importance increased, so their dance music was incorporated into the music composed for the church by professional musicians.

Two changes revolutionised music: firstly, some time around 800 AD, musicians and singers started playing two or more notes together instead of in succession. There were now two parallel lines of voices singing at the same time but singing different notes, a phenomenon Goodall compares to twin train tracks. Medieval church musicians labelled the technique of running two or more parallel notes *organum*, as it sounded like an organ. The Greek term for singing or playing more than one simultaneous vocal line is *polyphony*, i.e. many voices. It was what later came to be described as *harmony*. So if early plainchant was monophonic, after 800 AD, the introduction of two vocal or melodic lines made it polyphonic.

The second revolutionary change was the invention of notation by the Italian monk Guido of Arezzo around 1000 AD, a system still in use today. It was a time-saving device, aimed at avoiding the need for choristers to memorise long chunks of music. It was a system one could read and translate into song at sight. Guido gave each note its own identifiable mark on the page, placing them in the order in which they were to be sung.

 i. *monophony* which refers to music with a single 'part'—i.e. one vocal or instrumental melodic line;
 ii. *homophony* where multiple parts or melodic lines move according to the same rhythm, where they move together;
 iii. *polyphony* (which simply means 'many sounds'), where there is an interweaving of separate vocal lines; it can also be described as music in which the parts are of equal importance and when combined create both independent horizontal movement and also euphonious combinations of chords. Because the music was horizontal, the melodic movement of each individual part was of greater importance than the total sonorous effect of the whole.
 iv. *heterophony*, in which multiple parts or voices use the same melody but at different times, (i.e. it can perhaps be described as a specific kind of polyphony);
 v. *monody*, in which there was a single upper melodic line accompanied by instrumental parts to provide a chordal harmonic texture. More recent orchestral music is often monodic—a primary melody in the upper range with harmonic accompaniment. This combination of an upper melodic line and a lower harmonic accompaniment can be said to represent a vertical structure.

[See 'What Is Monophony, Polyphony, Homophony, Monody, etc.?' www.medieval.org/emfaq/misc/homophony.html].

Counterpoint was central—a relationship between two or more musical lines or voices which were independent in rhythm and melodic shape yet interdependent. These melodies were combined into a single harmonic texture on an instrument, that is, one or more melodies added to or below a given melody. The melodies or voice-parts were instrumental or vocal, and faced each other on treble and bass, generally scored for right and left hands.

The characteristic style of medieval music was a specific form of *polyphony*, a single line of music sung by all with little variation, in which every voice had its allotted place, each following the other in strictly regular *counterpoint*—with a second melodic line added to the first as an echo or accompaniment, creating a single harmonic texture. There was an orderly arrangement of notes and chords without competition or struggle between musical *themes*, and with little emotional variation, a style of music that emphasised order and stability. The element of *counterpoint* is present to some degree in all music but the high point of pure *contrapuntal* music was the sixteenth century, the period of Palestrina in Rome.

In the Renaissance period, 1450–1600, composers developed a different kind of *polyphony*. At the start of the period, they were writing music that differentiated them from medieval composers. Instead of focusing on a single voice with accompanying parts, they chose to emphasise the equal importance of the voices. There was a diversity of melodic and rhythmic material for each part. Typically, there were four vocal parts to a musical piece, two female parts, soprano and alto, and two male parts, tenor and bass [study.com: 'Rise of Renaissance Polyphony', Chapter 3]. The more modern composers chose to emphasise the equal importance of the voices rather than focusing on a single voice with accompanying parts.

A landmark innovation was *tonality* with its idea of a 'home' key which provided the focus for a piece of music. In relation to this home key, known as the 'tonic', other keys were said to be either close or distant. Rules were developed for the movement of the music between these keys—*modulation*. Compositions could *modulate* through various keys but eventually needed to return to the tonic or home key. Finally, composers developed the two 'modes', *major* and *minor*.

To add to the confusion, the term 'monody' is sometimes applied because in the development of Baroque music, and with it modern *tonality*, emphasis was put on a single, upper melodic line accompanied by instrumental parts to give the music a harmonic framework.

An additional change was in the way melody was created. In medieval or renaissance melodies, notes were close to each other, movement between tones limited. With the rise of Baroque music, composers wandered far more boldly across tones and keys.

MONODY AND THE BASSO CONTINUO

In Florence in the 1580s and 1590s, a small group of musicians and poets gathered to pursue some exciting new lines of research and experiment. Taking the name 'camerata', their aim was to revive Greek drama which, they believed, had combined music and poetry. Rejecting the existing polyphonic orthodoxy, they adopted the new system of *monody*—a single melodic line accompanied by an instrumental bass and a plucked or keyboard instrument. This humble beginning led through various developments to the production of the first real operas in Western music and, indirectly, to the style of music known as *basso continuo*. It was the compositional device that came to represent the musical style of the Baroque age.

Originally adopted by Italian composers in the early 1600s, it meant that they thought in terms of two lines of music, the melody and the bass. A typical *continuo* part would simply provide the bass line with figures above the notes to indicate which chords available on those notes should be used. A *basso continuo* was first clearly used by Monteverdi in his 'Orfeo' in 1607 as the accompaniment to all recitatives, arias and choruses, and is played either on harpsichords or chitarroni, or a combination of chitarroni and organ. *Basso continuo* or figured bass was further developed by Corelli. 'Figured bass allowed composers to jot down a minimum of information on their scores, assuming that their players already knew what their jottings meant, and to dash off their compositions much more quickly than before... it gave the players... artistic freedom to do a bit of on-the-spot improvisation' (Goodall 2013, p. 85).

The camerata did not invent accompanied solo singing—they must have experienced it in Tuscan folk music—but they did draw it into the field of 'art music', thus providing a strong impetus to the movement away from polyphony to the new Baroque style in which expressiveness and contrast were paramount. The new style abandoned the equality of parts, replacing it with the dual structure of treble and bass. European composers didn't completely abandon the language of polyphony; indeed, composers continued to use the old and the new styles. But as the sixteenth century drew to a close, so did 'The Age of Polyphony'. Composers now wrote their greatest music through exploring and developing the new style of vertical structure and chordal harmony.

An additional factor marking the transition from medieval and Renaissance polyphony to Baroque monody lay in the area of rhythm. The earlier styles were expressed through continuous, unbroken rhythms, whereas the later, more modern monodic style revealed more changing, fluid rhythmic styles. However, this fluidity was not as pronounced as it later became with the Classical style.

A further crucial modern innovation was 'equal temperament'. By 1600, Western music had worked out a possible nineteen subdivisions between one note and its octave. The existence of these nineteen pitches could be established by mathematical ratios governing the relationship between one string or pipe length and another. These tunings have been described as Pythagorean as it was the ancient Greek philosopher mathematician Pythagoras who devised the ratios for creating notes in music: he divided a taut cord and plucked it. The nineteen subdivisions could be easily sung or played on string instruments, as both the latter and the human voice allow for minute differences of pitch. But for keyboard instruments, on which the pitches of each step are firmly fixed, nineteen subdivisions were a nightmare. In other words, the division of the octave into nineteen notes conforms to the mathematical ratios that are found in nature. But this would have resulted in a huge and unwieldy number of sharps and flats. So the compromise arrived at for the sake of keyboard practicality was one that reduced the number of divisions between notes from nineteen to twelve, even though this meant eliminating some of nature's valid notes.

The next step occurred when tuners set about artificially moving the pitch of some of the twelve subdivisions so that they were re-positioned into twelve equally-spaced positions between the two ends of the octave rather than where they would have been allowed to remain if nature's laws had been the sole criterion. 'It would be like re-portioning the days, hours and minutes so that there were exactly twelve months of thirty days in every calendar year. It was re-calibration of pitch that became Equal Temperament—or equal tuning' (Goodall 2013, p. 101). The upshot of this revolution was that one could play any piece in any key without worrying that the piano or other keyboard instrument might sound out of tune if moving from one key to another. And Equal Temperament was achieved because of the growing dominance of keyboard instruments in sixteenth and seventeenth-century Europe.

The two poles of late Baroque music were the Italian and French styles and *forms*. The Italian contribution consisted, firstly, in the harmonic transformation represented by *tonality*. Secondly, the *forms* through which it was typically expressed were the concerto in instrumental and vocal music, and the sonata. Torelli's exceptional contribution to the concerto was the realisation of the concerto style and the creation of the Baroque concerto *form*. The Italians also contributed the instrumentalised *bel canto* of opera.

The French style consisted in the highly florid ornamentation of the melody and its orchestral discipline; crucial here were the orchestral innovations of court composer, Lully and the keyboard technique of Couperin: its typical *forms* were the overture and dance suite. Bukofzer also argues that whereas Lully's dominance was in orchestral music, Corelli's was in chamber music, so that in a sense, they complemented each other. Again, to the German composers, the two styles were not mutually exclusive: Georg Muffat studied first with Lully, then with Corelli; Georg Philipp Telemann (1681–1767) revealed his versatility in his fantasies through combining the French 'galanterie' style with the Italian concerto style. However, Telemann failed to synthesise the styles into a higher unity.

The German style is universally recognised as the third in the group of national styles. It was characterised by its determination to create a solid harmonic and 'contrapuntal' *texture*. Its role was that of mediator between the Italian and French stylistic poles which it reconciled in a higher unity. Bukofzer highlights this 'dialectical' function: the music that culminated in Bach attained its universality and distinction through the intentional fusion of national styles. Hence, while the German composers were imitators, they were not eclectics since 'they Germanised the forms they took over and assimilated them into the rich harmonic and contrapuntal idiom of the German style' (Bukofzer 1947, p. 262).

In short, the seventeenth and eighteenth centuries witnessed the rise, development and consolidation of a new musical language, that of *tonality*, one that found expression in new musical *forms* such as opera, the concerto and the symphony. The breakdown of the medieval modal system in which pitch, range and interval, had been linked in a purely melodic pattern, was caused by the growing complexities of the language of polyphony. Composers were developing a new sense of the organisation of sound, becoming increasingly concerned with the 'vertical' effect of many notes sounding together rather than the 'horizontal' lines of several melodies.

We can also now appreciate the growing importance of the chord of the *triad* as well as the coloristic effect of the *major* and *minor* third. These elements were increasingly adopted by musicians in the sixteenth century and later confirmed in the increasing use of the harmonic *basso continuo* in the early 1600s—two lines of music, the melodic and the bass. The inner parts might be written out in full or they might be left to the keyboard player to interpret.

As the seventeenth century progressed, the language of harmony became increasingly clear and sophisticated. This would not have been possible without the introduction of *tonality*, with its notion of a 'home' key which provided the focus for a piece or a section of music. Other keys were said to be either near or far from this home or *tonic* key. Rules were evolved for the movement—or—*modulation* between the keys of this tonal hierarchy, and with the spelling out of the separate *major* and *minor* keys, the essentials of a new musical language were created. The age of *polyphony* which had emerged from the music of church monody was replaced by the age of harmony.

THE ITALIAN AGE

As already mentioned, in the final years of the seventeenth century and a great part of the eighteenth, European music remained dominated by Italian composers, with France deriving inspiration from Italy's technical and formal developments. Both countries, though mainly the Italian tradition, contributed to the development of a European style that found its highest expression in the music of Germany and Austria—the Baroque masters Bach and Handel, followed by the classical composers Gluck, Haydn, Mozart and Beethoven. Italian supremacy was particularly marked in the areas of instrumental music and opera.

INSTRUMENTAL MUSIC

In the second half of the seventeenth century, the instrumental style of the Italian school developed apace. As regards keyboard instruments, we see the definitive separation of the styles of organ and harpsichord. At the same time, a distinctive style of writing for the violin was emerging. It was in the mid-seventeenth century that the first recognisable form emerged— the trio sonata, which was the harbinger of later types of chamber music and even played a role in the origins of the symphony.

The Italian composers of the later seventeenth century rapidly improved on the rudimentary but established musical forms which they inherited, while their music often heralds those of the eighteenth-century masters of Central Europe who gladly sought inspiration from them. For example, Bach studied the works of Vivaldi, many of which he transcribed for harpsichord. In the middle decades of the eighteenth century, both the technique and the inventiveness of Giuseppe Tartini paved the way for a great age of virtuosity, whose most prominent representative was G.B. Viotti (1755–1824).

THE BAROQUE ERA—MUSICAL FORMS AND STYLES

Much debate has surrounded the term 'Baroque' as applied to music composed roughly between 1600 and 1750. The term originates from the Portuguese word 'barroco' referring to irregularly shaped pearls, but thence applied more widely to mean distorted, dissonant, strange or even extravagant. As for its application to music, early in the twentieth century, it was generally confined to the work of Bach, Handel and Domenico Scarlatti. But by the end of the century, it was assumed to include, in addition, musicians as widely separated in time and compositional style as Monteverdi, Carissimi, Lully, Purcell, Schutz, Corelli, Vivaldi, Rameau, Telemann and Alessandro Scarlatti.

It seems the term 'Baroque' was first used to describe Rameau's operas, often criticised for alleged bad taste as compared to Lully. It is first found in 1734 when a French critic complained that Rameau's 'Hippolyte et Aricie' (1733) lacked 'coherent melody, was filled with unremitting disso-nances, constantly changed key and meter, and speedily ran through every compositional device' (Palisca 2001).

Beginning in the early twentieth century, German musicologists came to adopt a view of musical periodicity, according to which certain stylistic traits were seen as characteristic of a unified Baroque style even though it developed from simple to more complex, from early to late. The most influential attempt was that of Manfred Bukofzer, according to whom 'the Baroque era as a whole differs from the Renaissance era much more fundamentally than early, middle and late Baroque styles do among them-selves. In spite of their particular qualities, the three styles are linked together by the inner unity of the period…' (Bukofzer 1947, p. 18).

However, Buelow goes on to criticise Bukofzer on the grounds that he does not clarify the nature of that 'inner unity'. Moreover, he argues that Bukofzer has put forward a simplistic concept of musical Baroque. Specifically, he believes that using categories such as early, middle and late Baroque implies an organic development from a simple to complex style. And he asserts that this view is not justified by the evidence: for Buelow, a key feature of the music of the seventeenth and early eighteenth centuries is its great diversity: the development of essential new means of stylistic expression; the adaptation of old forms and styles that were welded to the new; the emergence of nationalistic and individualistic compositional styles; and the frequent debates over which style should be deemed the most successful; '… perhaps most challenging is any attempt to define a concluding borderline to these developments' (Buelow 1993, p. 2).

However, Buelow concedes that the term 'late Baroque' still serves as a convenient label for the abundant musical creativity of the last decades of the seventeenth and the early decades of the eighteenth centuries. Indeed, to abandon the term would obscure the fact that those decades did not witness anything radically new. To enter the Baroque around 1670 or 1680 is in most cases to discover musical achievements already formed by the changes initiated much earlier, harking back at least to the beginning of the seventeenth century. Leichtentritt argues similarly that Bach, Handel and Couperin sought not to create a new style but 'to perfect the style of the time, to surpass their rivals on their own ground'. the age differs considerably from the period around 1600 and from the later eighteenth century (Leichtentritt 1954, p. 141). More important, perhaps, is to examine what happened to the existing musical forms and styles in that period, and to see how those changes related to social factors.

What was the change that occurred at the crucial point of transition from Renaissance to early Baroque style? This point is characterised by 'discontinuity'. At a simple level, the new idiom was 'destructive' because it brought about the internal and external disintegration of traditional forms... Discontinuity prevails in virtually all forms of early Baroque music. An early symptom of the new Baroque style, seen in the music of Giovanni Gabrieli (1557–1612), is the contrast motive which abandons both rhythmic and melodic continuity. For example, one can see the disintegration of the madrigal (an unaccompanied and often complex secular song for several voices), effected internally by the new dissonance, and externally by the addition of the *continuo*. Gabrieli represents the climax of the Venetian style, at the time of the shift from Renaissance to Baroque forms. Nearly all early Baroque forms, in both instrumental and vocal music, had one formal trait in common: multisectional structure. This feature is the formal corollary of the discontinuity that characterises early baroque style. 'The nervous and erratic flow of early Baroque music merely reflects its intensely affective nature' (Bukofzer 1947, p. 353).

Bukofzer summarises his characterisation of early, middle and late baroque styles as follows:

(a) In early Baroque (1580–1630), two ideas dominated: opposition to *counterpoint* and a violent interpretation of the words, as expressed in an affective recitative in free rhythm. Accompanying this was a powerful desire for dissonance. The harmony was pre-tonal, that is, its chords were not yet directed towards tonal harmonies.

(b) Middle Baroque (1630–1680) ushered in the *bel canto* style in the cantata and opera, and alongside it the distinction between aria and recitative. The single sections began to grow and contrapuntal *texture* was restored. The modes were reduced to *major* and *minor*, and 'chord progressions were governed by a rudimentary *tonality* which restrained the free dissonance treatment of the early baroque. Vocal and instrumental music were of equal importance' (Bukofzer 1947, p. 17).

(c) Late baroque (1680–1730) is characterised by a fully established *tonality* which regulated chord movements, the treatment of dissonance, and the overall formal structure. Contrapuntal technique achieved its climax in the full absorption of *tonal* harmony. Furthermore, the forms grew to large dimensions: the concerto style appeared, with vocal music dominated by instrumental. Two caveats: these periods actually overlap in time; these spans indicate only the formative periods of the new styles with which the previous ones may run parallel. Secondly, the dates apply only to Italy from which Baroque received its main inspiration. In other countries, the respective periods began some ten or twenty years later. So, around 1730, when Italy had already turned to the 'style galant', Germany brought Baroque music to its glorious finale.

The early Baroque period witnessed some pre-tonal experiments and middle Baroque some development of a rudimentary tonality, whereas the definitive realisation of *tonality* occurred in Italy around 1680. It is the use of *tonality* in late Baroque that connects this period more closely than any other with the later living repertory. The creation of tonality affected all aspects of composition—above all, contrapuntal writing. 'The absorption of tonality into counterpoint gave the melodic design and the contrapuntal texture unprecedented harmonic support... The interpenetration of harmony and counterpoint resulted in the harmonically saturated or "luxuriant" counterpoint of the late Baroque period, which began with Corelli and culminated in... Bach' (Bukofzer 1947, p. 221). Also, in late Baroque music, the 'homophony' (multiple parts or melodic lines moving together, according to the same rhythm) that had characterised the Mannheim school was counterbalanced by the melodic orientation of the bass. The two opposite poles of late Baroque are 'luxuriant counterpoint' (the interpenetration of harmony and counterpoint) and continuo-homophony (multiple parts including bass moving according to the same rhythm). 'Continuo-homophony' differed from the ordinary 'homophony' of the Mannheim school in its rapid harmonic rhythm and its dynamic and sweeping rhythmic patterns that prevailed in both melody and bass.

The origins of continuo-homophony lay in the concerto style, arguably the most important stylistic innovation of late Baroque, as it permeated not just the concerto but all forms of music, both instrumental and vocal. In the concerto style, we see the consistent adoption of *continuo* homophony, frequent unison passages in all voices, rapid harmonic rhythm, and *themes* that circumscribed the key by emphasising the fundamental *triads* and the *diatonic* scale. The concerto style stressed its instrumental character, with *allegro* movements illustrating this by developing features such as rapid tone repetition, rhythmic energy, fast scale passages, and a wide range of *themes*.

In addition, contrapuntal writing broke up in the concerto style under the impact of continuo-homophony, surviving in the outer voices. Also, the instrumental character of the concerto style became clear in such features as rapid tone(note) repetition, fast scale passages, and the wide scope of the *themes*. This rhythmic energy was described as the 'fire and fury of the Italian style' (Bukofzer 1947, p. 222).

Tonality was not invented by a single composer but emerged at roughly the same time in the Neapolitan opera and in the instrumental music of the Bologna school. It was codified by Rameau more than a generation after its first appearance. *Tonality* established a system of chordal relations between a *tonal* centre (the *tonic triad* in a *major* or *minor* scale) and the other *triads* (or *seventh* chords) of the *diatonic* scale. These chords were not new but they now fulfilled a new function—that of restricting the keys, that is, ensuring that the keys were well-defined though not preventing movement between them. In the middle Baroque period, this function had been performed by the two *dominants—major/minor*—but in the late Baroque, it was extended to all chords. However, we should stress the crucial role played by Arcangelo Corelli (1653–1713) in the creation of the modern *tonal* system.

In the late Baroque period, the progression of *tonal* chords was governed by the drive to the cadence, whereby a sequence of chords moves to a harmonic conclusion or point of rest, at which the tension built up through the chordal movement away from the tonic is released. The movement towards the cadence consisted of a *diatonic* sequence of chords organised according to the circle of fifths. According to Bukofzer, 'the sequence in fifths crystallised as the most common and conspicuous harmonic formula that underlay the harmonic structure of an extended piece' (Bukofzer 1947, p. 220).

Goodall describes the circle of fifths as beginning with any note on the keyboard and dropping down five white notes in a sequence of chords. So the descending order of notes would be: B-E-A-D-G-C-F-B, and so on. When the sequence began to appear in the late seventeenth century, composers would write cycles of only three or four chords rather than work through the complete chain of twelve. There is a weakness in the first of two chords: if one plays a triad—say, G-B-D—it becomes vulnerable by the addition of the 'seventh' note, that is, F. Now, this triad of G plus F sounds lost and yearns to 'achieve cadence' by moving to the chord placed a fifth below it, that is C, in other words, the tonic triad of C-E–G. Adding a seventh to C will drive it to move to F, and so on (Goodall 2013, p. 91).

There is an abundance of these 'virtuous circles' of three or four, and occasionally five, chords throughout the music of Corelli, Vivaldi, Bach and Handel. 'What comes across in their work time and again is a relishing of the joys of chords for their own sake, the delicious transition from one to another... Sometimes they dispensed with melody altogether and simply allowed a lovely chain of chords to unfold'. An example is the opening 'Adagio e Spiccato' section of Vivaldi's second concerto in the collection labelled 'L'Estro Armonico' (the Inspiration of Harmony) (Goodall 2013, pp. 91–92). These fifth (and sixth) chords presented the tones of the *diatonic* scale systematically, usually in descending order, thus defining the key; but since they could be interrupted at any point, they also became the principal means of *modulation*.

The creation of *tonality* affected all aspects of composition, but above all, contrapuntal writing. According to Bukofzer, 'the absorption of tonality into counterpoint gave the melodic design and the contrapuntal texture unprecedented harmonic support... The interpenetration of harmony and counterpoint resulted in the harmonically saturated or "luxuriant" counterpoint of the late Baroque period, which began with Corelli and culminated in the works of Bach' (Bukofzer 1947, p. 221). Furthermore, tonality established a harmonic framework able to sustain large *forms*.

In addition, *tonality* re-defined the two structural voices of a composition. In the relation between melody and chord progression, the latter became more important than the former. Melodies were increasingly conditioned by the harmonic accompaniment—a process that culminated in the homophony (see p. 2) of the Mannheim School. Founded in 1741–1742 by Johann Stamitz, it had two features: a more independent treatment of wind instruments and a whole-orcherstra crescendo.

In brief, the late Baroque period established tonality, 'luxuriant counterpoint'—the interpenetration of harmony and counterpoint—and also 'continuo-homophony'. Definite formal patterns now emerge which are specifically characteristic of late Baroque music. 'Parts' become 'movements', with the order of the movements established as cycles—for example, the church sonata crystallises as a four-movement form in a sequence of slow-fast-slow-fast; similarly in the solo and trio sonatas and also in certain 'concerti grossi' and Italian overtures.

Earlier Baroque music was largely vocal in its forms and styles, with operatic styles the dominant factor in the origin and development of most of the music composed in the seventeenth century. However, by the turn of the eighteenth century, instrumental music had attained a level of sophistication that made it the primary influence shaping the future of music. Beginning with simple styles and forms in the late Renaissance period, the crucial decades of the 1680s to the 1740s witnessed the development of the final stylistic forms of the Baroque era—keyboard music, chamber pieces, and orchestral compositions. Most of these instrumental works originated in Italy, where the composers were most often violinists. Their ability to create string music of an increasingly demanding nature was closely bound up with the flourishing of string instrument building that started around 1680. And the drive to create string instruments with an enhanced beauty and sensuousness of tone came from the human voice which in opera had captured both composers and audiences.

Hence, for most of the seventeenth century, instrumental music was closely bound up with vocal composition, as, for example, in instrumental *ritornellos* in early operas and cantatas, orchestral introductions to operas called either sinfonias or overtures, and other semi-dramatic vocal forms. In fact, it was the disciplined orchestral playing of Lully's operas that provided the drive to create orchestras throughout much of Europe. Foreign musicians came to Paris to study Lully's orchestra which also inspired innumerable royal households to attempt to emulate the splendour of French operatic conventions. This created many additional positions for instrumentalists, at the same time raising their technical and artistic standards. Also, the early orchestral repertory was largely French—overtures, suites of dances from ballets, incidental music from operas by Lully, Campra and Destouches.

An orchestra, whether in the palace of a German prince or in the home of a rich Italian noble family, was as much a symbol of wealth and power as an expression of the latest developments in musical taste. Much instrumental music had a social function such as organ music in Catholic and Protestant liturgy, the trio sonata replacing sung sections of the liturgy, suites for social dancing or for background music at banquets, and town bands for civic celebrations. However, by the end of the seventeenth century, the upper social strata had profoundly shaped the growth of music composed for non-functional purposes—listening or playing for group or individual pleasure. Interestingly, there were many more non-professional musicians, creating a new amateur social force that influenced all aspects of music, both as art and as a business.

Corelli's composed instrumental works only in the forms already established by the turn of the century: the solo violin sonata (with *continuo*), the church and chamber trio sonata and the string ensemble concerto. His two collections of church trio sonatas Opus 1 (1681) and Opus 3 (1689), and two sets of chamber Trio sonatas Opus 2 (1685) and Opus 4 (1694) for continuo and two violins became models of their kind—chamber music with tolerable technical demands, exploiting the newly created balance between movements of vocal-like, *bel canto* melody and those of motivic contrapuntal *textures* enhanced by frequent clashes of dissonances. And the twelve solo violin sonatas Opus 5 (1700) helped to establish the primacy of the solo sonata over the trio sonata.

Corelli's music became popular on a scale unknown by previous composers of solo and ensemble string music. However, despite his popularity, Corelli's music seemed conservative in the way it placed the trio sonata as a solo (or concertino) group into the orchestral texture of the 'concerto grosso'—a form of Baroque music featuring a small group of solo instruments and the full orchestra. This is in contrast to the solo concerto which features a single solo instrument playing the melody line, accompanied by the orchestra. 'There was no thematic contrast, and the only change of instrumental colour involved solo string sonority against doubled ensemble strings' (Buelow 1993, p. 25). These works retained the older, multi-movement forms of either contrasting fast and slow tempos or a suite of dances. The future of the concerto lay in the changes launched in Venice by composers such as Albinoni, the brothers

Alessandro and Benedetto Marcello and, especially, Vivaldi. Each of these composers wrote operas while their instrumental compositions reflect the instrumental and vocal styles influenced by Venetian opera. Venice was where the final development of the Baroque concerto took place.

For Mellers, the basic conventional forms of Baroque music were the *binary* dance movement and the *aria da capo*. So, in the *binary* dance movement, a single melody is divided into two sections: in the first, there is *modulation* from *tonic major* to *dominant* or from *tonic minor* to *relative*; the second moves back to the *tonic* by way of related keys. In the *aria da capo*, there is an extended melody in dance rhythm, followed by a middle section based on a different aspect of the same *theme*, and often in the *tonic minor*, then a repeat of the first section with elaborate ornamentation. The *modulatory* sections in both the *binary* and *ternary* aria could be exploited as an effect of dramatic contrast as we see starting to happen in the later concerto grosso (Mellers 1957, pp. 8 and 9).

The concerto grosso resulted from the transformation into instrumental terms of the conventions of *opera seria* (heroic opera), whereby the soloist group took on the role of the singers, the *tutti* that of the operatic orchestra. The alternation of *tutti* and *soli* suggests that different or perhaps contrasting material associated with the two keys—*tonic* and *dominant* or *tonic* and *relative*—is being used. These keys are the orthodox props of the *binary* structure. Mellers argues that once the idea of contrast is accepted, *modulation* is sometimes used as a shock tactic rather than as a means of building the structure of a piece. This applies not only to Vivaldi's concerto movements, which emerged from the Baroque heritage, but even more so to the stock operatic overture, which was partly a reaction against that heritage. Here, the *modulatory* sections have to be dramatic or at least surprising, as there is no melody, as Bach or Handel conceived it, to extend (Mellers 1957, p. 9).

The end of the seventeenth century and the entire eighteenth century witnessed a rapidly intensifying search for unity of both *theme* and *form*. The sonata for two violins with *basso continuo* was the form preferred by most composers, but it was subdivided into *sonata da chiesa* (church sonata) and *sonata da camera* (chamber sonata). As we saw, *basso continuo* was the form of musical accompaniment used in the Baroque period. It was played by a keyboard instrument and another bass instrument such as a cello, violone (old double bass) or bassoon. The church sonata usually consisted of five or six movements, with indications of the different rhythms. It was generally in three parts, was stylistically imitative and intended for a small instrumental ensemble. The chamber sonata preserved the form of the old dance suite, and largely granted greater freedom of composition. In all these forms, composers tended to reduce the number of *themes*, sometimes writing mono*thematic* structures which, paradoxically, preceded the bi*thematic sonata*. Giovanni Legrenzi and G.B. Vitali in the late seventeenth-century outlined the first profile of this evolution, while Corelli gave it precision and Vivaldi built on it.

The other important development was the fixing of the number of movements at three. Vivaldi adopted the *ternary* form. At the beginning of the eighteenth century, more advanced composers were starting to abandon the *basso continuo* style, a development which entailed rescoring some instruments to give them heightened *colour* and *timbre,* and emphasising the individuality of instruments. This laid the basis for the transition from the early concerto grosso to, firstly, the orchestral symphony, and secondly, to the sonata and concerto for soloist.

Clearly, the development of instrumental technique contributed to the rise in importance of the soloist, paving the way for the emergence of a new era of outstanding *virtuosi*. The most noticeable development was among string instruments, particularly with the violin and cello, with composers such as Corelli and Boccherini. However, the invention of the pianoforte in 1709 by Christofori would have, at the end of the century, the strongest impact on keyboard music. Although the new instrument was not at once adopted, the style of works for the harpsichord gradually evolved towards the future style of the piano. An important marker in this evolution was Domenico Scarlatti, especially from the standpoint of form: he often foreshadows the bi*thematic* sonata, and although he retained the *binary* movements of the suites, some of his works have an incipient central development and a partial re-exposition which anticipates the classic *ternary* form of the sonata.

This development reached its full blossoming with Beethoven, while the Italian Muzio Clementi (1752–1832) also displayed great talent in his handling of form, and there was a degree of mutual influence between the two composers. The sonatas which Clementi wrote between 1788 and 1790 use elaborate *themes* and harmonies in a style that Beethoven only adopted some twenty years later. But in his suites of 1815 and 1820, it was Clementi who followed Beethoven, moving down a stylistic path that foreshadowed the lyricism of Chopin and even sometimes the symphonies of the great German Romantics. In short, this period—from around the start of the 1680s, that is, from roughly the time of the birth of Bach, Handel and Domenico Scarlatti to the end of the eighteenth century—is one of transition from the late Baroque to the Classical period. It is, furthermore, one that witnesses the first light of the dawning Romantic era.

Also, crucially, the seventeenth century witnessed fundamental changes in the type of instruments that were at the heart of the typical pre-Baroque and Baroque orchestras. The development of the violin and its family-members was central to this process. The violin emerged in the middle of the sixteenth century and was clearly a brilliant and powerful instrument, regarded at first as not fit for refined music but only for dances and 'mummeries' (traditional masked or mimed performance). So, at the start of that period, it was used for dramatic, coloristic effects but then achieved equal status with the viol, after which, due to its prestige in French court music, it displaced its rival. At the start of the seventeenth century, the language of music, as expressed in the music of Giovanni Gabrieli and the Venetian school, was that of contrast—contrasting sets of instruments using different tone *colours* and dynamics of volume. Such composers didn't try to achieve a blending of instruments into a homogeneous sound but revelled in the spicy contrast achieved by many *timbres*. This was probably influenced by the nature of the instruments themselves, particularly the wind family, which, with their strident tones, rendered blending impossible. The harsh tones of the shawms (medieval or Renaissance wind instrument) could not 'blend' with the tender sound of the viols, nor the nasal character of the crumhorns offer anything but contrast to the lucid, hollow sounds of the Renaissance recorder.

However, as the seventeenth century progressed, there was a shift of taste towards a more uniform instrumental combination, aided by two factors. The first was the choice of the sharp-toned violin as the basic string instrument, and the second was vital improvements in the design of the wind instruments. For the first time, these gradually achieved a more homogeneous tone within their range. The resulting loss of 'spice' was gladly surrendered in exchange for a newly discovered *euphony*. At the same time, composers were becoming more confident in the use of the new language of tonality which lent greater *colour* to their music. Hence, the thrills of contrasting instrumental *timbres* began to yield to those derived from changing and contrasting harmonies.

2 THE LATE BAROQUE STYLE   37

PART II: COMPOSERS

Counterpoint Supremo: Johann Sebastian Bach (1685–1750)

In the eighteenth century, Germany was divided into a number of small principalities, overshadowed by the larger kingdom of Prussia. However, the princes treated their musicians as lackeys. Bach came from a family of professional musicians. He worked as a court violinist, organist or composer for a series of princes. His work can be divided into five periods. During the early years (1703–1706), Bach worked as court violinist at Weimar and Arnstadt, then as organist at Muhlhausen (1706–1708). During his second Weimar period (1708–1717), he worked as organist, and from 1714 as 'Konzertmeister' (director of music) at the ducal court. In 1717, he fell out of favour and was forced to seek a new appointment. He accepted the directorship of music at the court of Prince Leopold of Anhalt-Kothen, but only obtained his release from Weimar after persistent lobbying and one month in prison for trying to leave the duke's employ-ment! (Blanning 2010, p. 14). From 1717 to 1723, Leopold, Prince of Anhalt-Kothen, employed Bach as his 'Kapellmeister' (director of music). The prince was a Calvinist, so Bach's music during this period was secular. 1723–1750: the Leipzig years when Bach was the Cantor (singing leader) at St. Thomas's church, one of the most important posts in Protestant Germany. His output during these years was mainly religious.

Although Bach composed hundreds of pieces, perhaps only half of which have survived, during his lifetime he was better known as an organist than a composer. He only became recognised as a great composer with a revival of interest in his music in the first half of the nineteenth century.

Bach's Late Baroque Style

Bach greatness lies firstly in his enrichment of the established German styles through his mastery of *counterpoint*, harmonic and *motivic* organ-isation, but secondly in his incorporation of Italian and French forms, rhythms and *textures*.

Counterpoint:

Bach didn't invent counterpoint but his contribution to its develop-ment was so fundamental that it became almost synonymous with his music. Counterpoint was central to his musical language. He defined it in the same way that the classical composers defined the sonata form (Eidam 2001, Chapter 20). For Bach, counterpoint was the fundamental set of rules governing the creation of music. To obey these rules was emotionally reassuring, and intellectually and aesthetically uplifting.

The musical embodiment of Bach's species of *counterpoint* is the *fugue*. Signifying 'flight' in Italian, it is a kind of *canon* or 'round' in which the same melody is repeated by successive singers or instruments, each new entry fitting on top of the others. In a typical Bach *fugue*, for example, the 'Gigue Fugue', the first voice is joined by three others who play the same tune though it is played by the same organist. Some of the entries are in new keys—it starts in G major, but there are versions in B minor, A major and also E minor, and some are 'upside-down', that is, the melody jumps up in one version and down in another. Another fugal device is 'retrograde' motion, in which 'the tune is played backwards against its forward-playing self' (Goodall 2013, p. 105). In some fugues, Bach introduces the incoming tune or echo at half or double the speed of the original. On other occasions, he uses several of these techniques at the same time, in the same fugue, but in different 'voices'.

Bach's music is permeated with religious influences as is clear from the hundreds of sacred works he composed. The traditional element in Bach's work can be seen in his adherence to Lutheranism and is expressed in the Lutheran chorale hymn tune. He worked these hymns into highly sophisticated and tightly integrated chorale preludes. And in composing massive religious works such as the 'St. Matthew Passion', the 'St. John Passion', the 'Mass in B Minor', Bach created pieces of the greatest profundity, that both give expression to the deepest emotional human experiences and also transform the existing range of artistic and technical potential present in every genre except opera. For example, his keyboard work 'The Well-Tempered Clavier' was composed in two parts, the first around 1722, the second in the late 1730s 'The Clavier-Ubung' series (Keyboard Practice) represented the climax of Bach's work as a pioneer of *Equal Temperament*.

Four-Part Harmony

Four-part harmony existed before Bach, and he himself sometimes reverted to the *modal* system (for example, his 'Chromatic Fantasia and Fugue in D' in *Dorian mode*, similar to D minor in the *tonal* system). Moreover, Bach lived at a time when Western music was completing the crucial transition from the *modal* to the *tonal* system. In the latter, a piece of music moves from one chord to another according to specific rules, each chord being made up of four notes. The new *tonal* system was at the heart of his style and his works prescribed the rules that were to dominate music in the following centuries.

These principles are found, not only in Bach's four-part choral music but also in his *figured bass* or *thoroughbass* accompaniment, that is, his method of notating a *basso continuo* (Spitta 1899, p. 315). In his teaching at Leipzig, Bach defined 'thoroughbass' as 'the most perfect foundation of music' (Wolff 2000, p. 309). However, from the late 1720s, Bach's organ music played *concertante* (i.e. as soloist), with the orchestra playing instrumental *cantata* parts. And in his sonatas for viola da gamba and harpsichord, neither instrument plays a *continuo* part but are treated as equal soloists, superceding the *basso continuo* role.

Modulation is another stylistic element in which Bach was an innovator. Baroque instruments were limited in their capacity to modulate. Keyboard instruments, lacking a system of temperament, did not cater for key-changing. Wind instruments, especially brass ones such as trumpets and horns, were tied to the key in which they'd been tuned, and it was roughly a century before they were fitted with valves facilitating *modulation*. Bach characteristically pushed the limits, adding 'strange tones' in his organ-playing which confused the singers. In the 'Suscepit Israel' of his 'Magnificat' of 1723, he had the trumpets in E flat play a melody in the *enharmonic* scale of C minor.

The most significant development in Bach's time, and to which he made a major contribution, was the development of a system of Equal Temperament for keyboard instruments that allowed musicians to play them in all available keys—twelve *major* and twelve *minor*. It also allowed for *modulation* without re-tuning. His early work 'Capriccio on the Departure of a Beloved Brother' already displays a talent for *modulation* greater than any of his contemporaries.

Bach's wrote quite elaborate *ornamentation* into his music, a feature generally left in his time to performers—for example, the second page of the 'Klavierbuchen fur Wilhelm Friedmann Bach', written for his nine-year-old eldest son, the 'Aria' of the 'Goldberg Variations'. Italian composers had written church music in which they adopted the ornamental operatic style of the Neapolitan mass. This was not a stylistic approach regarded as appropriate for liturgical music in Protestant societies. Indeed, one critical comment made after a performance of Bach's 'St. Matthew Passion' was that it sounded like opera!

Bach composed virtuoso music for specific instruments such as his sonatas and partitas for solo violin. These pieces are regarded as the peak of achievement for this instrument, extending its possibilities to the limit. He also wrote transcriptions of this music for other instruments. He scaled similar heights in his music for the cello and keyboard: again, his virtuoso music for these instruments seems to fit them perfectly. Bach was able to exploit the potential of these instruments to the fullest degree yet maintaining the essence and independence of the music.

In Bach's time, the concept of 'melody' was different from what it became by the beginning of the Classical era. By then—the 1760s or 1770s—a typical composition consisted of a melody, a bass line and harmony. Whereas melody was central to harmonic thinking in the Classical style and later periods such as the Romantic, the bass line was the important feature of Baroque music. Crafting a solid bass line was the vital first step in composition. From the early sixteenth century, the lowest (bass) line 'started to take on greater responsibility for the foundation of the harmony', facilitated by the development of the organ with its deeper pedal notes. The bass line had acquired a new role, as seen in Luther's chorale 'Ein feste Burg ist unser Gott'—'A Mighty Fortress is our God'. It was a fundamental structural change (Goodall 2013, pp. 62–63).

For Bach, however, the dividing lines between melody, bass line and harmony were blurred. He had a great gift for investing his bass line with strong, intriguing, melodies which easily co-existed with the top ones. Bach's music had a melodic richness that was extraordinary in the light of the constraints such as the need to compose canons or his use of counterpoint. His boldness was revealed in brave leaps, *melismas* or audacious *chromatic* runs.

Bach achieved a profound unique synthesis of the *contrapuntal* with the harmonic. And at the heart of this synthesis were his rich melodies. 'His musical structures, rich with melodic lines in all the parts and with beautiful and daring resultant harmonies, the profusion of which astonished and delighted Mozart, are built up into great units which possess an internal balance and overall sense of structure that may be described as architectural' (Hindley 1971, p. 199). In addition to his astonishing melodic gift, the harmonic assurance and boldness of his music and the powerful grasp of structural and formal perfection which inspires all his mature works, Bach had a vigorous and awe-inspiring sense of climax. In his instrumental music especially, he often takes a single melodic line or harmonic configuration and develops it comprehensively to construct a climax which depends not just on rhythm, or contrasting dynamics of volume, or crescendo, but on the accumulation of numerous musical assertions derived from the original *motif*. A classic example of this is the great 'Toccata for Organ in F Major' while in the 'Brandenburg Concerto No. 5', a series of smaller climaxes gives the strongest possible effect to the sense of liberation achieved in the last one.

Bach's work is reminiscent of Janus (the Roman God who faced two ways), pointing as it does to both past and future. He built up a large manuscript library of the works of composers such as Vivaldi, Corelli and Frescobaldi and borrowed freely from their material which he incorporated into his music. Both Bach and Handel studied the published work of the popular and prolific German Baroque composer Telemann (1681–1767). But although fully in tune with new developments, Bach's style also rests on the foundation of seventeenth-century German *polyphony*. It was, therefore, considered by some of his contemporaries to be outdated.

How did Bach interact with the stylistic norms of his era? On the one hand, his musical style reflected the conventions of his time, which express the climax, the final stage of Baroque. From an early age, Bach steeped himself in the music of his contemporaries and of earlier generations. He was certainly influenced by the French style, having been brought into contact with the French style and manners of performance at the Luneburg castle of the Duke of Celle between 1700 and 1702. The experience rounded off his study of French keyboard suites, overtures, and ballets.

However, if Bach gave expression to French and German musical ideas, his main influence was Italian. 'Bach's confrontation with the modern Italian concerto in the years before 1714 ultimately provoked what became the strongest, most lasting and most distinctive development toward shaping his personal style: the coupling of Italianism with complex yet elegant counterpoint, marked by animated interweavings of the inner voices as well as harmonic depth and finesse' (Wolff 2000, p. 174). Such Italian influence can be discerned in the titles of Bach pieces such as 'The Italian Concerto'.

The profound effect of Italian music on Bach's creativity is revealed in the new *thematic* sharpness and the lucidity of form that characterise the instrumental music of the (second) Weimar period. (1708–1717). On the other hand, Bach took over the stylistic conventions of the final stage of Baroque and, while absorbing their essence, developed them to their fullest potential. His adaptation, integration, and command of both modern and traditional compositional approaches represent a system-atic attempt at shaping and perfecting his personal musical language and expanding its structural possibilities and expressive powers.

A huge proportion of Bach's work, including nearly all his three-hundred-plus 'cantatas' and his huge output of organ music is based on hymn tunes, or 'chorales'. 'He would weave a tapestry of sound around a hymn being sung or played slowly through the centre of the work, as he does to majestic effect in "Jesu, Joy of Man's Desiring", in which what appears to be a lilting dance theme is transformed by the stately progression across it of a German hymn-chorale' (Goodall 2013, p. 104).

The German Englishman: George Frideric Handel (1685–1759)

Handel received important training in Halle, his birthplace, then worked as a composer in Hamburg and Italy before settling in London in 1712. He began his career as a composer of Italian style opera, a genre in which he distinguished himself with some fine work. Though conforming to the musical conventions of his time, he introduced greater variety by using choruses and instrumental interludes. But apart from their musical qual-ities, his operas have dramatic power and feature psychologically realistic human beings behind the mythological figures. Beethoven remarked that of all composers Handel knew best how to achieve grand effects with simple means while Haydn described him as 'the master of us all'.

Handel's Late Baroque Style

Handel's magic consists in the unique blend he achieved between the grace of French music, the harmonic intensity of Italian, and the polyphony of north Germany. Leichtentritt points out that Handel makes the most careful choice of keys for the arias in his operas and cantatas. Taking the five F keys—F major, F sharp major, F flat major, F minor or F sharp minor—'every one of these keys has a well-defined colour, atmo-sphere and meaning to which he adheres strictly during his entire artistic career of over fifty years' (Leichtentritt 1954, p. 143). So F major is the key of pastoral idyll, as also used by Beethoven in his sixth symphony.

A second important stylistic feature is Handel's use of *tonality* as the basic framework of an entire opera or oratorio highlighting Handel's mastery of *modulation*. Originally analysed by Rudolf Steglich, Leicht-entritt describes his 'ingeniously devised plan of tonalities, making use of

the various keys and grouping them in symmetrical order, or, when necessary, destroying this symmetry by a striking contrast' (Leichtentritt 1954,
p. 145). In Steglich's analysis, taking Handel's opera 'Amadigi di Gaula'
(1715), the first act moves through the following keys—g-g-C-B flat–e–B
flat–g-F-E flat-A-B flat-B flat-g. Furthermore, in each part, a completely
different key intrudes: E minor next to B flat major in the first part, and
A major between E flat and B flat major in the second part. For Steglich,
'these strikingly distant tonalities are carefully chosen for the purpose of
giving especial and definite emotional expression and colouristic effect
according to the demands of the dramatic situation. Melissa sings of her
amorous grief in the elegiac key, E minor, Amadigi of his amorous delight
in A major. The recitatives between the arias lead over in modulation
from one key to the next one, besides living their own harmonic life in
themselves' (Steglich 1924, p. 643, in Leichtentritt 1954, pp. 145–146).

Similarly, analysing Handel's operas 'Siroe' (1728) and 'Orlando'
(1733), one finds that in each score, Handel has created a different *tonal*
architecture. He constructs entire acts according to a progression through
various keys depending on their expressive and colouristic character, and
according to the demands of the dramatic situation. It is likely that this
approach was influenced by the Italian opera of the early 1700s. Keates
points to the influence of both Neapolitan and Venetian opera in the 'new
style' as developed by Handel (Keates 2009, pp. 169–170).

Again, like Bach, Handel used innumerable traditional contrapuntal
themes and *motifs*, but he also invented his own melodies that rose above
the conventional musical stock of his contemporaries. Both composers
had extraordinary melodic gifts. However 'Bach was happiest with *motifs*
that lent themselves to imitative-ornamental procedure, to that marvellous interplay of contrapuntal parts that is the essence of the linear
conception' (Lang 1966, p. 591). Handel's melodies are 'soaring and
sensuous', with a complicated structure... the melodies are broad, cutting
across different *registers* in quick succession. Handel's characteristic
melodies begin with opening strains of such expansive gestures that what
follows is almost irrelevant.

Two sides of Handel must be balanced: the 'heroic-pathetic' and the
'suave lyricist'. On the one hand, he produces 'choral thunder', on the
other pastoral melodies whose charm, whether expressive of Mediterranean languor or the quiet of the English countryside, never dims. We
can contrast the Handel of a 'Jupiter Tonans' (thundering Jove) with the
dainty grace of his late operatic tunes influenced by the Neapolitan style

of the 'opera buffa'. Against this there is Handel's Baroque tendency to create a 'certain melodic ecstasy that can result in a diffuse and flowery idiom, the melody luxuriantly overgrown with *coloraturas*' (Lang 1966, pp. 593–594).

Both Bach and Handel prefer the large melodic design but they express it differently. Handel adopts a freer stylisation whereas Bach adopts a more complex construction. Handel prefers vocal expression so that even his most typically instrumental works have a vocal basis. Also, his theatrical approach, his 'loyalty to the cause of drama', demanded a specific tone and pace, so that his 'sailing kite of melody is suddenly jerked from below by the composer's hand, the rhythmic flow exploded by a different accent' (Lang 1966, p. 595). In contrast, Bach tends to convert vocal melody into instrumental form. Frequently, Handel conveys an urgency, a certain recklessness, a stylistic quality also to be found in Verdi, which again requires the stage to produce its intended effect. In contrast to this, though also rooted in drama, are the extreme condensation and malleability of many of Handel's germinal utterances. Such compactness has a hidden propulsive, even an explosive, quality that demands immediate development. Again, Handel, who was interested in folk music and used to jot down street-cries he heard in London, could compose melodies with the touching simplicity of an English folksong. While Handel's great arias are usually *diatonic*, with *fugue themes* Handel sometimes followed the German Baroque practice, also found in Bach, of building on *chromatic*, even eccentric, *motifs*.

As for Handel's harmony, he did have a habit of adopting unaccompanied singing, of omitting the bass, or of accompanying his singers with violins alone, or even of leaving them to their own devices. This was probably due to his 'aural-theatrical imagination' rather than to any absence of harmonic sense. Handel's harmony is always interesting and often bold, with frequent use of *tonalities* such as B flat, E flat, and A flat minor, exceptional before the Romantic era. His *modulations* too can be very adventurous. Briefly, the flatness or boldness of Handel's harmony is governed by what is demanded dramatically. 'At times, the harmonies seem to have gone into hiding, while at others they glint in unexpected places, or fail where we expect them... his harmony is also determined to a certain degree by the vocal imagination that ruled his imagination' (Lang 1966, p. 598). His instrumental music is seldom adventurous: his harmony is dependably solid, but he relies mainly on his mobility, *counterpoint*, and eloquent *thematic* progression. However, in an accompanied recitative, he may wander far into uncharted future territory.

Handel had an exceptionally keen sense of rhythm and metric refinement. 'His musical sentences may be compared to blank verse whose rhythm is complicated by "enjambements" (continuation of a sentence without a pause beyond the end of a line)'. His frequent combinations and alternations of different *metres* and also his dance types are 'enchanting'. He liked to use the *hemiola*. This was a characteristic feature of Baroque music, resurrected by Brahms in a typically archaic North German spirit. Handel's favourite dance form was the 'siciliana', but even there he doesn't observe the traditional rhythm: 'the spirit of the dance is there, and so is the flowing, beguiling melody, but the rhythms are new and varied' (Lang 1966, p. 600). We can also see Handel's growing tendency to develop *themes* that may assume symphonic proportions. Examples of this can be found in his arias and choruses. He offers us *thematically* close-knit passages that clearly testify to the birth of the symphony from the spirit of opera. There is, in addition, his love of the Venetian *ostinato basso*.

Perhaps the most engaging and intriguing quality of Handel's music is his combination of asymmetric design with the urge for improvisation. The sudden mercurial turns, unforeseen internal repetitions, the abrupt tangential departures all derive from the inspiration of the moment. 'It is fascinating to watch how Handel, having presented the antecedent, will delay the consequent, continuing to develop his thought by introducing new antecedents or questions, then answer them summarily, or in a series of consequents' (Lang 1966, p. 601).

Bach and Handel

How should one compare and contrast the two giants of German late Baroque music, born within five weeks of each other eighty miles apart but who never met? Bukofzer puts forward a psychological explanation— Handel the extrovert, Bach the introvert. This difference emerges, he believes, in the manner in which they reacted to the musical styles of the period. Handel assimilated the various styles so that they became second nature, achieving in this way a complete coordination of national styles enabling him to master each one equally well. Conversely, Bach absorbed the different influences into his own personal style, thus arriving at a synthesis of national styles in which the individual elements are inseparable.

These different methods explain, firstly, why Handel's work revolves around his operas, which were composed from a supranational perspective for an international audience, and also around his oratorios, 'monuments of ethical humanism'. But, secondly, they explain why Bach's works centre around his cantatas, composed for the local churches of Saxony, and also his passions, those 'monuments of liturgical severity' (Bukofzer 1947, p. 349). This difference in their lives symbolises their artistic difference: Handel, always bent on success, gravitated to the international centres of music; Bach, unconcerned about worldly success, began and ended his career within the narrowness of central Germany.

Finally, the question of unity. According to Mellers, there were two kinds of unity in music prior to the sonata epoch of the late eighteenth century: each found a different expression in the work of Bach and Handel. Bach's unity was 'thematic and fugal', and was inspired by religious faith; that of Handel was 'architectural' and humanistic, based on the rituals of the state. Both types of unity, therefore, imply a connection to a central authority outside the self: Bach wrote for the church and expressed a theocratic and God-centred view of the world even in his instrumental music. Handel wrote for the opera house, for king and state, even in his church music (Mellers 1957, pp. 4–5). This difference in the two approaches to unity can be seen in two pieces: the first is Bach's last chorale prelude 'Vor Einem Thron tret'ich allhier'—'Before your throne I now appear' (1750) and Handel's 'How Beautiful are the Feet' from 'Messiah' (1741). Bach's piece was based on a hymn: the melody appears intermittently in long *note values*. And the other parts which seem to be accompanying the melody are, in fact, *thematic*—i.e. melodies in their own right. In other words, each phrase of the chorale is treated as a small scale *fugue theme*. The concluding phrase appears in its original hymn tune tempo. But every single note in the piece is derived from the original liturgical melody. Bach knew he was dying as he dictated this piece, so that 'Into Thy Hands I Commend My Spirit' in the extended *plagal cadence* (of a church mode) expresses the unity between humankind and God. 'There is some connection between fugal unity as a principle of composition and an age dominated by religious faith—by belief in something more than human potentiality' (Mellers 1957, p. 4).

Mellers confirms that Bach was in many ways an 'archaistic' composer, and that the *thematic* and fugal unity of this last chorale prelude is more typical of earlier periods. However, Bach's 'Janus' character meant that he assimilated both contemporary French and especially Italian styles, and took over the conventions of the final stage of Baroque, absorbing their essence and developing them to their fullest potential.

In contrast, Handel's piece is also an expression of unity but one that is not fugal but 'architectural'. There is one theme which falls into several well-defined segments. The first half *modulates* from *tonic* minor to relative major, whereas the second half returns to the *tonic* by way of related keys. Handel uses these *modulations* in order to stress the grouping of the clauses, not to provide a dramatic contrast. Bach's chorale prelude is an instrumental composition built on principles which are inherently vocal. On the other hand, Handel's aria is a vocal piece built on principles derived from the architecture of the dance.

The general principle here is: 'Bach tends to think fugally even when he writes dances; Handel thinks in terms of the dance even when he writes *fugues*. Bach's unity is the growth of the single melody in all the parts; Handel's unity is imposed on his melodies by a periodic dance *metre*, i.e. by a recurrent rhythmical pattern of beats per bar, and by the principle of tonality' (Mellers 1957, p. 50). While Bach always expresses a God-centred view of the world, Handel's vision is humanistic. Bach writes for the church even in his instrumental music; Handel writes for the 'opera-house' (the symbol of King and State) even in his church music.

A Man for All Seasons—Antonio Vivaldi (1678–1741)

Vivaldi is remembered as one of the most important figures in the development of the solo concerto, composing around 500 concertos, but he was equally innovative in symphonic writing. His remarkable productivity and brilliance made the solo orchestral concerto a definitive achievement of the late Baroque. Born in Venice, he gravitated to Vienna after the success of his meeting with Emperor Charles VI, wishing to take up the position of composer in the imperial court. Shortly after his arrival in Vienna, Charles VI died, leaving Vivaldi without royal protection or a steady source of income. Soon afterwards, he became impoverished and died. In modern times, Vivaldi's music has been criticised as lacking imagination, as having a simplicity of theme and a sameness of form. Stravinsky apparently remarked that he composed the same concerto over and over. In his own lifetime, these were perceived as displaying a freshness and vitality flowing from the current operatic styles. Although his music quickly lost its popularity after his death, one cannot perceive the closing phase of Baroque without acknowledging the seminal influence of his work on the future. His work was indeed criticised as eccentric by contemporaries, and after his death was almost entirely forgotten until its revival in the 1930s (Buelow 1993, p. 28; Hindley 1971, p. 206).

Vivaldi's Late Baroque Style

Vivaldi's concertos represented the first major orchestral repertory for concert audiences, establishing for more than a century the standard three-movement form of the concerto, and popularising instrumental virtuosity as an essential part of concert music.

However, according to Buelow, his compositions are structurally predictable: most use a three-movement form already familiar from the operatic overture, with a pattern of fast—slow—fast. The forms characteristic of these movements were I *ritornello;* II slow, often reflecting the pathos of the feelings expressed in operatic arias; III, a second *ritornello* or dance-like movement. The brilliant *ritornellos*, adapted from their operatic contexts, gave substance to the concertos. The orchestral *ritornello* would open the piece with the relevant musical ideas, to be followed by the solo instrumental music contributing new ideas through a virtuoso style. The *ritornellos* combined the familiar with surprises: the material of the opening might return incomplete or in variations and with harmonic surprises. Vivaldi entertained his audiences with an inexhaustible supply of musical ideas: melodic themes and symmetrical phrases of a strong rhythmic vitality. This melodic material clearly had operatic origins, but Vivaldi placed his own original stamp on them. The slow movements are usually extended solos for violin, or oboe or flute, in which the composer placed in a non-verbal, instrumental context some of Italian opera's most expansive and beautiful *bel canto* arias, extended beyond the limits of length usually associated with opera.

We saw how contrast could be used as a shock tactic rather than a means of building the structure of a piece (see p. 14). For example, in Vivaldi's concertos, the slow movements are based on continuous melodic development, in the heroic style of Handel or Bach. But the fast movements, especially the *finale*, already suggest a dualistic rather than a monistic principle of construction. "They exploit the exciting effect of tonal and rhythmic contrast; and that they do so is inseparable from the fact that their themes are no longer heroic, but popular in style" (Mellers

1957, p. 9). Moreover, the 'The Four Seasons' is an early example of what came to be known as 'programme music' (see Chapter 4).

Finally, Vivaldi's music had a direct effect on the first composers of the symphony, for example, Giovanni Battista Sammartini. For northern composers such as Bach, Vivaldi's style became synonymous with the Italian style. Bach's 'Concerto in the Italian Style for Harpsichord, BWV 971', is a brilliant imitation of Vivaldi's concerto music, testament to the extensive influence Vivaldi wielded on the music of his time. Moreover, that influence was the result of a composer responding to social factors, some requiring him to create a repertory of instrumental music attuned to the popular taste of his audiences, others deriving from wider factors.

PART III: SOCIAL AND POLITICAL INFLUENCES ON THE LATE BAROQUE STYLE

In feudal Europe, music was, like everything in society, dominated by religion and, therefore, largely sacred, intended to produce in its listeners an attitude of contrition for their sins and of reverence towards the church. In medieval Italy, 'there was a perpetual struggle between the religious authorities attempting to subjugate musical expression to the needs of church propaganda, while at the same time attempting to relate to the congregation through the popular idiom of the time' (Behrman, ISJ, 121, p. 125). Henry of Pisa, an early Franciscan monk, was an early evangelist who wondered why the devil should be allowed the best tunes: one morning, he heard a servant girl singing a love song. He liked the tune, so he gave it new words: 'Christe, Deus, Christe meus, Christe Rex et Domine' (Raynor 1972, p. 47, in Behrman, ISJ, p. 125).

We analysed the typical style of medieval music as a specific form of 'polyphony', starting with a single line of music sung by all with little variation, in which every voice had its allotted place, each following the other in strictly regular counterpoint—with a second melodic line added to the first as an echo or accompaniment, a style emphasising order and stability. This style, therefore, fitted well with, and seemed to express, a static society dominated by what were apparently timeless, ordered and God-given institutions, for example, the church, monarchy and feudal hierarchy. 'Plainchant' was a musical style intended to express the unity of a society overseen and controlled by the church.

As we also saw, in the medieval or Renaissance melody, notes were typically close to each other, with limited movement between tones. But the

Baroque era witnessed composers wandering boldly across tones and keys, an expression of the growing freedom of movement across the world—the voyages of discovery and the emergence of national and international markets.

As previously mentioned, in the Renaissance period, the more modern composers chose to emphasise the equal importance of the voices—treble and bass—rather than focusing on a single voice with accompanying parts. This again would seem to reflect the beginnings of capitalist society, its early bourgeois-democratic ideals of liberty, equality, individual aspiration and achievement, pitted against hierarchy and traditional authority.

Throughout the middle ages, the Roman Catholic Church, located in the Vatican, was the leading element in the European feudal structure, owning one third of the land and massively exploiting the peasantry. In the sixteenth century, the Church came under increasing attack from the European merchant classes and rulers who rebelled against its economic, political and ideological dominance. Europe began to fragment into national states and the feudal system to weaken. The Protestant Reformation represented the most serious challenge to the Catholic faith and the power of the Vatican. And of course, underlying the power of the Reformation was that of the rising merchant class, so that this religious rebellion was essentially the struggle of mercantile capitalism against feudalism and the Catholic Church. The Papal States were not only weakened by the Protestant Reformation which divided Europe into two camps, but also by the desire of the surviving Catholic princes to be masters in their own houses. This meant that they often clashed with the papacy over jurisdictional matters. Protestantism in its various guises was, therefore, the ideological orientation expressing the expressing the needs, attitudes and ideas of the rising class of bourgeois capitalists, an analysis developed most famously by R.H. Tawney in his classic 'Religion and the Rise of Capitalism' (1926), and Max Weber in 'The Protestant Ethic and the Spirit of Capitalism' (1904–1905). Furthermore, it was no accident that the Reformation first appeared in Germany where opposition and animosity towards Rome had long existed, fuelled by memori1992es of the conflict between the Papacy and the Holy Roman Empire, for example the 'investiture controversy'—a conflict between church and state over the right to appoint bishops (Rubinstein 2011, p. 18; Fulbrook 1992, p. 19).

With the decline of feudalism and the rise of the capitalist bourgeoisie, we no longer find single themes expressed monophonically but by a growing struggle between themes, by rising tensions, dramatic contrasts and climaxes, and, of course, by the composer's increasing expressiveness. Music was no longer performed for a stable, homogenous community but for a changing, heterogeneous audience. Thus, the seventeenth and eighteenth centuries (Baroque period) witnessed the creation of a new musical language—harmony—and of new musical forms—e.g. opera, the symphony. We saw how a new way of organising sound was being developed by composers increasingly concerned with the 'vertical' effect of many notes played simultaneously rather than with the 'horizontal' lines of several voices or melodies in sequence, as in medieval or Renaissance polyphony.

Could the new harmony, therefore, express the bourgeoisie's need to root themselves deep in their new society, to encourage a style of music that conveyed their social weight? It was, after all, the musical language of a society recently emerged from the Dark Ages, no longer simple and static but fluid and increasingly complex. It was the idiom of an economy no longer geared to production for use but to production for exchange.

Both Bach and Handel related to a central authority—Bach to the church, Handel to king and state—and in Handel's case, it is not surprising that the relationship between art and social ritual found in his music, and even more in the composers of Louis XIV's France, was becoming precarious. 'It depended on... a public small and unified enough for a system of values to be universally intelligible'. The decline of the aristocracy meant the end of that relationship, and, 'we can observe the beginnings of a change even in the work of Rameau (1683–1764) who regarded himself as an heir to the classical baroque tradition' (Mellers 1957, p. 6). Although many of Rameau's later operas were performed at Louis XV's court, unlike his predecessor Lully (1632–1687), he wrote with the Parisian public in mind. Significantly, his patron was the banker Le Riche de la Poupeliniere, one of the wealthiest members of the new bourgeoisie. Whereas Lully and Couperin had depended on melodic continuity and harmonic order, Rameau's operas often depend solely on instrumental *figuration* and rhythm to make a sensational effect. Perhaps the noise, force and restlessness said to characterise, for example, the earthquake in 'Les 'Indes Galantes' or the 'bruit de mer' in 'Hyppolyte at Aricie', 'with its shooting scales, percussive rhythms and picturesque orchestration', testify precisely to a society undergoing a gradual, at times unseen, but massive upheaval, reminiscent of the movement of the earth's tectonic plates prior to an earthquake. Rameau is significant in that he appears to be one of the first composers writing for a bourgeois audience.

Rise of Bourgeois Towns

The emergence of towns in the later medieval period provided a spur to the creation of more radical music inside the church. It created a way of life which needed music to express its dignity and elevate its ceremonies. Also, the nobility believed that their prestigious position required the salute of trumpets and drums, and that their pastimes and pleasures needed string and woodwind instruments. Equally, the rising bourgeoisie demanded that music add its symbolic and animated glories to their own proceedings. 'While the continental cities made it their business to glorify the churches and enlarge the church choirs as well as to employ the best available singer-composers for the service of religion, they wanted music socially, to enhance the dignity and civilisation of their lives' (Raynor 1972, p. 55) (The word 'bourgeois' means 'townsman').

The decline of music in the church meant its rise elsewhere, and the availability of musicians who had lost their church employment rapidly came to feed a growing appetite for music in society. Music became a prominent feature in the new wealthy houses of the rising middle class: in his Consort Lessons (1599), Morley shows that by 1597 music as a hobby was socially important in London middle-class circles. Young gentlemen were brought up with a private tutor 'who would insist upon some knowledge of music as a social accomplishment; they want to know about music because it is a social necessity in the circles in which they move' (Raynor 1972, p. 146).

Public concerts originated in England in the seventeenth century and became a regular feature of musical life in the eighteenth century. Many concert enterprises were now created in places such as dancing-schools and taverns. The latter were frequently hired for private music-making by members of a club or by concert promoters. In 1678, a music patron, Thomas Britton, amateur musician and charcoal merchant, set-up a series of evening chamber music concerts in a room over his shop. They were initially free and attracted a distinguished audience of both titled patrons and commoners. Handel's oratorio 'Esther' was first performed in 1732 at 'The Crown and Anchor' tavern in the Strand. But by the time Handel was giving public performances of oratorios, he needed theatres with large enough auditoriums to accommodate audiences sufficiently big to pay for the productions. A growing middle class was evident in British society in the eighteenth century, an important factor in the spread of concerts beyond London to large and small cities. Music was also performed in the various pleasure gardens in English cities. These concerts held from late spring to early autumn featured vocal and instrumental music, becoming a major institution in eighteenth-century England supporting English composers and performers.

In Europe, the social relations of the period, the musical taste of the public, and the way these impacted on composers, becomes clear in the successful career of Arcangelo Corelli. His music achieved popularity in the early eighteenth century, spreading across the borders of national tastes. Particularly popular were his solo violin sonatas and string trios, their collective style seen as a 'compendium' of the state of violin artistry. Their moderate technical demands enabled skilled amateurs to experience the joys of violin ensemble and solo performance "in a purity and refinement that established a concept of style." (Buelow 1993, p. 25). That concept was to endure well into the century, especially in England, where its influence was reflected in the work of Handel.

Until the nineteenth century, musicians had a definite if officially subordinate place in society, together with a clearly defined social function, composing and playing the music they were paid to write. But from the middle of the eighteenth century, the rising bourgeoisie and progressive elements within the aristocracy replaced the church as the principal patrons of music. This occurred mainly through the emergence of the public concert as the main venue for musical performance and 'the existence of a public which enjoyed listening to music as distinct from taking part in performances and which could afford to pay for its pleasures, and then on the existence of a municipal authority prepared to support music as a necessary civic amenity' (Raynor 1972, p. 314, in Behrman, ISJ 121, p. 125). The origins of the Leipzig Gewandhaus Orchestra lie in its creation in 1743 by a group of sixteen business men.

The new path leading from medieval and Renaissance *polyphony* to Baroque *monody* arguably expressed the competitiveness and individualism of the developing capitalist society, where the merchant was displacing the priest. However, modern harmony did not spring ready-made from *polyphony* but developed gradually within the old music just as the bourgeoisie grew within the womb of feudalism.

Italy—Dominance and Decline

It is clear that music and musical culture in the medieval feudal period and beyond—stretching into the early eighteenth century—was dominated by Italian musical culture. To this day, the vocabulary of musical expression—*forte, piano, allegro, dolce*, etc.—remains Italian. The bridge from medieval and Renaissance to Baroque music was largely built by Italian composers such as Giovanni Palestrina (c.1524–1594), Claudio Monteverdi (1567–1643), Girolamo Frescobaldi (1583–1643) and Arcangelo Corelli (1653–1713). The final twenty years of the seventeenth century and much of the eighteenth century witnessed the continuing domination of Italy over European music, especially in opera and instrumental music. Also, composers such as Francesco Cavalli (1602–1676), Alessandro Scarlatti (1660–1725), Tomasso Albinoni (1671–1750), Antonio Vivaldi (1678–1741), Domenico Scarlatti (1685–1757), Giovanni Gabrieli (1688–1733), Giuseppe Tartini (1692–1777) and Giovanni Pergolesi (1710–1736) belong to the Baroque period proper.

There are arguably three reasons for this Italian predominance: firstly, the hegemonic cultural role of the Renaissance, secondly, the political and economic power and cultural influence of the merchant class such as the Florentine Medici family and, thirdly, that of the Roman Catholic Church. Indeed, the last twenty years of the seventeenth century and during much of the eighteenth century, Italy maintained its musical dominance. Furthermore, French music was inspired by Italy's technical and formal discoveries, and contributed to the formation of that European style that achieved its full development in the German-speaking countries. But it was Italian music and musicians—the new expressive and formal concepts of Italian theorists and composers—that defined the typical forms and styles that put the stamp of modernity on European music as it emerged from the Renaissance into the Baroque era and beyond into the eighteenth century. Indeed, Italian music remained a key influence over European music until the end of the nineteenth century.

However, it is a strange phenomenon that the greatest composers of the late Baroque (and later the Classical) era, those that became the champions and leading exponents of the Italian style in the eighteenth century were not Italian, apart from Vivaldi, but German and Austrian. So, in the first half of the eighteenth century, the centre of gravity of European music moved north, across the Dolomites from Italy to German-speaking central Europe.

A word about the important role fulfilled by the city of Naples, the largest city in Italy in the eighteenth century and the most important centre of musical composition, including opera, for much of that period.

The city had witnessed experiments linking drama and music as early as the sixteenth century. Public performances of opera were first produced in Naples in 1650, only a few years after its introduction in Venice. In fact, 'it was in Naples' smaller theatres that traditional *commedia dell'arte* paved the way for *opera buffa*, in which the stock characters would sing and speak their drama in language, and rudimentary stage settings that were identifiably local' (Snowman 2009, pp. 41–42). It was also in Naples that Rome-born Pietro Metastasio, the eighteenth century's most influential librettist of 'opera seria'—operas with heroic or legendary subjects—came to work before moving to Vienna. As a young man, Handel spent three years in Italy honing his musical gifts and composing a *cantata* during a stay in Naples in 1708.

However, with the decline of the Vatican, the Italian city-state and the Italian merchant class, and the rise of the bourgeoisie and of secular empires in central Europe, the creative focus of music moved initially to France—where the work of Jean-Philippe Rameau (1683–1764) and ironically, of Italian-born, Jean-Baptiste Lully (1632–1687), established the form of French opera, in contrast to Italian, for more than a century (Einstein 1947, pp. 294–295). Music's focal points also shifted to Holland and England.

Role of Patronage

To fully understand the production and consumption of music in the Baroque period, the process must be seen in the context of patronage. Music had not yet become a commodity on the free market. Patronage, private or collective, guaranteed the composer a reasonably sound income, despite its disadvantages. The musician composed not for the sake of the art of music, nor for an ideal but non-yet existent audience, but for clearly defined occasions, and for specific social groups: the church, the court, the consort, or the 'collegium musicum'. Most compositions should, therefore, be classified as 'occasional' works, written for a practical purpose and generally forgotten thereafter. This applies to Bach's 'St. Matthew's Passion' and also to Handel's operas. Since each special occasion called for new music, composers became prolific. Because of the constant demand for new compositions, we have inherited incredible quantities of music of which printed music forms only a small part.

The Protestant Reformation

For Bach, the purpose of music was to glorify God, to reflect on and cele-brate the mystery of the Bible. The Protestant reformation had developed as a reaction against the corruption of the Catholic church, as an expression of disillusion with the traditional Roman hierarchy. At the heart of Lutheran ideology was an emphasis on the importance and sanctity of the law and the values of honesty and thrift. A vast proportion of his work is religious—his three hundred cantatas, masses, also his enormous output of organ music—is based on chorales (hymn tunes). Moreover, Bach's counterpoint technique was his way of expressing Lutheran ideals and priorities in music.

Also, Equal Temperament ushered in a sense of order out of chaos that would have appealed to Bach enormously as it was a product of his deeply-felt Lutheran faith. If one compares the atmosphere and architecture of an Italian church of the time, or of a Catholic church in southern Germany, with the kind of church Bach was familiar with in Saxony to see how deeply this difference of attitude might have affected every note he composed.

Bach's 'pietism', as he saw it, involved no contradiction between science and religion, as least as far as music-making was concerned, indeed his faith embraced both. His music was about illuminating the Gospel. 'Lutheran… churches were purged of decorative trappings, elaborate altarpieces, art that was potentially distracting, statues of saints and the kind of ornate, gold-leaf trinketry that sprawled across the walls of Catholic churches' (Goodall 2013, p. 104). This was the 'high Baroque' or 'Rococo' style. Lutheran congregations were expected to be active participants in the service, with communal hymn-singing accorded high status.

Pietism: Ideological Expression of the Rise of Capitalism

Bach's Lutheran Protestantism was part of the growing European social transformation that occurred with the decline of medieval feudalism and of the Roman Catholic church as the principal economic, political and ideological force in Europe, the power that underpinned feudal society. Bach's faith—German Pietism, and its English Puritan counter-part—stressed the need for congregations and individuals to find God themselves, not through the medium of the church. The founder of

German pietism, Phillipp Jakob Spener, launched the influential move-ment in 1675 as a tendency within the German Lutheran church, convinced of the need for a moral and religious reformation within it. The emphasis was on individual piety and living a life based on strong Christian values and principles. Pietism emerged 'strongly as a movement of renewed spirituality within the Lutheran church in the wake of the Thirty Years' War' (Gardiner 2014, p. 33). Though Pietism differs from Puritanism in its approach to the role of religion in government, they share an emphasis on personal behaviour, especially on the need for and the sanctity of labour, and a focus on inner experience and individual development. 'The Puritan's political radicalism grew directly out of his relationship to God: he was the elect, predestined to be God's chosen' (Sagall 2013, p. 146).

Furthermore, as Tim Blanning and Gardiner point out, German society in the eighteenth century (more in the first than the second half) was dominated by religion—with all the churches—Catholic, Calvinist and Lutheran (both Orthodox and Pietist) flourishing. It was both in its public and private discourse as much The Age of Religion as The Age of Reason. In that setting, music had a vital role to play (Blanning 2010, p. 82; Gardiner 2014, p. 50).

At the ideological level, the kings of Brandenburg-Prussia used the new, heterodox religious Pietist movement to centralise loyalty. They sponsored Pietism as the new state religion, displacing the established Lutheran orthodoxy which underpinned the local power of the impover-ished provincial nobility on whom the rulers, however, were dependent. Hence, on the ideological terrain, the battle between the kings and the nobility took the form of a struggle between Pietism and orthodox Lutheranism (Fulbrook 1992, p. 80).

Puritanism in England and Pietism in Germany were the ideological expressions of the decline of feudal landlordism and the concomitant rise of urban mercantile and rural agrarian capitalism. They put partic-ular emphasis on the role of the individual and the directness of her/his relationship to God, bypassing the mediation of the church, whose role was now simply to reinforce this direct relationship. The various branches of the Protestant religion were thus the ideological reflection of the profound changes occurring in society and the economy where the role of the individual was becoming paramount. The intensity of Bach's music, his relentless, forensic exploration of a melodic theme, its harmonic weight, his architectural sense of structure, may arguably be said to express his Pietism with its emphasis on dedication to duty and the sanctity of labour. Bach's architectural emphasis, but also Handel's somewhat different total structures, perhaps also reflect the growing confidence of the emerging bourgeoisie that they could reshape society in its totality.

Bach's Counterpoint and Melody

The upper and lower melodic themes Bach develops represent both the growing competitiveness of capitalist society and a striving for equality, an equality of higher and lower pitch, therefore, also, of treble and bass, of left and right. This striving for equality expresses, arguably, a democratic feature of Bach's version of counterpoint, a reflection of the democratic aspirations of the ascendant bourgeois classes across large sections of Europe. In addition, the melodic richness of Bach's music testified to the emergence of individualism.

For Bach, 'the point of music was to glorify God... to interpret and celebrate the meaning and mystery of the scriptures' (Goodall 2013, p. 104). Central to Lutheranism was the importance of laws, thrift and personal morality. *Counterpoint* was the 'ultimate set of laws in music', the ultimate arbiter. The new bourgeois individual believed that his life and work were the fulfilment of God's work on earth, ensuring he was one of the elect. Bach's counterpoint was an exploration of the new individualism with its radical transformation of human self-consciousness, of the bourgeoisie's perception of themselves, the elevated confidence in their potential to build a new world—in sum the courage of the rising bourgeoisie.

Influence of 'Zeitgeist' on Handel

To fully grasp Handel's style, we need, in addition, to understand the spirit of the time, or 'Zeitgeist', the dominant rationalism of eighteenth-century central and western Europe. The mathematical and philosophical trend was clearly towards creating holistic systems of thought that would explain the world as a whole and our human mental capacity for understanding it, as in the rationalist philosophy of Descartes, Spinoza and Leibniz. Gradually, the intellectual advances of the seventeenth and earlier eighteenth century reach music and influence it in important ways, resulting in the clear, well-proportioned music of Handel with its systematic construction of keys and *tonality* (Leichtentritt 1954, p. 146).

A further manifestation of the rationalistic spirit of the age can be found in Handel's operas in his treatment of psychological 'synthesis', the gradual building up of individual character through the addition of successive features. His characters present their audience with a sequence of isolated and pure emotions, leaving it to the listener to form an image of a whole character. This contrasts with Wagner's complex method which requires language, gesture, scenery, that is, more intensive theatricality, and orchestral underpinning to achieve its aim. Opera had developed according to the taste of the aristocracy. But Handel had no reason to keep faith with the wealthy but capricious and at times brutal upper echelons of English society who had twice caused his financial failure. Eventually, he turned his back on them and sought a new audience—the middle class, less frivolous and more reliable than the aristocracy, the class from which he himself had sprung (Leichtentritt 1954, p. 154; Bukofzer 1947, p. 331).

Moreover, Handel's 'sudden capricious turns, unexpected internal repetitions, the brusque tangential departures' (Lang 1966, p. 601) arguably reflect the new fluidity, the unpredictability of life, the opening up of unprecedented possibilities in the burgeoning capitalism, as is his capacity for *modulation*. His melodic gift testifies, like Bach's, to the individualism of the new age.

German Enlightenment

The rise of reason and tolerance found expression in the German version of the Enlightenment. At the end of the seventeenth and in the early eighteenth centuries, a powerful intellectual ferment swept across Europe expressed in a new cultural relativism, while rationalism replaced religious revelation as the basis of truth. As Fulbrook puts it, Enlightenment thinkers in Britain, France and Germany all grappled with the key questions of the day—the nature of good and evil, the best organisation of the state and society, the possibilities of education and social engineering. However, while British thinkers engaged in arguments about science, and French philosophers developed a more materialist, anti-clerical, republican version of the Enlightenment, the German 'Aufklarung' remained more aligned with established religion and authoritarian forms of rulership. Immanuel Kant defined Enlightenment as 'the courage to use one's reason to think independently and critically, refusing to accept the tutelage of another's authority' (Fulbrook 1992, p. 92).

Social Aspects of Instrumentalism and Tonality

The concerto form based on the individual instrumentalist would also seem to reflect a society in which individualism in the economy, in political careers and the professions has replaced the traditional values of a society based on inherited position. It represents, therefore, a society in which middle-class competitiveness and personal ambition has come to dominate every sphere of social life. However, the collective nature of most instrumental music, including the concerto, re-emphasises the social nature of human beings. It also perhaps reflects the need of the new merchant class for a strong mercantilist state to uphold the national market and protect them from foreign competition. McClary analyses the 'concerto grosso' as addressing 'the tensions between the dynamic individual and stable society—surely one of the most important issues of the increasingly prominent middle class' (McClary 1987, p. 9).

Furthermore, we may also suggest that the system of keys that became the norm at the end of the seventeenth century reflects a society which has overcome localism and the predominance of local centres of production; also, politically, a society which is witnessing the formation and consolidation of the system of nation-states and the rise of the centralised nation-state as the concomitant of music's key-centre. The central importance of *tonality*, with its emphasis on the home key, as these became established around 1680 again reflects the emergence of a number of strong centres of economic production as prevailed with the final elimination of feudal relations on the land and the guilds in the towns and their replacement by capitalist relations as ushered in by the class of bourgeois owners of capital, both rural and urban. McClary describes the new system as 'tonal procedures developed by the emerging bourgeoisie to articulate their sense of the world'... (McClary 1987, p. 40).

In addition, *tonality* was established in the aftermath of the Thirty Years' War (1618–1648) which had devastated central Europe. The century and a quarter following its end turned out to be a new era, one representing a new beginning. It was a time of social peace, when 'religious wars, peasant uprisings, civil wars and revolutions seemed a thing of the past' (Harman 1999, p. 233).

Tonality would also seem to express the rise of rationality as the guiding intellectual principle of the new post-feudal, burgeoning capitalist order. The trends in mathematics and philosophy were clearly towards creating holistic systems of thought that would explain the world and our human mental capacity for understanding it. Leibniz was one of the trio of great European rationalist philosophers whose work exuded optimism and a confidence in humanity's capacity to shape the world according to reason, the others being Descartes and Spinoza.

The German territories that emerged from the Thirty Year' War were diverse in size, and in their social and political character. Habsburg Austria possessed many non-German dynastic territories as well as its possessions within the Empire, and maintained a large court in Vienna. Other German states such as Protestant Saxony and Catholic Bavaria also had significant courts. The major ecclesiastical territories such as the more substantial bishoprics of Mainz or Wurzburg, as well as many smaller states, also wanted to project a newly discovered sense of status. For example, in the late seventeenth and early eighteenth centuries, many princely palaces were built, with ornate gardens, frequently modelled on Louis XIV's palace at Versailles.

This rise in the prominence and status of princes and courts resulted from certain socio-economic factors in part due to the Thirty Years' War. While certain towns were already in decline by the end of the sixteenth century, others actually improved their situation in the first half of the seventeenth century. But in general, in the later seventeenth century, urban life was less prosperous than a century earlier, with some notable exceptions such as Hamburg. 'The centre of gravity of European trade had moved westwards, to the Atlantic seaboard, and many German towns were no longer the flourishing, self-confident centres of trade and burgher life that they had been in the earlier sixteenth century' (Fulbrook 1992, p. 75).

Also, in many areas, the economic situation of the landed nobility deteriorated so sharply as a result of recurrent warfare that they grew to be dependent on the patronage of the rulers, becoming servants of the growing absolutist state. As for the peasantry, they were still enmeshed in the 'Gutsherrschaft' system of feudal obligation in which the noble landlords retained considerable legal and political rights over them. In short, 'a combination of relatively weak towns, an economically impoverished nobility, and an oppressed and servile peasantry permitted successive rulers of Brandenburg-Prussia to re-organise the administration of their diverse, territorially scattered possessions with a progressive centralisation of power' (Fulbrook 1992, p. 80).

However, by the early eighteenth century, the situation of certain towns had changed again. In this late Baroque period, those cities that were based on trade—Hamburg, Frankfurt and Leipzig—grew and became prosperous. From its very foundation, Leipzig had been a crossroads city, linking east and west, north and south. And during the Renaissance, Leipzig, Bach's city from 1723 until his death in 1750, was transformed from a 'moderately active' Saxon city to a 'teeming commercial town' (Stauffer in Buelow 1993, p. 255). In the early sixteenth century, Holy Roman Emperor Maximilian I granted royal trade privileges and guided commerce towards Leipzig while restricting business in rival cities. By the second half of the sixteenth century, Leipzig rivalled Frankfurt and Hamburg as a commercial centre.

After 1680, Leipzig merchants became manufacturers in the style of France and the Netherlands, and profits mushroomed. By 1747, local industry included 19 factories, 2000 artisans and 10,550 workers aged between 14 and 60. Leipzig also benefited from two waves of skilled immigrants: French Hugenots who fled the revoked Edict of Nantes in 1685, and Salzburg Protestants, expelled from Austria in 1732. There was a further extension of trade routes—west to the Atlantic, east to Moscow, south to Italy and north to the North Sea—that expanded the quality and sophistication of available goods, making Leipzig increasingly international.

A second example of large-scale urban development is Hamburg which at the turn of the eighteenth century had a population of 75,000, the second largest in the empire after Vienna. Originally a member of the Hanseatic League, by the seventeenth century, Hamburg had outgrown the other members in size and economic development. Then in the eighteenth century, Hamburg the free, imperial city-state, became one of the most important commercial and cultural centres in northern Europe. With its advantageous geographical position on the River Elbe, Hamburg prospered on shipping and trade. While much of central and northern Europe had been laid waste by the Thirty Years' War, Hamburg had remained neutral, dealing with the warring factions expediently, both economically and politically. As a free, imperial city-state, Hamburg had only a tenuous connection with the German Reich and thus escaped domination by the aristocratic forces that ruled most other cities in Europe.

It was, therefore, commerce that lay at the heart of the city's life, with visible benefits accruing to its citizens on both cultural and social levels. Moreover, an atmosphere of freedom permeated the city, clear to all visitors. Furthermore, the city flourished not only because of the financial and commercial acumen of its citizens, but also because it attracted wealth from various foreign enterprises, Hamburg being renowned as one of the most cosmopolitan European cities. Handel had arrived in Hamburg from his native Halle in 1704 aged 19 to play the violin and harpsichord in the opera orchestra. It was here that he learnt many of the vital aspects of composing and producing operas that would become a key focus of his career in Italy and London.

Our third case is Vienna. The Roman Empire built a military camp there. From such modest beginnings, it grew to be an important trading site in the eleventh century. It became the capital of the Babenberg dynasty, and subsequently of the Habsburg dynasty under whose rule it became one of Europe's most important cultural centres. Vienna's position in central Europe is marked by the intersection of two historical routes of trade and migration—the waterway of the Danube river linking east and west; and the road from the Adriatic to the Baltic connecting south and north. The city's geographical situation favoured its rise from its nucleus of a prehistoric settlement to the rank of an imperial city. (Vienna's importance will be discussed further in Chapter 3). In eighteenth-century Europe, there were frequent movements of musicians, so that a German-born but Italian-trained composer might then develop his career in London. In early eighteenth-century Vienna, this trend helped to enrich the musical court scene (Wollenberg, in Buelow 1993, p. 345).

In contrast to German cities, as we saw, Italian cities in the eighteenth century went into decline. By the end of the seventeenth century, Venice had enjoyed 100 years of undisputed power and a millennium of economic growth produced through commerce, mainly in the Mediterranean basin but also across land routes to the Middle East and Asia. Its power and stability had engendered an enlightened form of government, a doge elected by his fellow executives, a legislative assembly comprising all male nobles above twenty-one. Though not a democracy in the modern sense, power in Venice was vested in a corporate body rather than a single individual or group. Though it certainly was a hierarchical society, the elite was relatively large: in a population of around 100,000, there were some 3000 noblemen by the early eighteenth century. The Venetian territories stretched from the edge of the Piedmont across the northern plains of the Adriatic and into the Peloponnese. During its heyday, roughly from the ninth to the fifteenth centuries, its population was diverse, consisting of Muslims and Christians, Protestants and Catholics, Pontine and Levantine Jews.

Cultural diversity was prized. Although most Venetians were orthodox Roman Catholics, the state of Venice was notable for its freedom from religious fanaticism, with nobody executed for religious heresy during the Counter-Reformation. This apparent lack of zeal contributed to Venice's frequent conflicts with the Papacy. The antisemitism revealed in *The Merchant of Venice* was, therefore, perhaps a product of the beginning of economic decline.

During the Middle Ages and the Renaissance, the Republic of Venice was a major maritime power and a staging area for the Crusades and the great naval Battle of Lepanto against the Ottoman Empire (1571). Venice was also a very important centre of commerce (especially silk, grain, and spice) and art in the thirteenth century up to the end of the seventeenth century. This made Venice a wealthy city throughout most of its history. It is also known for its several important artistic movements, especially during the Renaissance.

Venice's long decline started in the fifteenth century, when it first made an unsuccessful attempt to hold Thessalonica against the Ottomans (1423–1430). The war against the Ottomans following the fall of Constantinople lasted thirty years and cost Venice much of its eastern Mediterranean possessions. Another crucial factor was Christopher Columbus' discovery of the New World in 1492. Following this, Vasco da Gama of Portugal found a sea route to India by rounding the Cape of Good Hope during his first voyage of 1497–1499, destroying Venice's land route monopoly. France, England and the Dutch Republic quickly followed. Also, Venice's oared galleys were at a disadvantage when it came to traversing the great oceans, and therefore Venice was left behind in the race for colonies. In general, the sixteenth century saw Italy enter a period of decline as the Age of Discovery shifted the European centre of trade from the Mediterranean to the Atlantic.

In the final two decades of the seventeenth century and the first two of the eighteenth, Venice began to feel the 'undertow of a shifting tide in the balance of power, as the Austrian Empire claimed much of the future Yugoslavia and Hungary from the Ottomans. The alliance of Venetians with the Austrians seemed to work more to the benefit of the latter...' (Selfridge-Field, in Buelow 1993, p. 66).

In the sixteenth and seventeenth centuries, the Roman School were a group of composers of mainly church music, thus spanning the late

Renaissance and early Baroque eras. And during the seventeenth and eighteenth centuries, papal authority and influence were apparent in both secular and religious music: in secular music-making, and particularly opera, papal interference was perhaps even more acutely felt. Against this, many cardinals, and even some popes, actively promoted plays and operas, and in some cases even wrote them. 'Under the pope, and often in conflict with his rulings, an ecclesiastical and lay aristocracy wielded immense influence as patrons of music…' (Boyd, in Buelow 1993, p. 43).

In Rome during the years 1670–1740, music fulfilled a 'decorative' role. 'Just as the statues, fountains and colonnades of Bernini adorned the city's public squares, so the music of Corelli, the Scarlattis, Caldara, Gasparini, Handel… adorned its churches, palaces, theatres and oratorios'. The role of this 'decoration' was to enhance the ideological power of the clerical ruling class lodged in the Vatican. Now Rome had depended for much of this musical creativity on the support of a small number of musical patrons. When the last and most important of these, Cardinal Pietro Ottoboni died in 1740, a significant chapter in Rome's musical history came to an end. But it ended because, with the eclipse of the Vatican and European feudalism, political and economic power had moved north, to German-speaking central Europe.

When Frederick II (Frederick the Great) (1740–1786) ascended the throne, Prussia was still an economically backward country whose power could not be compared with the major European states such as England, France or Austria. However, this changed dramatically during his reign: by the end of the Seven Years' War (1756–1763), Prussia had become a major European power, the equal of Austria in Germany. And during the second half of Frederick's reign, Prussia came to be regarded as the leading continental state (Fulbrook 1992, p. 81).

We can perhaps understand Bach's 'Janus' quality better if we understand the historical background of his music. We saw how the shift of power from the Venetian Republic, and from Rome and the Vatican, to the German and Austrian Empires provided the context for a similar shift of the hub of European music from Italy to Central Europe at the start of the eighteenth century. Interestingly, Venetian-born Vivaldi moved from Venice to Vienna at the end of his life and died there. In brief, late Baroque music in Germany and Italy emerged in the aftermath and as a result of this shift of economic and political power from Italy to German-speaking central Europe.

The absence of the German bourgeois revolution can be ascribed to some degree to the devastation caused by the Thirty Years' War which destroyed the cities economically and politically. But the decline of the cities also resulted from the discovery of the Americas and the shifting of international trade from central Europe and the Mediterranean to the Atlantic. Additional important factors were the defeat of the peasant revolts in 1524–1545 and the Thirty Years' War 'which destroyed the most important... productive forces in agriculture... the peasants, plebeians and ruined burghers were reduced to a state of Irish misery...' (Engels 1850/1969, p. 126). These factors resulted in an economically and politically weak bourgeois class.

These developments also strengthened the princes, who no longer faced a challenge from the middle classes to their position as great feudal landowners. The powerlessness of the German bourgeoisie, their exclusion from politics, induced a passivity which affected the entire cultural life of the period. The traditional element in Bach's work reflects this domination of the Lutheran princes over German society and its resulting backwardness.

On the other hand, Bach was open to wider social and political influences. And on the broader European canvass, we witness the steady growth of the bourgeoisie's economic and political power and of its cultural influence which was to culminate in the great French revolution of 1789. From this standpoint, Bach's music is testimony to the great struggle for human liberation that always continues despite numerous setbacks.

Legacy of the Baroque
Musical developments of the seventeenth and early decades of the eighteenth century gave birth to the modern world of music. An infinite variety of new music was generated through the rise of opera and its related forms—oratorios and concert arias—and the vitality of independent solo and ensemble forms. Virtually every musical form and style that came to characterise the art music of the later eighteenth and nineteenth centuries can trace its roots and often its substance to the Baroque. This is evident in the unabating relevance of opera to the present, the formation and definition of the orchestra, the growth of chamber music, including the string quartet, the solo keyboard literature, and the concept of the symphony as it developed from the French overture and particularly the Italian operatic overture. The realisation of the instrumental concerto is

but one of the many new Baroque forms to unceasingly enrich the future of music.

Karl Marx described how the German bourgeoisie funked its 'historical task' by failing to carry out the bourgeois revolution in the manner of its English, French and American counterparts. As a late developer in the field of industrial capitalism, when it did begin to occupy centre stage, it heard the stirrings of the fledging working class in the wings and promptly threw in its lot with the old, semi-feudal Junkers nobility (Marx 1962/1848, pp. 68–69). Following Marx, Herbert Marcuse remarked, that the German bourgeoisie had carried out the bourgeois revolution in philosophy instead. 'The German middle class, weak and scattered over numerous territories with divergent interests, could hardly contemplate a revolution. The few industrial enterprises that existed were but small islands within a protracted feudal system... Thus, while the French Revolution had already begun to assert the reality of freedom, German idealism was only occupying itself with the idea of it' (Marcuse 1954, p. 4). Could we not add that it also fulfilled its historic task in the field of music, together with its Austrian cousins?

In conclusion, late Baroque music absorbed the best of the past as it moved confidently forward into the future. With its rich melodic lines and sophisticated harmonic structures, its contrapuntal duality, it asserted reason as the defining principle of music, one which it expressed in the new system of *tonality*. This was the foundation stone on which successive generations of composers built the edifice of modern music, the richly diverse music of the capitalist era. As Susan McClary put it: '...its career of rise and decline happens to articulate through musical terms the course of the European bourgeoisie' (ed. Leppert and McClary 1987, p. 7). The nobility and petty princelings in Germany and Austria were determined to maintain feudal power, but 'the victory of the feudal landlords was more apparent than real. Their sun was setting, and a new aristocracy was arising in their midst. This aristocracy was bourgeois and middle-class, and rational rather than Catholic' (Mellers 1957, p. 7). Late Baroque was the music of the European bourgeoisie as it embarked on the creation of a new social order.

BIBLIOGRAPHY

Behrman, Simon. 2009. *From Revolution to Irrelevance: How Classical Music Lost Its Relevance*. International Socialism Journal 121 (January).

Blacking, John. 1974. *How Musical Is Man?* Seattle and London: University of Wasington Press.

Blanning, Tim. 2010. *The Triumph of Music: The Rise of Composers, Musicians and Their Art.* Harvard University Press.

Boyd, Malcolm. 1993. *Rome: The Power of Patronage*, in ed. G. J. Buelow. Macmillan Press.

Buelow, George, J. (ed.). 1993. *The Late Baroque Era: From the 1680s to 1740.* Macmillan Press.

Bukofzer, Manfred F. 1947. *Music in the Baroque Era from Monteverdi to Bach.* New York: W. W. Norton.

Cooke, Deryck. 1959/1962. *The Language of Music.* Oxford University Press.

Eidam, Klaus. 2001. *The True Life of Johann Sebastian Bach.* NY: Basic Books.

Einstein, Alfred. 1947. *Music in the Romantic Era: A History of Musical Thought in the 19th Century.* New York: W. W. Norton.

Engels, Frederick. 1850/1969. *The Peasant War in Germany.* Hamburg/London: Lawrence and Wishart.

Fulbrook, May. 1992. *A Concise History of Germany.* Cambridge University Press.

Gardiner, John Eliot. 2014. *Music in the Castle of Heaven: A Portrait of Johann Sebastian Bach.* London: Penguin Books.

Goodall, Howard. 2013. *The Story of Music.* London: Vintage Books.

Harman, Chris. 1999. *A People's History of the World, Bookmarks.* London.

Hindley, Geoffrey (ed.). 1971. *The Larousse Encyclopedia of Music.* Hamlyn Publishing Group.

Keates, Jonathan. 2009. *Handel: The Man and His Music.* Pimlico: Random House.

Lang, P.H. 1966. *George Frideric Handel.* New York: Dover Publications Inc.

Leichtentritt, Hugo. 1954. *Music, History and Ideas.* Cambridge, MA: Harvard University Press.

Marcuse, Herbert. 1954. *Reason and Revolution.* New York: Humanities Press.

Marx, Karl. 1848/1962. *The Bourgeoisie and the Counter-Revolution.* In *Marx Engels Selected Works*, vol. I, Moscow: Foreign Languages Publishing House.

McClary, Susan. 1987. The Blasphemy of Talking Politics during Bach Year in Music and Society: The Politics of Composition. In *Performance and Reception*, ed. R. Leppert & S. McClary. Cambridge University Press.

McComb, Todd M. 2000, March. *What Is Monophony, Polyphony, Homophony, Monody, etc.?* www.medieval.org/emfaq/misc/homophony.html.

Mellers, Wilfred. 1957. *The Sonata Principle From C. 1750.* London: Rockliff.

Palisca, Claude V. 2001. *Baroque. The New Grove Dictionary of Music and Musicians.* London: Macmillan.

Raynor, Henry. 1972. *A Social History of Music: From the Middle Ages to Beethoven.* London: Barrie & Jenkins.

Rubinstein, Jay. 2011. *Armies of Heaven: The First Crusade and the Quest for Apocalypse.* New York: Basic Books.

Sagall, Sabby. 2013. *Final Solutions: Human Nature, Capitalism and Genocide.* London: Pluto Press.

Selfridge-Field, Eleanor. 1993. *Venice in an Era of Political Decline*, in *The Late Baroque Era: From the 1680s to 1740*, ed. G.J. Buelow. The Macmillan Press.

Snowman, Daniel. 2009. *The Gilded Stage: A Social History of Opera.* London: Atlantic Books.

Spitta, Philipp. 1899. *Johann Sebastian Bach: His Work and Influence on the Music of Germany, 1685–1750*, vol. 3, p. 315. London: Novello & Co.

Steglich, Rudolf. 1939. *Georg Friedrich Handel.* Available only in German.

Study.com: *Rise of Renaissance Polyphony: Dufay, des Prez & Palestrina.*

Weber, Max. 1905/1930. *The Protestant Ethic and the Spirit of Capitalism.* London: Unwin University Books.

Wolff, Christoph. 2000. *Johann Sebastian Bach: The Learned Musician.* New York: W. W. Norton & Co.

Wollenberg, Susan. 1993. *Vienna Under Joseph I and Charles VI*, in *The Late Baroque Era: From the 1680s to 1740*, ed. G.J. Buelow. Macmillan Press.

CHAPTER 3

The Classical Style

The late Baroque era ends with the death of Handel in 1759. The Classical period emerged in the second half of the eighteenth century in Vienna, capital of the Austro-Hungarian empire ruled by the Habsburg dynasty. It is the age of Haydn (1732–1809), Mozart (1756–1791), Beethoven (1770–1827) and also Schubert. The latter two are rooted in the Classical style but their work forms a bridge to the early romantic movement: Ludwig Van Beethoven and Franz Schubert (1797–1827). So, arguably, the Classical age begins around 1760 with the start of Haydn's musical activity, and ends with Beethoven's death in 1827.

The achievements of Bach and Handel had been glorious. After them, an apparent barrenness appears spanning the years 1750–1770. But in reality, a new style was undergoing gestation, and the years 1750–1760 mark the gradual beginnings of a revolution in music, reminiscent of those of 1585–1722 which saw the invention of 'equal temperament' and of 1600 to the 1680s/90s which witnessed the creation of tonality (see Chapter 2).

Galant Music

'Galant' refers to the style which was fashionable from the 1720s to the 1770s but especially between 1755 and 1775. This movement featured a return to simplicity and immediacy of appeal after the complexity of the

© The Author(s) 2021   71
S. Sagall, *MUSIC and CAPITALISM*,
Critical Political Theory and Radical Practice,
https://doi.org/10.1057/978-1-137-52095-1_3

late baroque era. This meant simpler, more song-like melodies, decreased use of *polyphony*, short, periodic phrases. According to Arnold Whittall, "a period consists of two phrases, antecedent and consequent, each of which begins with the same motif", a reduced harmonic vocabulary emphasising *tonic* and *dominant*, and a clear distinction between soloist and accompaniment. [*The Oxford Companion to Music. Oxford Music Online*]. This musical style was part of the wider 'galant' movement in art at the time. The word 'galant' derives from French, where it was in use from at least the sixteenth century. In the early eighteenth century, a 'galant homme' described a person of fashion—elegant, cultured and virtuous. The rejection of so much accumulated learning and formula in music is paralleled only by the rejection in the early twentieth century of the entire structure of tonal key relationships.

This simplified style was melody-driven, not constructed, as so much Classical music was to be, on rhythmic or melodic motifs. "It is indicative that Haydn, even in his old age, is reported to have said, 'If you want to know whether a melody is really beautiful, sing it without accompaniment'" (Blume 1970, p. 19). This simplification also extended to harmonic rhythm, which is generally slower in Galant music than is the case in the earlier Baroque style, thus making lavish melodic ornamentation and nuances of secondary harmonic colourings more important (Palmer 2001, p. xvii). The affinities of Galant style with Rococo in the visual arts are easily overplayed, but characteristics that were valued in both genres were freshness, accessibility and charm.

Rosen suggests it is paradoxical that that 'period which owed so much to Christian and Emanuel Bach, which was so dependent on their craftsmanship and their innovations, could not produce a major style of its own until it had reabsorbed… the work of Handel and Sebastian Bach (i.e. J.S. Bach)' (Rosen 1997, p. 47).

As already suggested, two composers—with a shared surname, both German—are of prime importance in defining this transitional period, composers who built the important bridge between late Baroque and Classical. They are two of the sons of the great J.S. Bach—Carl Philip Emanuel Bach (1714–1788), and Johann Christian Bach (1735–1782). But in addition to the Bach brothers, some of Telemann's later music, that of Johann Quantz, Johann Adolf Hasse, Giovanni Battista Sammartini, Giuseppe Tartini, Baldassare Galuppi, Johann Stamitz, Domenico Alberti, and perhaps the early Mozart are also exemplars of the Galant style.

Carl Philipp Emanuel Bach developed a personal style known in German as 'empfindsamer stil' or 'sensitive style' which applied the principles of rhetoric and drama to music. His music forms an important milestone in the development of the Galanter Stil on the route to the new Classicism. Indeed, it was he who coined the term 'Galant' (Leichtentritt 1954, p. 162). His ample capacity to produce music of passion and sensitivity make his piano sonatas among the first great works for the recently developed, popular instrument. They had a significant influence on the work of Haydn and even the young Beethoven.

Johann Christian Bach developed a completely different, highly melodic style, the one, as already mentioned, referred to as 'Galant'. This involved balanced phrases, without too much *contrapuntal* complexity. This style opposed the complex lines of Baroque music, emphasising instead fluid melodies in articulated phrases. The Galant movement preceded the Classical style which fused the Galant style with a revived interest in *counterpoint*. Johann Christian's elder half-brother, Carl Phillip Emanuel, was a founder of the style, but Johann Christian carried it further, to the point where it approximated to the more complex Classical style. We can thus see a dialectical movement in eighteenth-century music with the Classical style being, in a sense, a synthesis of the opposites of *contrapuntal* Baroque and the Galant.

Johann Stamitz (1717–1757), Czech by birth but composer for Rameau's patron, the bourgeois Le Riche de la Poupeliniere, and for the Mannheim-based Elector of Palatine, created instrumental music in a theatrical style. He created a new type of melody and rhythmic accompaniment, introducing devices aimed at exciting and surprising his audience. In his orchestration, he concentrates on projecting the tune. We no longer hear the harpsichord *continuo* which in Baroque music provided the harmonic background to the interweaving melodies (see Chapter 2). Instead, we hear *ostinato* string figures and sustained notes on the horns filling in the middle parts since the melody only features in the treble or top, i.e., the upper, part of the instrumental or vocal tonal range. Stamitz develops Rameau's sound effects—necessary to express events like earthquakes—so that they become ends in themselves, for example, the *crescendo, diminuendo, tremolo*, sudden changes of *dynamics*. The 'bouncing upward *arpeggio* figures' across the strings (known as the Mannheim sky-rocket), the 'twiddling *figurations*' (Mannheim birdies), the 'long crescendo over a reiterated bass', to which 'the audience rose to its feet as one man' (the Mannheim 'steam-roller' became famous or notorious across Europe) (Mellers 1957, p. 11).

PART I: THE CLASSICAL STYLE

The years 1755–1775 may thus be designated as a period of transition, during which composers "had to choose between dramatic surprise and formal perfection, between expressivity and elegance." They could rarely have both. And Bach's sons had divided up the main stylistic possibilities among themselves. Only when Haydn and Mozart, separately and jointly, created a style in which a dramatic effect appeared both 'surprising and logically motivated', in which the expressive and the elegant could link arms, was the Classical style born (Rosen 1997, p. 44).

New stylistic developments emerged that became part of the musical language of the next half-century, ones that to help to shape a dramatic style based on *tonality*. Most of the typical features of the Classical style didn't appear in an orderly sequence, but sporadically, sometimes jointly, sometimes separately, though the final product has a logical coherence.

The Sonata Principle

A revolutionary principle of musical composition was created in the second half of the eighteenth century, a vital period of transformation in both European music and society: the emergence of the sonata form. It was a new approach to musical creation which, as Wilfred Mellers has pointed out, 'grew out of a particular set of circumstances... new human needs and desires', a period of revolutionary transformation (Mellers 1957, p. 3).

Classical Forms—Sonata Form

All the Classical forms—the *sonata*, the *trio*, the *quartet* and the *symphony*—used the basic three-part (or *ternary*) form, known as 'first movement sonata form', which evolved through the eighteenth century. It consisted of three sections: an exposition in which two distinct themes or melodies are stated, the first in the *tonic* of the piece, the second moving into the *dominant*, followed by a central *development* section in which the ideas of the two themes are elaborated. The movement is completed with a return to the main theme, which is in a different key or key-family and is repeated with modifications (*recapitulation*) (Goodall 2013, p. 129). The *bithematic* element of the *sonata* form had been fore-shadowed by Domenico Scarlatti, with C.P.E. Bach generally regarded as its creator, though it was perfected by Haydn. The music is mostly *homo-phonic*—a single melody line with accompaniment—made up using notes of the chord, or a texture where all parts keep in step with each other (often known as *chordal* style). There are short and clearly defined musical phrases with two or more contrasting themes [www.musicatschool.co.uk].

However, there is a difference between late Baroque and Classical melodies: with Bach, each musical voice is independent but the emphasis is on individual lines interacting and echoing each other. With Haydn and Mozart, there are clear divisions between melody and accompaniment, especially in *solo* works, though the bass line aspires towards equality in melodic development, particularly in orchestral and chamber music.

However, the Classical composers ended up developing and refining a more sophisticated version of the sonata, one based on a four-movement pattern. The first movement was typically an *allegro*, the second an *adagio* or *andante* the third a *minuet* or dance piece with or without a *trio*, and a *finale*, often in *rondo* form.

But the most important musical change in the second half of the eighteenth century was the emergence of the symphony as the key instrumental form. Pieces designated as 'symphonies' first appeared in Austria around 1740, emerging out of Vivaldi's concerto finales, the Italian operatic overture, and the 'concerto grosso' with its slow-quick-slow-quick sequence. Sometimes, the symphonies have three movements, quick-slow-quick, following the Italian theatrical fashion, with two *allegros* in *buffo* style, and a pretty aria in the middle. At other times, symphonies have five or six movements, including a suite which recreates one or more dance movements.

The symphony emerging out of these prior elements finally settled into a four-movement structure. A first movement—*allegro*—a brisk, lively movement was derived from the *opera buffa* which 'debunked the sublime' and dealt with the 'low life of Tom, Dick and Harry', and, of course, their young women. The musical style of the *opera buffa* was related to urban popular music, and the instrumental sections clearly modified the techniques of the Baroque musical style. *Opera seria* dealt with larger than life characters: humans swollen to the size of gods or monsters, mirrors of the great autocratic monarchs. *Opera seria* has been described as 'lifeless propaganda on behalf of the decaying ruling class'. It was well supported financially by them (McGarr 1991, p. 120).

The *allegro* might be prefaced by a slow introduction inspired by the 'concerto grosso' or by French heroic opera. The slow introduction was generally retained by Haydn, occasionally by Mozart and Beethoven. Slow movements were always based on the operatic aria. The third movement was a descendant of the dance suite, traditionally becoming a minuet, though its previous noble elegance was now infused with a rustic vigour. The finale might again be in the *buffo binary* style though it too might betray its dance origins by being a *rondo*. Whatever form their symphonies took, the Austrian composers found in the Italian *buffo* overture and the popular elements of the 'concerto grosso' the very materials they needed to create a 'democratic' instrumental style. Such "Italianate features could easily be reconciled with the urban and rustic popular music of their own country" (Mellers 1957, p. 10).

The symphony was defined by the French scholar E. Borrel as a 'sonata for orchestra characterised by the multiplicity of the performers on each instrument and by the diversity of tone colours'. It thus conforms to the plan which Stamitz and the Mannheim School had foreseen (Hindley 1971, p. 237). The founder, architect and initial master of the symphony was Haydn. He sometimes preceded the first movement with a slow introduction, and composed variations to serve as the finale. Mozart tended to follow this model, but Beethoven revolutionised both the sonata and the symphony.

There was much reciprocal influence on the part of these composers, but the most striking example is that of Haydn and Mozart. Haydn's mature late London symphonies (numbers 93–98 and 99–104) reflect the influence of Mozart's emotionally charged, fast-tempo movements, whereas in 1785 the young Mozart paid homage to his friend by dedicating to him the six quartets influenced by Haydn's opus 33 quartets.

As we saw in Chapter 2, the concerto, like the symphony, had its origins in the early eighteenth century in the 'concerto grosso'. It acquired its formal structure from the 'sinfonia' or Italian overture with its sequence of fast, slow, fast movements. But whereas the symphony received the addition of a fourth movement—a *minuet* or *scherzo*—the concerto remained a three-movement form.

INSTRUMENTS

In the pre-Classical period, the favourite *solo* instrument was the violin, although music was also written for the trumpet, oboe, cello, flute and viola. From the early Classical period, for more than a century, the piano was the favourite instrument, followed at some distance by the violin. But the Classical composers also wrote for other instruments: in addition to twenty concertos for keyboard, Haydn composed nine for violin, six for cello, one for trumpet, and several others for various instruments. Among the fifty or so concertos composed by Mozart, twelve are for different instruments.

The importance of the *solo* instrument was enhanced in the Classical first movement because of its role in the initial *thematic* exposition, and also in the central development. Moreover, the soloist's virtuosity could be given free rein in the *cadenza*, previously improvised but now written out.

A concerto for several soloists didn't contrast a small group with the *tutti*, as did the 'concerto grosso', but rather several soloists conducted a dialogue with the orchestra. This resulted in an amplification of the traditional three movements, as can be seen in Mozart's concerto for flute and harp or in Beethoven's triple concerto (Hindley 1971, p. 237).

Forerunners of the great trio of Classical composers had written keyboard works using the sonata form. J.C. Bach had composed symphonies full of charm and grace. However, in the field of keyboard and chamber music, it was Haydn and Mozart who scaled the heights of Classical achievement. Their favoured instrument remained the piano, but Haydn also composed sonatas for the tenor string instrument, the 'baryton', and sonatas for piano and violin. Mozart composed sonatas for two pianos, for piano for four hands, for violin and piano, and for bassoon and cello. The amplification of the second subject, the duality of themes in the central development, i.e. two distinct melodies, and Haydn's bold *modulations*, prepared the ground for Beethoven.

Chamber music developed rapidly. In some ways, it was more suitable for the expression of the composer's inner emotional life. Hence the trio, quartet and quintet became vehicles of the deepest personal expression, especially the quartet. The roots of the string quartet lie in the mid-eighteenth century, the first forays in this form in Germany and Austria, in the works of Stamitz, Starzer and Leopold Hofman. Both Haydn and Mozart adopted the sonata form in their first movements.

The early Viennese symphonies represent the first appearance of a pattern that was to become a regular feature of the music of Haydn and Mozart—the return to Baroque complexity and the recapturing of some of the richness lost with the advent of Galant music (Rosen 1997, p. 45).

The Classical style consists broadly of nine features: (1) the primacy of melody; (2) an atmosphere of drama created by abrupt dramatic shifts and breaks in both melody and rhythm; (3) therefore, an uneven rhythmic flow with frequent changes of tempo; (4) a homophonic texture with a single melodic line and accompaniment consisting of a limited range of chords or plain harmony to emphasise the primacy of the melody (Goodall 2013, p. 125): the three main chords are expressed as I, IV and V because they are the *triads* belonging to the first, fourth and fifth notes of the scale—*tonic, subdominant* and *dominant*; (5) the short articulated phrase with two or more contrasting themes; (6) the relation between principal voice and accompanying voices is transformed: in one bar, the melody is given to one instrument, say the cello, with the other instruments taking up the accompanying figure but in the next bar, the accompanying figure becomes the principal voice carrying the melody. Haydn himself claimed that his opus 33 quartets represented a revolution in style (Rosen 1997, p. 116); (7) the central role of tonality; (8) a melodic framework consisting of the tension between *tonic* and *dominant* followed by a climactic resolution to the *tonic*; and (9) finally, the supremacy of sonata form.

Firstly, the primacy of melody. Leichtentritt believes that symphonic music of the mid to late eighteenth century was marked by a new stress on melody as 'the main factor of the entire composition; everything else—harmony, construction, *counterpoint*—becomes subservient'. This new melody was indebted to the folk songs and dance tunes of the ordinary people; 'it was indeed of the same type, but a little more finished, shaped by an artist's hand, fitted for use in a composition of larger dimensions' (Leichtentritt 1954, p. 164).

What is melody? A broad definition is that it consists of a rhythmical succession of single tones producing a distinct musical phrase or idea. Classical melody consists of short and clearly defined musical phrases with two or more contrasting themes [www.mostlywind.co.uk].

It is mainly homophonic, that is, with multiple parts or melodic lines moving together according to the same rhythm, the clear melody line having a subordinate chordal accompaniment. This creates a layered structure and a clearer contrast between treble and bass parts—that is, between the melodic lines and harmonic accompaniment. Brighter contrasts also appear in more frequent *modulations* and greater *dynamic* changes. Also characteristic of the Classical melody is a predominance of the *tonic* and *dominant* notes of the scale, which form a kind of context, though the interplay between notes that makes up the Classical melody also takes in the other notes, including the subdominant, *mediant* and *submediant*.

Goodall provides two examples of melodies at either end of the sixty-year period after 1760. They are Gluck's charming, gentle 'Dance of the Blessed Spirits' (1762) from his 'Orfeo ed Euridice', and a more powerful, more dramatic piece—the final movement of Beethoven Fifth Symphony (1808) (Goodall 2013, p. 126).

Secondly, the atmosphere of dramatic tension. In his analysis of the origins of the Classical style, Rosen describes a dualism, a pair of conflicting ideals, between which balance had to be struck: dramatic sentiment and dramatic action. The High (ie, Late) Baroque had given musical expression to dramatic sentiment, in dance movements or in opera, for example Handel's 'Jeptha' which gives voice to the daughter's courage, the father's tragic sternness, the mother's despair, and the lover's defiance. But the later eighteenth century demanded more: dramatic action had to replace mere sentiment. An operatic example is the lovers in Mozart's 'Die Entfuhrung Aus Dem Serail', Konstanze and Belmonte, who move from joy to suspicion and outrage, then to final reconciliation. The necessity of action applies also to non-operatic music, for example, the *minuet*. Every one of Bach's minuets has an uninterrupted seamless flow, whereas in Haydn they become articulated, dramatic events, with abrupt melodic changes and sudden rhythmic breaks.

The first significant examples of this new dramatic style can be found not in Italian theatrical works but in the harpsichord sonatas of Domenico Scarlatti (1685–1757), composed in Spain in the second quarter of the eighteenth century. In his sonatas, the *periodic* phrasing, the changes of key and of *texture* are the dramatic events, clearly delineated, "that were to become central to the style of the generations that came after him. It was, in fact, under the weight of this dramatic articulation that the High Baroque aesthetic collapsed" (Rosen 1997, p. 43). (In the Classical era, periodic phrasing consisted of finely balanced antecedent and consequent phrases. An antecedent phrase is a 'question' phrase, often ending on the *dominant* and therefore sounding incomplete. A consequent phrase is an 'answer' phrase, invariably ending on the *tonic* and therefore sounding complete.)

Thirdly, frequent rhythmic changes. The typical and most common form of Baroque rhythm is a simple, unified or homogeneous rhythmic texture. We may also describe it as an even or fluent flow of music without sharp breaks of rhythm or interruption of melody. However, in the late eighteenth century, rhythmic transition is achieved with separate, well-defined elements, each being twice or half as fast as the preceding one.

But the movement from one rhythm to another is heard 'as a transition and not as a contrast' (Rosen 1997, p. 64). There is, here too, a sense of unbroken continuity which is achieved partly by starting the faster rhythm in a subsidiary or accompanying voice so that its arrival is less noticeable, and partly by the use of accents, but also by harmonic means. "Haydn and Mozart were the first composers to understand the new demands on harmonic movement made by the periodic phrase... Much of their success hangs on a comprehension of dissonance and harmonic tension: it is often an exceptionally dissonant chord that introduces new and faster rhythm, and both composers made full use of the added animation that is so natural at the end of a musical paragraph in its drive towards a cadence and resolution." (Rosen 1997, p. 65).

Fourth, composers of the mid to late eighteenth century confined themselves to a limited range of chords, partly as a reaction against the harmonic style of their predecessors and partly in order to stress the primacy of the melody. They believed that the tune should 'glide unencumbered across the aural landscape, without the listener being too distracted by chordal complexities lurking beneath it' (Goodall 2013, p. 125). Goodall points out that there are three chords in the shortened list that were used time and again, since they were the ones that most clearly brought out the sense of 'home' in the music, strengthening the 'melody's typical journey away from home and back again'. The reams of music composed in the sixty or so after 1750 clung on to these chords.

These three chords can be expressed as the numbers I, IV and V, because they are the *triads* belonging to the first, fourth and fifth notes of the major or minor scale. So, in C major, they are the C, F and G *triads*. In G major, they are G, C and D, and so on. These three chords for every key-family are also described, as we've seen, as the *tonic*, *sub-dominant* and *dominant*. Leichtentritt argues similarly that 'contrapuntal complexity finds no place in the new symphonic type, which, in accordance with its plain melodic material, is perfectly satisfied with a very plain harmony, with chords that hardly go beyond the range of tonic, dominant, and sub-subdominant' (Leichtentritt 1954, p. 164). The tunes by Gluck and Beethoven mentioned above demonstrate the ubiquity of the I, II and IV chords.

Both tunes are harmonised by chords I, IV and V of their respective scales (F major and C major). In the case of the Beethoven movement, the first chord we hear that isn't one of those three is in the thirty-sixth bar, some forty-eight seconds into the work. However, it is also true that

Beethoven had to stick to those basic chords if he wanted to include brass instruments which in 1808 were only able to play a limited number of notes belonging to the 'home' chords. By the time he came to write his ninth symphony, completed in 1824, technology in the form of pistons and valves had come to the rescue, providing brass instruments giving a much fuller menu of notes and available keys. The reason that these chords appear over and over again is that these three harmonic centres are the most powerful, that is, they are created from the most 'natural' ratios of sound (Goodall 2013, p. 126).

However, even if the Classical composers limited themselves to a small number of chords, their music was far from simple. Beneath the surface of the music of Gluck, Haydn and Mozart, lies an intensely sophisticated infrastructure. These composers were influenced by the models of order bequeathed by the ancient Greek world, seeking in its 'Apollonian' equilibrium the Classical ideals of harmony, elegance and rationality. But being unable to reinvent the music of ancient Greece, they had to discover their own methods of inserting grand, formal structures into the foundations of their pieces. Rather than just composing pretty tunes with accompaniment, they constructed them according to a model: every piece they produced was written according to a 'musical map'. An opera would pursue the path laid down by its narrative. A sacred choral work would navigate through the religious texts as ordained by the Church.

Fifth, the short, articulated phrase with two or more contrasting themes, perhaps the most distinctive element in the newly created Classical style: when this first appeared, it disrupted the Baroque style which relied on an 'encompassing and sweeping continuity' (Rosen 1997, p. 57). The model is the four-bar phrase, though at first, two-bar phrases predominated, for example with Domenico Scarlatti. However, Haydn, in his Quartet opus 20, no. 4 (1772), begins with seven independent six-bar phrases. Three-bar and five-bar phrases often appear at the beginning of works and seven-bar phrases become possible towards the end of the century.

Sixth, the relation between principal voice and accompanying voices is transformed: in one bar, the melody is given to one instrument with the other instruments taking up the accompanying *figure* but in the next bar, the accompanying *figure* becomes the principal voice carrying the melody.

Seventh, the musical language which underpinned the Classical style was that of *tonality* (ushered in by Corelli around 1680). However, from its inception, this had never been a massive, immobile system but a living, changing language, one which reached a new and important turning point just before the style of Haydn and Mozart took shape (Rosen 1997, p. 23). What develops is a new emphasis on the tension between *tonic* and *dominant*. The *dominant cadence*—the climactic resolution of tension by returning from the *dominant* to the *tonic*—becomes a key harmonic feature of the Classical style, reinforced by the increased importance of the *dominant seventh* chord (a seventh chord consisting of the root—lowest note of a chord—major third, perfect fifth and minor seventh notes).

Ninth, the supremacy of the *sonata* form as outlined above.

Clearly, not every Classical composer gave equal weight to all nine features though our three main protagonists certainly featured most of them.

Counterpoint was not forgotten, especially in the later period, and there was also an echo of the Galant style which stressed light elegance in place of the Baroque's impressive dignity, seriousness and grandeur. In general, there was a greater emphasis on variety and contrast within a piece. In the previous two centuries, as many writers have pointed out, most instrumental music originated in dance music. Dance once again, therefore, forms a musical template. The periodic, articulated *phrase* is related to the dance which requires a pattern of phrases that corresponds to its steps and groupings.

However, as composers grew more ambitious, they resolved to compose works not to dance to but to be listened to. This required alternative ways of determining a piece's structure, pace, duration or changes of mood. So rules were devised—what Goodall calls maps or 'design templates'—whose most sophisticated expression was to be found in the growth and popularity of the symphony. We know that 'the form that underpins every symphony composed between around 1750 and 1900 actually has a name inherited from a smaller-scale instrumental work: "Sonata Form"' (Goodall 2013, p. 129).

Articulated, *periodic* phrasing brought about two fundamental changes in the character of eighteenth-century music. The first was a heightened sensitivity to *symmetry* which can be seen in an ascending scale or series of notes followed by a descending scale. The dominance of *symmetry* came from the *periodic* character of the Classical phrase. It implies, therefore, *symmetry*, recurrence and closure.

Arguably, historically *symmetry* preceded drama. We find *symmetry* in the Rococo style from the early eighteenth century on, a feature that facilitated the growth of the dramatic concentration of tension in the later Classical style (Rosen 1997, p. 77). The suggestion here is that a phrase is heard and is then followed by the next phrase which balances or complements it. This provides a comfortable 'predictability' for the ear which then makes the non-symmetry that follows all the more unexpected and, therefore, dramatic. The second change brought about by periodic phrasing is the rhythmic *texture* of great variety mentioned above, where the different rhythms are neither contrasted nor superimposed, but flow naturally into each other.

In the second half of the eighteenth century, there develops what Mellers describes as the split between a 'popular style' and a 'style of sensibility', that is, between 'people's music' and 'artists' music'. He believes this is exemplified in the career of Johann Christian Bach who started out as a composer of Italian opera, then settled in London, writing instrumental music for the drawing-room in a superficial Rococo style with pretty tunes and mildly titillating harmonies and *modulations*. But he also wrote a few works, notably a 'Piano Sonata in C Minor', which hint at a deeper world. There are further examples of this dualism in the work of Johann Christian's two half-brothers—Carl Philip Emanuel and William Friedman. These two styles interacted with each other to produce the mature sonata style of the Age of Enlightenment. This conflict grows increasingly intense within the development of the sonata in the eighteenth and indeed the nineteenth century as it is related to a conflict within society itself. This conflict is both economic, with the industrial revolution sweeping aside earlier forms of production, and political, as the French and American revolutions sweep away the old order (see Part III).

In 1812, the German writer and critic E.T.A. Hoffmann listed three great figures, Haydn, Mozart and Beethoven, who, he said, "developed a new art" (Rosen 1997, p. 19). These three composers were of different character, with often opposed ideals of expression, but they reached analogous solutions in most of their work. Around 1775, we can see a major change in the music of both Haydn and Mozart: it was around this time that Haydn became more fully acquainted with the Italian comic opera tradition to which the Classical style was so indebted. And in 1777, Mozart composed his 'E flat Piano Concerto K. 271 ('Jeunehomme') which was perhaps the first large-scale work in which his mature style was in complete command. Earlier dates could have been chosen, but, arguably, it is only from this point on that the new sense of rhythm which displaced that of the Late Baroque) became completely consistent.

Haydn himself claimed that the 'Scherzi' or 'Russian Quartets, Opus 33' of 1781, were composed according to completely new principles (Rosen 1997, pp. 23/59). The creation of the Classical style seems to be a natural one, a step in the progressive realisation of the musical language as it had developed from the fifteenth century. Yet, in relation to the preceding style, it seems more like a revolutionary leap.

Rosen emphasises the dramatic element in the Classical style, a key factor differentiating it from Baroque which is sometimes described as decorative. Now a Baroque work is undramatic in that its tension remains fairly constant until the final *cadence*, rarely rising above the level set at the start. But the opening and closing pages of a Classical sonata are a crucial part of its form, facilitating the increased tension of the middle sections. A crucial contrast with the Baroque style lies in the moment and location of the dramatisation created by *modulation*. *Modulation* already exists in all early eighteenth-century dance forms. But in High Baroque, a pause marking the arrival of the *dominant* is placed at the end, hardly ever in the middle of a piece. The music gradually flows to the *dominant* with a resolution at the end of the section. But early in a sonata, i.e. a Classical work, there must be a dramatic moment when we are aware of the new *tonality*. It can be a pause, a strong *cadence*, a new theme or anything else chosen by the composer. This 'moment of dramatisation is more fundamental than any compositional device' (Rosen 1997, p. 71).

This need for dramatisation is the reason the Classical style required more forcible means of stressing new keys than the Baroque: it employed for this purpose the new expedient of 'filling', which Rosen defines as 'conventional material, superficially unrelated to the content of the piece'. All musical styles depend on some form of conventional material, mainly at *cadences*, which generally followed traditional formulas. But the Classical style magnified and lengthened the *cadence* so as to strengthen the *modulation*. A Baroque composer worked mostly with 'vertical filling', i.e. the 'figured bass' or *continuo*, and the Classical composer with horizontal, i.e. long phrases of 'conventional passagework'.

The two basic forms of such conventional material are *scales* and *arpeggios* and they fill Classical works to an extent that Baroque composers would only have used in order to create an improvised sound. An early eighteenth-century composer would have used certain material to convey the impression of freedom, whereas for Mozart this became quite basic to the way he developed the form. Mozart used entire *phrases* of *scales* and *arpeggios* the way Handel used *sequences*—to link sections of the work. However, in the finest Baroque music, the *sequence* is usually covered by *thematic* material, while even in Mozart's or Haydn's greatest work, the 'filling' is displayed openly and even seems to have been partly prefabricated.

Rosen suggests that the Classical style created a sense for a large area of stability, impossible before and lost since, which established what might seem to be the one fixed rule of sonata recapitulation: 'material originally exposed in the *dominant* must be represented in the *tonic* fairly completely, even if rewritten and reordered..' (Rosen 1997, p. 72). The point is that in the eighteenth-century music presented outside the *tonic* must have created a feeling of instability which demanded *resolution*. But with the reaffirmation of the *tonic* in the second half of the piece, the material already presented in the *tonic* was often severely cut, while the rest of the exposition demanded resolution in the *tonic*. Whereas at that time, the musical culture prescribed a sensitivity to *tonal* relationships, after Beethoven, harmonic sensibilities became coarsened by the *tonal* instability of music, i.e. frequent shifting of keys and, with modernism, the rejection of *tonality* and, therefore, of any resolution to the *tonic*.

Philip Downs puts forward a similar analysis, suggesting that as the size of musical pieces grew larger, the relatively homogeneous *textures* of Haydn and Mozart gave way to a kind of 'layered structure', defined by melody alternating with 'passagework', i.e. rapid *scales* or *arpeggio* passages. With Beethoven or Schubert, the dimensions of all movements tended to expand, just as the number of movements increased, with four movements becoming the norm in virtuosic sonatas. We described above how Mozart used *scales* and *arpeggios* to link sections of a work. 'Layered structure' refers to the vertical layers of notes or entire phrases made up of the melodic top line and the counter melodies and harmonies on the bottom line. So the complex interplay of textural change of the previous period became simplified, and a typical sonata exposition came to consist of 'an extended melodic section in the *tonic*, leading to a *modulated* section of short *note values* exploiting some pianistic *figure* and often built around a small rhythmic *motive* derived from the opening melody' (Downs 1992, p. 362).

Having established a new key, composers would once again dip into their 'well of lyric inspiration' and produce a melody comparable to the opening one, which in turn was followed by passagework lasting until the closing theme. This might be either *cantabile*, like the first two melodies, probably derived from the first, or a 'combination of melody and virtuosity'. By the end of the century, this scheme remained basically the same for the concerto and string quartet. Downs believes that this underscores the error of separating form from content, that is, seeing structure simply as a container for certain elements—melodies, harmonies or rhythmic movements—in a fixed order. In other words, with the late Classical style, structure *is* these elements, not a separate feature outside them.

['Form' appears to refer here to the overall shape of the work, for example, in the Sonata Form, we have the Exposition, Development and Recapitulation of the piece which we might also see as the 'horizontal journey' through the piece. 'Structure' usually refers to the division of music into different sections, identified as keys, melodies, lyrics or chord sequences. These various sections form the structure of a piece. 'Content' refers to the elements of melody, harmony and rhythm that constitute the heart of a work].

The Classical style has an emotional force which is linked to this contrast between dramatic tension and stability. A fundamental change took place towards the middle of the eighteenth century. 'In most Baroque music, a relatively low level of tension is created and sustained, with certain fluctuations, only to be resolved at the end of the piece: the music works cumulatively—it is rare that one moment is notably more dramatic than another'. There is a decline of tension and gravitas towards the middle, for example Bach's *Chaconne* for unaccompanied violin, or the great A minor *fugue* for organ. The climax of a Baroque work can be heard in the faster rhythm leading to the final *cadence* (Rosen 1997, p. 75).

In contrast, the climax of a Classical work is nearer its centre, which means the final area of stability must have correct proportions. However, the resolution of harmonic tension, and the *symmetry* of the music (the whole piece) and the phrasing were not the only factors affecting Classical proportions: there were various large-scale rhythmic factors within a dramatic structure which demanded that the rhythmic tension be resolved, a resolution that had to be combined with the need to keep the piece flowing until the end. With the interacting of these various elements, the proportions of each Classical work are specific to it, torn in each case between drama and *symmetry*. However, one requirement cannot be altered: 'a long, firm, and unequivocally resolved section in the *tonic* at the end, dramatic if need be, but clearly reducing all the harmonic tensions of the work' (Rosen 1997, p. 75).

There is an insistence on stability at the beginning, but even more, at the end of each Classical piece, a feature which enabled the Classical style to create a form with a 'dramatic violence' that the earlier Baroque style never attempted and which the Romantic style left unresolved, leaving its musical tensions simmering. A Classical composer didn't always require themes of a particular harmonic or melodic energy for a dramatic work: this was because in a Classical work, the drama arises out of the structure.

A Baroque piece reveals its dramatic character in the first bar by the nature and structure of its melody. But if we take a late Classical—some would say early Romantic—piece such as Beethoven's 'Appassionata' piano sonata, only the pianissimo of the first two bars provides any hint of the coming storm. Classical melodies are generally rounded off or resolved as they end, and the fact that they do end is what differentiates them from the Baroque melody. The latter is almost indefinitely extensible. None of the three great Classical composers could have written a melody anywhere near as long as the one in the slow(second) movement of Bach's 'Italian Concerto'. It seems to end only when it has to, when a *tonic cadence* is finally unavoidable, although its climax is left somewhat undefined, its tension diffused rather than concentrated, which enables Bach to sustain the melody at such length. In contrast, 'the energy and tension of a Classical theme (often uniting a variety of rhythmic elements) are much more clearly concentrated, and this climax logically demanded a symmetrical resolution of the melody' (Rosen 1997, p. 77).

A glorious feature of the Classical style is its capacity for reinterpretation, that is, giving a completely fresh significance to a phrase by entering it into a different context, for example a phrase in Mozart's 'Piano Sonata in G major, K 283', which in the exposition is a *modulation* to the *dominant* (moving from *tonic* G major to D major), and in the *recapitulation* is a return to the *tonic*.

Arguably, the feeling for *timbre*—the quality of sound not related to pitch, volume or duration, but which enables the listener to identify a sound as being produced by a specific instrument and to differentiate between different instruments or instruments of the same type (a violin whose strings are made of horsehair compared to strings made out of nylon)—is 'one of the most important distinctions between the style of the three great Classical masters and the preceding generations'. Haydn and Mozart both used the *subdominant* to relax harmonic tension, Haydn less consistently.

The Classical style also had great sensitivity towards the secondary *tonalities*—the keys to which a piece *modulates*—and their relation to the *tonic* can produce moments of sheer poetry. An example is the opening theme of Beethoven's 'Eroica' symphony which is really a horn-call, but the horn only plays it solo at the *recapitulation*. The orchestra then *modulates* from the *tonic* (E flat) to the *supertonic*, i.e. F, and the horn enters *dolce* with the theme, followed by the flute playing it in D flat major. There is a sweetness, a delicacy and an air of stillness which come from the new keys as well as from the orchestration.

This complex, even contradictory, emotion is a further achievement of the Classical musical style. And it is surely not the emotion that has changed since the early eighteenth century—Bach's emotions were no doubt as complex as Beethoven's—but the expressive language. 'The affective character of a Baroque piece is much less complex; the emotion is sometimes deeply poignant, and it can attain an expansiveness that the Classical style reaches with much greater difficulty, but it is generally more direct, and always more unified. The emotional complexity of the Classical language is what makes the operas of Mozart possible. Even irony was possible in music now, as E.T.A. Hoffmann remarked of *Cosi Fan Tutte*' (Rosen 1997, p. 80).

This complexity rested in large measure on the Classical harmonic relationships. The early Classical, Mannerist or Rococo composers, for example, Gluck or J.C. Bach, heightened the tension between *tonic* and *dominant*, and for most of them, this was the limit of large-scale harmonic effects. It fell to Haydn and Mozart to carry this tension further, understanding its implications for the entire area of harmony—the circle of fifths (Goodall 2013, pp. 90–92, see my Chapter 2)—in order to create a new emotional language of music.

Therefore, while contrasting themes are an inevitable aspect of the Classical style, perhaps even more significant are the themes of internal contrast. 'As for the dramatic effect of contrasting themes, the power of the same theme played in different ways is as great, if not greater, and it is through the transformation of themes and not their contrast that the Classical composer affects us most' (Rosen 1997, p. 81).

So, what was important was dramatic effect combined with a profound sense of *symmetry* and proportion. These required a clear sense of the degree of tension and stability in each part of the composition, and also a clear articulation of these parts, but these can be achieved without any contrast of character, either in the various themes or in the different sections of a movement. For example, the first movement of Haydn's 'Military Symphony' has two similar themes, both jaunty and rhythmically stable. The different sections of the movement are developed by orchestration and not by contrasting themes—each begins only with woodwind, continuing with strings alone, finally giving way to the full orchestra with timpani.

Before 1750, such contrast is almost always external—it is between voices or different phrases—and rarely internal, that is, within a melodic line. But in Classical melodies, internal contrast is not only frequent but essential to the style, which relies heavily on *dynamic* inflection, that is, a change or variation of pitch or loudness in a musical line. The Classical style, therefore, is unique in the way in which the whole and the parts reflect each other so clearly.

However, there is a need to resolve *dynamic* contrast. This reconciliation or mediation can take many forms. One of the simpler methods of resolving a contrast between loud and soft is to follow it with a phrase that proceeds gradually from one to the other. Rosen believes that this reconciling of *dynamic* opposites is at the heart of the Classical style. It is a synthesis that constitutes the basic Classical form. He claims not to want to turn Haydn, Mozart and Beethoven into Hegelians, but he argues that the simplest way to summarise the Classical form is as 'the symmetrical resolution of opposing forces'. If this seems too broad a definition of artistic form in general, that is because 'the Classical style has largely become the standard by which we judge the rest of music—hence its name' (Rosen 1997, p. 83). The shape or structure of Mozart's 'C Minor Fantasy' (K475) provides a good example of *symmetry* or balance. It proceeds as follows:

1. *Tonic*: it begins in C minor but modulates quickly away from the tonic, going finally to B minor.
2. *Dominant* of the *dominant*: it goes from the weakened *dominant* G major to the latter's *dominant* D major.
3. Continuous *modulation* through various keys.
4. *Subdominant* of the *subdominant*: B flat major (used as *subdominant* in place of F major, similarly to stage 2).
5. Continuous *modulation*, affirmation of C minor.
6. *Tonic*: return to C minor (Rosen 1997, p. 93).

In contrast, the Late Baroque does contain *resolution*, but the rhythmic and dynamic forces are not sharply defined. And there is a contrast with the Romantic movement—the generation of 1830—where the *symmetry* is less marked, and a refusal of complete resolution can be part of the poetic effect, the new take on a more uncertain world.

One could summarise the *sonata form*, or Classical style, as 'an immense melody', an expanded, articulated phrase, whose harmonic climax is located three-quarters of the way through followed by a *symmetrical* resolution that rounds it off in a careful balance with the opening. Expansion of the end of a phrase is the articulated form of an older technique, and the basis of the *cadenza*. It is essentially the High Baroque method of expansion which proceeds by extending and developing the final few notes of the phrase. However, 'the expansion of the centre of the phrase is peculiar to the Classical style, and is the key to its sense of proportion' (Rosen 1997, p. 87).

An illustration of Classical *sonata form* is Haydn's 'Piano Trio in G Minor' (1793): the first movement contains two themes, with the second theme's second variation becoming a complete *sonata* movement. Haydn expands this second theme (in G major) most significantly in the central *modulation* and the end, a feature that reflects the historical development of the *sonata*, and explains the growing importance during the century of the *development* section and the *coda*. But the greatest master of the development of the centre of a phrase was Mozart. It is here that we find part of the secret of his broad capacity for dramatic composition. His string quintets offer the most impressive examples of this central expansion.

Important changes are also apparent in rhythm, as previously indicated. In the first half of the eighteenth century, the beats are nearly equal in weight or length; the first or downbeat note in a bar is heavier or longer, and the last or upbeat note in a bar is accorded greater importance through a slight lift. In contrast, in a Classical work, half a century later, each beat in a bar has a distinctive weight of its own: in 4/4 time, the upbeat has a much greater weight than the second beat. If one compares a *minuet* written by Bach with one by Haydn, the different is clear: in Bach, the beats are almost exactly equal in time, whereas the sequence in Haydn is uneven: strong or long, weak or short and moderately strong or intermediate notes follow one another in every bar. 'No minuet of Bach attains the strong characterisation of the beat so clear in Haydn, while no minuet of Haydn reduces the beat to something so close to undifferentiated pulsation'. The life and energy of Classical rhythm was based on this possible isolation of each beat (Rosen 1997, p. 90).

Rosen argues that the relation of individual detail to the large form, and the manner in which the form is freely shaped in response to the smallest parts, give us the first style in musical history in which the organisation is completely audible and where the form is never externally imposed. In the Baroque period, the form of the chorale prelude is clearly imposed from outside; it is not simply that the *counterpoint* accompanying the 'cantus firmus' ('plainchant' or simple Gregorian melody as prescribed by ecclesiastical tradition) is usually inspired by the first phrase of the chorale, but that even in some of Bach's greatest works there isn't a total conception but a 'successive modification to respond to the changing phrases of the chorale' (Rosen 1997, p. 93).

Rosen analyses this as a way of writing that suited the 'additive' nature of the Baroque style: it is like a building that has been designed little by little, modified as the construction proceeded. It may give us an impression of unity, but it is a unity different from that of a building designed as a whole, or as a single form, although the former may be no less beautiful. Pursuing this building metaphor, Baroque or *polyphonic* music is like a modern building where the tall inner core, for example the lift shaft, is erected first and the rest of the building constructed around it. The music is built layer upon layer around and below the chant melody, with each line viewed as a melody, where the composer writes one line to the end, then returns to the beginning to add the next line, and so on.

In Classical music, however, the overall structure is vertical, focusing on harmony almost as much as melody. A composer will concentrate on the movements of their chords, how each harmony progresses from the one to the next so that the overall sound, from one chord or key to another, takes the listener on a musical journey. As violinist and broadcaster Lucie Skeaping put it: 'A composer might have a melody at the ready, then make choices of how to harmonise it (and there are always several options) and move through various keys or chords in order to stir the ear of the listener, but still taking "instruction" from the original melody'. [Footnote: private correspondence]. In Baroque music, the bass line becomes its harmonic basis and doesn't constitute a principal melodic line, except, as we saw, in the late Baroque style with Bach and Handel; whereas in Classical music the bass line generally becomes an equal partner in the melodic dialogue, for example, the cello part in a string quartet.

The independence of music can be seen in the realm of humour. 'Even humour becomes possible in music without outside help; the music of the Classical style could be genuinely funny, not merely jolly or good-natured' (Rosen 1997, p. 95). Examples of musical jokes are Beethoven's 13th 'Diabelli' Variation with its contrasts of *dynamics* and *register* and a *presto* passage at the end of Haydn's Quartet Opus 33, for which he was attacked as a 'buffoon' by his contemporaries. The buffoonery of Haydn, Mozart and Beethoven is merely an exaggeration of the essential quality of the Classical style. This style was originally a comic one. This doesn't mean by this that the deepest tragic feelings could not be expressed by it, but simply that 'the pacing of Classical rhythm is the pacing of comic opera, its phrasing is the phrasing of dance music, and its large structures are these phrases dramatised' (Rosen 1997, pp. 95–96).

As we saw, in the two previous centuries, most instrumental music was composed for two purposes: either for dancing or for religious practice. But with the rise of lay, middle-class audiences, composers now became more ambitious and, therefore, needed new methods of determining structure, tempo, length and mood shifts. The result was the rise of the symphony with its 'design templates' for instrumental music.

Instrumentation and Musical Forms

In the course of the eighteenth century, the orchestra grew in size, range and power. The principal forms of instrumental music were the *sonata*, *trio*, string quartet, symphony and the solo concerto. Vocal works were also important—songs for a singer and piano, choral works and opera.

Solo and Chamber Music—1780–1800

Decline of the Continuo

The practice of *basso continuo* or *thoroughbass*, continued throughout the eighteenth century, but after 1760, it was rapidly abandoned (Leichten-tritt 1954, p. 164; Downs 1992, p. 353). During the final decade of the century, this two-hundred-year tradition of *basso continuo* ceased to be part of the texture of composition. Some string composers wrote *sonatas* for violin and continuo until the end of the century but these were exceptions: they can be considered as works for solo violin with cello or double bass accompaniment. Even the way composers wrote for the cello was changing: as we saw, the purely harmonic function of the bass line declined as its melodic function increased. The result was a 'much closer relationship between the bass line and the total musical texture' (Downs 1992, pp. 353–354). But it's also true that where the *symphonic* composer needed plain harmony, they used chords largely limited to the range of *tonic*, *dominant* and *subdominant*.

From the Harpsichord to the Fortepiano

One ideal of the eighteenth century composer was to cater to the tastes and abilities of the amateur as well as the professional. But the keyboard *sonata* of the Classical period demanded a more professional level of technique, a virtuosity only occasionally glimpsed in the earlier period. And as the popularity of the clavichord and harpsichord declined in favour of the piano, there was an astonishing number of virtuoso keyboard composers writing for it in the second half of the eighteenth and early nineteenth centuries.

The Accompanied Keyboard Sonata

The accompanied keyboard *sonata* continued to be popular with composers manifesting a range of different approaches. A standard version was the keyboard *sonata* accompanied by a subordinate 'melody' instrument (violin or flute) that never gets the melody! There was also the 'dialogued' *sonata* in which each instrument has a roughly equal share of the material, but which is still referred to by composers and publishers as 'a keyboard sonata with accompaniment of...' Equally common was the keyboard *sonata* with two accompanying instruments with an even greater range: a piano sonata in which other instruments such as violin or flute have no initiative at all, a piano *sonata* in which there is dialogue only between the piano and the upper melody instrument with the cello having no initiative, and the *sonata* in which the dialogue embraces all the instruments in different degrees. The great pianist composers of the time—Muzio Clementi and Jan Ladislav Dussek—wrote as much for these combinations as for piano solo.

Chamber Music for Strings

In music written for the home, developments in combined string instruments without piano were highly important for two reasons: firstly, because the number of published works ranging from duets to quintets greatly increased; and secondly, because the greatest composers, Haydn and Mozart, produced some of their greatest works in this field, with Beethoven's contribution consisting of his first set of quartets, opus 18, as well as his finest string trios.

String Trios

The string trio remained a kind of 'stepchild' of music, with the combination of two violins and cello predominating, and the combination of violin, viola and cello less popular. It is hard to understand why the string trio was largely ignored, as there are important representatives, mainly for two violins and cello, by Boccherini, Haydn, Pleyel, Viotti, and many others. Mozart's Divertimento K. 563, and Beethoven's String Trios, Opus 3, 8 and 9, are all large-scale imposing works for violin, viola and cello, completely worthy of standing beside these masters' contemporary string quartets. Few other composers of the period thought to use the string trio in this way.

String Quartets

The string quartet covered the full range of the musical needs of the period. Arguably, no other form was able to fill the gamut of social demands as well. 'The great works of the masters, with their immense expressive range from the humorous to the serious, from the naïve and rustic to the sophisticated and refined, satisfy the eternal human longing for the highest attainable in art'. On the centrality of melody, there are original string quartets that 'embody the then-modern trend of emphasising the primacy of melody by using folk tunes, either quoted directly or used for re-working...' (Downs 1992, p. 374). There were even multi-movement string quartets that were constructed on the most popular operatic arias of the time.

Music for Voice and Piano

During the final quarter of the eighteenth century, the song for voice and keyboard became imperceptibly more popular. Charming, innocent songs continued to be written by many composers, but an increasing number of them felt an urge to deepen the effect of the *strophic song* and the theatrical effect of ballad settings or narrative songs. The function of the keyboard in songs of the 1790s was much more developed than in earlier times. Especially important at this time, and for the first half of the following century, was the musical setting of the poetic ballad.

The Pre-Eminence of the Symphony and Concerto

As we saw, in the late eighteenth century, the symphony came to constitute the core of what has been called the 'Great Repertoire' in concerts in all the major, wealthy music centres: Vienna, London, Paris, New York. And the first genuinely international symphonist was Haydn. However, officially, in London and Paris, it was the concerto that formed the heart of the public concert, not the symphony. The terminology is interesting: a concert was divided into two 'acts' and each 'act' was opened by an 'overture'. However, this overture might be a Haydn symphony, so, formally, it might be perceived as the introduction to the arias and concertos that followed (Downs 1992, pp. 379/385).

PART II: COMPOSERS

It is universally agreed that the music composed during the last twenty years of the eighteenth century includes some of the greatest ever written, indeed that its finest representatives embody some of the most extraordinary artistic achievements of Western civilisation. These creations were the achievement of two giants: Joseph Haydn and Wolfgang Amadeus Mozart. During the final decade of the century, they were joined by Ludwig Van Beethoven.

THE LIBERATED SERVANT—JOSEPH HAYDN (1732–1809)

Prior to this period, one could have pointed to 'composers of roughly equal stature, whose works had local currency, but whose names were less likely to appear on public concert program in other cities… But beginning around 1779/80, the works of Haydn came to dominate the symphonic portion of concerts' (Downs 1992, p. 379). There are some revealing concert statistics: in 1777, Haydn's symphonies occupied 3.5% of the time allocated to symphonies, in 1790, 78%. Nothing comparable had ever happened, for Haydn's work made the symphonies of all his contemporaries seem commonplace and mediocre by comparison. Haydn is known as 'the father of the symphony' (he composed 104) but he could even more accurately be described as 'the father of the string quartet'. This is not because he invented these forms but because in his music they first attained their full stature. An important milestone, dating from the 'Russian' quartets of 1781, was the conscious exploitation of the *bithematic*, three-part *sonata form* which gave the development section its full significance (Hindley 1971, p. 240).

His fourteen masses have often been described as 'sacred music of the concert hall' rather than as liturgical music for use in a church service. Haydn also gave fresh impetus to the *oratorio* and *cantata*. In these, his deep religious feeling blends with basic descriptive musical features, expressing his belief in God and highlighting the picturesque in nature. His *oratorios* 'The Creation' (1798) and 'The Seasons' (1801) were written under the influence of Handel whose music he had heard in London.

HAYDN'S CLASSICAL STYLE

Haydn achieved a unique combination of quality, output and historical significance. His work over six decades testifies to a gradual but steady growth of complexity and sophistication. His early work—roughly 1750–1760—dates from a presto in which the compositional style of the Late Baroque as exemplified by Bach and Handel, had gone out of fashion, with C.P.E. Bach a key influence. He is preoccupied with formal problems: how to integrate his varied material—the 'quirks and quiddities' of the Mannheim style—by means of a developed sense of *tonality*. It was a period of uncertainty and exploration. At first, Haydn is not hugely concerned with the profound meaning of his music as human experience, but to describe it as 'entertainment' is in no way to discredit it. This becomes clear in his approach to both the string quartet and the symphony which, for him, were initially interchangeable.

Haydn's numerous trio sonatas were often charming but trivial works, a Galant simplification of the Baroque style. Virtually all the *sonata* movements contain diverse material, though Haydn makes no more attempt at *thematic* development than did the composers of *buffo* overtures. His first quartets differ from them in discarding all heroic traces. These were 'cassations'—a minor musical genre related to the 'serenade' and 'divertimento'—intended for outdoor performance by orchestral or chamber ensembles, revealing the influence of the suite. The *trios* of the *minuets* are peasant *Landler* rather than courtly dances. The low-pitched movements are perhaps more stimulating in performance than on paper. 'Haydn was a practical musician, who wrote music to be heard, in given conditions' (Mellers 1957, p. 19).

These works, composed between 1750 and 1760, can be seen as either rudimentary quartets or rudimentary symphonies. They don't approximate Stamitz in 'fire or precision of effect'. But before long, Haydn begins to acquire his own character as a symphonist. Symphony No. 22, 'The Philosopher' (1764), is clearly a transitional work, halfway between Baroque and Rococo. However, Haydn's approach to the orchestra recalls the chamber style of the Baroque rather than the 'modern' style of Stamitz; the wind instruments, in particular, are given solo parts.

As the 1770s approached, Haydn's music underwent a stylistic transformation. The main reason was the rise of the 'Sturm und Drang' ('Storm and Stress') artistic movement, most famously in literature, though initially in music. It lasted, broadly, from the late 1760s to the early 1780s: it stressed individual subjectivity, with extremes of emotion given free expression in reaction to the perceived constraints of rationalism imposed by the Enlightenment and associated aesthetic movements.

The musical language of this period resembles the preceding one but it is found in compositions more intensely expressive, for example in works in minor keys. The works of this period are 'longer, more passionate, and more daring' (Webster 1991, p. 18). Some of Haydn's best known compositions are of this period: the 'Symphony, No. 44 ('Trauer'— 'Mourning) the Symphony No. 45 ('Farewell'), the Piano Sonata in C Minor, and the six String Quartets Opus 20 (the 'Sun' Quartets), all written in 1771–1772. They generally have a strong melodic emphasis, exemplifying the first point of the Classical style. But it was also around this time that Haydn became interested in writing *fugues* in the Baroque style, and three of the Opus 20 quartets end with a *fugue*.

What was the reason for the rise of the new movement? Mellers argues that it was the same set of impulses that had prompted C.P.E. Bach to create a music based on conflict between a 'popular style' and a 'style of sensibility', that is, between 'people's music' and artists' music'. However, in the music Haydn composed in the 1770s, he also exploits the dramatic potentialities present in the Rococo style. In the 'G Minor Symphony, No. 39', for example, he uses stock Rococo features—shooting scales, repeated notes on the horn, sudden breaks, contrasting *dynamics*, dissonant *appoggiaturas*—not because they titillate the senses but because of their dramatic intensity. The music is fiercer but less melancholy than Mozart's G minor mood as exemplified in the latter's Symphony No. 40. Indeed, there is little lyricism in the whole work. The *modulations* jump to extravagant keys, while most of these stormy symphonies are in minor keys, or, if in major, then in a strange key such B. Haydn still prefers to derive his second themes from his first, and, reacting against Rococo variety, feels the need to give his music cohesion. He seeks unity in diversity and links his themes ever more closely without sacrificing the dramatic tension which is the essence of the *sonata* style. These various examples of dramatic tension, including Rococo features, again exemplify point two of the Classical style (see p. 10).

The stormy features of these works are immediately striking, but they not should obscure the fact that they also represent an interesting development in Haydn's humour. The comic elements in his earlier work were mainly an expression of *buffo* frivolity. Those comic expressions that occur in 'Sturm und Drang' tend to startle as much as to amuse—for example, an abrupt contrast of key, a melodic ellipsis, a sudden pause or contraction of rhythm. This feature illustrates the third Classical feature—frequent changes of tempo—and the fifth—the short articulated phrase.

Passages that may in some contexts be dramatic are in others witty. 'All through Haydn's mature music—and in a more poignant way in Mozart's also—one finds this precariousness: the sudden defeat of expectation, the interruption of a norm of behaviour, whether of tonality or of melodic, harmonic, or rhythmic formula' (Mellers 1957, pp. 22–23). It is a feature one doesn't encounter in composers who lived in the pre-modern, pre-capitalist era, the Age of Faith, before the Age of Reason, 'Bach and Handel are sometimes comic, seldom if ever witty'. Haydn's music is also known for its humour, a talent for the facetious that no other composer developed, for example, the sudden loud chord in the slow movement of his 'Symphony, No. 94 in G Major' ('Surprise') (1791).

At about the same time that he was composing his 'Sturm und Drang' works, Haydn was also developing his distinctive quartet style. His Opus 9 appeared in 1769 and his Opus 17 in 1771. Both collections reveal the tempestuous fire of 'Sturm und Drang' and strong *thematic development*, while Haydn writes independently for each instrument (Mellers 1957, p. 23). These traits of Haydn's work—startling humour, the storm-like quality,—illustrate again the second feature of the Classical style—increased dramatic tension (see pp. 13–14).

The 'Sun' quartets, Opus 20 (1772), intensify all these features but add another—many of them have a *fugue* in their finales. And all use *counterpoint* in a manner remote from the 'style Galant'. Nor was Haydn intent on recreating the Baroque *fugue*. He merely sought to impart dignity and coherence to the quartet and *counterpoint* was a means to that end. Therefore, the type of *counterpoint* he employed 'was not Baroque, but symphonic, and therefore reconcilable with the pathos of a movement such as this quartet's opening allegro' (Mellers 1957, p. 23).

However, Mellers argues that Haydn's 'phase of overt passion and protest' didn't last long. In his music of the 1780s, passion is mitigated by acceptance, both because of the creative path he himself went down and because of the influence of Mozart. Yet it was in 1785 that Haydn joined the Freemasons, at that time a radical movement, arguably under Mozart's influence (Robbins Landon and Wyn Jones 1988, p. 179). The mature Mozart also taught Haydn how he could adapt both *counterpoint* and lyricism to the dramatic purposes of the symphony. The transitional 'D Minor Symphony No. 80' (1784) exemplifies this: apart from the *finale*, all the movements have melodies which are more Italian and Mozartian than those of Haydn's previous works. Although Haydn had not yet learned to create a lyricism appropriate to his own developing symphonic style, nevertheless, this development illustrates again the centrality of melody in Haydn's work.

It was only in the group of symphonies composed for Haydn's first visit to England that he finally achieved his synthesis of protest and acceptance. He had solved the problem of composing lyrical themes which can also be treated in a *sonata* style, and no longer sound like Mozart. 'The search for unity in diversity, which must be attained without impairing dramatic tension, here reaches its apotheosis' (Mellers 1957, p. 24). However, Haydn's approach to sonata form in his mature works is unpredictable, and no two movements are similar in structure. If one compares 'Symphony No. 104 in D' with the earlier symphonies, what is most immediately striking is the song-like melody of the opening theme, its serenity and powerful dramatic intensity which does not disturb the continuity of the music's *texture*. In the recapitulation, the material is 'creatively modified', 'it has been born afresh in the course of the development'. Indeed, Mellers believes that Haydn's mature movements are all *development*, which begins in the *exposition*, as the second subject is a *development* of the first. If one compares Bach and Handel with Haydn, the two late Baroque composers are concerned in their different ways with states of Being, whereas Haydn's sonata movements deal with growth and change—with Becoming (Mellers 1957, p. 25).

Towards the end of his life, stimulated by his journeys to England, Haydn developed what Rosen calls his 'popular style', an approach to composition that created highly popular music but which nevertheless retained a rigorous musical structure. A crucial feature of this style was its increasing use of folk material. This style can be heard in his later work, including twelve symphonies, fourteen string quartets, fourteen piano trios, six masses and two *oratorios* (Rosen 1997, p. 329).

The Opus 33 Quartets (1781), and also the symphonies of the same period, reveal a 'Mozartian leaning towards a more lyrical type of melody'. Haydn himself wrote that these quartets were written in an 'entirely new and special style'. Rosen points to a number of important advances in Haydn's compositional technique that mark the arrival of the Classical style in full flower. These include a fluid form of phrasing in which each *motif* emerges from the previous one without interruption, the practice of letting accompanying material evolve into melodic material, and a kind of 'classical *counterpoint*' in which each instrumental part maintains its own integrity. This is perhaps an additional example of the articulated phrasing mentioned earlier as point five of the Classical style.

As an illustration of Haydn's 'manifesto', his 'revolution in style', Rosen points to the opening page of Haydn's first Opus 33 Quartet (1781) (beginning in D major but settling in B minor). We see the relation between principal voice and accompanying voices 'transformed before our eyes. In bar 3, the melody is given to the cello and the other instruments take up the little accompanying figure. In bar 4, this accompanying figure has become the principal voice—it now carries the melody'. It's not clear at what point in bars three and four the violin becomes the main melodic voice, and where the cello shifts to a subordinate position: all we hear is that the violin starts bar three as an accompaniment and ends the bar as melody (Rosen 1997, pp. 116–117). This illustrates the sixth characteristic of the Classical style.

Rosen believes this is the true invention of Classical *counterpoint*, in no way a revival of Baroque technique, where 'the ideal (never, of course, the reality) was equality and independence of the voices... The opening page of this quartet... affirms the distinction between melody and accompaniment. But it then transforms one into the other' (Rosen 1997, p. 117). However, as we saw, late Baroque aspired and arguably, came remarkably close to establishing a degree of equality between melodic treble and harmonic bass lines (see Chapter 2). We shall examine in Part Three the political significance of this 'revolution in style'.

Even the most melancholy of the quartets such as the F Sharp Minor opus 50 (1787) or the B minor opus 64 (1790) are not marked by the feverishness of the 'Sturm und Drang' years: they are mellowed by their lyricism. Mellers believes that Haydn achieved his 'Apollonian' equilibrium in the last series of quartets, opus 71, 74, 76 and 77. Comparing his last quartet, the F major opus 77, with the early *quadri* or the well known 'Serenade' quartet from an opus 3, it seems clear that Haydn's achievement is not so much the development of a new technique as the creation of a new world of thought and feeling.

Haydn's piano *sonatas* follow a pattern of *development* identical to his symphonies and quartets. An early work like the A Major of 1762 follows the orthodox *binary* structure of a dance by Bach or Handel. But it is different in having almost no melody, merely twirls and twiddles. Later, Haydn discovers the dramatic potential in such superficial frolics. 'Abandoning Baroque unity and continuity, he creates contrasting and heterogeneous material based around two different key centres. The focus of the piece is no longer an unfolding melody, but the conflict between two groups of material and different keys'. This dramatic atmosphere is even more marked in those *sonatas* like the fierce B Minor that are strongly influenced by the mood of 'Sturm und Drang'. We see again the importance of dramatic tension in the Classical style; also, the tension between the *tonic* and *dominant* with a resolution to the *tonic*—feature eight of the Classical style. In Haydn's late *sonatas*, especially those composed after the first London visit, both the themes and keyboard writing acquire a new maturity; again, the themes tend to be closely linked. The great 'Sonata in E flat' is a worthy counterpart of the London Symphonies and the Opus 76 and 77 Quartets. 'In sonatas, symphonies, and quartets equally the dramatic urgency is increased rather than diminished, as compared with earlier works; only the drama is now resolved in a structure radiant with light. 'Apollonian' order implies a new kind of belief. Haydn's God was not the mystical divinity of Bach, nor the Lord of earthly glory of Handel; but all his later music is religious in the sense that it reflects the beliefs that had meaning for him—an ethical humanism based on reason and the love of created nature' (Mellers 1957, p. 28).

Rosen also refers to one of Haydn's 'best-loved and most dramatic effects'—the surprise return for example, in the finale-theme. 'A great deal of ingenuity is expended upon the return of the theme, almost always with rollicking effect: the trick is to keep suggesting the return but to delay it until the listener no longer knows when to expect it...' (Rosen 1997, p. 337). We discussed above the dramatic effect of the contrasting themes. Examining the quartet Opus 74, no. 3, we see how Haydn derives the second theme directly from the opening phrase. Haydn operas were insubstantial, but his sense of a dramatic musical gesture closely linked to the action was extremely sharp.

A central feature of Haydn's music is the development of larger structures out of short, simple *motifs*, often derived from standard, accompanying *figures*. The music is also formally concentrated, with a movement's main musical events unfolding quite rapidly (Sutcliffe 1989, p. 343). Haydn was also partial to the 'monothematic exposition' in which the 'music that establishes the dominant key is similar or identical to the opening theme' (Hughes 1950, p. 131, in Rosen 1997, p. 331).

Haydn's inventiveness—his role in the pioneering of the *sonata* form—led him to integrate the *fugue* into the Classical style and to enrich the *rondo* form with more cohesive tonal logic. In other words, in the *development* section, existing themes may appear in new harmonic and textural contexts, and new material may be introduced, but the *development* changes into the *recapitulation* where all themes from the *exposition* are now presented in the tonic key. Haydn was also the main exponent of the 'double variation form', that is, variations on two alternating *themes*, which are often major and minor-mode versions of each other. Following the twilight of 'Sturm und Drang' in the early 1780s, Haydn returned to a lighter, more entertaining style. He produced no quartets during this period, and the symphonies assume new traits, often featuring trumpets and timpani.

Haydn's return to Vienna in 1795 witnessed the final turning point in his style. His oratorios 'The Creation' (1798) and 'The Seasons' (1801) address lofty themes such as the meaning of life and humanity's purpose, and express an attempt to feature the sublime in music. He attains his 'Apollonian' equilibrium in the final series of quartets: Opus 71, 74, 76 and 77. As in Symphony No. 104, the finale is a magnificent piece of symphonic *counterpoint*, the first movement opening with a theme that is 'rich, ample, *cantabile*'.

In the late sonatas, especially those composed following the first English visit, both the themes and the keyboard writing achieve a new maturity. The great 'Sonata in E Flat' is a 'worthy pianistic counterpart' of the London symphonies and the Opus 76 and 77 quartets. In Haydn's late sonatas, symphonies and quartets, the dramatic urgency is heightened compared with earlier works, except that 'the drama is now resolved in a structure radiant with light. "Apollonian" order, with its emphasis on rationality, order and prudence, suggests a new kind of belief. Haydn's God was not the mystical divinity of Bach, nor the Lord of earthly glory of Handel; but all his later music is religious in the sense that it reflects the beliefs that had meaning for him—an ethical humanism based on reason and the love of created nature' (Mellers 1957, pp. 28–29). In a crisis-ridden world, Haydn's music inspires love and hope.

OVERTURE TO REVOLUTION: WOLFGANG AMADEUS MOZART (1756–1791)

Mozart was undoubtedly the most prolific musical genius Europe has ever produced, demonstrating his prodigious gifts from the age of five when he began composing—he was already competent on keyboard and violin. His astonishingly abundant output covers some 626 works from operas to symphonies and string quartets painstakingly catalogued by Ludwig von Kochel in 1862. He died at the absurdly young age of 35.

Mozart's Classical Style

In childhood, Mozart had acquired extensive knowledge of European music, both past and present, and a special familiarity with Italian music. Any composer brought up in eighteenth-century Austria would have been nurtured on Italian opera. Indeed, most of the music Mozart heard on his continental travels was operatic and Italian. As for *sonata* composers, two composers made a deep impression on the youthful Mozart—one was Johann Schobart (1720–1767), a composer from the Polish border who had settled in Paris, the other was J.C. Bach whom he met on his travels and in whom he found a kindred spirit. J.C. Bach's music was 'modern' and imbued with a *cantabile* lyricism. Whereas Stamitz and the early Haydn had achieved symphonic drama by sacrificing lyricism, J.C. Bach had preserved lyricism by rejecting the dramatic implications of *sonata*. But in Mozart's mature music, he achieves a unique synthesis of lyrical melody and *tonal* drama, according to them equal status. The equilibrium between lyricism and drama, the glorious achievement of Haydn's last years, appears in Mozart's music almost from the moment he becomes a person. This illustrates the first and second features identified as essential to the Classical style—the primacy of melody and an atmosphere of dramatic tension created by abrupt shifts and breaks in both melody and rhythm.

Mozart's early works are technically more assured than those of Haydn which have a 'popular virility' but are at times wilfully uncouth. But whether Mozart writes serenades for weddings of the local bourgeoisie or symphonies not radically distinct from them, they have 'an Italianate sweetness and polish'. At puberty, he began to adapt the tired formulae of *opera buffa* and of J.C. Bach to his own modest aims. His 'Symphony No. 5 K. 22' (1765) contains a *chromatic andante* which transcends existing fashion; even his accompanying *figurations* become *cantabile*, i.e. unusually melodious.

Interestingly, virtually the first group of works to reveal a Mozartian personality is a set of Violin Sonatas, K. 55–60, composed in the early 1770s. In the Baroque violin sonata, string melody had been the music's heart backed by the keyboard. In the Rococo period, the roles of the two instruments were reversed. Haydn's early violin and piano sonatas sound like piano solos—a violin part is available if a fiddler is around! That is why Haydn favoured the piano sonata and largely ignored the violin as solo instrument. But in his early youth, Mozart rehabilitated the violin as an instrument allied to the singing voice. His mature violin and piano sonatas are real duos that achieve a balance between symphonic drama and song. This exemplifies again the first two features of the Classical style—melody and dramatic tension.

In the 1770s, Mozart, like Haydn, went through a 'Sturm und Drang' ('Storm and Stress') phase. His 'Symphony no. 20 in D Major, K. 133', composed in 1772, at the age of sixteen, is poetic and lyrical, but its grace gradually becomes dramatic, especially in the first movement's *recapitulation* and *coda*. Haydn's influence, and his own development, are starting to deepen the Rococo charm he acquired from J.C. Bach. The following year witnessed an even more remarkable development: the 'little' 'G Minor Symphony, K. 183', composed in 1773, both resembles and differs from Haydn's minor moods in his 'Sturm und Drang' works. It has similarly passionate repeated notes and sudden changes of dynamics apparent in Haydn's G Minor Symphony No. 39. But whereas Haydn is fierce, Mozart is melancholy; and the difference consists in that Mozart's themes have a sweetly singing quality whereas Haydn's are explosive, and in the persistently sighing *appoggiaturas*. However, Mozart's tone is inherently dramatic. Even his Symphony in A major K. 201 (1774), a radiant work, combines 'sinuously *chromatic* melodies alongside airily dancing *buffo* tunes...' (Mellers 1957, p. 39). Mozart achieved a unique equilibrium between lyricism and drama, one that also balanced joy and sorrow: we are never quite sure whether his music is happy or sad. Arguably, it conveys the rich and profound complexity of human emotion, especially at a time of far-reaching social and political change. Another example would be the 'E Minor Violin Sonata No. 21, K. 304'. Again, this exemplifies the first two features of the Classical style identified above— the supreme importance of melody and a dramatic ambiance created by sudden contrasts.

Mozart reached full maturity in the early 1780s. We saw that his development was deeply influenced by Haydn's quartets Opus 33 of 1781. In 1783, Mozart composed the six quartets which he dedicated to Haydn (see p. 7). These quartets contain movements modelled on Haydn's, yet they testify to Mozart's independence. For example, Mozart's E Flat Quartet K. 428 'with its *tritone* and sinuous chromaticism, is as personal and un-Haydnesque an utterance as the hauntingly seductive andante'. (Mellers, 1957, p. 41). In contrast, Haydn's great lyrical melodies are never *chromatic*, whereas Mozart's are always liable to become *chromatic* even if this feature isn't present at first.

It was a while before Mozart followed the 'Haydn' set with new quartets. He began, instead, to experiment by combining strings, and sometimes wind instruments, with piano, composing the 'G Minor Piano Quartet No. 1, K. 478 (1785), one of his most passionate instrumental works, and the Trio in E Flat for Clarinet, Viola and Piano, K 498' (1786), one of his most 'enigmatically profound'. Lacking an existing model, Mozart initiated this kind of dialogue between melody instruments and piano. We find here another example of the new relation between the different instrumental voices mentioned above: the melody is initially given to the piano with the strings playing the accompaniment; but the roles are soon reversed, with the strings playing the melody and the piano the accompaniment (Rosen, 1997, pp. 116–117). This is the sixth feature of the Classical style.

Moreover, it was in the piano concerto that Mozart developed the most accomplished form of his synthesis of operatic technique and sonata. Significantly, the cycle of piano concertos was composed during Mozart's greatest period of operatic creation, years during which he composed only one symphony. It is no exaggeration to say that Mozart created the Classical concerto. Before him, the *Rococo* concerto had developed a pleasant *euphony* but it had a stubborn and unpredictable character that did not lend itself to the drama and insistence of the sonata. Arguably, Mozart's early violin concertos, written at Leopold's instigation as showpieces for Wolfgang's virtuosity, are unambitious. The exquisite Sinfonia Concertante K. 364 (1779) for violin and viola, translating operatic aria into instrumental form, remained an isolated experiment.

The first unambiguous masterpiece of the Classical style which has shed all 'mannerist' (or *Rococo*) traces is Mozart's Piano Concerto No. 9 in E flat, K. 271', nicknamed 'Jeunehomme', composed in 1777 when he was 21, during his 'Storm and Stress' period. With it, Mozart becomes 'Mozart'! It hinted at the importance this form would have for him later on. It was a breakthrough comparable to Beethoven's as he moved from the second to the 'Eroica' symphony. The most striking thing about this concerto is that Mozart was trying to give the form a stature comparable to the symphony. Compared with *Rococo* concertos, it is long and difficult, with its operatic influence clear, from the slow movement to the *cadenzas*. The piece was badly received, Mozart's public regarding it as too noisy and 'overburdened with notes' (Mellers 1957, p. 45).

The very opening reveals a bold and delightful rhythmic variety, with the orchestra and piano playing in different tempos. In subsequent bars, there is a fusion of the two kinds of beat. It is a rhythmic transition that is the touchstone of the Classical style: 'never before in the history of music had it been possible to move from one kind of pulse to another so naturally and with such grace' (Rosen, 1997, p. 60). In contrast, the most common Baroque form is characterised by a unified, homogeneous rhythmic *texture*: it continues unwaveringly until the pause before the final *cadence*. A change of rhythm is then possible without creating the impression that something unusual is happening.

Rhythmic variety in the Classical period is also associated with two additional factors: (a) articulated phrasing: this required its individual elements to be discrete, set off from each other so that its shape and symmetry would be clearly audible; (b) this in turn created a greater variety of rhythmic textures. In the opening phrase of Mozart's Piano Concerto No. 9 K. 271, mentioned above, what would have been a Baroque style contrast between a section of music for orchestra and another for solo has been concentrated into a single phrase. Such a conflation requires a style that can mediate between these sections: this is simply because a work consisting of such dramatically juxtaposed contrasts without a protracted transition between them would be intolerably compressed. The mature Classical style created this style of transition, whereby it became possible for the first time to mediate between different kinds of rhythm. A common practice was to introduce a faster rhythm into the accompaniment and some bars later into the main voices, thereby smoothing over the join until no rupture is felt. This illustrates again the third and the fifth features of the Classical style—an uneven rhythmic flow with frequent changes of tempo, and the short, articulated phrase with two or more contrasting themes.

The fourth feature of the Classical style—a *homophonic texture*—a single melody line with accompaniment consisting of a limited range of chords or plain harmony to highlight the primacy of the melody—is evident in innumerable works by Mozart. Mozart is the first composer to consistently use the *subdominant* fully sensing the way in which it achieves a relaxation of long-range harmonic tension. Generally, he introduces it as a feature of the *recapitulation* following the re-entry of the *tonic*. Another frequent device is Mozart's use of secondary *dominants*—the *dominant* of the *dominant*—to intensify harmonic movement. Mozart's approach to harmony his sensitivity to large *tonal* areas (several chords within the same scale facilitating enlarged harmonic potential) remained unmatched until Beethoven.

The eighth Classical feature was identified as a melodic framework based on the tension between *tonic* and *dominant* with *modulations* ending in a *resolution* to the *tonic*—in Mozart, this was exemplified above in his C Minor Fantasy where we discussed the related question of *symmetry*. As for the ninth feature—the supremacy of the *sonata* form—it is surely clear that a major part of Mozart's *oeuvre*—his symphonies, instrumental sonatas, chamber works—are all conceived according to the rules and conventions of the sonata form.

Mozart seems to have had a hard time composing his violin concertos and found the Flute and Harp Concerto a 'sore trial'. When he engaged seriously with the concerto form, he ignored melody instruments in favour of the piano, thus preferring the *cantabile* violin to the piano for solo sonatas but choosing the piano over the violin for concertos. He preferred the piano to the violin since its power and contrasting *timbre* made it a worthy partner to the orchestra. He unconsciously regarded the piano concerto as a 'duality in unity', it seemed to him a kind of metaphor of the separation of the individual (the soloist) from society (the orchestra). But this separation is only carried out so that the soloist and orchestra can forge a new unity in a kind of dialectical movement. For Mellers, "the Mozartian concerto threatens, only in order to vindicate, civilisation" (Mellers 1957, p. 44).

Mozart's cycle of mature concertos begins in 1782, in tandem with his cycle of operas. If the violin concertos are modelled on the operatic aria, the piano concertos are based on the operatic ensemble, the first movement being more complicated than in his symphonies. Soloist and orchestra always have equal status. The orchestra opens with its *thematic* material in a long prelude, the soloist then entering with a different set of *themes*. Hence there are two complementary *expositions*, with four to six separate *themes* interlinked in a changing sequence. This technique implies a new conception of orchestration. Mozart's scoring is not purely linear like the Baroque, nor purely harmonic like the *Rococo*: it combines the two, a mixture whose parts are volatile, whether they be themes or melodic *figurations* that underpin the harmony. This technique is comparable to Mozart's mature operatic ensembles in which several characters sing together phrases that differ in mood and mentality, yet the result is not turmoil but a harmonious blend.

Mozart's great cycle begins with two lightweight concertos, K. 413 and K. 414. Did Mozart deem it necessary, when introducing his audience to his new kind of ensemble concerto, to let them down gently? These early works display pastoral charm and serenity but also unsuspected profundity. But K. 449 is grand, powerfully sorrowful, and full of intimate connections with Figaro. K.482 has a similar relationship to 'Cosi Fan Tutte', and the 'demoniacal' No. 20 in D Minor K. 466, to 'Don Giovanni', with its tragedy similarly completed in '*buffo* merriment'. (Mellers, 1957, p. 46).

The high point of the Mozartian concerto, however, is No. 24 in C minor, K. 491 (1786) which has the passion of the D minor 'ennobled with a classical grandeur'. There is a long orchestral introduction, the piano entering with a new solo theme, while the final variations are grand and resiliently sombre, consistently inventive in their treatment of the dialogue between soloist and *tutti*. The final concerto, the B flat, K. 595, is again as different from the severe K. 491 as can be. It sounds child-like only because its subtlety is so translucent. Yet this exquisite music was composed under conditions of dreadful physical and psychological suffering.

Mozart had the gift of absorbing the valuable stylistic features of other musicians, his travels helping him to create a unique compositional language in which he synthesised many different elements. In his mature years, he used *counterpoint* as an important element in his music. He embarked on a detailed study of Bach, observing that here at last was something from which he could learn. Half operatic, half symphonic in character, the *contrapuntal* complexities of the late Baroque re-emerged, adapted to and disciplined by new forms, and shaped by a new artistic and social context. Some of the works Mozart consciously wrote in a Bachian style have a strange emotional effect—for example, the Adagio and Fugue for String Quartet in C Minor, K. 546— in which he packs in the *contrapuntal* devices of *inversion, augmentation, diminution*, and *stretto*. This creates a sparkling harmony that makes the music resonate with a driving energy strained almost to breaking point.

But the Bachian works also helped Mozart develop the Masonic style of his later years. This is apparent in his great, final trio of symphonies, Nos. 39 in E flat, K. 543, 40 in G Minor, K. 550, and 41 in C Major, K. 551 (the 'Jupiter'). The only symphony he had composed during the period of the piano concertos was No. 38 in D Major, K. 504, which contains much 'operatic' *polyphony*, and, like the D minor concerto, has an affinity with 'Don Giovanni'.

But the final three symphonies he wrote not for a commission but for himself. They contain statements about life and death which he had incor-porated in his reinterpretation of Freemasonry. 'He has transformed the symphony from rococo entertainment into a personal testament' (Mellers 1957, p. 48). The G Minor Symphony No. 40 is a refining of suffering in which the features of 'Storm and Stress' are divested of rhetoric, so that the music and drama are fused, and the suffering is not personal but that of humankind. The 'Jupiter' Symphony is an assertion of, and perhaps a plea for, order and harmony. In the last movement, Mozart's synthesis of sonata conflict and operatic ensemble *counterpoint* represents a triumph over pain and darkness. The concertos are the instrumental embodiment of the operatic Mozart, where in the last symphonies he offers a musical expression of his newly discovered religion—Freemasonry with its Enlightenment ideals.

Mozart's musical trajectory ran somewhat parallel to that of Haydn: both culminate in a distinction between their attitudes to the orthodox creed of their time, Catholicism, and to the 'religion' which they discovered in the course of their creative lives, the Enlightenment. Haydn modified traditional Catholicism according to the Enlightenment rational humanism of his age, though he never formally broke with Catholic dogma. But the features which infuse his last 'ethical' works such as 'The Creation' also leave a stamp on his final masses.

Mozart's two unfinished choral works were the great 'C Minor Mass and 'The Requiem Mass. Mozart's reasons for writing these two works were personal rather than officially religious. He wrote the Mass at the time of his marriage, as an expression of praise and gratitude. It is modelled on the great Baroque masters—Handel, Caldara, Alessandro Scarlatti, and above all, Bach's *polyphony*. The Mass incorporates *symphonic* and dramatic features of the Baroque, as Haydn had done in his final masses, and relates the Italianate vocal style of the Baroque to Mozart's own kind of operatic lyricism.

Mozart wrote The Requiem for himself, and its spirit is personal and Masonic. The story of the 'dark stranger' is well known. To the dying Mozart, he seemed like an emissary from another world arrived to escort him out of this one. The reality is more mundane: he was the emissary of a count who wanted to remain anonymous so as to pass off the work as his own. Elements of Mozart's Masonic style are all present in 'The Requiem': Bachian *counterpoint*, which is both tense and serene; moreover, in the Introit the suspensions, tied notes and syncopations create a suppressed turbulence beneath the surface solemnity. This is intensified by the dark Masonic orchestration featuring clarinets, basset horns, and bassoons. There is, however, another style in 'The Requiem' which is as purely *homophonic* as the Bachian movements are *contrapuntal*. The 'Hostias' is a hymn-like melody in the Masonic key of E flat with simple harmonies. This kind of melody is present in 'The Magic Flute where it is associated with the triumph of light.

Mozart always retained his belief in human potentiality, but he came to accept humankind's natural limitations, and similarly an acceptance of life and death. He wrote to his father: 'Since death... is the true goal of our lives, I have made myself so well acquainted during the last two years with this true and best friend of mankind that the idea of it no longer has any terrors for me, but rather much that is tranquil and comforting'. (Mellers 1957, p. 51). His life was ludicrously short but extraordinarily intense, and the completeness and perfection of his music provide the last word. Had he lived longer, he would doubtless have added something to a musical experience that already seems all-encompassing, but it is impossible to imagine what. Nevertheless, we can see how, for example, the great E Flat Divertimento for String Trio K. 563 is far removed from his early cassations (informal instrumental composition) and serenades, and it appears as though Mozart has abandoned the attempt to compose music for a society in which he no longer fully believed. We shall see that whatever Mozart's conscious beliefs and attitudes, a deeper radicalism was expressed in his music including his operas, the latter pervaded by an array of anti-feudal servants.

THE TRAGEDY AND MIRACLE
OF LUDWIG VAN BEETHOVEN (1770–1827)

Beethoven was a revolutionary composer, one whose work immediately conjures up non-musical, radical political as well as musical, ideas. He was strongly attracted to the ideals and values of the Enlightenment and scorned traditional authority and social rank. The influence of French revolutionary music on, for example, his fifth symphony, has been frequently remarked on. He famously dedicated his third, 'Eroica' symphony to Napoleon whom he believed to be a great revolutionary, democratic leader. However, when, in 1804, Napoleon declared himself Emperor, Beethoven scratched out the dedication, making a hole in the paper, and declaring: "Now he too will trample on the rights of man!" Beethoven was the first composer to consciously desire to build a new, different world, and who saw his music as a means to that end. His deafness is perhaps the greatest tragedy in the history of European art. The way he overcame it, indeed harnessed it to his creativity, is arguably the greatest miracle in European art.

BEETHOVEN'S CLASSICAL STYLE

Beethoven's career is generally divided into early, middle and late periods. According to this scheme, his early period lasts until roughly 1802, the middle period until 1814, with the late period beginning around 1815.

Early Beethoven

In the early period, Beethoven's work bears the strong imprint of Haydn and Mozart. However, he began to explore new directions, gradually expanding the scope and ambition of his work. Between 1800 and 1803, he came to be regarded as one of the leading members of the generation of young composers who followed Haydn and Mozart. His first six String Quartets, Opus 18, composed between 1798 and 1800 and dedicated to Prince Lobkowitz, were published in 1801. With these, and the first and second symphonies first performed in 1800 and 1803, Beethoven established his early reputation. His versatility was also revealed in his piano compositions, including his first two piano concertos and a dozen piano sonatas. In 1799, he also completed his 'Septet in E Flat Major Opus 20', one of his most popular works during his lifetime. For the premiere of his First Symphony, he hired the Burgtheater, staging an expensive programme including works by Haydn and Mozart as well as his Septet and one of his piano concertos. The 'Allgemeine Musikalische Zeitung' described the concert as 'the most interesting... in a long time' (Cooper 2008, p. 90).

If one examines the three Piano Trios that comprise Beethoven's Opus 1 (1793/1795), and even more his String Trio Opus 3, it is clear that although they are remarkably daring and express a strong personality, Haydn would have recognised them as having an affinity with his own music. However, the three Piano Sonatas of Opus 2 inhabit a new world of feeling. Although the first, Sonata in F Minor, is conventional in its dimensions and form—indeed, the first movement is more orthodox than most of Haydn's mature works—the opening theme is a 'Mannheim skyrocket' (a swiftly ascending passage typically having a rising *arpeggiated* melodic line together with a *crescendo*); the second subject is a free *inversion* of the first theme; and a *modulatory* scheme in the *development*. Beethoven differs from Haydn, and even more from Mozart, 'in the almost complete subservience of the melodic element to a dynamic treatment of piano technique'. This is even more marked in the final movement (*prestissimo*), a 'ferociously whirling *toccata*... an assault on the listener's nerves' (Mellers 1957, p. 56).

The Second Sonata of Opus 2 in A major (1796), is subversive in a subtler way. According to Rococo convention, the *exposition* of a *sonata* was meant to establish the basic tonalities of *tonic* and *dominant* associated with the first and second themes. But Beethoven begins his second theme in the minor of the *dominant*. The theme then develops through eight keys, touching on tonalities as remote from the home key (A major) as G major and B flat major. These are extreme *modulations*, normally reserved for the climax of the *development* section. Here they occur in the *exposition*, the conventional purpose of which is to establish *tonality* before *development* begins. The effect is startling, if not anarchic, as the passage has a bass line which rises step-by-step up an octave from E and finally establishes the *dominant* in which the *exposition* ends. Beethoven then achieves his climax by building his *modulations* not on step-wise progressions but on a series of descending thirds (harmonic combination of two notes at an interval of three *diatonic* degrees) (Mellers 1957, p. 57). Descending thirds arguably express crisis or drama.

Such passages are a musical counterpart to Beethoven's flouting of social etiquette—his rudeness to duchesses and his throwing crockery around. Identical motives prompted both Beethoven's musical and social bad manners. The artistic and the social rebellion were both rooted in Beethoven's personality which in turn was a product and an expression of the social upheavals being experienced across Europe. It is also significant that the most characteristic music of Beethoven's youth are his piano sonatas, the piano being for him a dynamic rather than a melodic instrument. His early violin sonatas are rather less aggressive than the piano sonatas of the same period.

This is especially evident with Beethoven's 'Piano Sonata No. 13 in C Minor, Opus 13— ('Pathetique')—composed in 1798, described as a 'call to arms' (Mellers 1957, p. 58). After a slow introduction, there is a tempestuous first movement. The Classical mould is still evident here, though the way Beethoven uses the introduction threatens to break it. Also significant here is Beethoven's interweaving of dramatic silences in the course of the introduction. The 'Pathetique' surpasses any of his previous compositions in originality, emotional depth, strength of character and ingenuity of *motivic* and *tonal* diversity. Its emotional content, exploring the concept of pathos, 'seems to herald the era of Romanticism in which the sublime rather than the rational holds sway'. Also, analytically, this sonata is highly original. 'Thus both emotionally and technically, Beethoven was here pushing the bounds of Classical convention well beyond their previous limits...' (Cooper 2013, p. 48).

By the time we get to Opus 27—the piano sonata he described as 'Quasi Una Fantasia', subjective experience has 'remoulded the mould': the so-called 'Moonlight' Sonata, completed in 1801, no longer even looks like a *sonata*. There is a slow introductory prelude—the calm before the storm. Beneath the surface lurks a powerful intensity. It has a *binary* structure which makes it resemble a miniature sonata movement without a second subject. There are some *modulations* followed by a return to the *tonic* and *recapitulation*. The second movement, an interlude, is free of tension: it is a kind of 'dream-minuet', which, however, is abruptly shattered by the tornado of the last movement, a full-scale sonata *presto* which, with its fierce *modulatory* conflict and dynamic keyboard technique, far outpaces anything Beethoven had attempted previously. The work does not follow the traditional movement arrangement in the Classical period of fast–slow–fast–fast. Instead, the rapid music is held off until the third, final movement which is described as 'a bursting of dykes' (Mellers 1957, p. 60).

The work was composed during the first of Beethoven's two spiritual crises, sparked by the difficulties experienced in his relations with women, or perhaps his love for Countess Giulietta Guicciardi to whom the 'Moonlight Sonata' was dedicated. Moreover, we cannot fail to appreciate Beethoven's extraordinary melodic gift, prominent throughout his music—the first Classical feature.

Middle Beethoven

Beethoven's middle, also known as the 'heroic', period—roughly 1802 to 1814—began shortly after the onset of his second personal crisis sparked by growing awareness of encroaching deafness. It includes large-scale works that express heroism and struggle such as Symphonies Nos. 3–8, the last three Piano Concertos, including the heroic Fifth or 'Emperor', the Triple Concerto, the Violin Concerto, five String Quartets Nos. 7–11, several Piano Sonatas, including the 'Waldstein', 'Appassionata', the 'Kreutzer' Violin Sonata, and his only opera, 'Fidelio'. Beethoven is pitting himself against the dark forces of a malevolent Fate, but the more ferocious its blows, the more energetically must his will subdue them.

His music becomes his weapon in his battle against external forces, his art imposing order on chaos. The musician must shape the world afresh. The earlier Classical struggle to achieve equilibrium between the artist and his world has gone. However, the word 'heroic' is not always appropriate: the Sixth Symphony ('Pastoral') would hardly be described thus.

Beethoven's first two Symphonies while anticipating his later technique, are based on Classical principles but don't attain the level of Haydn's and Mozart's greatest works, being significant largely as the music of a revolutionary genius composing within the established tradition. But the Third, 'Eroica' Symphony, completed in 1802, represents a new chapter in music, the first movement opening with Fate's two hammerblows. The opening theme enters, an *arpeggio* that sounds like a challenge and climaxes in conflict. The symphony has many difficulties such as cross-rhythms (or *hemiola*), and *modulations* to strange keys 'that would catch players unawares at the first attempt, as well as tricky and rapid *figuration* that would require careful practice' (Cooper 2013, p. 71).

The first movement, in ¾ time, is in *sonata* form. The initial two hammerblow chords in E flat played by the whole orchestra establish the movement's *tonality*. The first theme is introduced by the cellos, and by the fifth bar of the melody, a *chromatic* note (C sharp) appears, which establishes the harmonic tension of the piece. The first theme is followed by a calmer, second theme that leads to the *development* section. Remarkably, Beethoven introduces a new theme in the *development* section, thus breaking with the tradition of Classical composition—that the *development* section works only with the existing material. The second movement is a funeral march in C minor with a trio in C major, and comprises multiple *fugatos*. Musically, the *thematic* solemnity of the second movement has lent itself for use as a funeral march proper. The fourth movement is a set of variations on the only theme which Beethoven had used in earlier compositions, for example, the finale of the ballet 'The Creatures of Prometheus', Opus 43 (1801) or the Piano Variations Opus 35, ('Eroica') (Lockwood 2015, p. 58).

The power of the entire, greatly enlarged orchestra is displayed in a *fortissimo* F major chord, with the second (E) added to the F. The strings *modulate* to E minor and to the first development theme that is introduced on the oboes. The work was published in 1806, acquiring the title by which it has become known: 'Sinfonia eroica… composta per festeggiare il sovvenire di un grand uomo' (composed to celebrate the memory of a great man, ie. Napoleon).

It does seem that Beethoven had republican sympathies. According to John Clubbe, 'Beethoven's ideal for Austria would have been a republic'. He adds: 'Admittedly Beethoven did regard republics as the best solution'. In a letter to Theodora Johanna Vocke, dated 22 May 1793, Beethoven wrote in a clear indication of his opposition to the Austrian monarchy. 'Love liberty above all else' (Clubbe 2019, pp. 50/65/66). Also relevant is his 'Wellington's Sieg'— 'Wellington's Victory' which celebrates the British victory over the French at Vitoria in 1813, as is his use of 'God Save the King' and 'Rule Britannia' as themes for variations. These perhaps testify to his admiration for the British parliamentary system (Cooper 2013, pp. 70–71). Nicholas Mathew describes 'Wellington's Sieg' as 'the grandest of all such compositions' (Mathew 2013, p. 39). However, it is generally considered to be musically inferior. With Napoleon's defeat, Beethoven's hopes for a better Europe evaporated.

Beethoven had long been attracted by the idea of heroism—his 'heroic' ballet, 'The Creatures of Prometheus', of 1801 was an early example, followed by the Piano Sonata Opus 26 containing a 'Funeral March on the Death of a Hero'. The Prometheus Variations (Opus 35) renewed the idea of the ancient hero. It is also significant that the *chaconne* theme from the first movement of the 'Eroica' is one that Beethoven first used in the ballet Prometheus and again in the 'Eroica' variations, opus 35. Prometheus' importance is that he challenged the gods, offering humankind the gift of fire and, therefore, the potential to control our destiny. Beethoven's hero is the man of struggle who is the architect of a new world. Napoleon turned out to be the architect of a new tyranny. Could Beethoven himself be the real hero of the symphony in his solitary 'Heiligenstadt' battle to pit his genius against his affliction? He did believe that the battles for Europe's and his own salvation were closely intertwined.

Opera

Shortly after completing the 'Eroica', Beethoven's attention turned to an opera for the 'Theater an der Wien' whose director Emanuel Shikaneder had written the libretto for The Magic Flute. Rejecting a number of proposed themes on the grounds that he needed 'something moral, edifying', Beethoven eventually hit on a 'rescue opera', a subject popular in

France at the time with composers such as Cherubini and Kreutzer. At the end of 1803, he found a French libretto, 'Leonore, ou l'Amour Conjugale', about a Florestan, wrongfully imprisoned by the wicked jailer Pizzaro. Florestan is rescued by his wife Leonora who has disguised herself as a boy called 'Fidelio' and obtained a job as Pizarro's assistant.

Beethoven was attracted to this theme for three reasons: firstly, he had always hated all forms of despotism and arbitrary power. Secondly, he could empathise with Florestan's isolation which conjured up his own isolation caused by his deafness. Thirdly, Leonora's heroism, risking death to save her husband, created for him an image of the kind of woman he had long hoped to find. Fidelio contains much music of the heroic kind and was first performed in November 1805.

Another work Beethoven began to compose shortly after completing the 'Eroica' was his Fifth Symphony in C Minor, devoting most of 1807 to its composition. The Fifth can be seen as the natural successor to the 'Eroica' as it develops still further the technique of *thematic* transformation. 'The Fifth is the state of Becoming in music, as Bach's last chorale prelude is the state of Being... The four movements... are evolving facets of experience which grow, or are willed, to an inevitable end' (Mellers 1957, p. 64).

First performed in Vienna's Theater an der Wien in 1808, the work achieved its prodigious reputation soon afterwards. The symphony consists of four movements. The first begins by stating a distinctive four-note "short-short-short-long" *motif* twice. It is one of the most famous *motifs* in Western music, described as 'Schicksals-Motiv' (theme of destiny) and the symphony coined 'Schicksals-Sinfonie'.

There is an assertion of the Will in the 'Eroica' which required a great expansion in the dimensions of the Classical symphony. In the Fifth, Beethoven concentrates and intensifies his power. There are aggressive *metrical* patterns of *tempo* and rhythm and contrasts of *tonality*, making it the most vehement conflict-piece ever composed. Again, Beethoven's intention was to overcome a hostile world and a dogged destiny. Each movement is dominated by the same 'thematic contour'—i.e. the way in which the *pitch* of music or the pattern of *tones* varies—and this is transformed in the course of the symphony.

In the first movement, it assumes the following shape: rising minor sixth and seventh, expressing yearning, followed by the falling and rising third, followed by the minor *triad*. 'The music continually seeks the stability of this *arpeggio* phrase, with its implied *tonic* and *dominant*, and

is repeatedly frustrated by the interjections of the rhythmic Fate motive...'
i.e. the four-note theme (Mellers 1957, pp. 64–65). In the slow movement, each of these three elements reappears, in modified form, in the
passive key of the flat *submediant*. The more lyrical version of the theme
is a dream of serenity, which is destroyed by the Fate rhythm (associated
with a *tonally* disruptive diminished seventh), and then transformed into
a battle-cry in C major. *Rondo* form is here used to express unresolved
fluctuations between submission to dream and challenge to reality.

Moreover, Beethoven's orchestral arrangement was unprecedented:
no composer had used trombones in the way he did in the eventual
finale: previously, they had been used only for church music and occasionally opera. Beethoven also added a contrabassoon and piccolo for
the movement, thus creating 'a sense of climactic power that was quite
overwhelming' (Cooper 2013, p. 77).

Mellers asserts that in the Fifth, Beethoven has 'imposed unity on
chaos, integrating highly disparate modes of experience'. This unity is
expressed both within individual movements, and in the relationship
between the movements. The first three movements are only fully intelligible if seen in relation to the last. This interrelation also exists between
groups of works: the Third and Fourth, the Fifth and Sixth Symphonies,
and also, the Seventh and Eighth should be seen as complementary.

On completing the Fifth, Beethoven set to work on its companion
piece, the Sixth or 'Pastoral'. He loved the countryside, as he indicated in
a letter in 1810: 'How delighted I shall be to wander for a while through
bushes, woods, under trees, plants, rocks. No one can love the country
as much as I do' (Cooper 2013, p. 78). He succeeded in conjuring up
suitable moods in a work which is completely symphonic, not merely
pictorial, yet evoking rural imagery throughout. The pastoral feature is
indicated both by the title of the work as a whole—'Pastoral-Symphony
or Recollection of Country Life, more expression of feeling than painting'—and by the titles of the individual movements: 'Scene by the brook',
'Merry gathering of country people', 'Thunder, storm', 'Shepherds' song:
glad feelings with thanks to the Godhead after the storm'.

Many works with pastoral associations have been composed, both
before and after the Pastoral Symphony, and they were especially common
in the eighteenth century; but Cooper believes that no composer has
succeeded in creating such 'a perfect musical representation of the
countryside and the feelings associated with it' (Cooper 2013, p. 78).
Arguably, however, Schubert was equally successful (see Chapter 4).

The year 1809 falls close to the middle of Beethoven's middle period, and might thus be expected to witness consolidation rather than innovation. However, the year marked a turning point in his life. He completed the fifth Piano Concerto in E flat—the 'Emperor'—early that year, having composed over the previous decade six symphonies and five concertos. Yet over the remaining eighteen years of his life, such large-scale orchestral works all but disappeared. He wrote only three more symphonies, one of which was also a choral work. Towards the end of his 'heroic' period, in 1809, he embarked on smaller forms, notably *lieder*, and on many settings of folk songs, mainly British. A work closing this period was his Seventh Symphony (1811–1812), a powerful piece arguably on the threshold of his late period. The fourth movement consists of a relentlessly repeated rhythmic pattern: it is the bridge taking Beethoven to the glory of his final works.

Late Beethoven

The late period—roughly 1817–1827—contains works of an unprecedented intellectual and emotional depth, of a *formal* and *thematic* innovativeness, and of a profound intensity of personal expression.

For about five years (1812–1816), Beethoven composed comparatively little, but when these years were over, he produced radically different music. The return of creativity found initial expression in the Piano Sonata No. 29, Opus 106 ('Hammerklavier') written in 1817 and 1818, a work that beckons us to cross the threshold into Beethoven's reborn world. The piece contains four movements, a structure often used by Beethoven, one that was imitated by contemporaries such as Schubert, in contrast to the usual three movements of Haydn and Mozart sonatas. Rosen has described how much of the piece is organised around rising and falling sequences based on descending thirds. It is most clearly recognisable in the opening fanfare of the *allegro*, in the *scherzo*'s parody of that fanfare, as well as in its *trio* theme, in bar two of the *adagio*, and in the *fugue* (Rosen 1997, pp. 407, 409, 423).

The first movement carries on from the Seventh and Eighth symphonies and is one of Beethoven's most titanic conflict pieces, based on assertive *metre* and *modulation*. But these characteristics are modified by several features: the second subject is very *cantabile* and is accompanied by extended *trills*; there is much *fugato* writing in the *development*. The slow movement contains a song-like *theme* in Italian aria style, even with quasi-vocal *coloratura*. The movement does not sound like that of a *sonata*: the second subject does not provide a dramatic contrast but is an unbroken lyrical evolution from the first. The final movement bursts out of a kind of recitative into a *fugue* of unprecedented, titanic power.

The last three *sonatas* represent the achievement of what he strove for in the 'Hammerklavier', especially the last, No. 32 in C Minor, Opus 111, written between 1821 and 1822 and dedicated to his friend, pupil and patron, Archduke Rudolph. The piece consists of four movements, a structure often used by Beethoven, in contrast to more usual three movements of Mozart and Haydn sonatas. The first movement is stormy and impassioned, and abounds in diminished seventh chords (three superimposed minor thirds—e.g. B-D-F-A flat—which is two *tritones* a minor third apart plus a note forming an interval of a seventh note above the chord's root). It has been used, for example, as a symbol of 'Sturm und Drang', or in *modulation*, especially in late Classical and Romantic music. The second, final movement is a set of eight variations on a sixteen-bar theme, with a brief *modulating* interlude and final *coda*. The last two are famous for introducing small notes which constantly divide the bar into twenty-seven beats (as heard, not as written) which is very uncommon. The pianist Robert Taub called it "a work of unmatched drama and transcendence... the triumph of order over chaos, of optimism over anguish" (Taub 2004/2012, online article).

Beethoven worked out the plan for his final three Sonatas (Opus 109, 110 and 111) during the summer of 1820 while he worked on his 'Missa Solemnis', or Mass in D, Opus 123. However, the string quartet is the quintessential medium of Beethoven's late years, as the piano was of his youth and the symphony orchestra of his middle period. Earlier, he had not devoted much attention to the quartet which, as a gathering of equal-voiced instruments, did not naturally lend itself to his dynamic style. His early quartets Opus 18 are clearly inspired by Mozart's G Minor Quintet. And in the three main quartets of his middle period, Nos. 7 in F major, 8 in E minor and 9 in C major, Opus 59, the 'Rasumovsky' Quartets—undoubtedly major works, he inflates the quartet into a symphonic style. Also, the 'linear nature of quartet writing prompts him to create themes rather more lyrical than his symphonic motives...' (Mellers 1957, p. 75). ['Linear music' is where the melody is the primary feature and harmony secondary].

The cycle of late quartets begins with No. 12 in E flat major, Opus 127 and ends with No. 16 in F, Opus 135. Arguably, the most comprehensive and certainly the most complicated of Beethoven's last works is the C Sharp Minor Quartet, No. 14, Opus 131, which he also believed to be his greatest work. It is generally regarded as having seven movements but the third and sixth are so short as to merely introduce the movements that follow. The resulting effect is one of fragmentation, but Beethoven counteracts this by making the quartet the most unified of all as regards the *thematic* relationships between movements, the way the end of one movement joins on to the next, and also the work's grand, overarching structure.

The archaic style of the opening *fugue* declares an intense seriousness, but the ensuing *allegro* provides a sharp contrast. The work's core is the fourth movement—a gentle theme with six variations, the last of which is in the unusual metre of 9/4 and is followed by a long *coda*. However, the mood changes in the subsequent *presto*, and the quartet climaxes in a tempestuous *finale* which contains echoes of the opening *fugue* theme before surging to a tortured but defiantly ambiguous conclusion [Cooper', Complete String Quartets' CD, Introduction, p. 18].

The Grosse Fuge in B flat, Opus 133 (Great Fugue) was originally composed as the *finale* of Quartet Opus 30. But the audience found it impenetrable and bewildering, so he wrote a new *finale*, and the Grosse Fuge was published as a separate work. It consists of a brief introduction marked 'Overtura' followed by three main sections. The *fugue* theme, first heard in the 'Overtura', reappears rhythmically altered in each of the three sections. As Barry Cooper puts it: 'The overall impression is one of overwhelming size and power—a Mount Everest among quartet movements' [Introduction, CD, 'Complete String Quartets', p. 17].

But it is in the Missa Solemnis in D major, Opus 123 that 'late' Beethoven attains his most profound, monumental expression. It is generally considered one of Beethoven's supreme achievements, and together with Bach's Mass in B Minor, is one of the most profound Mass settings. It is a choral composition that sets the invariable portions of the Eucharistic liturgy—principally that of the Catholic Church, the Anglican Communion, and Lutheranism—to music of the 'common practice period', i.e. the era between the formation of the *tonal* system around 1680 until its dissolution around 1900. It was dedicated to Archduke Rudolph of Austria, Archbishop of Olomouc, Beethoven's principal patron as well as pupil and friend. The mass illustrates Beethoven's characteristic disregard for the performer: in several places, it is technically and physically exacting, with many sudden changes of *dynamic, metre* and *tempo*. Like most masses, it is in five movements: 'Kyrie', 'Gloria', 'Credo', 'Sanctus', 'Agnus Dei'. It features a quartet of soloists, a large chorus and the full orchestra, with each being used in virtuosic, *textural* and melodic capacities.

Beethoven frequently described it as his 'greatest work' even after completing the Ninth Symphony. The music operates on several levels, 'ranging from almost absurd directness of expression (such as huge downward leaps to illustrate the word "descendit") to amazing technical complexity in the *fugue* for the words "et vitam venturi saeculi" ("and the life of the world to come")...' (Cooper 2013, p. 121).

Some critics have been troubled by the problem that, as Theodor W. Adorno put it, "there is something peculiar about the Missa Solemnis" (Adorno 2002, p. 570). In many respects, it is an atypical work, for example, Beethoven's continuous exploration of themes through *development* is absent. The *fugues* at the end of the 'Gloria' and 'Credo' have the mark of his late period, but his simultaneous interest in the theme and variations form is missing. Instead, the 'Missa Solemnis' presents an uninterrupted musical narrative, virtually without repetition, particularly in the 'Gloria' and 'Credo', the two longest movements. Its five parts are almost completely unified movements. Most remarkable is the 'Gloria' 'with its use of a recurrent *texture* to organise the form'. 'Even the relations between the large sections are closely knit: the 'Credo' opens with a brilliant and rapid *modulation* to the new key, a *modulation* which becomes itself a *thematic* element. The unification of each of the separate parts of the Mass derives from Beethoven's tendency, at the end of his life, to combine a four-movement work within the frame of a first-movement sonata' (Rosen, 1997, p. 375).

Adorno refers to 'certain archaicising moments of harmony—church modes—rather than by the advanced compositional daring of the great 'Grosse Fuge'... Altogether it, reveals a sensuous aspect quite opposed to the intellectualised late style, an inclination to splendidness and tonal monumentality... usually lacking in that late style' (*Essays on Music* 2002, pp. 572–573).

Adorno also suggests in typically enigmatic style that Beethoven had become mistrustful of 'the unity of subjectivity and objectivity, the roundness of symphonic successes... of everything that gave authenticity up to now of the works of his middle period... At this moment, he transcended the bourgeois spirit whose highest musical manifestation was his own work' (Adorno 2002, p. 580). We will suggest in Part III the political meaning of this.

Donald Tovey connected the work to the earlier tradition: 'Not even Bach or Handel can show a greater sense of space and of sonority… There is no choral and no orchestral writing, earlier or later, that shows a more thrilling sense of the individual colour of every chord, every position, and every doubled third or discord' (Tovey 1937, p. 165).

A key feature of Beethoven's late style is his retention of 'out-of-date formulas' and the success with which he rehabilitated them through a technique that was uniquely his and which no one could have imitated, as exemplified throughout the 'Hammerklavier', Opus 106, most strikingly at the end of the *development* of the opening movement. Beethoven returned, in his final phase, to his early stylistic technique, launching an amazing expansion of that style beginning with opus 106. This was 'so formidable that its origins are clouded, but some of the power of the last works depends on Beethoven's incessant efforts to reincorporate the tradition that he knew best into what he himself believed was a radically new conception of the musical work' (Rosen, 1997, p. 487).

As for *counterpoint*, in his last piano sonatas, Beethoven took on the task of imparting new life to the old *fugal* forms. The massive shape of the 'Hammerklavier' *fugue* was a 'manifesto'; the first movement of Piano Sonata Opus 111 produced a synthesis of *fugue* and first movement sonata form.

A further, highly original, feature of Beethoven's late style is his reworking of the Classical convention of moving to the *subdominant* after the start of the *recapitulation* this complex harmonic approach occurring here rather than in the *development*. He develops the *exposition* in the *subdominant*, then *modulates* to a remote key, culminating in *resolution* to the *tonic*. This reveals his approach to the fourth and ninth principles of the Classical style: harmonisation through the three main Classical chords—*tonic, dominant and subdominant*. And, of course, Beethoven remained committed to the *sonata form*.

In his 'Piano Sonata in A flat major, No. 31, Opus 110' (1820–1822), the opening four bars of the *exposition* are initially reworked with a new, rich *texture* representing a genuine *development* of another part of the *exposition*. The 'melody is transferred to the left hand for a simple transition to the *subdominant*… The dynamics descend slowly to *pianissimo* as we reach the only *modulation* in the opening movement to a remote key. The most complex harmonic treatment takes place, therefore, not in the *development* but in the *recapitulation*... The transition to E major is a moment of intense lyrical expression but the eventual return to the *tonic* is even more extraordinary' (Rosen 1997, pp. 491–492). However, here the *dominant* chord is absent.

Between 1819 and 1824, Beethoven's composed the 33 Variations for Piano on a Waltz by Anton Diabelli. Beethoven's approach to the *theme* is to take some of its smallest elements such as the opening melody, the descending fourth and fifth, the repeated notes, and construct variations of great imagination, power and sophistication. It takes a simple, almost commonplace tune and, on its basis, constructs an extraordinary musical edifice. According to Maynard Solomon, 'Beethoven extends to its furthest limits the distance between the theme and its spiritualised metamorphosis. And he accelerates the animated character of the theme in a variety of *prestos, vivaces,* and *allegro assais,* which convey the sense of hastening toward a desired destination...' The piece contains an implied protagonist who looks back to the theme which links him to the home s/he left to pursue 'the metaphor for a desired goal—God, Paradise, reason, wisdom, order, peace, healing, and love' (Maynard 2003, p. 25). It is also, arguably, within the Hegelian dialectical tradition, according to which the real is the potential.

Beethoven's world was clearly no longer that of Haydn and Mozart, yet he continued to use the stylistic conventions he learned as a child even when expanding them beyond recognition, aware of their energy and the depth of their expressive power. So much of Beethoven seems incompatible with eighteenth-century style that it's difficult to see how much of his greatest work synthesises late eighteenth-century ideals. He maintained his belief in basic power of the *dominant;* even when using *mediants* within the form, he prepared them with a strong *dominant* introduction, while younger contemporaries preferred *chromatic* shifts. He preserved the Classical balance between *dominant* and *subdominant,* a 'dead letter' to subsequent generations, and never discarded the long final section in the *tonic* leading to the final *resolution.* Arguably, his greatest achievement was understanding the latent potential of the contemporary *tonal* language and greatly enlarging its expressive capacity. Beethoven's paradox is that while steeped in the Classical tradition, he yet inaugurated a new era (Rosen 1997, pp. 508–509).

The movements of the Ninth Symphony are not in the traditional order. He does begin with an *allegro,* albeit a weighty one, but puts the *scherzo* before the slow movement. From the opening rumbles of the first movement, Beethoven takes us through the frantic conflict of the *scherzo*, then on to the sublime, prayer-like lyricism of the slow movement, concluding with the joyful explosion and triumphant vision of the *finale*. The music is a symphony, oratorio, allegory and inspired declaration of hope rolled into one. The *finale*, with its four vocal soloists and chorus breaks all musical conventions. Beethoven had discovered Friedrich von Schiller's 'Ode to Joy' poem (1785) in his early youth and been intoxicated with its romantic vision of liberty and brotherhood.

Sachs vividly describes the flow of the symphony from the vantage-point of the *finale*: 'we have survived the first movement's brutality and despair, participated in the second's harsh struggle, and been purified by the third's glowing acceptance of life as it is. What Beethoven wants us to experience now [i.e. with the fourth movement) is all-embracing joy. For this is the moment in the work in which Beethoven most unequivocally declares his aim of helping to liberate mankind through art' (Sachs 2010, p. 154). As many commentators have observed, Beethoven's Ninth is one of the crowning achievements of European culture.

Although his major works had been premiered primarily in Vienna, Beethoven contemplated having the Ninth premiered in Berlin as he thought that musical taste in Vienna had declined due to domination by Italian composers such as Rossini. When his friends and financiers heard this, they urged him in the form of a petition signed by a number of prominent Viennese music patrons and performers to premiere the symphony in Vienna. Beethoven was flattered by the adoration of Vienna, so the Ninth Symphony was premiered on 7 May 1824 in that city's 'Theater am Kärntnertor'. The hall was packed with an audience that included many of Beethoven's aristocratic patrons, many admirers from the cultured bourgeoisie, and many musicians, mostly regarded as belonging to the lower class.

The premiere of Symphony No. 9 involved the largest orchestra ever assembled by Beethoven and required the combined efforts of the Kärntnertor house orchestra, the Vienna Music Society ('Gesellschaft der Musikfreunde'), and a select group of capable amateurs. Many of Vienna's most elite performers are known to have participated.

PART III: SOCIAL AND POLITICAL INFLUENCES ON THE CLASSICAL STYLE

From Feudalism to Capitalism

Feudal society was based on local production and consumption. Economic and political power was decentralised, vested in the landowning nobility who exploited the peasantry compelling them to surrender either part of their labour or their produce. But improved production and the growth of trade stimulated urban development. Decentralised political structures meant that the towns which developed as commercial centres could achieve relative independence from the feudal lords. The town became the focus of economic activity of a new class, the bourgeoisie, ancestor of today's capitalist class, also new political structures and ideas. Its economic power in society grew, its social and political weight striving to align themselves to it.

These changes produced a modified form of feudal rule, in particular the growth of centralised absolute monarchies. 'Economic and social life had begun to outgrow the local horizons of feudalism. This laid the basis for the development of bigger, more unified "national" economies and states' (McGarr 1991, p. 97). Absolutism expressed this transformation, with kings acting to curb the independent power of local feudal lords and build a unified, centralised state. Although the feudal nobility retained its political domination of society, it was increasingly subordinated to the centralised monarchy.

In France, the economic rise of the bourgeoisie and the market steadily undermined the power of the monarchy and the nobility, developments which culminated in the great French Revolution of 1789. The rise of the capitalist bourgeoisie and the decline or overthrow of the feudal aristocracy found expression in many areas of social endeavour: not only in music but in the arts generally, and also in science and in people's economic and political lives. The seventeenth and eighteenth centuries in Europe witnessed a historically unprecedented growth of scientific enquiry the fruits of which were an enormous expansion of knowledge and its application to the economic development of society. By 1760, that process had changed people from agricultural labourers into machine-builders and mechanical workers whose individual productive capacity was multiplied many times over.

In Austria and Germany, as we saw in Chapter 2, the Thirty Years' War had bequeathed a legacy of destruction and chaos, as well as the dominance of a foreign power—France. In this situation, the petty princelings attempted to maintain the prevailing feudal serfdom, while emulating French and Italian aristocratic splendour, and the way of life, the art and music, of those societies.

In the mid-eighteenth century, the Galant style was part of the decline of the Rococo style, when it was taken over by the bourgeoisie. Rococo art now 'lost its fantastic, exuberant aspect, and degenerated into a somewhat sober, artificial grace, fit for everyday life' (Leichtentritt 1954, p. 163). Music was thus adapting to the growing bourgeois control of society. As for Stamitz's sound effects, his sudden changes of dynamics, they powerfully expressed the feelings of a growing public which had been unrepresented in the aristocratic art of the previous generation. However, the bourgeois forces in the Age of Enlightenment were convinced that the future was with them. Their self-confidence is reflected in the jaunty dynamism of Stamitz's music.

Rise and Dominance of Vienna

The crucial development in the final part of the eighteenth century is the emergence of Vienna as the music capital of Europe, the home of the new art of the symphony and the sonata, and of Italian-style opera. How was this possible? Could the new forms not have succeeded equally well in the other great musical centres—Naples, Rome, London, Paris, Mannheim, Dresden or Berlin? First-class artists lived in all these cities, as did wealthy patrons of the arts. But Vienna possessed particular social and cultural conditions which made it especially fertile soil for the emergence of great music, superior to any other city for the growth of instrumental, chamber and orchestral music.

As we saw, Italy had dominated the operatic scene to the point where orchestral music never attained a similar importance: instrumental solo and chamber music, for example, the violin concertos, sonatas and concerti grossi of Vivaldi, Corelli and Tartini, were preferred to symphonic orchestral music. In Paris, too, musical interest focused characteristically on opera, the form in which the most exciting developments occurred: for example, Lully and Rameau. For many years, Paris music lovers were in a state of expectancy over the arguments between the adherents of French opera—the 'bouffonists', the Lully party—and Italian opera—the anti- 'bouffonists', the Rameau party, and later, the Gluckists against the admirers of Piccini. This situation accounted for Paris' success in opera while according only secondary importance to new symphonic work.

Germany, especially Prussia, had been further impoverished by the Seven Years' War (1756–1763). Moreover, after the death of Bach in 1750, the Saxo-Thuringian area, having been the cradle of Protestant church music, went into decline. Berlin became a centre of music due to the sponsorship of Frederick the Great, but he favoured Italian and French music over German, despite having once complimented Bach. Moreover, the famous Mannheim orchestra was unable to maintain its supremacy indefinitely: after one generation, its innovations were no longer supported by outstanding musicians, and its technical achievements became the common currency of orchestras throughout Germany and France.

Austria was different—a country brimming with musical talent, with an atmosphere that had been saturated in music for centuries. It wasn't only the imperial court in Vienna that patronised musicians. Every noble family had a private orchestra and even a private opera company in their castle. There was an abundance of good orchestral musicians, with every butler and manservant expected to double up as an instrumental musician. Every small town had its music master who laid on orchestral music for every occasion: parties, weddings, funerals. Typically, a dozen or more talented apprentices lived in his house, ready to play at any hour. Bohemian musicians known as 'German bands' became famous all over Europe: Gluck and Haydn began their careers as players in such bands. In sum, a well-established tradition, a deep well of musical talent, an enthusiasm for music permeating all classes of the population, great wealth and musical ambition on the part of the aristocratic ruling class—all these factors combined to foster the musical talent, devotion and skill that created the unique context within which Viennese music could flourish. The great noble families rivalled one other in the musicianship of their private orchestras. In summer, they lived in the country in their magnificent castles, with music as a daily gratification. In winter, they moved to their Vienna palaces, accompanied by their musicians.

By the late eighteenth century, Vienna had become a major economic and political hub, no doubt a small city by twentieth-century standards but highly sophisticated and cosmopolitan. Traders from all nations and constellations of Italian singers and composers proliferated in this stimulating, glittering world. Vienna was a city permeated by intense musical activity, both in the area of aesthetic theorising, composition, publication and the manufacture of instruments, and in that of performance—private or official concerts. 'Vienna was expanding rapidly... a great deal of activity was spilling out of the old city walls into the new suburbs. Voluntary associations sprouted up all over Vienna—reading groups, choral societies, the Masonic lodges...' (Snowman 2009, p. 91).

The wealthy bourgeoisie and the nobility enthusiastically cultivated chamber music, and in 1778 founded the National and Court Theatre, while Mozart's works were performed at the 'Theater auf der Wieden' founded by his librettist Emanuel Shikaneder. Vienna also became increasingly influential as a music publishing centre, reducing the need for German or Austrian composers to succeed in Paris or London.

Italian styles dominated the Viennese musical scene in the latter half of the eighteenth century. *Opera buffa* was all the rage: while influenced by the declining *opera seria*, it was doubtless a reaction against the heroic view of life showcased by the established order. However, Vienna was gradually able to throw off the Italian influence in favour of a German style, characterised by a solid harmonic and *contrapuntal texture*. This was due both to the intensity of its musical life and the genius of its composers. Salzburg in the eighteenth century was also a centre of musical achievement. The French style had been introduced at the end of the seventeenth century by Georg Muffat, a pupil of Lully's, while Caldara had developed the Italian style there. But a group of German musicians, among them Leopold Mozart, adopted the German style.

In the early nineteenth century, Vienna's musical life was enriched more than that of any other European capital, not by public concerts but by small, semi-private performances in the homes of the well-off middle class as well as in the aristocratic mansions. Beethoven's chamber works—sonatas, quartets, trios—'disrupted the character of this musical life to some extent even while they exploited it' (Rosen 1997, p. 510). Although during his lifetime, the piano sonatas were almost never played in public, but only in private gatherings, many of them—for example, the 'Waldstein', 'Appassionata', 'Hammerklavier'—'implied a public domain'. No doubt these works were of such depth and on a such grand scale as to transcend in performance scope the private salon. After his death, it was his instrumental compositions—rather than those of Haydn or Mozart—that became the staple of the public concert.

In Austria and Germany, the ancien regimes survived, but the power of the old aristocracy gradually became eroded. However, the reforming Austrian Emperor Joseph II, following in the footsteps of his mother Empress Maria Theresa, attempted to abolish serfdom but fell foul of the continuing entrenched power of that class. His Patent of Toleration of 1781, a good example of enlightened despotism, granting religious freedom of worship to Lutherans, Calvinists and Serbian Orthodox, in opposition to the papacy, was followed a year later by the Edict of Tolerance, which extended that freedom to Jews. Joseph II was also motivated by economic considerations as the emigration of Austria's Protestant population would have led to a slump. But these measures were defeated by the Esterhazys, Haydn's patrons. Their palace, an attempt to recreate Louis XIV's glory in Austria, was "an oasis, even a mirage, in a desert of misery, for it depended on serfdom for its existence" (Mellers 1957, p. 7). Moreover, the outbreak of the French Revolution in 1789 prompted Joseph to reverse his reforms.

Nevertheless, on a European-wide canvass, the days of the feudal landlords and Catholicism were numbered, their system and ideology gradually undermined, their power overthrown by the rising bourgeois class whose mercantile and industrial system proved to be economically far superior. This had already happened in Britain, and the French Revolution had a major impact on countries in Europe and the New World, not least the USA, inspiring the creation of liberal regimes and heralding the end of many traditional, feudal laws and practices. The waning of the ancien regimes, the setting of the feudal sun and the rise of that of the bourgeoisie, could thus be seen even in Austria where Freemasonry upheld the power of reason, as embodied in the Enlightenment, to reshape society. Haydn, apparently a pious Catholic, aroused the ire of the Church because of the Masonic implications of his oratorio 'The Creation'. Mozart's Masonic opera 'The Magic Flute' was famously regarded with suspicion by the Church as a subversive work. In the Temple of the Sun, Sarastro, high priest of the Sun, announces the sun's triumph over the night, and hails the dawn of a new era of wisdom and brotherhood. These developments indicate how powerfully democratic ideas permeated the work even of musicians who had been aristocratically nurtured.

Moreover, Mozart's operas are permeated with the characters of feudal noblemen whose days are numbered or rebellious servants who challenge their masters' authority. In 'The Marriage of Figaro', Figaro defies his master Count Almaviva's hitherto undisputed feudal right to the first night with a servant bride. 'Don Giovanni', with his all-conquering reputation, spends the entire opera chasing potential female conquests, failing dismally in every case, a singularly unsuccessful rake. His servant Leporello sings of his wish to cease being a servant and to become the lord: 'Voglio Far Il Gentiluomo-Non Voglio Piu Servir'. In 1787, when Don Giovanni welcomes his masked guests with 'Viva La Liberta', Mozart unleashes the full orchestra with trumpets and drums *maestoso* in an invigorating passage full of martial rhythm, would the audience not have seen a link with the American revolution of 4th July? (Rosen 1997, pp. 94–95). In 'Cosi Fan Tutte', Despina the maid, asserts the need for women's independence as she urges her mistresses to take new lovers while their existing ones are apparently fighting at the front. Finally, 'The Magic Flute' is the opera in which Mozart gives full expression to his commitment to the Freemasons, at that time, of course, not a businessman's mutual aid society but a genuinely progressive movement upholding the ideals of the Enlightenment—the primacy of reason, scientific progress—and the values at the heart of the French Revolution—liberty, equality, fraternity (Arblaster 1992, p. 37). The sun that floods the stage at the end symbolises the truth and light of the Enlightenment, the power of reason, progress and constitutional government, to liberate society from the darkness of the old order. Mozart's 'music and operas are rooted in the contradiction between the decaying old society which has yet to die and the growing new society yet to be born... the curtain had lifted on a Parisian drama in which Figaros in the mass were not only defying their lords and masters, but would soon bury them and their society for ever' (McGarr 1991, p. 127). Moreover, in 1781, Mozart himself had vented a strong mutinous spirit when defying Archbishop Colloredo's refusal to release him from his duties as a feudal servant. He wrote to his father: 'I have perhaps more honour in me than many a Count; and lackey or Count as soon as he insults me he is a scoundrel' (Stone 1996, p. 143).

Haydn had created a new order in the orchestra, as Joseph von Holzmeister, Chief Clerk of the imperial war ministry, pointed out in a speech on the occasion of his admission to the Masonic Order, "for if every instrument did not consider the rights and properties of the other instruments, in addition to its own rights, if it did not often diminish its own volume in order not to do damage to the utterance of its companions, the end—which is beauty—would not be attained" (Mellers 1957,

p. 8). The symphony orchestra, therefore, reflected a democratic ideal—the new orchestral set-up can be said to have incorporated all three values at the heart of the French Revolution: equality and fraternity, with liberty emerging as each instrument expresses itself through its specific performance.

Again, it seems that the birth of the string quartet was also a democratic process: 'music moved not merely from Church and court to the chamber or living-room, but even into the streets. Vienna was a-jingle with serenading parties playing in the open air' (Mellers 1957, pp. 18–19). Furthermore, if this music was to be effective, its style needed to be even simpler than that of *opera buffa*. It needed jaunty melodies, accessible rhythms and a basic harmonic accompaniment. Again, we highlighted Haydn's sense of the comic: this often has a profoundly subversive significance, indicating the extent to which Haydn expressed in his work the growing instability and rebelliousness of the revolutionary age in which he lived.

We also saw how in the Classical style the relationship between principal voice and accompanying voices is transformed. In Haydn's Opus 33 quartet, at first, the cello has the melody and the violin the accompaniment, but later the violin acquires the melody. The Classical bass line becomes the treble line's equal partner in melodic development. 'It is as if the principles of Liberty, Equality and Fraternity, so much in the air at the time, were emancipating the bass from its role of service to the upper instruments' (Downs 1992, p. 354).

This undermines the Classical hierarchical structure by introducing a new fluidity into the relations between melody and accompaniment, one which no doubt reflects the growing fluidity of social relations, the beginnings of social mobility in late eighteenth-century European society. With the development of industry, it began to be possible for individuals to enter into different roles in a lifetime—small traders becoming wealthy merchants, independent artisans combining to become factory owners, the factory system replacing cottage industry, peasants casting off feudal subservience to become independent farmers (Rude 1967, pp. 98–100).

The primacy of melody conceivably testifies to the rise of individualism in European society: the growing confidence of the bourgeois class that they have the right and the capacity, as individuals, to intervene in society and the economy, to transform it according to Reason without reference to higher authorities. 'Career Open to the Talents' was an important slogan governing the lives of a growing number of rising middle class individuals.

Secondly, there is an atmosphere of drama created by abrupt shifts in melody and rhythm, which creates an uneven rhythmic flow with frequent changes of *tempo*. This arguably testifies to three factors: firstly, as just seen, the rising aspirations of the mercantile class in the eighteenth century, and their increasing interest in music as a mark of aristocratic taste and social distinction; secondly, the increase in population and the number of amateur musicians which provided a new, affluent public; thirdly, unceasing change, the growing unevenness and unpredictability of economic and political life in a Europe that was emerging from the dark ages, less and less subject to the control of Church and Monarchy. Crucially, in the eighteenth and nineteenth centuries, Europe experienced greater change than in the previous five–ten thousand years.

We also saw that while contrasting themes are an inevitable aspect of the Classical style, perhaps even more significant are the *themes* of internal contrast, that is, within a melodic line. However, the prevalence of both forms of *thematic* contrast can perhaps be interpreted as expressive of a revolutionary age, of an intensifying dynamic of events, in which the unexpected, the sudden twist and turn of events, is becoming the norm. Examples abound: the intensification of agriculture and of urban development, the scientific revolution, the growth of national and international markets, the accelerating pace of colonialism. This is in contrast to the static predictability of the pre-capitalist order. A further important element in this developing scenario is intensifying rivalry between social classes and political groups pitted against each other.

Another crucial feature, as we saw, is the limited range of chords—plain harmony—intended to stress the primacy of melody: I, IV and V—the triads belonging to the first, fourth and fifth notes of the scale—*tonic, sub-dominant* and *dominant*. Musically, these three chords are those that best bring out the sense of 'home' in the sound, 'reinforcing the melody's typical journey away from home and back again' (Goodall 2013, p. 125). Arguably, the drive to resolution in the *tonic* expresses the aspiration towards a harmonious settlement of tension and conflict, expressing the bourgeoisie's need for a strong centralised state guaranteeing peace, enabling them to create new markets, accumulate wealth and pursue unhindered the construction of their new society.

As for the prevalence of *sonata* form, this again surely testifies to the growing complexity of a rapidly developing capitalism and the boldness of its bourgeois creators, their ability to generate new needs and desires, their willingness to explore uncharted territories, confident that they would return home (closure through a return to the home key), a period of revolutionary transformation. And arguably the development of the eighteenth century sonata style is the musical expression of the new bourgeois democracy.

In sum, Haydn and Mozart express the turbulent atmosphere of pre-revolutionary Europe which, despite living and working in a feudal environment, they conceivably experienced at an unconscious level. So Mellers describes Haydn as 'a revolutionary composer... without conscious awareness' (Mellers 1957, p. 16). Therefore, his claim that Haydn's phase of protest had dissolved into acceptance is questionable. In the case of Mozart's final three symphonies, especially No. 40 in G Minor, we find again sharply expressed the tension and conflict of a European society undergoing the most profound changes certainly since the collapse of the Roman Empire and the rise of feudalism.

Mozart's 'Jupiter' Symphony, No. 41 in C Major', is, in contrast, expressive of the resolution following on the conflict between opposites. The final movement has achieved the 'Apollonian' equilibrium, that resolution of the conflict between opposites sought by the composers of the Classical era, which many thinkers of the bourgeois age, for example Hobbes, thought they had found in the capitalist state. Moreover, the focus in Haydn's sonata movements on change, dramatic contrast and thematic enlargement also ostensibly expresses the turbulent atmosphere of pre-revolutionary Europe.

Haydn's 'Apollonian' equilibrium achieved in the final quartets are arguably the expression in music of the deepening of the transformation of thought and social action that swept across Europe in the last decades of the eighteenth century, a radicalisation that was to achieve its practical apotheosis in the French revolution. Moreover, the centrality of drama in Haydn's music, as indeed throughout the Classical age, surely reflects the tensions and conflicts of a European social and political world that was undergoing the most profound change in its history, though, of course, the dramatic transition to the bourgeois order had already occurred in England in the seventeenth century. Again, Haydn's fondness for folk melodies is no doubt due to the 'republican' enthusiasm and the rise of national cultures of the end of the eighteenth century.

Mellers argues that Haydn's God was not Bach's 'mystical divinity', nor Handel's 'Lord of earthly glory' but that his later music reflected the belief that had meaning for him—'an ethical humanism based on reason and the love of created nature'. Haydn's religious music reveals him gradually discovering 'the religion... implicit in his later instrumental music' (Mellers 1957, pp. 28–29). The ethical humanism of eighteenth-century Europe expressed the moral and political ideals of the rising bourgeoisie striving to transform society according to its ideals of liberty, equality and fraternity. It was a world that could only be ushered in through the application of reason to social goals, though interestingly, the love of nature is an early harbinger of a future romantic ideal. Returning to the *andante* in Symphony No. 104, Haydn has here achieved a new resolution of the conflict between the artist and his world. He celebrates the Enlightenment's 'Discovery of Man': it was an era in which humankind were striving for democracy, recreating themselves through the reconstruction of civilisation in the light of Reason. Human passions were only the means towards the 'Apollonian' equilibrium which, as we saw, became the Classical ideal epitomised in Haydn's late symphonic *allegro*s and hymn-like *andante*s, as it is also in Mozart's Masonic music. This ideal also features in the *scherzo* and *finale* of Symphony No. 104: the minuet includes sudden breaks and trills which give it an almost Beethovenian power, and the rustic conviviality of the *finale*, with its folk-like theme and bagpipe drone, evolves 'through its symphonic *counterpoint* into a paean of praise. It is both comic and majestic' (Mellers 1957, p. 26).

Again, it was argued earlier that whereas Bach and Handel are concerned in their different ways with states of Being, Haydn's sonata movements deal with growth and change—with Becoming. This would seem to reflect the beginnings of the industrial transformation of European society with its unprecedented change in the methods of production and patterns of exploitation, leading to a transformed class structure, habits of work, way of life and culture.

Beethoven's early artistic and social rebellion were rooted in his personality which in turn was a product and an expression of the social upheavals being experienced across Europe. The most characteristic works of his middle period—the Third ('Eroica') and Fifth symphonies, and the 'Emperor' Piano Concerto—surely also express the urge to change the world. The Eroica's assertion of the Will described above, the Fifth's famous opening four notes—knocking on the door of history— the Emperor Concerto's heroic exhortation—the way the soloist opens with a *cadenza* followed by a propulsive, thrusting opening *theme*—all seem to communicate the longing to sweep away the old order and usher in the new. These works, therefore, surely reflect the profound influence on Beethoven of the French revolution and its democratic, republican ideals, inspired as they were by the ideas of the Enlightenment. As Adorno wrote: 'the din of the bourgeois revolution rumbles in Beethoven...' (Adorno 1989, p. 211).

Social and Political Influences on Beethoven's Late Style

Beethoven can be said to be the musical embodiment of the ideals of the French revolution—reaching the heights of our potential for self-liberation and brotherhood. Haydn and Mozart had not been politically engaged, at least at a formal or conscious level, though Mozart, as we saw, privately expressed anger and contempt towards members of the aristocracy. Beethoven, however, was ardently convinced of the revolution's democratic, republican ideals, enthusiastically embracing its watchwords: 'liberte, egalite, fraternite'. As Leichtentritt puts it: 'Spiritually, he is a son of the French Revolution' (Leichtentritt 1954, p. 183).

As a young man in Vienna, studying with Haydn, Beethoven was already aware of his artistic capabilities, showing a lack of respect for the established powers, 'a proud demeanour, and a self-assertiveness that shocked the modest Haydn' who dubbed him the 'grand mogul', and 'Turkish pasha' (Leichtentritt 1954, p. 183). Beethoven became the darling of the Viennese aristocracy. But unlike Haydn and Mozart, he refused to be ranked as a servant to the noble families, considering himself socially their equal, and spiritually their superior by dint of his genius. Meeting the great writer Wolfgang von Goethe in Teplitz, they were walking in a park when the imperial family approached: Goethe bowed respectfully, infuriating Beethoven who stormed off in the opposite direction (Suchet 2012, pp. 226–227). He was the first composer able to maintain such an independent attitude, and, by standing fast against this time-honoured custom, raised the social status of the musician from aristocratic servant to independent artist, for his own and later generations. He raised music to a new level, putting it on a pedestal it had never previously occupied.

Musical culture proceeded down a new path. In the previous century, the patrons of music had been almost exclusively the wealthy nobility, though England had witnessed the beginnings of a bourgeois audience. But in the nineteenth century, music ceased to be exclusive entertainment for royal courts and aristocratic families. It was now maintained on as high a level as before by the rising bourgeoisie, whose political emancipation came to match their prior socio-economic and cultural emancipation.

The European Political Context

Between 1796 and 1815, Europe had been devastated by the French revolutionary and Napoleonic wars. From the Atlantic seaboard to Moscow, ideological clashes had been converted into national military clashes. The banner proclaiming 'liberty, fraternity, equality' had been bloodied by The Terror of 1793–1794, and with Napoleon as military leader, France embarked on a campaign that transformed defence of the revolution into its export as a cover for achieving European domination. However shocking the excesses of the infant French Republic's guillotine may have been (some 16,594 were executed), they were dwarfed by the carnage of the wars between 1796 and 1815 when some two and a half a million soldiers and one million civilians died (Sachs 2010, p. 62). The final movement of Beethoven's Seventh Symphony arguably expresses his dual rage at his continuing deafness but also the turmoil overwhelming Europe, including the French occupation of Vienna.

In 1815 with Napoleon's final defeat and exile, an enormous sense of relief engulfed Europe. In the period of relative calm that followed the Battle of Waterloo, one watchword and one phrase describe the scene: restoration and balance of power. At the Congress of Vienna four key victorious nations were represented—Britain, Russia, Prussia and Austria, together with the vanquished France, officially present as an observer.

The main concern of the principal governments was to return to the traditional 'balance of power'. They believed that a balance of political and military force would deter any state or alliance of states from attempts at domination. It was also agreed that each state should receive compensation for their struggle with France in the form of territory. So, Britain received colonies and outposts it had won during the wars. Austria surrendered Belgium but received territory in southern Germany and the northern Italian provinces.

The allies restored the Bourbon dynasty and France's 1792 boundaries (larger than those of 1789). Negotiating with arch-diplomat Talleyrand, no reparations were demanded, on the understanding that France would support Austria and Britain and help to prevent Russia from expanding westwards and linking up with Prussia (Sachs 2010, p. 64). Leniency towards France was dictated by the need to maintain its state strong enough to be able to resist possible future revolutionary upheavals. However, measures were taken to prevent renewed French aggression: Belgium and Holland were united under a single Dutch monarchy capable of standing up to France militarily, while Prussia was awarded additional territory on France's eastern border enabling it to be the 'sentinel on the Rhine'.

The Congress of Vienna reformed the numerous German-speaking states into thirty-nine independent states, of which Prussia and Austria were the most powerful and over which Austria presided. The confederation's members pledged to come to the aid of any state that was attacked. This gave Austria a pulpit from which to bully the smaller German states. The outcome was not a move towards German unification but rivalry between Austria and Prussia for domination of Central Europe.

Under the leadership of Austrian chancellor Metternich, the alliance that became known as the 'Concert of Europe' planned to intervene in any country threatened by liberal or nationalist ideologies of the kind that had kindled the French Jacobins and which might threaten the status quo. It was also important that no country should dominate Europe as France had under Napoleon.

However, despite these Herculean efforts to prevent a second French revolution or a 'catastrophic' spread of revolution on the French model to the rest of Europe, they were battling against the tide. As Hobsbawm remarked: 'Rarely has the incapacity of governments to hold up the course of history been more conclusively demonstrated than in the generation after 1815' (Hobsbawm, 1962, p. 137). Throughout Europe, the revolutionary atmosphere was endemic and combustible, as likely to be ignited by a spontaneous spark as by deliberate agitation. The revolutions of the post-Napoleonic period differed from the 1789 revolution in that whereas the latter had been spontaneous, the former were intended and even planned. This doesn't mean they were the product of individual, disaffected agitators, as the numerous spies of the time told their superiors. They happened because the political systems reimposed on Europe in a period of rapid social change were profoundly and increasingly inadequate for the political conditions of the Continent. Moreover, the economic and social discontents were so acute as to make a series of outbreaks almost inevitable.

The model of 1789 gave the discontent a focus, helping to transform unrest into revolution, and, most crucially, linking European countries in a current of subversion. During the Restoration period, the 'blanket of reaction' covered all those dissenters equally, the distinction between Bonapartists and Republicans, moderates and radicals, hardly visible. There were as yet no working-class revolutionary socialists, and most continental mass discontent 'was as yet non-political... a dumb protest against the new society which appeared to bring nothing but evil and chaos' (Hobsbawm 1968, p. 142). Political opposition in Europe was confined to small groups of the well-off or the educated. Members of the labouring poor who were consciously 'leftwing' accepted the classical demands of middle-class revolution, though perhaps in the radical-democratic rather than the moderate version, but so far with only a hint of defiance.

Throughout Europe, the united front of the absolutist states excluded peaceful reform. Revolutionaries saw themselves as 'small elites of the emancipated and progressive operating among, and for the eventual benefit of, a vast and inert mass of the ignorant and misled common people, who would no doubt welcome liberation when it came, but could not be expected to take much part in preparing it' (Hobsbawm, 1962, p. 143). They saw themselves as combating the one enemy: the union of absolutist monarchs under the leadership of the Tsar. They regarded revolution as 'unified and indivisible', a single European phenomenon rather than 'an aggregate of national or local liberations'.The years 1820–1821 witnessed a crop of revolutionary initiatives—some launched by brotherhoods such as the 'good cousins' or Carbonari, apparently descended from Masonic or similar lodges in Eastern France, which then took shape in Southern Italy after 1806 and spread north and across the Mediterranean after 1815. These were found as far away as Russia, where the Decembrists mounted the first insurrection in modern Russia in 1825. These insurrectionary attempts failed everywhere except in Greece where the 1821 people's rising against the Turks inspired a generation of international liberals and nationalists, including the poet Lord Byron, who rallied the European left, organising support and volunteer fighters reminiscent of those who fought in the Spanish Civil War in the 1930s.

One possible explanation for the decline in Beethoven's creativity during the years 1812–1816 could, therefore, be disappointment in the failure of the French revolution to result in any major liberation for humanity as a whole. Although the French bourgeoisie had inscribed on their banner 'Liberty, Equality, Fraternity', they meant it only for themselves. Once they had won political power, they chose to consolidate, and the mantle of struggle fell on to the shoulders of other social forces to extend the boundaries of freedom and democracy beyond the limits laid down by the bourgeoisie. Later years indeed witnessed other social formations in France and elsewhere taking up the cudgels of revolution.

Nevertheless, the French revolution retained a powerful influence on Beethoven, and arguably the late works—his late quartets and piano sonatas, the 'Missa Solemnis' and the Ninth Symphony—combine sadness and anger at the failure of humanity to break free from the shackles of oppression, but also optimism that future generations would achieve this. As we saw, the key stylistic features of these works—for example, preserving the Classical balance between *dominant* and *subdominant*, not discarding the last section in the *tonic* leading to the final resolution—express the late Classical style reworked into a new, revolutionary idiom. '...Beethoven's originality reveals itself most often not by frustrating the conventions that he learned as a child, but by magnifying them beyond the experience or expectations of any of his contemporaries'. He preserved 'the traditional formal procedures of his youth until, at the end of his life, he was alone in continuing a late eighteenth century style that he so transformed into the sensibility of a new age that he seemed to have reinvented it' (Rosen 1997, p. 460).

Beethoven in his late works perhaps expresses, no doubt unconsciously, his sorrow at the burden reimposed on Europe by Napoleon and the victorious monarchies, but reasserts his faith in the capacity of future generations to rise up against servitude. The third, slow movement of the Ninth Symphony expresses a tragic lyricism that mourns the failure of the French revolution to fulfil its political and moral promises, whereas the fourth, choral movement reasserts a belief in humanity's long-term capacity to usher in such a world.

Regarding the 'Missa Solemnis', Beethoven himself was not a practising Catholic. Early biographies suggest he did not believe in divine revelation or a transcendental Supreme Being. His secretary Anton Schindler suggested he inclined to Deism, which rejects revelation as a source of religious knowledge, asserting that reason and observation of the natural world are sufficient to establish the existence of a Supreme Being: God ceases to intervene in the world after he sets its physical laws in motion. In later life, Beethoven probably did come to believe in a transcendental being but he also became interested in eastern religions, especially Hinduism and Egyptian polytheism. As Swafford put it: 'He will grow up nominally Catholic and, in his fashion, close to God, but he will be no lover of priests, ritual or magic' (Swafford 2014, p. 2). The Missa's upward surges followed by downward leaps ('descendit') suggest, rather, a desire to create heaven on earth. The Mass is perhaps contradictory: a theological work with a significant secular dimension.

Beethoven aspired to light the way for humanity, to help human beings realise their high ethical potential. And despite the defeat of the ideals of the Great French Revolution of 1789, struggles for national liberation did continue after 1821, with a new social revolution erupting in Paris in 1830. 'The uniquely expressive power of the Ninth Symphony... [is] one of the most striking products of human beings' attempts to continue the struggle [for liberation], as well as to deepen their individual relationships to life...' (Sachs 2010, p. 111). Also important here is that for Beethoven, it is not only heroes but also 'common people' who are included among the 'all men' who one day 'will be brothers!'.

Central to Beethoven's existence was the longing to help mankind raise itself out of the muck of ignorance and suffering. In his final decade, this moral imperative became increasingly pressing, linked as it was to his 'strange and acute personal misery'. It elevated Beethoven 'to levels of abstract expression and of rarefied, distilled emotion that no one else in the history of Western music has reached' (Sachs 2010, p. 129). This doesn't mean that Beethoven is 'greater' than Bach or Mozart, just that he had a unique ability to channel his most intimate experience into sounds that also expressed his powerful drive to transform the human condition.

Social Origins

Haydn came from peasant stock, while Mozart and Beethoven came from middle-class backgrounds, but there is a line of increasing radicalisation that passes through that Classical trio. Haydn accepted his socially but not spiritually or artistically subordinate status; at a conscious level, Mozart struggled to integrate himself into the sophisticated Viennese upper-class society, though we have seen how the radicalism both of his operas and his music embodied an inherent attack on the aristocracy and the status quo, with contempt for the nobility expressed in his letters. Beethoven, like Haydn and Mozart, was also dependent on the Viennese aristocracy but, unlike his predecessors, pitted himself against them, not just in his music but in his conscious ideas. If Haydn and Mozart were covertly revolutionary composers, Beethoven is overtly so.

Conclusion: Beethoven and Hegel

In one of those strange historical coincidences (Western music has several), two German cultural giants—Beethoven and Hegel—were born in the same year—1770. Hegel was writing at the time when Beethoven composed his Ninth Symphony, arguing that 'philosophy has the universal for its object, and, in so far as we think, we are universal ourselves' (Hegel in Sachs 2010, pp. 129–130). Hegel saw his work as the culmination of Western philosophy, as humanity's realisation of its possibilities, its achievement of self-consciousness, the fulfilment of the Absolute Idea. There is a sense in which Beethoven is the musical counterpart to Hegel: if Hegel represents the high point of bourgeois philosophy, Beethoven marks the fulfilment, the apotheosis, of the line of development that begins with the invention of tonality around 1680 and journeys through the late Baroque and Classical eras. As Adorno expressed it: 'his music expressed the same experiences which inspired Hegel's concept of the World Spirit' [Beethoven, The Philosophy of Music, p. 32]. Perhaps the dialectic is present within Beethoven's own work, the early period being the thesis, the middle period the antithesis, with the late period absorbing and synthesising elements of both. Beethoven expresses in his music the peak of bourgeois social and ideological creativity and confidence but also looks forward to a future society based on human solidarity.

Bibliography

Adorno, Theodor W. 1989. *Introduction to the Sociology of Music*, New York: The Continuum Publishing Company.
Adorno, Theodor W. 2002. *Alienated Masterpiece: The Missa Solemnis*, in *Essays on Music*, ed. Richard Leppert. Berkeley and Los Angeles, CA: University of California Press.
Arblaster, Anthony. 1992. *Viva La Liberta: Politics in Opera*. London: Verso.
Blume, Friedrich. 1970. *Classic and Romantic Music: A Comprehensive Survey*. New York: W. W. Norton.
Cooper, Barry. 2008. *Beethoven*, 2nd ed. Oxford and New York: Oxford University Press.
Cooper, Barry. 2013. *Beethoven: An Extraordinary Life*. London: ABRSM Publishing Ltd.

Clubbe, John. 2019. *Beethoven, The Relentless Revolutionary*, NY, London: W. W. Norton.

Downs, Philip G. 1992. *Classical Music: The Era of Haydn, Mozart, and Beethoven*. New York: W. W. Norton.

Goodall, Howard. 2013. *The Story of Music*. London: Vintage Books.

Hindley, Geoffrey (ed.). 1971. *The Larousse Encyclopedia of Music*. London: Hamlyn Publishing Group.

Hobsbawm, Eric. 1962. *The Age of Revolution: 1783–1815*. World Publishing Company & George Weidenfeld & Nicolson, Ltd.

Hobsbawm, Eric. 1968. *Industry and Empire*. London: Weidenfeld and Nicolson.

Hughes, Rosemary. 1950/1970. *Haydn*, revised ed. New York: Farrar, Strauss and Giroux.

Leichtentritt, Hugo. 1954. *Music, History and Ideas,* . Cambridge, MA: Harvard University Press.

Lockwood, Lewis. 2015. *Beethoven's Symphonies—An Artistic Vision*. New York: W. W. Norton.

Mathew, Nicholas. 2013. *Political Beethoven*. Cambridge Univesity Press.

Maynard, Solomon. 2003. *Late Beethoven: Music, Thought and Imagination*. London: University of California Press.

McGarr, Paul. 1991. *Mozart: Overture to Revolution* in International Socialism Journal 52 (Autumn), reprinted as Redwords pamphlet.

Mellers, Wilfred. 1957. *The Sonata Principle from C. 1750*. London: Rockliff.

Palmer, Kris. 2001. *Ornamentation According to C.P.E. Bach and J.J. Quantz*. Bloomington: 1st Books Library.

Robbins Landon, H.C., and David Wyn Jones. 1988. *Haydn: His Life and Music*. Bloomington: Indiana University Press.

Rosen, Charles. 1997. *The Classical Style: Haydn, Mozart, Beethoven*. London: Faber and Faber.

Rude, George. 1967. *Revolutionary Europe: 1783–1815*. London: Collins.

Sachs, Harvey. 2010. *The Ninth: Beethoven and the World in 1824*. London: Faber & Faber.

Snowman, Daniel. 2009. *The Gilded Stage: A Social History of Opera*. London: Atlantic Books.

Stone, J. 1996. *Mozart's Opinions and Outlook*, in *The Mozart Compendium*, ed. H.C. Robbins Landon. London: Thames and Hudson.

Suchet, John. 2012. *Beethoven, the Man Revealed*. New York: Atlantic Monthly Press.

Sutcliffe, W. Dean. June 1989. *Haydn's Musical Personality*, Musical Times Vol. 130, No. 1756 pp. 341-344.

Swafford, Jan. 2014. *Beethoven: Anguish and Triumph*. New York: Houghton Mufflin Harcourt Publishing Co.

Taub, Robert O*n the Beethoven Sonatas,* http://voxcd.com/taub_beethoven.htm
   / Taub, Robert, *The Beethoven Sonatas,* Hal Leonard Corporation, 2009,
   Milwaukee, USA.
Tovey, Donald. 1937. *Essays in Musical Analysis* (Vol. V). London: Oxford
   University Press.
Webster, James. 1991. *Haydn's 'Farewell' Symphony and the Idea of Classical
   Style: Through-Composition and Cyclic Integration in His Instrumental Music.*
   Cambridge: Cambridge University Press.
[www.mostlywind.co.uk].

CHAPTER 4

The Romantic Style

The Romantic movement was an artistic and intellectual movement that arose in Europe in the late eighteenth or early nineteenth century. Its ideological heart was a reaction against the Enlightenment and its key offshoots—the appropriation of nature by scientific rationalism, the crucial precondition for its subordination through industrialisation. One of the first to apply the term to music was the German writer E.T.A. Hoffmann in a review of Beethoven's Fifth Symphony published in 1810 in which he identified the origins of Romantic music in the later works of Haydn and Mozart. Romanticism had a triple birthplace—England, Germany and France—the latter two being the dual womb of its music.

Four features lay at the heart of musical Romanticism. Firstly, discontent with existing formulas and conventions. The Classical style in the arts including music tended to be a concentrated, closed form, whereas the Romantic style was open and loose. The Classical style had clear-cut contours in contrast to the Romantic preference for a picturesque, *colourful* treatment and shadowy outlines. The Classical tradition was rationalistic, logical, in search of harmonious proportions, as opposed to the experimental approach of Romanticism with its focus on the irrational—on mystery, fantasy, remoteness, the infinite, the nocturnal and the supernatural. There is a contrast between the objective, orderly language of the Classical era and the subjective, individualistic, irregular

S. Sagall, *MUSIC and CAPITALISM*,
Critical Political Theory and Radical Practice,
https://doi.org/10.1057/978-1-137-52095-1_4

musical idiom of the Romantics, the free rein given to the imagination and emotional self-expression (Leichtentritt 1954, p. 197).

Secondly, there was a new absorption in nature, and a fascination with the pre-industrial and pre-capitalist medieval past. Thirdly, the universal ideas and values of the Classical ideal were replaced by a love of one's nation, stimulating a preoccupation with the folk song and the development of national musical styles.

Fourthly, the Romantics celebrated the individual. The artist was seen as a free spirit, without family or social ties, who opposed capitalism and sometimes became a fighter against national oppression, for example, Lord Byron. Romanticism unleashed wild and exotic visions and yearnings, inspiring artists to aspire to unlimited horizons. The greatest Romantics admired Napoleon, the 'unbounded personality' (Fischer 1963, p. 55). A contradiction therefore arose between the Romantic hostility to the economic individualism of the new capitalism and the assertion of their artistic individualism.

However, there were contrasts within the Romantic movement itself, for example, between theatricality and intimacy. On the one hand, Romanticism leads to withdrawal into the secret, intimate areas of the personality as in the pianistic art of Chopin or Schumann. But this intimacy sits alongside brilliant virtuosity as in the piano music of Weber. Again, Wagner penetrates to our deepest emotional level, yet his art is that of theatrical performance (Einstein 1947, pp. 4–5).

Despite the stress on the mysterious mentioned above, the Romantics also pursued clarity in their music: for example, Mendelssohn was a Romantic by virtue of his new feeling for sound, but he hated any disturbance of harmonic rules. He was a master of clarity and *symmetry*. On the other hand, Berlioz hated the strict observance of rules. Both derived from Beethoven, but whereas Mendelssohn saw in him the master who perfected form, and brought order into chaos, Berlioz saw in him the master who revolutionised the symphony while unchaining forces of darkness and chaos (Einstein 1947, p. 6).

Another contrast within Romantic music is that between 'absolute' and 'programme' music. Programme music aimed to extend music's expressive potential by giving a musical interpretation to a poem, a story or dramatic scene. An early example, of course, was Beethoven's Sixth ('Pastoral') symphony (Leichtentritt 1954, pp. 222–223). An even earlier example was Vivaldi's 'The Four Seasons' (see Chapter 2). For Berlioz, music inevitably contained features from the other arts: it needed fantasy and, therefore, the stimulus of poetry even when following musical rules. In that sense, it was programmatic.

On the other hand, Mendelssohn saw his music as 'absolute', composing instrumental works which were never based on a programme in the sense of Berlioz, Liszt or Wagner. In general, the Romantic composer was no longer 'her/his own poet' but sought inspiration in the sibling art of poetry, for example, Berlioz in Victor Hugo's Romantic thrillers, in Byron's 'Weltschmerz'-coloured scenes, in Walter Scott's novels, and Shakespeare's dramas. The Romantics sought to erase the boundary line between music and poetry, with music helping out poetry by seeking to represent by more direct, sensuous means the essence of the poem or painting. This entailed a mixture of literary and musical elements, unthinkable for the eighteenth century. However, these contrasts are not mutually exclusive but resemble the positive and negative poles in an electro-magnetic field. Tension exists between them, but they are united by a lively stream that flows from one to the other. Historical examples abound: Weber and Schubert, Liszt and Brahms, Wagner and Verdi.

But what is it that links these composers? Clearly, a powerful musical affinity binds them together, particular sonorities, the new sounds, including the new harmonies that sprang up in the post-1800 period. 'Sound took on new meaning. It was a stronger factor in the body of the music than it had ever been before" (Einstein 1947, p. 8). And the expression of their new relationship to sound was the development of the orchestra in the nineteenth century. This new relationship to sound was the 'new refinement' in music, yet it was also a 'regression' to the primitive relationship to music that humankind had previously created—precisely to the mysterious, the exciting, the magical. It was a union of the refined and the elemental, the latter a rejection of the cultural values at the heart of modernism, the scientific and philosophical rationalism embodied in the Enlightenment.

Another key characteristic of Romantic music is the central importance attributed to nature, especially landscapes, a feature also present in poetry and painting. The Romantic composer isn't interested in a precise photographic reproduction of a landscape but in projecting her/his emotional world into a vision of a landscape. The contrast between Romantic and non-Romantic musical landscape painting can be illustrated by comparing Haydn and Weber. The scores of Haydn's oratorios 'The Creation' and 'The Seasons' are full of charming, idyllic sounds: the lion's roar, the cock's crows, the bird calls, the dogs' excitement in the hunt; in addition, he sketches in the beauty of the flowers, the hills and fields, of sunrise and sunset and of rain. But despite his love of nature and delight in its beauty, his portrayal remains descriptive and doesn't go beyond the idyllic stage. Mozart had virtually no interest in nature and Beethoven's was limited to its sublime aspect with rare exceptions such as the Pastoral Symphony which does have a pronounced Romantic atmosphere.

In contrast, Weber's 'Der Freischutz' is ground-breaking in its power to lay bare the essence of a landscape, its ability to evoke the sounds, the mood, of nature and its dark forests. It is partly the way Weber captures in sound the elemental force of the German forest, with its endless clusters of dark trees, its clouds and winds, its mystery. But it is also the way these features influence the inhabitants. The 'Wolfsschlucht' scene with its "... dark nocturnal powers of hell, projected into the bright sunlight of day, gives 'Der Freischutz' its weird and fantastic atmosphere, its Romantic colour...' (Leichtentritt 1954, p. 204). Weber's evocation of such landscape impressions by the peculiar *colour* of orchestral sound is one of his greatest achievements. This scene became the breeding ground in which future Romantic operatic composers were nurtured, the workshop from which they forged their tools, including Berlioz and Wagner.

Another important Romantic setting is fairyland as inhabited by air phantoms. The leading exponent of light, aerial music is Mendelssohn, with a vision of nature almost as an idealised benign parent. Romantic music also became 'orphic', supernatural, expressing an escape into a semi-darkness that hosted visions of nocturnal wonder. The night itself became a powerful symbol of the Romantic movement, of immersion in the unconscious, the location of magic and mystery. Wagner's prelude to 'Lohengrin', an early exemplar of Romantic opera, has this magical quality of pure sound, with a sonorous, *dynamic* crescendo leading up to the entrance of the trumpets. An A major chord contains the unfolding theme which 'shimmers and dies away in a magical pianissimo' (Einstein 1947, pp. 34–35). The magic of music takes us back to the philosopher of the Romantic movement, Arthur Schopenhauer, who recognised the 'orphic' power of music and saw it as the fountainhead of all the arts.

This leads to two musical forms especially cherished by Romantic composers: song and opera. As Rosen puts it: "...the representation of the past through the immediate sensation of the present made possible one of the greatest achievements of the Romantic style: the elevation of the song from a minor genre to the vehicle of the sublime' (Rosen 1996, p. 124). Nevertheless, in Schubert's songs, melody and accompaniment are two weights in equilibrium; Italian opera preserved the predominance of the human voice. And in the later Romantic song and opera, the accompaniment claimed an ever-increasing proportion of the music.

The Romantic movement flows along two separate but related streams, the German, springing from a literary source, and the French, from a revolutionary ideal. Similar factors were at the origin of Romanticism in the two countries, but their reaction to the new ideas was quite different. In Germany, the Classical spirit of clear-minded eighteenth-century rationalism had exhausted itself by the end of the century. The years from 1780 to 1830 witnessed the struggle of the new Romantic spirit, one finally decided after the deaths of Beethoven and Goethe in favour of Romanticism. But even after its victory, the Classical spirit is not completely dead: elements survive and find their way into Romantic music—observable in the work of Mendelssohn, Schumann and Brahms.

The eighteenth century had kept the various arts separate. But an important feature of the Romantic movement is their integration. Up to now, music had been separate from literature and painting: when the different art forms did meet on common ground, each retained its own character, for example in 'The Marriage of Figaro', both a play and an opera. But the Romantic ideal developed the notion of integrating the different art forms, in composing music that was poetic and picturesque, while poetry adopted musical norms. The German *lied*, created by Schubert, Schumann and Brahms was a quintessentially Romantic product, its aesthetic basis the marriage of poetry and music. The pre-Schubertian song maintains the separation between poetry and music, whereas post-Schubert poetry, vocal melody and instrumental accompaniment are thoroughly integrated so that words and melody cannot be disentangled. '…The words interpret the meaning of the music just as the music unveils the inner sense of the words, and the rhythms and harmonies of the instrumental accompaniment give characteristic colour, light, and shade, accents and climax, and thus paint the scene of the poem' (Leichtentritt 1954, pp. 209–210).

Music and painting thus achieve a close affiliation in Romantic music. Conceptions of light and shade, of finely graded distinctions between lighter and darker *colour*, had until now been found in music only accidentally and exceptionally. In the Romantic work of art, the idea of *colour* becomes a necessary factor, and it was achieved by an exemplary refinement of harmony and orchestration.

Chromatic harmony is the essence, the heart, of Romantic harmony. The frequent use of *chromatic* progressions diminishes the distinction between major and minor *tonalities* and greatly increases the possibilities of varying *cadences* and *modulations* from one key to another. Arguably, this sensitive new harmony is the main achievement of the Romantic movement in music, given that it contributed a feature that did not previously exist in such intensity and richness. Schubert's music is full of such subtle *modulations*, achieving that vague Romantic *colour* which is neither bright nor dark but various shades of twilight. But the real creator of this wonderful Romantic harmony in all its richness and sensitivity is Chopin.

Another aspect of this integration was the emergence of dual talents. The straightforward musician of the eighteenth century became, in the early nineteenth, a 'musical artist'. Weber, Berlioz, Schumann were both musicians and writers. Wagner revealed his immense literary talents as a dramatist in the 'Ring Cycle'. The composer had acquired a kind of 'high-priestly power' (Einstein 1947, pp. 25–26/31).

Indeed, it is suggested that the Romantic poets actually viewed music as the womb from which all the arts were born. The language was seen as inferior to music. The more 'musical' a poem, the greater seemed its capacity to penetrate into new, uncharted areas of feeling. Music became the medium that could make sense of the unspeakable, the mysterious and the magical. Reacting against the Classical, rationalist tradition, the Romantics began to respect and to delve into the unconscious. Beethoven was revered because he had broken the established form and had penetrated new areas of feeling and agitation. He was similarly honoured because of his transformation of instrumental music, which, for the Romantics, became the heart, the kernel of all music.

Moreover, of all the instruments that Romantic music used, it was the piano that became its 'home', that was best suited to the performance of the new sound—neither the organ nor strings nor wind instruments could achieve the same emotional effects. Earlier versions of the piano—the clavecin, cembalo, spinet and clavichord—had been ideal instruments for eighteenth-century piano music by Couperin, Rameau, Bach, Handel, Scarlatti and even Mozart. But these delicate, thin-toned instruments were unsuited to the performance of the new Romantic music, so that technical changes became essential. Hammer action gave the piano a more brilliant and powerful tone, but of even greater importance was the pedal which enabled sound to be extended, a device unknown in previous types of keyboard instrument. Even the sustained tone of the organ is different from that of the piano, a contrast that enables the piano to produce its Romantic spell, its specific capacity to express *colour*, atmosphere, light and shade. The prolonged organ sound is rigid, grows abruptly or declines in volume, whereas the pedal tone of the piano shades off delicately, becoming softer before fading away. 'Pedal resonance is to sound what the air, the sunlight, penetrating layers of clouds, is to *colour* in painting. It makes possible an amazing variety of *colour* effects, and Chopin, Schumann and Liszt with admirable inventive genius achieved a practical realisation of these captivating possibilities, these fleeting shadow effects' (Leichtentritt 1954, p. 213).

Whereas the Classical composers, Haydn and Beethoven, trans-formed the *dynamics* of music, the Romantic composers brought funda-mental change to these other aspects of musical experience—resonance, pedalling, *tone colour*. If we look at transcriptions, the Classical musicians didn't seek to retain the instrumental qualities of the original instru-ment. Beethoven's transcription of his Violin Concerto for piano didn't try to make the piano sound like a violin. He has merely transferred the original series of *pitches* to another instrument. But for the 1830s generation, reproduction of the original *sonority* on the new instrument becomes a crucial preoccupation. For example, Liszt composes great pianistic illusions of orchestral instruments and of the interplay between voices and instruments. For the Romantic generation, a fully pedalled *sonority* becomes the norm. 'The change of pedal is crucial to the concep-tion of rhythmic movement and to the sustaining of the melodic line over the bass' (Rosen 1996, p. 24).

Romantic music broke the mould of Classical form: for example, the three or four-movement *sonata* or symphony, each movement passing through definite phases such as main *theme*, *development*, second subject, *recapitulation* and *coda*. The emphasis was now on the expressive content of music at the expense of traditional form, with the composer giving free rein to ideas, feelings or fantasies. Music now attached great importance to meaning, content, expression. Fantasy acquired an important role, with strictly formal problems relegated to a secondary level, though, of course, they couldn't be entirely neglected. Instead, they were refashioned for the new task, which was less architectural, constructive and mathematical than before. Words like 'tension', 'dynamic accent', 'contrast' gained a new important meaning.

In addition, Romantic composers preferred short pieces in one move-ment, and turned their backs on complicated designs. They sought inspiration, poetic magic and mystery, ecstasy. However, the flame of inspiration is likely to burn itself out quickly, which helps to explain the many short or fragmentary compositions. The architectural structures of a Bach, Handel or Beethoven require intellectual power and are absent from Romantic music. *Sonata* form is replaced by less exacting and schematically determined forms—by small-scale lyrical and descriptive genres, for example, the *fantasia, arabesque, etude, intermezzo, impromptu,* and variation. Musicians write short intense pieces burning with inspiration: Chopin's 'Waltzes' or 'Etudes', Mendelssohn's 'Songs Without Words'. Schumann's 'Carnaval' or Liszt's 'Annees de Pelerinage' resemble a painter's sketch-book: they contain highly evocative lyrical or impressionistic details but abandon any attempt to create a total impression and an organic unity from the beginning. They are no longer 'the acts of a drama but the scenes of a revue' (Hauser 1962, p. 210).

Hence, Romantic music is not static, no longer a comprehensive elaboration of a single idea or mood. It is essentially *dynamic*, constantly in flux, changing from one idea or mood to another. The Beethoven *sonata* and symphony became models for the future Romantic movement: they develop according to a dialectical principle of conflict and resolution, expressing the composer's experiences and perceptions of the world. In chamber music as well as symphonic and instrumental music, Beethoven's work reached such a pinnacle of achievement as to lay down a marker for his successors: he gave them no alternative but to follow or to deviate from him. Eventually, the deviations led further away from the main line.

A final factor to be considered is that of the changing *tonality*. As we saw in chapter three, the foundation of Western *tonality* is the relation of *tonic* to *dominant*. In the early nineteenth century, the attempt was made to substitute third, i.e. *mediant*, relationships, for the Classical *dominant*. This represented an attack on the principles of *tonality*, contributing eventually to the collapse of *triadic tonality*. 'A new chromaticism, largely arrived at through the use of mediant relations, blurs the clarity of the tonal system: one is no longer so certain which harmonies are most distant from the central tonic, a doubt which never arises with the music of the Bach, Haydn or Beethoven' (Rosen 1996, p. 237).

In eighteenth-century music, movement to the *dominant* raised the tension of the music whereas a shift to the *subdominant* decreased it. So, in a Bach *fugue* or Mozart *sonata*, the music goes first to the *dominant*, then usually emphasises *subdominant* harmony in a later section of the piece. This distinction was very useful for dramatic expression in the eighteenth century but practically disappeared for composers born around 1810. Beethoven often tried to replace 'third' relationships (*mediant* to *tonic* chords) for *dominants*, and to create a direct polarised tension from *mediant* to *tonic*. *Mediants* for Beethoven were not mainly *colouristic* episodes, as they were for Mozart, but harmonies of greater tension than the more ordinary *dominant*. Beethoven replaced the polar opposition of the *dominant* with a *mediant*, one of the main features of eighteenth-century harmony that is weakened in the Romantic style. In this style, a Classical opposition is retained but has become blurred. The new keys are not formally established: the music slips from *tonic* to *mediant*. But in Chopin and Schumann, such formal enunciations are often so hidden as to virtually disappear. By 1830, the complementary function of *dominant* and *subdominant* had been forgotten. 'The strictly defined hierarchy of diatonic relationships was traded for a new conception of the *chromatic* continuum, in which a dazzling variety of harmonies could blend with one another in a kaleidoscopic exchange of energy. This opened up not only new harmonic possibilities but also a novel and much more fluid conception of rhythm and tempo' (Rosen 1996, p. 257).

PART II: ROMANTIC COMPOSERS

Into the Dark German Forest—Carl Maria von Weber (1786–1826)

Despite his relatively short career, Weber composed over 300 works, in which dramatic music is represented by some dozen 'Singspiele' (a type of German opera with spoken dialogue alternating with ensembles, songs, ballads and folk-like arias), several melodramas and three operas. His contemporaries saw him as embodying the spirit of the new Germanism that had arisen in response to the challenge of Napoleonic France. During his lifetime, among his best-known music was his settings of the patriotic poems by the young Theodore Korner, 'Lyre and Sword'.

Weber's Romantic Style

We discussed above Weber's ability to uncover the essence of a landscape, to evoke the sounds and mood of nature and its dark forests. This is why Weber is regarded as the first Romantic, a composer who, like Beethoven, was deeply inspired by nature. However, for Beethoven, nature is a serene, pantheistic force, above humanity, whereas for Weber it participates in and interacts with our emotional life. He interweaves the sublime and the comic, and boldly uses the entire range of the full orchestra's tone *colours*, revealing particular originality in his approach to the brass, especially the *staccato* tones of the horns, but also in the deep *register* of the clarinets, the gloomy accents of the trombones and the shrill flutes (Hindley 1971, p. 270; Einstein 1947, p. 114). Weber's musical drama achieves a new expressiveness through both individualising and enriching tone *colours*, and uniting them in an original manner.

But it was in the creation and use of melody that Weber was to make a lasting impact, whether expressed in a single line or in choruses of great beauty. These choruses seem to express a key element in German Romanticism—that a people should not be viewed simply as a collection of individuals but as a 'collective soul' possessing a reality of its own. Indeed, one aspect of Weber's Romanticism is that he was steeped in German folk songs: although none of the melodies in 'Der Freischutz' are actually derived from folk music, his command of the idiom created that impression (Blanning 2010, p. 122). Through his striking melodic powers and increasing free *modulation*, his choice of specific harmonic progressions and varied ways of marshalling them, he contributed to the creation of a new musical language that considerably influenced Wagner (Leichtentritt 1954, pp. 206/230).

The Tragic Lyricism of Franz Schubert (1797–1828)

Schubert's music is more Austrian, or rather Viennese, than that of his three great classical Viennese predecessors. He is principally a lyrical composer, his early, apparently effortless gift for songwriting having leapt ahead of his more slowly emerging genius for *sonatas* and symphonies. He was brought up on Italian-style opera, but also influenced by Gluck, Mozart and Rossini whose sparkling recreation of *bel canto* was very fashionable in Vienna. The earliest works of his adolescence were operatic *scenas* with *recitative* and in *arioso*. They deal in German with German folk-myth subjects, though musically, 'they transfer Italian opera to the drawing-room', the piano replacing the orchestra (Mellers 1957, p. 84).

Schubert's six hundred + songs have a melodic simplicity and an emphasis on subjective feeling which make them akin to folk songs. His feat is to have developed the song from a popular to a 'high art' form. Indeed, the prestige of the great song cycles testifies to their key role in Romanticism: they achieved one of its ideals—to impart to the lyrical expression of Nature 'an epic status, a genuine monumentality, without losing the apparent simplicity of a personal expression' (Rosen 1996, p. 125).

All Schubert's circle wrote new-style lyrical poems, highly subjective work, with Novalis, for example, writing about frustrated love, consumption and heavenly aspirations. This thoughtful poetry found its ideal partner in the early nineteenth-century piano, whose evocative quality (compared to the harpsichord) and range enabled it to be warmly *cantabile* but also to efface itself so as to create a poetically 'orchestral' background. Song is a union between lyric poetry, the human voice and the piano, each element being equally important.

Schubert's Romantic Style

Lieder:
Schubert virtually created the new German song ('lied'), laying its foundation-stone at the age of seventeen with 'Gretchen am Spinnrade'— 'Gretchen at the Spinning Wheel'. Its robust piano accompaniment was an innovation in its independence from the main theme. In many songs or song cycles, the accompaniment, like the bass part of many piano pieces, evokes the natural world, for example, the flow of water, the blowing of the wind or the rustling of leaves, as in 'Die Forelle'—'The Trout', 'Schwanengesang'—Swan Song,' or 'Winterreise'—'Winter's Journey'. These convey an urge to recapture a lost unity with nature, a favourite romantic theme, also expressed in 'The Trout Quintet'.

In his adolescence, Schubert composed two kinds of song: domesticated, operatic *scenas* already mentioned, and simple *strophic* songs in folk. Schubert's earliest songs fuse these two types. Two of the most famous were composed in his teens—'Gretchen am Spinnrade' 'Gretchen at the Spinning Wheel' and 'Erlkonig'. Both have melodies of outstanding beauty and use *figuration* in the piano part suggested by the poem (the spinning wheel and the galloping horse), also using *figuration* as a way of organising the music: both uses create great dramatic urgency from the interplay of vocal line and piano embellishment.

Over the coming decade, Schubert deepened his music, permeating his songs with the enriched melodic and harmonic inventiveness revealed in the symphonic sophistication of his later instrumental works. 'Die Junge Nonne'—'The Young Nun' (1825) is a lyrical and meditative song with dramatic overtones. It tells of a young woman retired to a convent because of frustrated love. It achieves this through a tight melody and a piano *figuration* suggested by Craigher de Jachelutta's poem. The change from agitation to ecstasy is implemented by the alternation of minor and major—this *modulation* is a key characteristic of Schubert's music. The nun is one of many masks for Schubert himself: his use of the mask reaches its climax in the two song cycles of poems by Wilhelm Muller 'Die Schone Mullerin'—'The Fair Maid of the Mill' and 'Winterreise', Schubert's supreme achievement as a songwriter. In the former, the young woman is stolen from him by a mysterious green huntsman (perhaps representing Beethoven); alone, he contemplates suicide. In 'Winterreise', winter has followed spring and the pilgrim trudges down a lonely road. He dreams of spring but awakens to a cold, hostile world. Walking down his lonely road, the solitary human figure is the hurdy-gurdy man grinding out a tune no one listens to. His surroundings—the brook, the trees, the raven, the hurdy-gurdy man—become unconscious projections. In the Muller cycle, Schubert expresses the frustrations of his life and love, whereas in 'Winterreise' he was thinking of his illness and death. Almost immediately after completing them, his health broke down. The two cycles represent the peak of the expression of personal life in lyrical song (Mellers 1957, pp. 88–89).

Instrumental Works:
Schubert's existence was racked by disappointment, humiliation and poverty. However, musically, a rich inheritance was bestowed upon him, and, in his unique position as the Romantic Classic, he created a new world. In his early instrumental music, his *motifs* and *themes* bore the influence of Mozart, Haydn and Beethoven. It was perhaps his good fortune that he reached full maturity before he could be influenced by Beethoven's final works, His achievement is all the more extraordinary in that he lived and composed in the shadow of Beethoven, 27 years his senior, whose influence dominated the European musical scene. Perhaps in Schubert's early period, he concentrated on songs rather than instrumental music because of Beethoven's supremacy in this field, needing to distance himself from his mighty contemporary. However, Schubert always composed within the framework of the Classical sonata form: even in a late work like the 'Octet' (1824), he adopted the model of Beethoven's 'Septet', both in the instrumentation—clarinet, horn, bassoon, string quartet and double bass—and also in the succession of movements (Einstein 1947, p. 89).

Around 1815, Vienna was stirred by the new Italian style of Rossini. Schubert ceded to his influence, composing Italianate overtures and 'canzonets' (light and graceful song) on Metastasian texts (Pietro Metastasio, was an eighteenth-century Italian poet and librettist, considered the most important writer of *opera seria* libretti). He also incorporated into his instrumental works many captivating Italianisms. Despite these derivative features, Schubert was from the outset a distinctive, original figure whose pioneering creations marked him out as a Romantic. By the age of 21, he had composed six symphonies. In these works, he followed the model of Beethoven's early rather than later symphonies, the first or second whose *larghetto* had profoundly impressed him. In his modestly instrumented 'Symphony No. 5 in B Flat Major' (1816) Schubert tried the brighter combinations of Haydn and Mozart. It was almost like writing chamber music, and one can see the Classical influence in each of the four movements (Einstein 1947, p. 90).

However, in several respects, Schubert's early symphonies are closer to Mozart than to Haydn. He normally avoids the close-knit *thematic* unity of much of Haydn's instrumental work: like Mozart, he distributes his melodies with generous abandon. The melodic and harmonic motion at the start of the Fifth Symphony in B flat is typically Mozartian. The 'Symphony No. 4 in C Minor' ('Tragic') begins with a *chromatic* dissonant introduction reminiscent of that of Mozart's String Quartet in C Major, K. 465. Indeed, Schubert is closer to Mozart than to any other composer, but "the lyrical and dramatic bases of his art are more widely separated: from the struggle to reconcile them sprang the mingling of passion and nostalgia which is his music' (Mellers 1957, p. 104). Yet these early symphonies often don't resemble either Haydn, Mozart or Beethoven. For example, the last movement of the Fourth Symphony is a 'perpetual motion' piece with almost continuous movement in *quavers*. Against these, he repeats simple, dance-like melodies with kaleidoscopic shifts in harmony and instrumentation. Such leisurely repetition of material is a hallmark of Schubert's music. The difference from Beethoven can be gleaned by listening to the perpetual motion *finale* of the latter's Fourth Symphony: instead of gay Viennese dance tunes, we hear terse themes and fragmented melodies punctuating the unvarying rhythm. These gather momentum and build towards tense climaxes. In contrast, Schubert sounds 'lyrical, placid, and agreeably static' (Plantinga 1984, p. 84).

Two features mark these early works: a new *sonority* arising from the new sensitive treatment of the wind instruments, and an abundant harmony full of feeling. A new kind of melody is linked to these elements, not derived from the *development*, as so often in Haydn and Beethoven but self-generated, 'cradled in its own felicity'. Other composers have written beautiful melodies, for example, Beethoven, but with him, it is an element of contrast, as in *counterpoint*, whereas for Schubert, it is an end in itself. His themes are 'pure, unminted gold' (Einstein 1947, p. 91).

The year 1822 marks the line of division between those symphonies in which he was still learning and those in which he took his place beside Beethoven and even pointing the way past him to the post-Beethoven era. In October, he composed the two movements of 'Symphony No. 8 in B Minor' ('Unfinished'). The title is bizarre as the two movements contain everything that can be said about sadness or melancholy. The glory of this symphony consists of its exquisite lyrical melodies, its fine instrumental *colouring* and its novel harmonies. Pursuing the classical scheme, Schubert introduced as the first movement's second theme a *Landler*. Schubert thus establishes himself as more 'Viennese' than Beethoven, Haydn or Mozart, who also wrote Viennese dances. But their pieces are more neutral and Classical than Schubert's, which are full of disarming melodies and rhythms and *colourful* harmonies. One of the most magical sounds ever written is the symphony's second movement, with its immortal dialogue between oboe and clarinet above the shimmering background of the strings. Schubert once complained: 'Who can do anything more after Beethoven?' He supplied his own answer with the 'Unfinished Symphony'.

The Ninth C Major Symphony' ('Great') (1825–1826), often considered Schubert's finest piece for orchestra, is also one of the composer's most innovative pieces. Beethoven's influence is still evident in the work's *thematic* development though Schubert puts far more emphasis on melody, to be expected from the composer of some six hundred *lieder*. Beethoven had always used the trombone as an effect, and therefore sparingly, or, in the case of his Ninth Symphony, to double the alto, tenor, and bass parts of the chorus as was common in sacred music and opera at the time. However, in Schubert's 'Unfinished Symphony' and also the Ninth, the trombones become essential members of the orchestra playing throughout the piece and even receive important melodic roles.

Schubert's harmonic innovations include movements where the first section ends in the key of the *subdominant* rather than the *dominant* (as in the final movement of the 'Trout Quintet'). This represented a forerunner of the common Romantic technique of relaxing rather than raising tension in the middle of a movement, with the final *resolution* postponed to the end.

What applies to Schubert's symphonies applies equally to his string quartets, the difference being that the line of demarcation between the experiments and the independent masterpieces is drawn earlier. His eleven quartets took as his model either Mozart or the Beethoven of opus 18. In 1820, he composed a quartet movement as finished as the 'Unfinished' Symphony, full of Schubertian grace and magic. And he followed it with three masterpieces: the 'Quartets in A Minor' (1824), D Minor (1826), and G Major (1826), notable for being uninfluenced by Beethoven's Opus 59 Quartet or his subsequent quartets up to opus 130. The Seventh Symphony reveals another of Schubert's Romantic features: his habit of taking a *motif* rooted in a song 'Die Gotter Griechenlands' ('The Gods of Greece') and expanding it fully into the instrumental realm. In the melancholy D Minor Quartet, we find a similar relationship with his song 'Death and the Maiden'. Death's gentle answer provides the seed which in the quartet blossoms into full lyricism, expressing confidence in a blissful release into eternal peace.

One should add to the three quartets his last work, the 'String Quintet in C Major' composed in 1828. Whereas Mozart and Beethoven doubled the violas, Schubert creates something unique by doubling the violoncellos. There is a new quality of sound, which also reflects the invention of new themes. When the C major *triad* at the beginning 'bursts into a diminished seventh chord (a semi-tone lower), to come again into the pure heaven of C major... the door of the Romantic era has been surreptitiously opened' (Einstein 1947, p. 94). However, there is in the theme a faint echo of Mozart's C Major Quartet. But the *adagio* in E, the Trio of the D flat Scherzo, and the unrestrained *finale*, have no precedent. The C Major String Quintet 'most comprehensively embraces every facet of his genius... The first subject group combines lyricism with the dynamic manner of the big C Major Symphony... the second subject is one of the most acutely nostalgic of his song-tunes. The wild conflict between these two moods has already been anticipated in the dissonant *cadential* harmony of the opening phrase' (Mellers 1957, p. 102).

Piano Works:

Schubert's piano works fall into two categories—*sonatas* and 'modest' pieces, such as 'Moments Musicaux', Impromptus', Landler, Waltzes, Marches, *Rondos*. In these works, as in most of Schubert's instrumental compositions, one hears outlines of Viennese popular music, especially dance-rhythms and close-position chords (its tones as close together as they can be) of the part-song (a form of choral music that consists of a secular song having been written or arranged for several vocal parts.

Among Schubert's finest works are his last three Piano Sonatas—D 958 in C Minor, 959 in A, and 960 in B flat. The last of these is a masterpiece in which Schubert displays to the full his extraordinary gifts for melodic invention, piano *sonority* and original key changes. All four movements evoke the dance. But however decisive is Schubert's personal stamp, as a *sonata* the music carried the traditions of Haydn, Mozart and especially Beethoven. The first movement is an excellent example of Schubert's reconciliation of the demands of tradition with his own unique gifts. It begins with a theme that captures the warm resonance of Romantic piano music: *octave-plus-sixth doubling* which disseminates the melody's shape throughout the texture. In the *finale*, there is a special homage to Beethoven, recently deceased. The dance-like movement begins with a long-held *octave* G, the major sixth of the *tonic* B flat but also the *dominant* to C minor. The harmonic similarity to the opening theme, also dance-like, of the *finale* of Beethoven's String Quartet No. 13 Opus 130 in the same key of B flat, completed just before his death, is unmistakable. 'Thus, in his last major composition, Schubert acknowledged the sort of debt to his older contemporary that was to prove a burden to nearly every composer of instrumental music of the nineteenth century. But he did so in a composition that fully established his own greatness in the very traditions to which Beethoven seemed to have gained a proprietary claim' (Plantinga 1984, pp. 105–106).

In sum, with the flowering of Schubert's talent, he developed a unique and original 'free' style, marked by new post-classical forms. An important Schubert trademark is frequent *modulation*. In the course of this, he often passes from minor to major, the minor mode conveying sadness or grief, the major mode consolation, tenderness or confidence. The less frequent reverse shift, from major to minor, expresses a change of mood from playfulness to poignancy, or from joy to sorrow.

Whereas previously, melody had been one element in the development of a piece, with Schubert, it becomes an end in itself and he produces an apparently endless stream of exquisite tunes. His chamber, instrumental and orchestral works all exhibit the influence of his song-writing, with its melodic inventiveness and rich harmonies. For example, the 'Trout' Piano Quintet, whose main theme is also a song, reveals Schubert at his most spontaneously joyful. His singing melodies and 'harmonic ambiguities' also express his 'consciousness of mutability', an essentially Romantic trait. Despite his respect for the past, Schubert's late music is 'inexhaustibly prophetic'—especially of Wagner's 'sensuous individualism'. Furthermore, his anticipation of future Romanticism carries a 'sense of doom which hung over his world and himself' (Mellers 1957, p. 104).

In his later works, Schubert achieved an extraordinary depth of expression, perhaps best described as tragic lyricism. There is a profound sense of desolation, as though he is mourning a lost world of human unity. Yet at other times, he achieves a unique serenity, as though glimpsing the capacity of human beings to create a world based on love and solidarity. 'Swan Song', the last of three song cycles, written in 1828, turned out to be Schubert's own farewell.

The Pictorial Romanticism of Hector Berlioz (1803–1869)

Berlioz is the sole outstanding representative of French Romantic music. French Romanticism has a militant, radical spirit, and Berlioz is the main exponent of this agitated music: together with Liszt and Wagner, he makes up the triad of great composers that represent the 'new music' of the nineteenth century, the 'Music of the Future' (the term is derived from three essays by Wagner, published between 1849 and 1861).

Berlioz's Romantic Style

Berlioz exploded on to the debilitated scene of French music, like a volcano in the middle of the sea. During his lifetime, his music was either ignored or denigrated, yet the establishment was sufficiently impressed by his 'Requiem Mass' to award him the Legion d'Honneur. His music embraces extremes: it can be either gentle and lyrical or stormy and passionate. His works have a theatrical quality, but the staging of his works is problematical. He both reshaped existing forms and developed new ones. Berlioz's contribution to the new music consists in the development of 'programme music', the aim of which is to stretch the potential of musical expression by interpreting a poem, a story or scene. The idea wasn't new though the method was. His overtures, for example, are in fact symphonic tone poems, liberal interpretations of the writings of Scott, Shakespeare and other heroes of literary Romanticism. Programme music was not musical photography, that is, a means of illustrating literary or other verbal or visual descriptions, in the way that film music might attempt. Rather was it developed as a new means of meditating upon the world, on life, different human characters or situations (Leichtentritt 1954, pp. 222/227).

Berlioz's programme music certainly weakened the symphonic form. But he did not destroy it. Rather did he set up a new conception of it that combined the purely instrumental and the vocal. 'Romeo et Juliette' (1839) is a 'symphonie dramatique', with choruses, vocal 'soli' and a prologue in choral recitative. 'La Damnation de Faust' (1845–1846) is a 'legende dramatique'. And Berlioz himself did what he could to stress the symphonic nature of 'Romeo et Juliette'. However, most of his works are accompanied by literary texts and voices.

Also, the originality of 'Symphonie Fantastique' lies in the coincidence of the programmatic with the Classical *sonata* form: in the first movement, the coincidence of the 'Reverie' with the introductory *largo*, of the 'Existence Passionnee' in all its changing moods with the *allegro*. The following four movements—the 'Bal' in waltz form, the 'Scene aux Champs', the dreamlike 'Marche au Supplice' ('March to the Scaffold'), and the 'Songe d'une Nuit de Sabbat' ('Dream of the Night of the Sabbath')—abandon this correspondence with the classical pattern. Freer and bolder, they are welded together by the theme in the first *allegro*, which returns either as variation or parody. Another *leitmotif* is the musical representation of the beloved in a melody that returns in each movement (Plantinga 1984, pp. 208–209). After this piece, the entire Romantic movement is imbued with this reminiscent, returning *leitmotif*, a feature central to Wagner.

Berlioz's harmonisation and rhythm reveal the contradictory nature of his music, his originality and rejection of the Classical tradition, but also his retention of certain Classical elements. In the initial presentation of the *leitmotif*, an opening phrase of eight *bars* is succeeded by one of seven, an irregularity that upset a contemporary critic. But the forty *bars* of the theme are governed by a regular underlying rhythm of four *bars*: the change in the phrase length is merely 'the sign of a more important shift of accent applied to the unchanging four-bar group' (Rosen 1996, pp. 545–547). Shifting the accent enables Berlioz to give the melody its dramatic character, increasing the excitement and tension towards the centre, and giving the final *bars* their broad, singing resolution.

Specifically, for the first fifteen *bars*, the accent is on the first and third of each four-*bar* group: that is, if we regard each *bar* as a single beat, the *downbeat* and the third beat are stressed. Suddenly, in *bar* sixteen, the phrases begin on the fourth bar of each four-*bar* group, as if making the *upbeat* important. With the increased harmonic motion as well as the use of harmonies other than simple *tonic* and *dominant*, this augments the agitation, shaping the melody by breaking it into smaller units. We can also see Berlioz's use of surprise in the harmonic resolution in *bar* thirteen of the *motive*: his phrase leads us to expect a resolution on the *dominant* chord but he then harmonises the phrase with a *tonic* chord, a Classical feature (Rosen 1996, p. 549).

Was Berlioz a Romantic, given Romanticism's rejection of Classical antiquity and Berlioz's lifelong cherishing of Virgil and the Aeneid together with his love of Rome? His symphony 'Harold in Italy' testifies to his affection for Italy, as in a way does his opera Benvenuto Cellini. Berlioz's radical Romanticism is evident in his orchestral *colouring* or *timbre*, an artistic achievement comparable to Chopin's *chromatic* harmony. Before Berlioz, orchestral instruments associated with the Classical style (melody and harmony mainly in the strings, with winds used for periodic reinforcement and soloistic *colour*) had remained standard. Exceptional instrumentation, as in some passages in the operas of Gluck and Weber, was reserved for special dramatic effects. But for Berlioz, the creation of specific *tone colours* for individual passages was a normal part of composition (Plantinga 1984, p. 212).

His orchestral writing doesn't fall easily into the category of 'instrumentation' or 'orchestration': for example, the recurring *leitmotif* in the first movement of 'Symphonie Fantastique' reveals both an original instrumentation and an unconventional musical texture. He presents a lavishly ornamented melody and orchestral *colour* or *timbre* with only the barest bass harmony. He thus displayed phenomenal sensitivity to the ways in which music can associate itself with scenes, ideas and feelings. According to Blanning, the piece has a good claim to be seen as the 'summit of French romanticism' (Blanning 2010, p. 89).

Berlioz was neglected in France for much of the nineteenth century, but his music is considered as highly influential in the development of the symphonic form, instrumentation, and of *programmatic* ideas, central to musical Romanticism. Although he never achieved success in opera, he became one of the century's most outstanding composers of dramatic music. And it was in his opera 'Les Troyens' that he displayed to the full this talent for expressive, pictorial music, one that laid the foundations for the music of Liszt, Wagner, Richard Strauss, and Debussy, an achievement comparable to that of Chopin's *chromatic* harmony.

Searching for a Lost Paradise—Felix Mendelssohn (1809–1847)

According to Rosen, Mendelssohn was the greatest child prodigy in the history of Western music. Not even Mozart or Chopin before nineteen had his gift for lyrical, melodic lines and delicate, transparent *textures* and control of large-scale structures. Many of his *scherzos* express delight in the play of delicate *tones* that suggest dancing spirits floating in the air like clouds soaring lightly in graceful undulations. The *scherzo* of his 'Octet', with its light, delicate touch, though composed by a sixteen-year-old, yet displays the firm hand and imagination of a great artist. And the incidental music to 'A Mid-Summer Night's Dream', written a year later, is the creation of a precocious 17-year-old genius.

In the joyous 'Octet', written in 1825, the subtlety of the way the return of the *scherzo* is integrated into the *finale*, or the beginning of the *recapitulation* of the overture to 'A Midsummer Night's Dream', where the flute harmonies of the opening simply reappear and are poised delicately over the gentle, profound final *cadence* of the *development*, exemplifies craftsmanship amounting to genius (Rosen 1996, p. 569). Schumann described Mendelssohn as the Mozart of the nineteenth century.

Mendelssohn's Romantic Style

Although Mendelssohn composed music of amazing mastery at a very early age, he never outgrew his precocious youthful style, retaining a basic conservatism, a fidelity to the status quo, the Classical forms as developed by his great predecessors (Taruskin 2010, pp. 180–183). So, like all composers, Mendelssohn imitated his great forbears, in his case, the *sonatas* and quartets of the late Beethoven. However, his 'Piano Sonata in E Major', for example, written at the age of 17, though modelled on Beethoven's Opus 90 and Opus 101 Sonatas, was far from being simple reproduction, but expressed an individual personality. Mendelssohn also composed impressionistic works, as in his 'Italian' and

'Scottish' symphonies in which the music depicts landscapes of those two countries. His 'Fingal's Cave Overture' vividly evokes the surging sea, waves echoing in rocky caves, the shrill cries of the seagulls. His light aerial music expresses at times almost a certain nature worship.

Wagner had asked why Romantic composers after Beethoven still wrote symphonies. According to Einstein, it was 'just because Beethoven had preceded them in this field'. Mendelssohn, Schumann and Berlioz had composed symphonies that settled their accounts with this great inheritance in different ways. Mendelssohn's particular talent gave him the least trouble. Beethoven's symphonies had created the means of conveying his great message to humanity. Mendelssohn accepted the framework and filled it with a more modest content. He was the 'romantic classicist' in contrast to Schubert who was the 'romantic classic' (Einstein 1947, p. 124). Both retained Classical forms but filled them with different content, Schubert's melodic and harmonic structures remaining closer to the traditional style. The harmonious nature of Mendelssohn's music appears in the fact that the Classicistic element in his work could be combined with the Romantic. There is a unique *symmetry* of form in his movements and his cycles which is of Classical vintage: yet his entire work glistens with a Romantic light, a glow of feeling, a mixture of grace and humour.

We see this expressed in the elfin music of his 'Midsummer Night's Dream' overture. There is also a passion in his music that takes you by surprise with its almost 'purposeless', Romantic effect. Mendelssohn is the only composer who introduces fire and passion for their own sake, often indicating in the *allegro* movements the directions *con fuoco* or *appassionato*. Another Romantic characteristic is his tendency to begin with an introduction in a light key—his favourites are A major, E major and G major—and then *modulating* in the main movement to the corresponding minor, leading us into a region of dark passion or melancholy gloom (Einstein 1947, p. 125).

Mendelssohn can be said to have composed pure symphonies and chamber music though with less strict unity than a pure Classical composer. He didn't follow the Beethoven of the Third ('Eroica'), Fifth, Seventh and Eighth symphonies so much as the Beethoven of the Sixth ('Pastoral') Symphony, with its more pictorial succession of movements, All his symphonies, beginning with Symphony No. 1 in C Minor Opus 11 composed when he was 15 (1824), avoid expressions of 'power': they are, rather, expressions of lyricism. In their first movements, they display clever examples of *development*. But while, for example, in Beethoven's 'Eroica' one recalls especially the *development* as the focal point in a great battle, in Mendelssohn's symphonies, it is the enchanting details that linger: in the Symphony No. 1, the divided strings with timpani solo in the 'Trio of the Scherzo', in the Scottish' Symphony No. 3 (1829–1842) the bagpipe in the *Scherzo*, in the Italian Symphony No. 4 (1833), the *Tarantella* or the beautiful melody in the slow movement.

Mendelssohn is probably consistently at his best in his chamber music, where he displays great facility in part-writing (music for a particular voice or instrument in concerted music) and in strong idiomatic handling of instruments. These virtues are especially noticeable in the four later String Quartets Opus 44 and 80, the early Octet Opus 20, and in the two Piano Trios in D Minor, Opus 49, and C Minor, Opus 66. However, of these works, only the Octet and the Piano Trio in D Minor have survived as a standard part of the modern chamber repertory. Much of Mendelssohn's piano music belongs in the post-Mozartian tradition, a category in which Hummel's virtuosity is also influential: Mendelssohn wished to remain within conventional limits. The 16-year-old's 'Capriccio' is a brilliant example of Hummel-like *prestissimo* but the seriousness of its *theme* raises it far above mere virtuosity. The E Major Piano Sonata bears traces of Beethoven's last two sonatas—Opus 101 and 110—while the *finale* has echoes of Weber with its Galant rhythms and violoncello-like melodies. Of the Seven Characteristic Pieces Opus 7, the majority are 'Bachian' though no. 2, the '*Sarabande*', is to be played 'with longing'.

This phrase hints at the criticism levelled at Mendelssohn's style: sentimentality. But it is a feature present in all the Romantic composers—Schumann, Liszt, Brahms—one on which Mendelssohn merely put his own stamp. It represents a searching, a reaching-out for something intangible. It features in his probing the musical hinterland for the ghosts of Bach and Handel. But his 'sentimentality' emerges most clearly in the eight volumes of his 'Songs Without Words'—his melodies in song form with delicate, shy accompaniment, idealised duets, mostly striving for something indefinite, though many having a distinct character: spinning songs, hunting songs, cradle songs, funeral marches, folk songs. They express an unsatisfied longing for a 'lost paradise of simplicity, for the original womb of music' (Einstein 1947, pp. 201–202).

The Sadness of Exile: Frederic Chopin (1810–1849)

We saw that it was the piano that became the 'home' of the new, romantic sound, the instrument that was best suited to its performance. Schumann and Liszt began as purely pianistic composers and only later did they seek more universal forms of expression—triumphing in the genres of the symphony, chamber music, and large and small forms of vocal music. But all of Chopin's known works involve the piano, with only a handful venturing beyond piano solo music, such as either the piano concerto, songs or chamber music. Significantly, at his Vienna concerts, he played his own concertos as solo pieces. Polish by birth, he lived most of his life in Paris but always hankered after his homeland.

Chopin's Romantic Style

Chopin's early works are in the style of the 'brilliant' keyboard pieces of his time, the influence of Polish folk music and Italian opera coming later. Much of what became his characteristic style of ornamentation was derived from vocal music. His melodic lines were increasingly reminiscent of the features of Polish music, for example, drones (unvarying sustained bass notes).

Chopin took the new salon genre of the nocturne, invented by John Field, to new heights of sophistication. He was the first to develop the genres of the *ballade* and *scherzo* as individual concert pieces. And he established the free-standing *etude* as a completely new genre, expanding in his two sets of Etudes Opus 10 published in 1833 and 'Opus 25 in 1837 the poetic potential present in the works composed in the 1820s and 1830s by Liszt and Clementi. As Blanning points out, the night of Field or Chopin's 'Nocturnes' is a 'gentle, melancholy, wistful, yearning, languorous sort of time… a time for romance' (Blanning 2010, p. 74).

Chopin also bestowed upon popular dance forms a greater range of melody and expressiveness. His 'Mazurkas derived from the Polish dance 'Mazurek' but differed from the traditional kind, being written for the concert hall rather than the dance hall. The series of seven '*Polonaises* published in his lifetime (another nine were published posthumously) set a new standard for the genre. He also composed his '*Waltzes* for salon recitals rather than the ballroom: hence they are often at faster *tempos* than their dance-floor equivalents.

All Chopin's orchestral works carry early opus numbers. He later turned to a smaller, more select public, combining great artistry with intimacy, avoiding brilliant but showy works. His contemporaries report that his dynamics never exceeded *forte*, but retained all their relevant shading.

Improvisation was at the heart of Chopin's creative impulse. He abandoned early on large-scale multi-movements forms in favour of pieces of simple design but with subtle and complex internal structures. An important aspect of his unique style is his flexible handling of the four-bar phrase as a structural unit. Chopin's mastery flows from his ability to keep the four-bar grouping while varying the metrical significance of the bars (Rosen 1996, p. 271). The four-bar phrase amplified music's time scale, turning short pieces into 'genuine miniatures', as if, for example, Chopin's Prelude in G Major were only seven bars long and not thirty (seven times four plus one bar of introduction and one of suspension). It gave a larger sense of motion to long works and altered the significance of the smaller details. This laid the basis for the gigantic forms of Wagner's operas (Rosen 1996, p. 278).

Among the works intended for the concert hall, the four 'Ballades and four 'Scherzos reign supreme, while the *Barcarolle* Opus 60 provides an example of Chopin's repository of rich harmonies linked to an Italianate melodic warmth. These works express a broad range of moods, *thematic* material and structural detail, and are based on an extended 'departure and return' form: 'the more the middle section is extended, and the further it departs in key, mood and theme, from the opening idea, the more important and dramatic is the reprise (repetition) when it at last comes' (Temperley 1980, pp. 298–307, W).

Chopin's 'Mazurkas' and 'Waltzes' are all in the straightforward *ternary* form (Jones 1998, in Rowland 2011, pp. 176–191). The 'Mazurkas' frequently contain more folk features than many other works, including *modal* scales and harmonies and also drone basses (unvarying sustained bass note). Some are exceptionally sophisticated, for example, 'No. 3 Opus 63', which contains a rare *canon* at one beat's distance.

In contrast to the *polonaise*, which was danced by the Polish aristocracy in the seventeenth and eighteenth centuries, the different forms of the *mazurka* remained folk dances and were rarely played in European art music before Chopin's time. Some of his early efforts in this genre closely resemble folk tunes: for one, the Mazurka Opus 68, No. 3' (1829), a specific model was identified. Many of his later *Mazurkas* are highly

stylised and abstract; a lifelong preoccupation of Chopin's, 'this miniature genre became a vehicle for his most individual and advanced musical
ideas' (Plantinga 1984, p. 199).

Chopin's two sets of *Etudes*, Opus 10 and Opus 25, are universally seen
as the most accomplished of all such piano studies. While comprehensively
probing the new brilliant and demanding keyboard *figurations* with which
the modern virtuoso was expected to be familiar, they maintain an unwaveringly high level of musical interest. Although the *Etudes* are sometimes
performed as cycles, they don't reveal any consistent overall design of key
or nature, and there is no reason to believe that Chopin wanted them
heard together. Like his *Mazurkas* and *Waltzes*, the *Etudes* are mainly in
ternary form. He used them to teach his own method of piano playing—
for example, playing double thirds (successive chords consisting of the
first and third notes of the scale), as in Opus 25, No. 6, playing in *octaves*,
as in Opus 25, No. 10, or playing repeated notes as in Opus 10, No. 7
(Jones 1998, pp. 160–161). Plantinga points out that the *Etudes* stand
in a respected tradition: from the seventeenth century onwards, 'serious'
music with a didactic purpose was common in keyboard composition.

In these *Etudes*, Chopin invents sound with a powerful imagination
reminiscent of Liszt, though the latter's invention is more imitative,
his sonorities resembling sleigh bells, horses' hooves, fountains, rustling
leaves, or imitating instruments—violin, flute, trombone, percussion.
This effect is rare in Chopin. The etudes express pure, abstract piano
sound. The essence of this is his structure of subtle 'layers of sonority, a
counterpoint of colour' (Rosen 1996, p. 377).

The twenty-four '*Preludes* reveal a surprising variety of *textures*,
harmonies and moods: stormy virtuoso pieces coexist with innocent,
lyrical presentations; extremes of harmonic uncertainty Prelude No. 2 in A
Minor contrast with pure *diatonic* composition Prelude No. 7 in A Major.
A famous example of Chopin's predilection for obscure *tonal* syntax by
means of linear *chromatic* motion is the Prelude No. 4 in E Minor. The
Preludes follow a clear *tonal* plan: modelled on the *preludes* and *fugues* of
Bach's '*Well-Tempered Clavier*', they encompass the 24 *tonalities* of the
major-minor system. They move up the circle of fifths, each one accompanied by its relative minor mode. They are very short, some occupying
only a single page, consisting of one homogeneous section, with Chopin
exploring a single musical idea. The collection displays an astounding
variety of keyboard *textures*, harmonic styles and moods.

Chopin's *Polonaises* reveal a marked advance on those of his Polish predecessors in the form. As with the traditional *polonaise*, Chopin's are in *triple* time while his melodies, accompaniments and *cadences* express a martial rhythm. They differ from most of their precursors in demanding a formidable playing technique (Reiss and Brown 1980, p. 51). By 1825, when he composed the Polonaise in D Minor, Opus 71, No. 1, he had clearly struck out on his own: the respectful domesticated dance of the eighteenth century has become a heartfelt virtuoso composition.

Chopin can be said to be the first great nationalist composer: the spirit of Poland radiates from his work. Though he spent twenty years in Paris, the most cosmopolitan city in the world, and was welcomed in the most exclusive Parisian society, his heart never left Poland. Some speak of Chopin almost as having created Polish music, and, by this, it isn't meant that there had been no Polish music or musicians before him. As early as the second half of the sixteenth century, collections of instrumental dances had included Polish tunes with their typical rhythms. The *polonaise* was an internationally fashionable dance in the eighteenth century. The point is that Chopin took typically Polish themes and elevated them into the highest musical art. On the other hand, the 'national' compositions make up only part of Chopin's output. He composed over fifty *mazurkas* and thirteen *polonaises*. But he also wrote fifteen *waltzes*, a *tarantella*, a *bolero*, a *barcarolle*, and three *ecossaises*. Are they Viennese, Neapolitan, Spanish, Venetian, Scottish? Or do they express a universal musical spirit? Chopin was prone to embrace a particular style and rhythm, and use them to weave a light, airy, imaginative fabric, one that linked that style to the universal, Romantic mood of his age.

Chopin wrote three piano sonatas. Composed between 1828 and 1844, they are regarded as his hardest compositions, both musically and technically. The second in B flat minor, Opus 35 (1839), contains as its third movement the famous Funeral March. The *sonata* has proved irresistible to generations of pianists and audiences, replete as it is, with the ornamented melodies and sonorous accompaniments for which Chopin is famous. At the beginning of the contrasting central section of the Funeral March, there is an example of Chopin's gift for maximising Romantic piano *sonority*: the pedal sustains the slow-moving harmonies in each bar, enhancing the resonance of both the melody and the wide-ranging *arpeggiated* accompaniment (Plantinga 1984, p. 195).

The four *Ballades* are single-movement though multi-sectioned virtuoso pieces with complex construction. The pieces are an innovation of Chopin's which don't fall into any other category, for example, the *sonata*. However, the genre is a variant of the *sonata* with specific differences, such as the 'mirror reprise' (presenting the two *expository* themes in reverse order during the *recapitulation*). Chopin also introduced dramatic and dance-like features into the form. Composed between 1831 and 1842, the *Ballades* seem to be the first instrumental compositions to appear with that name. Chopin apparently derived the name from the eighteenth-century English or German ballad, and he probably intended it to evoke associations with an idealised, folk-like, narrative style of poetry and music. According to Schumann, Chopin claimed that his Ballades were inspired by some poems of the Polish nationalist writer Adam Mickiewicz. This illustrates again the close links between Romantic music and national folklore.

Chopin wasn't just an imaginative genius but a great craftsman, the greatest master of *counterpoint* since Mozart, with the proviso that *counterpoint* should not be equated with a strict *fugue*. His principal training, in both composition and piano playing, came from a lifelong study of Bach, though other influences were important: his ideas of the concerto form came from Hummel, Friedrich Kalkbrenner and John Field. His delight in Italian opera, and its overwhelming popularity, would have rendered it an additional influence; also important were the rhythms and harmonies of native Polish dances.

Colour is the new, crucial aspect of Romantic music, expressed through light and shade, delicate gradations of lighter and darker *colour*, *colour* itself being achieved through a refinement of harmony and orchestration. This new harmony is perhaps the main achievement of Romantic music, an innovation first developed by Schubert in his major-minor *modulation*, but later taken further by Chopin, the real founder of 'this new land of luminous shadows, of transitions from brighter to darker levels of sound, of genuine scales of musical colour' (Leichtentritt 1954, p. 210).

Chopin, like Berlioz or Liszt, was a Romantic revolutionary, but one who reacted against some of his contemporaries: he disliked what he felt were Berlioz's bizarre features and Liszt's exhibitionistic and 'charlatanic' brilliance. Beyond Polish themes, there are many musical ingredients that Chopin smelted and poured into his mould. They are so faultlessly blended that on hearing Chopin's work, we are not aware of the presence of Bach, Hummel, Rossini, Mozart, John Field or Weber, but only of Chopin's unique offerings.

To study Chopin is to reveal the intimate relation between line and *colour* in music. Chopin's poetic power resides in his control of all the melodic lines of a complex *polyphony*. On this, he based the subtly shifting *phrase* accents and the unique experiments in harmony. The superb sonorities of Chopin's compositions—the 'exquisite spacing, the vibrant inner voices'—flow from an 'abstract structure of lines'. The pianist and listener are conscious, as in Bach, both of the sustaining of an individual line and of the passing of the melody from one voice to another, both in small details and in the larger forms. Chopin's lyricism and dramatic shock are equally indebted to this craft. Indeed, the paradox of Chopin is that 'he is at his most original in his use of the most fundamental and traditional technique. That is what made him both the most conservative and the most radical composer of his generation' (Rosen 1996, p. 471).

Chopin's influence was international. Just as no symphonic composer of the nineteenth century could avoid Beethoven, so no piano composer after 1830 could fail to take account of Chopin's work.

The Tormented Inner World of Robert Schumann (1810–1856)

In the music of each of the Romantic composers examined so far, there is a different balance between classical heritage and Romantic innovation. Schumann began his career as a revolutionary Romantic. No other Romantic, not even Chopin, compares with him in youthful originality. In common with Chopin, the piano was his exclusive vehicle for the expression of his 'Storm and Stress' up to his 'Nachtstucke Opus 23', a set of four 'character' pieces for piano, composed in 1839. Like Chopin, he was able to use the piano to express his deepest feelings. At the same time, he was able to use his new, virtuoso style to protest against the shallow, brilliant 'drawing room virtuosity' which, after Hummel and Weber, dominated the scene alongside genuine virtuosi like Liszt. After twenty-three piano works, the twenty-fourth blossomed into a song cycle. As for his mental breakdown, 'he was the composer who achieved the most powerful musical representations of pathological states of feeling before Wagner, and some of his music has, because of its modest scale, a concentration denied to... more diffuse forms of large-scale works'

(Rosen 1996, p. 648). In 1854, he attempted suicide by jumping into the Rhine and died two years later in a mental asylum.

Schumann's Romantic Style

In Schumann's fiery and dreamlike music, there is an element of the esoteric which excludes the uninitiated. "Carnaval, Opus 9 (1834–1835) was subtitled 'Scenes Mignonnes sur Quatre Notes', and consists of 21 short pieces representing masked revellers at a festival before Lent. The four notes are A–E flat (E flat is pronounced as the letter S)—C–B (representing H). The notes spell ASCH which was the home of the young woman he loved at the time. In the second number, among the 'Intermezzi, Opus 4', the first line of Gretchen's spinning-wheel scene from Faust is unexpectedly quoted above the music. But it needs intimacy with Schumann's work to decipher these clues. 'Like all the romantics, he loved the mask, so that he might behave all the more sentimentally and exuberantly. He was too completely the artist to present his confessions baldly and openly' (Einstein 1947, p. 207). Later, Schumann avoided such hints. Among his twenty-three early works were three piano sonatas—in F Sharp Minor Opus 11, the F Minor Opus 14, and the G Minor Opus 22—which were a compromise of the revolutionary spirit with the Classical form: the *sonatas* adhere to the Classical four-movement form but are filled with very different content.

The complexity and many-sidedness of Schumann's creativity were symbolised in the Davidsbundlertanze,—'Dances of the David's League', composed in 1837. This was an imaginary group, a secret order rallying all progressive forces, and opposed to all philistinism, to everything shallow and mediocre. It consisted of two main characters representing the two sides of Schumann's character—the passionate side expressed in passages signed F(Florestan), and the dreamy side in sections signed E(Eusebius), but also the even-tempered Raro who required Schumann to express himself in a more objective form than hitherto. The work is widely regarded as one of Schumann's greatest achievements and as one of the most important piano works of the Romantic era.

His three string quartets have not become classics, although they reflect Beethoven's influence, as is evident from their slow movements: in the first quartet, it echoes the *adagio* of his Ninth Symphony; in the second, it resembles a variation of the *adagio ma non troppo* of Beethoven's quartet Opus 127. Also, there is an imbalance between the lyrical heart of the three quartets in their first movements and the lack of depth and fullness in the other movements. This contrasts with Beethoven's quartets, which are characterised by a comprehensive balance between the movements. Schumann's quartets seem another marker of the breakup of the Classical structure and the replacement of the Classical style by the Romantic style, a necessary development if Romanticism was not to remain mere academic imitation. 'There is no development above and beyond that which is perfect—in this instance, the Beethovenian string quartet' (Einstein 1947, p. 129). Indeed, of Schumann's chamber music, the piano works are generally considered the most successful, with the Piano Quintet a much-admired piece in which his musically creative ideas are superbly adapted to their medium.

Similar considerations apply to the Schumann symphony. For Einstein, it becomes livelier, more youthful and Romantic than Mendelssohn's, the further it strays from the Classical pattern. Like Mendelssohn's two great symphonies, Schumann's No. 1 in B flat major, is descended from Beethoven's Pastoral. Schumann labelled his the 'Spring Symphony' but it contains far less programme music, less 'painting' than Beethoven's: depiction of the outside world has given way to expressions of feeling. Schumann's Symphony No. 4 in D Minor Opus 120' , first composed in 1841, but re-orchestrated in 1851, is his most typical, and actually originated a few months after the first, in 1841, so must really count as the second. It links five movements into an uninterrupted whole and in its original form bore the title 'Symphonic Fantasy'. This unity is not externally imposed but flows from the movements' melodic seeds 'planted' in the Introduction. This is a new form of the symphony—one possessed of a *thematic* homogeneity. But alongside this homogeneity stands a characteristically Romantic feature—disintegration of the Classical structure, as seen in one of Schumann's most enduringly beautiful works—the Piano Concerto in A Minor, Opus 54 (1841/1845). We no longer have Mozart's Classical balance between piano and orchestra, nor Beethoven's dramatic give and take. Instead, 'the soloist is carried, supported and caressed by the orchestra' (Einstein 1947, p. 131). However, Schumann, in common with most Romantic artists, wrote his most successful compositions when he was young, notably his early songs and the piano music.

Schumann's songs make him the successor to Schubert. In 1840, the *lied* suddenly became the focal point of his creativity. Previously, as a Romantic, he had composed only piano music, believing that only through instrumental work could the 'inexpressible be expressed', his innermost feelings be reached. He had hitherto regarded words as too rational, therefore a limitation. But when, with 'Liederkreis, Opus 24, Heine's song sequence, he did begin writing *lieder*, he resembled an erupting volcano. In this, his first and richest year, he wrote no fewer than 138 songs. He rejected a rational interpretation of the word, wishing to liberate it from the 'curse of reason, and, by means of the unity of feeling between language and music, to fuse them into something like a universal art-work' (Schultz 1930, p. 256 in Einstein 1947, p. 187).

It was important for Schumann's turn to *lieder* that he had already composed twenty-three piano works, that behind him lay a body of original pianistic, virtuoso music. He created a different balance between song and accompaniment from that of Schubert. In Schubert, although the melodies are exquisite, the word leads, the piano subordinates itself. In Schumann, the piano is more refined in *sonority* as it undertakes the task of stressing the poem's finer features, of creating bridges in the song cycles, expressing the overflow of feeling—, of contributing to a 'more highly artistic and more profound kind of song', as Schumann himself put it. (Einstein 1947, p. 187).

In Schumann's songs, one can see how the Romantic spirit had intensified the nationalist mood. Haydn and Beethoven had arranged Scottish songs but in a Classical style. Einstein claims that Schumann's songs are more Scottish than the originals; Schubert 'came out' in Hungarian costume but Schumann changed costume 'with still greater delight'. In 1840, Schumann 'descended to the people's level', composing his 'Album of Songs for the Young Opus 79' though occasionally its simplicity rose to a higher level of refinement. A folk quality also became the hallmark of Schumann's later ballads and romances. (Einstein, 1947, pp. 188–189).

Schumann is the embodiment of the Romantic spirit. His Romantic qualities were rooted in and inspired by literary sources. Jean-Paul (Richter), E.T.A. Hoffmann, Ruckert, Eichendorff, Heine are the poets close to his heart. No composer prior to Schumann had devoted his art to making his music 'poetic' to the same degree. For him, the words 'poetic' and 'musical' were synonymous, two aspects of identical artistic essence. 'The poetic quality he seeks to achieve is that ideal aspect, that elevation above the commonplace, that escape into a world of fantasy which is the desire and final aim of the Romantic soul' (Leichtentritt 1954, p. 213).

Schumann's Romanticism is very individual and different from that of Weber, Mendelssohn, Chopin or Liszt. He is not primarily interested in nature, 'Waldszenen' notwithstanding, and landscape painting, nor in fantastic visions of fairyland, as are Weber and Mendelssohn; nor in Chopin's picturesque sound-fantasy; but rather in 'poetic exaltation, youthful exuberance, and soulful lyricism of Romantic art' (Leichtentritt 1954, p. 213). His compositions resemble pages from a personal diary—fragmented, condensed and profusely inventive. His preoccupation with the inner world of romantic feeling puts him in close rapport with Romantic novelists such as Jean-Paul (Richter) and E.T.A. Hoffmann, whose writings deal with both humorous and grotesque types and with beautiful and enchanting ones. Schumann's exquisite 1830s dance fantasies—'Papillons', 'Faschingsschwank aus Wien', 'Davidsbundler', 'Carnaval'—illustrate the difference between his German dance and Chopin's no less magnificent *waltzes, polonaises, mazurkas*, authentically Slavic, more specifically, Polish in character.

Schumann has been criticised for his technical weaknesses in construction and orchestration. But the emotional power of his music is so strong that in the works of his early period he reaches the pinnacle of creative achievement. His melodies express our deepest feelings, of sadness, yearning and joy. They continue to have the most powerful emotional impact, as they did on later composers in Germany, France and Russia (on musicians such as Gounod, Saint-Saens, Bizet, Cesar Franck, Massenet, Liszt, Rubinstein, Brahms, Tchaikovsky, Borodin and Rimski-Korsakov).

The Programmatic Drama of Franz Liszt (1811–1886)

Liszt is best known for his piano works, but he did write orchestral and other ensemble works, though nearly always including keyboard. His piano music is noted for its difficulty. These pieces are usually divided into two categories—firstly, original works, secondly 'transcriptions', 'paraphrases' or 'fantasies' on works by other composers. Liszt invented a new form—the 'symphonic poem'—an orchestral piece in one movement in which an extramusical programme provides a narrative or illustrative feature. The programme may derive from a poem, a story or novel, a painting or other source. The term was used by Liszt to describe his thirteen single-movement works of this kind. They were not pure symphonic movements in the Classical sense since they dealt with descriptive themes adopted from mythology, Romantic literature, history or fantasy.

Liszt's Romantic Style

Liszt applied for the first time the principle of 'cyclical' construction, by which he developed all the various themes of a symphony or *sonata*-like work from a few basic *motives*. He then proceeded to transform these through rhythmical or melodic changes. This was a remarkable musical application of the Romantic notion of evolution: in Liszt's 'symphonic poems', his 'Faust' and 'Dante' symphonies, and also his concertos, Liszt illustrated superbly the potential of this principle of organic structure. This cyclical method had been widely used in the sixteenth or seventeenth centuries, in forms such as the *ricercare, canzone or fantasia*. But it had been forgotten in the eighteenth century, and Liszt probably derived it from his studies of Beethoven's last sonatas and quartets, where an ingenious and complex use is made of a similar transformation of themes (Leichtentritt 1954, p. 225).

Like Chopin, Liszt developed new methods of conveying impressions of landscapes. His 'Album d'un Voyageur' and 'Annees de Pelerinage' (Parts I and II) translated his impressions of travel in Switzerland and Italy into vivid, imaginative piano music. His three 'Sonnets of Petrarch' are transcriptions of his songs to those texts, and in a piece entitled 'Les Cloches de Geneve', the bells are clearly audible. Towards the end of his life, Liszt turned to ecclesiastical music, becoming the principal exponent of a peculiarly Catholic Romanticism, with its mystic, angelic *sonority*. His masses, oratorios and psalms anticipate the atmosphere and mood of Wagner's 'Parsifal'.

Liszt's notion of programme music reveals an advanced stage of development compared with Berlioz's more extravagant, theatrical music. His 'symphonic poems' are lyrical or dramatic scenes or *cantatas*, or operatic intermezzos without words, but with imaginary scenery or action. He derives his subject matter and titles largely from poetry (Victor Hugo, Lamartine, Goethe, Shakespeare, Dante). In true Romantic style, Liszt increasingly sought to relate his music to literary images and ideas, to works of art, and also to scenes from nature. Piano compositions appear with the titles 'Apparitions' (1835), perhaps borrowed from Lamartine's poem 'Apparition', 'Harmonies Poetiques et Religieuses'

(1835 and 1853), and 'Consolations' (1849–1850), following Sainte-Beuve's poems. Liszt's motto was 'renewal of music through its inner connection with poetry.' He rejected the tradition of Classical *sonata* form, though he admired Bach, Beethoven and Schubert, whose works he performed, he prevented them from influencing his own creative output, whose aim was to be 'more free... more adequate to the spirit of these times' (Einstein 1947, pp. 140–141).

Liszt deserves credit for having taken his ideas to their conclusion. His unusual artistic career and spiritual development led him to become the most independent of the Romantics. He was supranational—born in Hungary of German parents, he never mastered Hungarian fully, went to Paris at the age of twelve and kept that city as his artistic and intellectual home though his virtuosity led him all over Europe. After 1848, he settled in Weimar, apparently abandoning his nomadic life. However, in 1861, he visited Rome, and in 1865 he became Abbe Liszt, fleeing into the arms of the Catholic Church. This was a familiar Romantic move, less common, however, among musicians than poets: it was the act of a Romantic who, after numerous attempts to get to grips with contemporary, fashionable philosophical currents, became tired and disappointed and offered his soul to the church. But the 1860s were also years of great sadness: he lost his son in 1859 and his daughter in 1862. Ironically, no Romantic composer was more 'worldly' than Liszt: none enjoyed such success or remained so closely in touch with the surrounding artistic world, yet felt so lonely and homeless.

Liszt's homelessness, together with his virtuosity, also influenced his creativity. As a 'free' artist, he used the titles 'sonata' and 'symphony' but they no longer referred to the Classical forms. His B Minor Sonata (1852–1853), for example, is a 'great, rhetorical rhapsody' on a few themes largely set out in the first fifteen bars. The *sonata* doesn't have an *exposition* and *recapitulation*, though it does have a first and second theme, and a contrast between *allegro* and *andante*, and a large dramatic *development* section (Einstein 1947, p. 142). There is no separation of individual movements, but instead, recitative-like linkages and transitions. In other words, the three 'movements' become linked into a single piece, the connection achieved through elaborate *thematic* relationships. This process, known as 'thematic transformation' reveals Liszt in command of strikingly advanced techniques.

Moreover, his 'symphonic poems' are less dependent on poetry and painting than seems the case at first. As a musician, Liszt doesn't follow closely an external programme, or tell a story, but embarks on composition in an independent frame of mind. He seeks to lay bare the heart of his subject. He no longer writes cyclical works of four or more movements, like Berlioz's 'Symphonie Fantantique', nor does he give us naturalistic touches (imitating real life or nature) such as, again, we find in Berlioz.

In the 'Annees de Pelerinage', the first piece, 'Sposalizio', from Part II, 'Italie', takes its title from a Raphael painting depicting the marriage of Mary and Joseph. For Liszt, although music without words does not have a 'meaning'—yet the feelings and impressions it evokes find correlates in other spheres of human activity such as the visual arts, language, especially poetry, or communing with nature.

In later years, Liszt created an abundance of transcriptions—converting Beethoven symphonies, Berlioz's 'Harold in Italy', the overtures to 'William Tell', 'Oberon', 'Freischutz', and Wagner's 'Tannhauser', into immense piano pieces. He finally took the unprecedented step of removing the orchestra and other soloists from his concerts. Although Liszt no longer now composed cyclical pieces like Berlioz's 'Symphonie Fantastique', he did compose two symphonies—the 'Faust' and 'Dante' symphonies. However, their movements are not episodic, as they had been in Berlioz. 'A Faust Symphony in Three Character Sketches After Goethe' (1), Faust, (2) Gretchen, (3) Mephistopheles (premiered 1857) doesn't tell the story of Goethe's drama; rather does it create musical portraits of the principal protagonists. Einstein argues that the masterpiece here is the final movement, 'Mephistopheles', which consists of negative elements: parody, distortion, mockery of the Faust themes (Einstein 1947, p. 146). 'A Symphony to Dante's Divine Comedy', is a programme symphony (also premiered 1857), and is perhaps not so much a symphony as two descriptive symphonic poems. It consists of two movements, both in a loosely structured *ternary* form, with little *thematic* change. There remains to mention Liszt's two Piano Concertos, in E flat Major and A Major (1848–1849). Inspired by Weber's 'Concertstuck' in F Minor (1821), Liszt excels him in *thematic* inventiveness and virtuoso *bravura*. Typical of Liszt is the free form, which unites the individual virtuoso and *cantabile* passages.

Liszt's achievements sent waves of creativity in various directions. Debate is possible over the enduring value of Liszt's music, but not over his inventiveness in developing new technical means of expression and his extraordinary sense of sound and *colour*. From Berlioz, he derived his ideas of orchestral tone *colour* and programme music, though he developed them in his own individual style. Chopin bequeathed to him his sensitive new *chromatic* harmony, though he enriched it and passed on to Wagner a perfected instrument which he used in 'Tristan und Isolde' (Leichtentritt 1954, p. 224). Although many regarded Liszt's work as 'flashy' and superficial, his work criticised for being marked by an excess of emotionalism and rhetoric, nevertheless, his legacy was highly significant. Many of his works, such as 'Nuages Gris', 'Les Jeux d'Eaux a la Villa d'Este', which contain parallel fifths, the whole-tone scale, parallel diminished and augmented triads, and unresolved dissonances, anticipated and influenced key twentieth-century composers such as Debussy, Ravel and Bartok. A piece like the 'Dante Sonata' engages in 'heaven-storming virtuosity' that overextends the physical limits of both soloist and instrument. Liszt's harmonic style in this work is often astonishingly advanced: sections of the 'Vallee d'Obermann', for instance, verge on *atonality* (Plantinga 1984, p. 186).

The Teutonic Mythology of Richard Wagner (1813–1883)

Wagner's musical output is listed by the 'Wagner-Werk-Verzeichnis' (WWV) as comprising 113 works. But his operas are his principal artistic legacy. He always wrote his own libretti, which he called poems, unlike most opera composers who engaged others to write the text and lyrics.

Wagner's Romantic Style

Early Period (to 1842):

In his early period, Wagner revealed a strong preference for the Italian style. But his three-year Parisian stay (1839–1842) witnessed a turning point in his artistic outlook, initiated by the hearing of Beethoven's Ninth. He could not renounce opera to become a composer of symphonies and chamber music. But Germany had few significant operatic landmarks and no operatic tradition—'The Magic Flute', 'Fidelio' and 'Der Freischutz' were the highlights—so he was unable to take an existing national operatic form and build it up into something superior, a solution that was available to Verdi. He rejected traditional Grand Opera in the style of Auber, Spontini or Meyerbeer. His first opera to be successfully staged was Rienzi (1842). Its style was conventional, though it did reveal the lingering influence of Grand Opera.

Middle Period: 'Romantic' Operas' (1843–1851):

This middle period, during Wagner's tenure as conductor at Dresden (1843–1849), began with 'Der Fliegende Hollander—'The Flying Dutchman' (1843) a more original German Romantic opera. The story suggests the exhilaration of the supernatural and the charm of local colour as provided by the sea storm. It also revealed the first example of an omnipresent theme in Wagner—redemption through love. Also displayed in rudimentary form is Wagner's extensive use of particular themes—the *leitmotif*—to refer to characters, objects, events and ideas which he later develops. Harmonically, 'The Flying Dutchman' belongs to Wagner's early work: it has a largely *diatonic* syntax disturbed by occasional *diminished-seventh* sonorities at moments of high emotional tension.

'Tannhauser (1845) recounts the medieval legend of the Christian knight torn between the carnal pleasures offered by Venus, Goddess of Love, and the pure, redeeming love of the saintly Elizabeth. In Act Three, where Tannhauser describes his pilgrimage to Rome and his impending return to the Venusberg, Wagner creates a dramatic 'style of declamation' enlivened by important orchestral themes, notably the magical glimmer of the Venusberg music from act one. In the 'Pilgrims' Chorus' in act one, Wagner provides a foretaste of his own *chromatic polyphony*. Here, and elsewhere in 'Tannhauser', Wagner reveals his growing ability to create musical characterisation, providing situations and characters with their own distinctive melodies and *textures*.

Wagner's linking of musical *themes* with dramatic elements is extended in 'Lohengrin'. The narrative, replete with symbolism, combines medieval legend and history. The major characters, events and ideas, all have their identifying *motifs*. Harmonically, the music is conservative when viewed against the emerging backdrop of Wagner's development as a composer: traditional *diatonic* procedures and clearly laid-out *tonal* areas dominate. Much of the music is rhythmically *symmetrical*, with traditional patterns of earlier and later phrases and a preference for *duple meter* (Plantinga 1984, p. 267).

An important innovation in 'Lohengrin' is the substitution of a *homogeneous* prelude to the drama for the customary overture with its musical overview of the opera. This prelude has a dramatic significance revealed in the third act when the music accompanies Lohengrin's account of his origin. The celestial gleam of its *tremolos* and slow-moving harmonies refer to the land of the Holy Grail, the Templars who guard it, and the dove that descends each year to reactivate its miraculous powers. Another brilliant orchestral piece—the prelude to act three—highlights the orchestra's role as equal partner to the singers, and points to the direction that Wagner is taking, towards a synthesis of forces and a homogeneity of *texture* aimed at serving new dramatic objectives materialising in his mind.

Wagner was preoccupied with creating music for a future world. His unique twofold genius as dramatist and composer were bolstered by his reading of German Romantic philosophy, resulting in the 1850s in his writings about the 'Music of the Future' and his concept of 'Gesamtkunstwerk'—total work of art. Closely linked in with Wagner's philosophical interests was his strong commitment to practical revolutionary activity. He was powerfully affected by the two revolutions that swept across Europe in 1830 and 1848. A teenager during the first, he was on the barricades in May 1848 in Dresden during the second, fighting for a united German constitutional monarchy, forfeiting his post as 'Hofkapellmeister' at the Royal Opera.

Late Period—(1851–1882):

Wagner's late operas—his 'music dramas'—are regarded as his masterpieces. 'Der Ring des Nibelungen'—'The Ring Cycle', is a set of four operas based on characters and features of German medieval mythology, especially Norse mythology. Wagner wrote the libretti for these operas according to his interpretation of 'Stabreim', highly alliterative rhyming verse-pair used in ancient German poetry. They were also influenced by Wagner's concept of ancient Greek drama. 'The Ring' is an intricate series of tales describing the actions of Germanic gods, demigods and giants, all of them lusting after the gold controlled by the dwarfish race of the Nibelungs, and especially for the ring moulded from it by Alberich the Nibelung.

In 'Das Rheingold', with its 'relentlessly talky "realism" (and) the absence of lyrical "numbers"' (Grey 2008, p. 86), Wagner came close to the musical ideals of his 1849–1851 essays—synthesising the musical, poetical and dramatic elements of an opera. 'Die Walkure', whose first act includes a virtually traditional aria (Siegmund's 'Wintersturme'), and the quasi-choral appearance of the Valkyries themselves, has been described as 'the music drama that most satisfactorily embodies the theoretical principles of 'Oper und Drama'… A thoroughgoing synthesis of poetry and music is achieved without any notable sacrifice in musical expression' (Millington online article, undated).

The music of 'The Ring', is, like the dramatic action, conceived as a whole. Themes are used consistently from beginning to end, with a consistency of style that is astonishing given the twenty-six-year span over which the work was composed. 'Vocal writing in 'The Ring'... is dominated by a style of declamation that moves easily between two poles: rhythmically regular melody and a kind of disjunct vocal *counterpoint* to the music in the orchestra' (Plantinga 1984, p. 273). The orchestral part remains independent, flexible and powerfully expressive. Wagner's mature style, famously, though ambiguously, described as *chromatic*, functions within a harmonic framework that is complex but remains thoroughly *tonal*. (Chopin's music has more *chromatic* inflection of a traditional *diatonic* structure). 'Wotan's Farewell' in 'Die Walkure' begins and ends in E, but the music explores that key's possible relationships, starting in E minor, moving into G, its *relative major*, followed by a passing reference back to E minor, then to C, the *subdominant* of G. Moving into A minor, it lurches towards B minor which in the major mode becomes the *dominant* leading back to E. But before reaching the final *cadence*, a further short excursion produces sonorities based on C and F that we heard before in the C major section. Wagner inserts such 'parenthetical sonorities' before a *cadence* as one means of averting or delaying return to the *tonic*.

Wagner's *leitmotifs* enter into different *contrapuntal* combinations, and change their form through numerous variations of harmonic *colouring* and dynamic accents. From Act Three of 'Siegfried onwards, the 'Ring' becomes melodically more *chromatic*, harmonically more complex and developmental in its treatment of *leitmotifs* (Puffett 1984, pp. 48–49). The end of the cycle reflects Wagner's post-1849 obsession with a 'fire-cure' to cleanse the world. But the question remains: if the gold is returned to the Rhinemaidens, why do the gods nevertheless perish? We are frequently told that the return of the gold will save the gods from their doom. But finally it doesn't, which highlights Wagner's apparent determination that the gods must perish to make way for the new order since they represent the old order of states and laws (Arblaster 1992, p. 175).

Wagner's final opera, 'Parsifal' (1882), has a storyline suggested by the legend of The Holy Grail. It also contains features of Buddhist renunciation suggested by Wagner's reading of Schopenhauer. It is controversial because of its treatment of Christianity, its eroticism, and, according to some interpretations, its German nationalism and antisemitism (Glenn 2008, in Grey 2008, pp. 151–175).

Like all great artists, Wagner was happy to appropriate from other composers. He took over from Berlioz an orchestra glittering with all shades of *colour*, full of novel powerful and suggestive sound effects. However, as a dramatist, he was not interested in writing descriptive operatic symphonies Berlioz style. But he did incorporate into his dramas shorter stretches of such descriptive music: the 'Feuerzauber' ('Magic Fire') in Die Walkure, Siegfried's Rhine-journey in 'Gotterdammerung, and the 'Rhinegold' prelude depicting the quiet flow of the Rhine. These scenes are all strongly suggestive of Berlioz. From Liszt, Wagner learned the affective, refined new harmony which Liszt in turn had derived from Chopin. Of course, Wagner was no crude imitator: Berlioz had perhaps mastered the new orchestral possibilities earlier than Wagner, Liszt was maybe a decade ahead in his consummate supremacy over the new *chromatic* harmony, but Wagner enriched these achievements, incorporated them into his work, making them his own, effective instruments of a 'style superior to that of both Berlioz and Liszt'.

Furthermore, Wagner drew on Beethoven's symphonies for their constructive principles, on Weber for his sensitivity to the moods of nature, and on Meyerbeer for his theatrical expertise. Wagner was also enthusiastic about ancient Greek drama, the vitality of his work flowing from a felicitous union of Romantic and Classical ideas. Whereas Gluck had reformed opera by reviving ancient Greek mythology, Wagner drew inspiration from Germanic, and sometimes, Celtic, mythology, while applying ancient Greek ideas of form and technique. 'The tetralogies of Aeschylus are the distant models of Wagner's Nibelungen tetralogy. In 'Tristan und Isolde' and 'Parsifal', a certain Euripidean spirit becomes manifest, and in the 'Meistersinger von Nurnberg reminiscences of the comedy of Aristophanes are undeniable... The cool marble beauty of antique form is infused with the warm blood of the romantic imagination...' (Leichtentritt 1954, p. 231). Wagner's genius is perhaps revealed most clearly in the creative union of the severity, sculptural lucidity, and architectural grandeur of ancient art, and the rich detail and imaginative exuberance of the Romantic era. Wagner strikes a balance between Romantic formal vagueness and the firm constructive approach of ancient tragedy.

In the later operas, the orchestra's dramatic role includes the use of *leitmotifs*—their complex interweaving and development illustrate the unfolding of the drama. Indeed, the orchestra became as important as the singers, being assigned the role played by the chorus in Greek drama.

Where the Greek chorus approves or disapproves of the events and actions, so in Wagner the orchestra comments on the drama, interpreting the inner meaning of the actions, especially where the libretto fails to fully convey this. In order to equip his orchestra to fulfil this task, Wagner drew on the entire array of Romantic orchestral tools: its *tone*-painting, subtle and *colourful chromatic* harmony, and rich palette.

Wagner transferred Beethoven's symphonic style and technique to the theatre. The 'Eroica' and the Ninth Symphony have an elaborate and complex structure of *themes* in the 'working out' sections which gives the effect of coherence, of dramatic tension and excitement. Similarly in Wagner's art, many typical, leading themes are used throughout a work. They enter into various *contrapuntal* combinations, changing their effect or impression through multiple variations of harmonic *colouring* and *dynamic* accentuation. A significant trait is Wagner's ability to achieve a convincing transition from one complex of emotions to another, moving through successive sets of *colour*, rhythm and melodic design, a feature absorbed from Beethoven's symphonic technique that Wagner ingeniously adapted to the needs of his own *tone*-language (Leichtentritt 1954, p. 232).

As a music dramatist, Wagner saw himself as a combination of Aeschylus, Shakespeare and Beethoven. Since this fusion appeared to be formidable, he saw the nation, indeed the entire world, as the recipients of his artistic and philosophical message. He wanted to conquer the world, and did really conquer the nineteenth century, having forged the artistic tools with which to achieve this conquest. It was this path that led him to music drama. In a mood of Rousseauesque primitivism, he denounced the corrosive effects of civilisation, exalting the uncorrupted, 'natural man', a representative of that product of the Romantic imagination, the Folk or People. 'Not you, the intelligentsia… are truly inventive, but the Folk, for it was need that drove them to invention' ('Gesammelte und Dichtungen', 3, p. 53, in Plantinga 1984, p. 269). Wagner advocated overthrow of the state for the sake of art, denigrating all materialism and privilege as the adversaries of art and the Folk. But also swayed by the atheist philosopher Ludwig Feuerbach, he specified Christianity as the main enemy, the force principally responsible for the decay of art and for human enslavement. In 1850, he wrote the scurrilous essay 'Judaism in Music', in which the villain is Jewish control of the arts. The influence of Jewish composers such as Mendelssohn and Meyerbeer is, for Wagner, unfortunate, a reflection perhaps of his own hitherto lack of success. And there have been frequent suggestions that his operas contain antisemitic stereotypes, for example, the character of Mime in 'The Ring', Beckmesser in 'Die Meistersinger', and Klingsor in 'Parsifal'. However, Wagner had, throughout his life Jewish friends, colleagues and supporters. Also, Wagner's anti-semitism was a product of nineteenth-century European culture (Weiner 1997, p. 11; Katz 1986, p. 19; Conway 2012, pp. 258–264).

According to his book 'Oper und Drama, - Gesammelte Schriften und Dichtungen', No. 3, (p. 231, in Plantinga 1984, pp. 270–271), the constituent arts—poetry, music, and dance, but also the plastic arts—must all function as means to a central end, the living drama whose subject must be myth rather than history, as mythology has the advantage of originating among the Folk.

Wagner demanded a large orchestra, greatly expanding all sections—strings, woodwind, brass, percussion. His creative and flexible management of this ensemble produced effects ranging from overwhelming virtuosity to the frailest and delicately *coloured* orchestral discourse. Though indebted to Berlioz and Meyerbeer and Weber, this was in his time a unique achievement. 'Wagner saw his work as lying in direct succession to that of such quintessentially romantic German figures as Beethoven and... Weber' (Snowman 2009, p. 114).

The music of 'Tristan' represents an extension of the stylistic innovations of the first parts of 'The Ring'. The evolution and transformation of characteristic motives are raised to new heights. There is a comprehensive orchestral exposition and explanation of musical themes, with individual melodies serving as the basis for endless pages of the score. As in 'The Ring', the themes have dramatic associations. However, their identification is risky as the drama is internal, so that melodies do not easily refer to external events. The familiar opening of the 'Prelude' illustrates several aspects of the opera's musical style: three times the cellos, playing in a high *register*, reveal a descending *chromatic* figure which is answered by the woodwinds with a rising one.

In 'Tristan', the extreme *chromaticism* of the lines and harmony, the continuity of the rhythm, the *enharmony* of the *modulations* themselves represent the liberation of the individual spirit, or rather the striving for liberation. The succession of harmonic tensions, reinforced by the impact of the orchestra, becomes an 'emotional orgy', and virtually all the musical principles that had characterised the Classical *sonata* until Beethoven's final works have disappeared (Mellers 1957, p. 176).

Despite Wagner straying far from the Classical tradition, 'Tristan und Isolde' has its own set of rules. The entire symphonic *texture* is unified by the dominance of a single personality. This becomes clear in the musical unity which emphasises the dramatic and symbolic unity of the *leitmotifs*. The three 'Tristan chords', structured on overlapping fourths, with which the work opens, reappear in altered form at every critical point in the work. They end up as the melodic basis of the 'Liebestod' itself, and the harmonic basis of the final, immaculate resolution into B major.

The prelude's 'overwhelming intensity derives from the fact that Wagner concentrates on the dissonant harmony at the expense of its resolution; it is always the dissonant chord that falls on the strong beat... the effect of the passage as a whole depends on the way in which the brief, upward-yearning, *chromatically* falling phrase, underlined by its dissonance, is repeated several times at progressively rising intervals' (Mellers 1957, pp. 177–178). This heightened excitement leads one to expect a grand climax when the discord is finally resolved on to the *tonic*. Instead, we hear an unexpected chord—the *submediant*. So we hear a buildup of harmonic tension which is partially frustrated and a tendency towards rhythmic fluidity which is counteracted by the continuous repetition of the phrases in sequence.

'Die Meistersinger von Nurnberg' 'The Mastersingers of Nuremberg' - has a libretto that is comic and, like all Wagner operas, historical. It has aria-type singing and imposing choral scenes, contrary to Wagner's theoretical tenets, and also long stretches of *diatonic* harmony (without *chromatic* deviation). Set in the narrow, gabled streets of sixteenth-century Nuremberg, this opera offers a comic but sympathetic picture of the codified art of the Mastersingers. Their complex of rules governing poetry and song, upheld by the pedant Beckmesser, is ridiculed, whereas the genuine artistic impulse is represented by the young hero Walther von Stolzing. Their disaccord is mediated by Hans Sachs, Mastersinger who represents both past and present, tradition and innovation, but also by the enlightened judgement of a wise people. The rapid *fioritura* with which Beckmesser adorns his songs is made to sound ridiculous, while Walther's contest song comes off all the better by comparison. The orchestra also provides him with helpful accompaniment that is denied to Beckmesser. But Wagner emphasises through the music that this is no simple triumph of modernism over tradition. A poem by Hans Sachs is set in a deliberately archaic style: a Mastersinger melody is used for the 'guild march', and the opera opens with a chorale reminiscent of church music in the German Reformation. These features, together with a *polyphonic* mixture of themes in the overture, pay homage to musical tradition, to the foundations on which innovation rests.

In 'Parsifal', Wagner drew upon various past techniques. He no longer felt bound by the theories that had informed much of 'The Ring' and 'Tristan' and wrote a poem based mainly on end rhyme—having lines ending with words that sound the same (e.g. star light, star bright). Much of the drama is organised in static tableaux reminiscent of grand opera. But the intention and effect are not designed to overpower the listener with scintillating scene and sound, but to offer ritual and an epic story, and to uncover complex layers of symbols.

Wagner again uses referential musical themes to elucidate the actions and thoughts of the characters. And the motives themselves seem attuned to their dramatic meaning. Following the long-established traditions of Western music, suffering and adversity are expressed through *chromaticism*, while *diatonic* structures illustrate the simplicity of the character Parsifal and the sublime nature of the Holy Grail. Whereas the texture of 'Tristan' is consistently *chromatic*, Parsifal' is both *chromatic* and *diatonic* but in the Holy Grail at times *modal*.

Wagner explored the limits of the traditional *tonal* system which since the late seventeenth century had given keys and chords their identity. The 'Tristan chord' points the way towards twentieth-century *atonality*: the harmonic revolutions of Debussy and Schoenberg (works of both contain examples of *tonal* and *atonal* modernism) have often been traced back to Tristan und Isolde' and 'Parsifal'.

The Rebellious Nationalism of Giuseppe Verdi (1813–1901)

Like Wagner, Verdi's career was devoted exclusively to the composition of operas, with the exception of his 'Requiem (1874). His creative development over the five decades spanning the years 1839 to 1893 revealed a line of continuity, yet it is clearly divisible, like Wagner's, into three periods. Although, in contrast to Wagner, Verdi was no theoretician, like Wagner, his synthesis of music and drama reached soaring artistic heights.

Verdi's Romantic Style

Verdi was the heir to the Italian *bel canto* tradition, a vocal style that dominated singing in most of Europe during the eighteenth and early nineteenth centuries. Verdi's rapid-paced ensembles often recall Rossini, and his smooth, seamless melodies reflect the influence of Bellini and Donizetti. Verdi absorbed this style and enhanced it into a medium of powerful tragic expression. However, a new simplicity, a freshness and energy characterise his music. The proportion of *recitative* is reduced so that the extended vocal *solo* including aria and recitative becomes compressed. Straightforward marching rhythms proliferate, and the chorus often sings simple melodies in unison while revealing a wide range of styles.

Early Verdi:

Verdi's first period was inaugurated with 'Nabucco (1842), an opera based on the Biblical theme of the Babylonian oppression of the ancient Hebrew slaves, which immediately became a metaphor for the subjugation of Italy by the Austrians. Its famous chorus of the slaves, 'Va Pensiero sul'Alli Dorate' ('Go, Thought, on Golden Wings'), expressed the pent-up yearning for freedom and hope of the Italian people, acquiring the status of the unofficial anthem of the Italian national liberation movement. At the first rehearsal, the stagehands shouted their approval, beating on the floor with their tools (Phillips-Matz 1993, p. 116). 'Va Pensiero' contains a broad *cantabile* melody with a special lilt achieved by a *cadential* ornament in triplet motion.

The sixteen operas Verdi composed between 1839 and 1850 comprise his early style. Four of them seem especially significant in his development: Nabucco (1842), 'Ernani' (1844), 'Macbeth (first version 1847), and 'Luisa Miller (1849). Verdi always urged his collaborator to accept his ideas, so that the dramatic form and language of Franceso Maria Piave's librettos were frequently strongly influenced by the composer. In 'Ernani', Verdi's familiar conflict pitting love against honour is played out in an almost melodramatic manner.

Verdi's growing stature as a dramatic composer is evident in his next opera, 'Macbeth', in the creepy supernatural atmosphere of the witches' scenes, and in the strength of the title role, now a fully fledged Verdi baritone. But perhaps the most memorable single feature of the work is Lady Macbeth's sleepwalking scene in Act 4 in which the effect of the highly expressive *arioso* part is intensified by a compulsively repeated rhythmic *figure* in the orchestra. As for 'Nabucco', its success could not have depended on external, political factors were it not for its musical brilliance. Also significant is that, although the main characters are well delineated, the great heights of the opera lie in its choral moments. 'Nabucco' is all the more remarkable an achievement as Verdi composed it at a difficult moment in his life, following the death of his wife and two children.

Perhaps the most striking stylistic feature 'of the early Verdi operas, and the one most obviously allied to the mood of the Risorgimento, was the big choral number...' The success of 'Va Pensiero' was followed by 'O Signor, dal Tetto Natio' in 'I Lombardi (1844) and by 'Si Ridesti il Leon di Castiglia' in 'Ernani' (1844), the battle hymn of the conspirators seeking freedom (Taruskin 2010, pp. 570–575).

Middle Period:

During the following four years, Verdi wrote five operas—'Luisa Miller' (1849), 'Stiffelio' (1850), 'Rigoletto' (1851), 'Il Trovatore' (1853) and 'La Traviata' (1853), all of them famous for arias and choruses gloriously rich in drama and melody. The first two can probably be best considered as transitional works bridging Verdi's early and middle periods, whereas the last three belong to the middle period proper. Verdi considered 'Rigoletto' as an especially significant milestone in his career.

The original Victor Hugo play 'Le Roi s'Amuse' presented scenes of royal dissoluteness, causing it to be banned in 1832 by the relatively liberal regime of Louis Philippe. 'Verdi's appetite was once again whetted by a subject that was bound to be politically sensitive' (Plantinga 1984, p. 308). But he was also attracted by a dramatic situation in which a doting father (Rigoletto) unknowingly participates in the death of his daughter (Gilda), and in which the two male leads, Rigoletto and the Duke, display contradictory traits: they are villains, yet both reveal positive human emotions.

Immediately striking in 'Rigoletto' is the way Verdi juxtaposes the threatening prelude in C minor, with *tremolando* lower string, with the opening scene that exudes energetic bonhomie. The ball scene expresses a rhythmic gaiety and bland harmony as Rigoletto, the Duke's hunch-backed jester, assists his master in his amorous conquests among the wives and daughters of his courtiers. The story, however, assumes a tragic irony as he discovers that his master has seduced his own daughter. A *stretta* of ensemble singing and dancing suddenly breaks off as Monterone, father of one of the Duke's victims, curses Rigoletto in the ominous style of the prelude. The dramatic and musical unfolding of the opera reveals the inevitable consequences of the curse in scenes in tones ranging from merriment to horror.

Much of the drama is pursued in duets, a powerful example being the *scena e duetto* between Rigoletto and Gilda in Act I, scene 2. Opening with Rigoletto's solemn soliloquy on his tragic status as a hunchback and a clown, he sings in a powerful declamatory voice, while the orchestra uses different devices of accompanied *recitative* that change with the protagonist's shifting moods: vigorous orchestral interjections, string accompaniment with *chordal tremolando*. The orchestration creates an atmosphere of spirited frivolity by doubling the tune in the violins with all the treble winds, a stylistic feature of earlier nineteenth-century Italian opera. 'Rigoletto' reveals Verdi's maturity, being a masterpiece of powerful characterisation and unforgettable music. It contains, in addition, a strong element of class hatred, pitting, as it does, the tragic jester against the hedonistic duke who has seduced his daughter.

Several of Verdi's 'middle period' operas, i.e. of the late 1840s and early 1850s, emphasise duets, harnessing his dramatic and musical genius to explore individual personalities or particular human relationships such as the father–daughter relationship in 'Rigoletto', or that between Violetta and Alfredo in 'La Traviata' (The Fallen Woman). 'La Traviata' (1853), usually regarded as sentimental, is, in fact, a forceful indictment of bourgeois hypocrisy. Violetta, a courtesan, seeks respectability through marriage to her lover Alfredo, whose father, however, persuades her to give him up. Violetta emerges as a victim of conventional morality but also, crucially, as a heroine morally superior to her detractors.

In the 1850s, Verdi embarked on a further change of direction. Up to now, he had composed operas that were compact, swiftly moving. In this new, late middle period, his operas were on a larger scale, in keeping with the tradition of French 'grand opera' which examined historical themes, frequently with a strong political element. In these operas, personal conflicts reflect the relations between larger social or national groups. Verdi thus returns to political questions, but interweaves them with personal conflicts, striking a balance with great conviction. Italian nationalism was approaching its moment of fruition and Verdi sought to deal with the new problems it faced. Significantly, most of the works composed between 1855 and 1871 were written for theatres outside Italy: 'Les Vepres Siciliennes (1855), 'Don Carlos (1867) and a revised Macbeth (1868) were first performed in Paris, 'La Forza del Destino in St. Petersburg (1862), and 'Aida in Cairo (1871).

An important issue running through these works is the kind of government that is desirable for modern nation-states. Verdi presents us with a range of possible rulers. King Gustavus in 'Un Ballo in Maschera— A Masked Ball - has vision and magnanimity. Verdi was clearly hoping that the future unified kingdom would overcome the vestiges of feudal barbarism and usher in a new era of civilised democracy. Philip II in 'Don Carlos' and Ramfis (Egyptian high priest in 'Aida'), on the other hand, are harsh rulers whose unforgiving nature results in destruction.

Of these works, 'Don Carlos' is perhaps Verdi's classic treatment of politics and personal life. A love triangle unfolds against the backdrop of broader struggles among nations and between church and state (Plantinga 1984, p. 312). In each of the four leading characters, there rages a conflict between political obligations and personal feelings. The revolt of the Netherlands against Spanish rule is seen as the point of departure for the modern struggle for freedom, whether national, religious or individual. It also contains Verdi's most unreserved condemnation of the Catholic Church. The music encompasses a wide emotional range, expressing passion, dramatic conflict and tragic lyricism. The scene between Philip II, the upholder of traditional authority, and Posa, the champion of liberty, is one of the most dramatic Verdi ever composed. And the fourth act contains the unforgettable duet between the King and the Grand Inquisitor—two basses who represent the clash between temporal and ecclesiastical powers.

'Aida' represents 'a crowning synthesis of the best of the Italian and French traditions that Verdi had been cultivating ...' (Plantinga 1984, p. 312). 'Aida' inaugurates the final period of his musical life. Commissioned for the celebrations in Cairo on the opening of the Suez Canal in 1871, the work is on a grand scale and rich in festive pageantry. The story is, again, one of conflict between love and honour, private passion and public duty, played out in a context of a struggle between nations: ancient Egypt and Ethiopia.

Although 'Aida' is an opera of 'numbers', it has a continuity of action and music that is new in Verdi. *Recitative* is at a minimum, while the drama advances mainly through a powerfully expressive declamation that moves easily to *arioso*. Both are underpinned by a rich, versatile orchestral accompaniment. The ensemble scenes are on an epic scale, beyond anything in Verdi's earlier work. Most spectacular is the second scene of Act II, a grandiose act-finale involving a brass band, choruses of the people, high priests and prisoners in a mammoth victory parade, with extensive dancing. Solo singing by the principals *counterpoints* the grandiose brilliance of the massed forces. The harmonic language of

'Aida' is more complex than was customary in the Italian tradition up till then. Even Radames' famous *romanza* 'Celeste Aida' (Heavenly Aida) reveals a well-developed harmonic complexity. The initial two sets of two half-phrases in the first eight bars proceed to the third (D major) of the *tonic* (B flat major) instead of to its *dominant. Chromaticism* and *counterpoint* in the *Prelude* must have alerted the audience to unaccustomed levels of musical complexity. Critics noted these innovations and, to the annoyance of Verdi the Germanophobe, attributed it to Wagner's influence.

There develops, in addition, a 'growing freedom in the large-scale structure... and an acute attention to fine detail'. Verdi wants to move away from standard forms such as *'cavatinas,* duets, trios, choruses, finales, etc.... and if you could avoid beginning with an opening chorus...' he would be quite happy (Kimbell 1981; Chusid 1997; Budden 1984, p. 61).

Two factors conditioned this shift: firstly, Verdi's growing reputation gave him greater freedom to choose his own subjects; secondly, the changed political situation—the defeat of the 1848 revolutions, which resulted in a weakening of the Risorgimento ethos (at least initially) and a marked increase in censorship. This is reflected in Verdi's move away from political themes towards personal issues. There are 40% fewer choruses compared to the early period: whereas virtually all the early operas begin with a chorus, only one of the middle period ('Luisa Miller') does so. Instead Verdi experiments with a variety of means—a stage band in 'Rigoletto', an aria for bass in 'Stiffelio', a party scene in 'La Traviata'. Chusid also notes Verdi's increasing tendency to substitute shorter orchestral introductions for full-scale overtures (Chusid 1997, pp. 9–11).

In 1873, the death of the poet Alessandro Manzoni, persuaded Verdi to embark on a quite different type of composition: a 'Requiem Mass' in his memory (1874). It is not, therefore, fundamentally a religious work but an act of homage to human greatness. For Verdi, despite living in a Catholic country, was an agnostic and convinced humanist. His own life, following the tragic death of his young family, was calm and uneventful. But in his operas, he expressed through his characters the extremes of turmoil, passion and despair.

In the 'Requiem', Verdi deals with the themes of living and dying with the same immediacy and splendour as 'Aida'. It has a sublime passion, expressed in its soaring *cantabile* themes and its violent harmonic and *tonal* oppositions, and in its intense and glittering orchestration. The essence of both the 'Requiem' and of Verdi's final masterpiece, 'Otello, is the opposition of life and death (Mellers 1957, p. 219).

Late-Verdi:

In Verdi's final phase, consisting of two operas, he gave expression to his lifelong love of Shakespeare. In 'Otello' (1887), Verdi's great sense of theatre reached a remarkable level of dramatic sophistication. Verdi and Boito were both fascinated by the character of Iago, Verdi at one point considering calling the opera 'Iago'. Because opera hasn't the space that spoken drama has to allow such an elusive character to unfold his nature, Iago declares his true colours in his monologue 'Credo in un Dio Crudel' ('I Believe in a Cruel God'). These words are at first set as an impassioned declamation similar to the most dramatic kind of accompanied *recitative* with strong orchestral interjections accentuating the baritone in the upper reaches of his vocal range. This enhanced declamation then assumes a melodic regularity as Iago's 'articles of disbelief' (starting with the word 'credo'—'I believe') receive the same *head-motive* in a *chromatically* rising sequence. The entire monologue is bound together with subtly recurring instrumental themes, especially by a sixteenth-note triplet *figure* which in the initial scenes of Act II is as prominent in the orchestra as Iago's personality is on the stage.

If there was one principle governing nineteenth-century opera, it was a striving for continuity. The former succession of aria and *recitative* had provided a convenient vehicle for alternate action and reflection, but the shifting *textures* and *tempos* of events were in large part governed by operatic convention, not by the needs of the developing drama. This became less and less acceptable to nineteenth century composers for whom realism (*verismo*) became their highest ideal. In his later operas, Verdi worked systematically towards a continuous musical fabric whose changing *textures* responded to the dramatic objective at hand.

The first two scenes of Act III of 'Otello' illustrate Verdi's consummate skill in handling theatrical complexity. His task was to provide music expressing the shifting emotions and attitudes of the main characters—Iago's cunning and unscrupulous ambition, Otello's intensifying suspicion and rage, Desdemona's innocence, bewilderment and final terror. For the second, crucial scene of Act III, Verdi has created music perfectly geared to the shifting sentiments of the characters: Otello's volatile anger and erratic moods are subtly expressed in the 'movement between *arioso* singing and emotionally charged declamation' (Plantinga 1984, p. 321).

Perhaps the most remarkable, and most Shakespearean, quality about 'Otello' is its restraint. And maybe his wildest music is the opening storm scene or Otello's hysterical *arioso*. But the ultimate climax lies in the eternal tranquillity of 'The Willow Song' and 'Ave Maria', and in Otello's unaccompanied sob, 'Come sei pallida, e muta e bella'. There is a marked difference between 'Tristan' where an external cruel fate consigns the guilty lovers to mutual doom; in 'Otello', Otello and Desdemona had the option of life but human frailty destroyed their love and their lives.

Verdi's musical language in 'Otello' reveals an enrichment of his earlier style. He uses inventive *diatonic* procedures and *chromatic* elements that seem at home in the late nineteenth century. Even harmonically stable songs such as Desdemona's melody 'Io Prego' is subjected to *chromatic* inflection rare in Verdi before 'Aida'. However, Verdi rightly rejected allegations of Wagnerism ascribed to his late operas. His elaborations of the inherited *tonal* language are more decorative than substantive and his music retains the outlines of regular tempo. His orchestra, though important, never acquires the dominant role it plays in Wagner's music dramas. His operas focus on human dramatic characters who develop and are revealed through singing.

This was also true of Verdi's final masterpiece, 'Falstaff' (1893). Verdi brings his mature powers to bear on a work that is in the finest traditions of the *opera buffa* of Mozart and Rossini. It concludes with a bubbling fugue to the words 'Tutto nel Mondo e Burla' ('All the World's a Joke'). He concludes his career with a scintillating display of musical virtuosity, as vigorous and dramatically incisive as ever characterised his work (Plantinga 1984, p. 323).

The Italian operatic tradition had decayed, but Verdi's genius renewed and surpassed the past. Verdi had the most profound understanding of theatre, one open to the great mass of spectators. His music is always sensitive to the needs of the drama and plot, not in the manner of Wagner with his elaborate network of *leitmotivs* but in a spontaneous manner that fits dramatically and expresses a feeling for a *phrase* rather than the literal text.

Verdi's methods are usually simple and direct, always making a real dramatic impact. He was a fighter, politically as well as artistically, and his taste for conflict, which generally involved an element of amorous passion, inspired some of his loftiest music. The directness of his music also means it does not feature the symbolism present in Wagner. Verdi fears neither convention nor theatrical excess, but at the same time, he succeeds in grasping those conventions of Italian opera and sublimating them into the highest art.

Both Verdi and Wagner achieved a synthesis of music and theatre which provided vehicles for the highest flights of dramatic art. Verdi's plots perhaps lack the carefully ordered structure of Wagner's, yet they have an innate vitality that expresses both the composer's instinctive passion and his debt to Shakespeare. With Verdi, Italian opera emerged transformed but the clear heir to its monumental past and the pinnacle of an outstanding tradition. Verdi's art grew organically out of the native tradition which he inherited. He took the *bel canto* style and sculpted it into a style of great tragic expressiveness, the outstanding Italian contribution to European romantic music.

Verdi's Nationalism:

As a Romantic composer, Verdi sought to anchor his music both in his inner emotional life and in fidelity to melodic expression. But as an ardent patriot, Verdi strove to incorporate in his work the Italian musical tradition. Italy's national musical form was opera, and its medium of expression the human voice. True, he had composed a string quartet but it was a very Italian one. This is the key difference between Verdi and Wagner: though influenced by Wagner in his later works, this influence extended mainly to form, to harmonic purification and subtle orchestration.

A final word on the contrast between Wagner and Verdi: Verdi was the straightforward 'peasant', musically Italian to the core, with his direct, at times overpowering, strength, whereas Wagner, with his supreme German intellectualism, his 'Protean versatility', his 'demoniac, magical art', was a supreme German artist. '...these two were too far apart to meet on common ground' (Leichtentritt 1954, pp. 235–236).

The Janus Figure of Johannes Brahms (1833–1897)

Brahms was born in Hamburg to a musician father. At the age of twenty, he became a protégé of Robert Schumann and his pianist wife, Clara, and at twenty-nine, he moved to Vienna where he spent the rest of his uneventful life.

Brahms' Romantic Style

Brahms later curbed his Romantic strivings by a growing reverence for the music of the great Classical masters. It was this seemingly backwards-looking tendency that estranged him from the 'Music of the Future' (Romantic music). Nothing would have been easier than for Brahms to throw in his lot with the revolutionary party of Berlioz, Liszt and Wagner, and even to become a leading member, but even as a twenty-year-old Brahms felt that his artistic ideals beckoned him down a different path. This marked the onset of the rupture which culminated in the publication in 1860 of the manifesto against the 'Music of the Future' or the 'Neudeutsche Schule'—the 'Neo-German' school of Liszt and Wagner. This declaration of war was signed by 'traditionalists' such as Brahms and Joseph Joachim, the great violinist, splitting German music into two hostile camps for roughly thirty years.

Brahms was the driving force of this countercurrent to the 'Music of the Future.' For him, the extreme tendencies of Romantic music had to be opposed: the history of German music in the second half of the nineteenth century may, therefore, be summarised in this opposition: Wagner v Brahms. For decades, militant Wagnerians fought a fierce battle for their champion's sole glory, scorning Brahms as the epitome of bourgeois complacency. There was also a less brassy campaign supporting Brahms. Eventually, around 1900, the clamour abated and music lovers discovered that it was unnecessary for enthusiasts of Wagner and Brahms to be mutually hostile—the music of both are outstanding achievements, which complement each other. Brahms himself remained aloof from the conflict, 'expressing profound admiration for the mature Wagner' (Scholes 1970, p. 125).

Brahms was both a Classical and a Romantic composer. He established the balance between Beethoven, the Classical composer who built the pathway to Romanticism, and Schumann, the Romantic who tried unsuccessfully to be Classical. As a conservative, he favoured order and strict form. But his character was contradictory, influenced by his readings of the German Romantic writers and poets who fostered a dreamy, imaginative side to his nature. Hence his work, while mainly couched in Classical forms, is Romantic in spirit. So Brahms borrows Classical forms for use as a basis but which he then moulds to suit his own creative goals. His *sonatas*, symphonies and concertos adhere to the traditional style established by Beethoven while enlarging their scope. Instead of the usual two themes, the *allegro* movements of his *sonatas* often consist of as many as three or four, while his variations have unprecedented breadth of vision and freedom. His slow movements are similar, while his *finales* assume the form of a *chaconne* or *rondo*. Romantic artists looked to and admired the past. Because he went further than other Romantics in clinging to conventional, Classical forms, he has been dubbed a 'posthumous' musician (Einstein 1947, pp. 149–154). The years 1862–1863 saw a major reawakening of interest in Schubert. Brahms came under his influence and the first important piece of his maturity, the powerful 'Piano Quintet in F Minor Opus 34' (1865), reveals the impact of Schubert's great 'C Major String Quintet' (Webster 1979, pp. 52–71).

In his orchestral writing, Brahms was haunted by the ghost of Beethoven. It took him twenty years to complete his First Symphony. Its fourth movement pays tribute to Beethoven with an echo of the 'Ode to Joy' from his Ninth Symphony—when first performed, Brahms' symphony was described as Beethoven's Tenth. However, Brahms subverts Beethoven's revolutionary optimism with brass themes reminiscent of Wagner in the way they conjure up German folk life.

Hence, the content of Brahms' music is infused with a deeply Romantic spirit. His symphonies and concertos, chamber, piano and vocal music have remained relevant and popular because of their emotional power. They have a melodic richness, a rhythmic vitality and a generosity that gives them the freedom to express a wide range of feelings. Brahms' music is full of tension and contrast, moving from passages of striking dramatic power, violent struggles or declamatory protests, to ones of dark, melancholy brooding. An example is his 'Third Symphony' which opens with a theme of impassioned eloquence which is then dissipated in a passage of reflective intimacy. Each of his four symphonies establishes this balance between 'outer' and 'inner' elements, between public oratory and private yearning. And despite official opposition to Wagner, there are distinct traces of his influence in Brahms' work.

In fact, Brahms has been described as a 'pathbreaker', among the first to see the complete range of present and past music as a source from which to draw upon in creating his own highly original work, an approach we find regularly in composers of the twentieth and twenty-first centuries. By introducing new features into traditional forms and attempting to meet the master composers on their own ground, he was undoubtedly pursuing a harder course than those who stamped their mark through innovation.

Associated with Brahms' *contrapuntal* mastery was his subtle handling of rhythm and *metre*, inspired by his contact with Hungarian Gypsy music. It seems that the teenager Brahms heard Romani bands playing in Hamburg. Another influence was the Hungarian violinist Eduard Remenyi whose concert Brahms had attended aged seventeen and for whom he later became an accompanist (RomArchive).

The teenage Brahms' contact with Hungarian and gypsy folk music led to 'his lifelong fascination with the irregular rhythms, triplet figures and use of *rubato*' (Sadie 1995). An example of rhythmic ambiguity is Brahms' sole 'Violin Concerto (1878). In the first movement, there is a *hemiola*. Such manipulation of rhythm and *metre* has the force it does (reminiscent of Stravinsky) precisely because there is an underlying regularity to be thwarted. Again, Brahms is expanding the boundaries of tradition (Musgrave 1985).

The Violin Concerto, modelled on Beethoven's, is full of a deep yearning for love. The orchestral exposition presents a 'Classical' series of short themes while remaining in the *tonic*; the following exposition for soloist and orchestra, *modulates* to the *dominant*. The opening bars reveal the influence of Beethoven but also Mozart. The rhythmic pattern and melodic colouring of its final movement, *all'ongarese*, drew clear inspiration from the national, folk tradition of Hungary. But there are important ways in which Brahms departs from Beethoven's concerto models. For example, the relationship of *tutti* and *solo* sections differs from the traditional approach adopted by Mozart and Beethoven. After the orchestral exposition, Brahms writes genuine *tuttis* at certain structural points, marking the endings of the second *exposition*, the *development*, and the *recapitulation*, in addition to a short one during the *development*. Mozart and Beethoven had habitually included a number of shorter *tuttis* within the second *exposition* and *recapitulation*, emphasising the comings and goings of the soloist. Brahms' texture is more continuous: the relationship between soloist and orchestra is one of interaction rather than competition. Many of his typical stylistic features can be heard in this concerto, for example, a predilection for low-lying sonorities can be heard in the opening bars of the orchestral exposition. The harmonic style of this concerto is also vintage Brahms, especially his passion for pedal points.

The D Minor Piano Concerto (1858) is the culmination of the Romanticism of Brahms' youth. He enters a new phase with a renewal of his *contrapuntal* work. Unlike most sonata composers, Brahms, a northern Protestant, had always inclined towards the use of *counterpoint*: some of the works composed at this time, such as the choral motets, were revivals of archaic styles whose harmony was infused with a personal *timbre*. Their climaxes are a series of compositions based on the static *principle of variation* (melody or harmonic sequence is stated, then repeated in the same key). The finest of these are the 'Handel Variations' of 1861. They end with a *fugue* similar to Beethoven's in his 'Hammerklavier Sonata'. Generally, Brahms' *counterpoint* is closer to Handel than to Bach despite his veneration for the latter. For example, he displays little of Bach's tension between melodic line and harmony (Mellers 1957, p. 119).

Brahms' accomplished expertise in *counterpoint* and rhythm are abundantly expressed in 'A German Requiem Opus 45' (1855–1868). The seven movements have a Lutheran character. The style is free, combining various older techniques with Brahms' own developing musical style. The chorus has the principal role, the two solo voices intervening periodically in short passages. The 'Requiem' resembled most nineteenth-century religious texts in having a certain bygone air: *contrapuntal* textures abound and at certain points, the choral writing resembles ancient 'points of imitation' (when a phrase recurs exactly as before). 'Skilfully combining various older techniques with Brahms' evolving personal style, this composition served more than other to establish him... as one of the leading composers of Europe' (Plantinga 1984, pp. 418–419).

In 1873, the success of the 'Variations on a Theme by Haydn', based on the St. Anthony Chorale theme, emboldened Brahms to finally complete his First Symphony. The shadow of Beethoven had loomed large over Brahms, but he finally freed himself from the inhibition, completing the symphony in 1876. Beethoven's influence continued to hang over the work, infusing it with his spirit, its C minor *tonality* that of Beethoven's fifth symphony. Brahms retorted angrily that 'any jackass' could see that: he knew that the spiritual heart of the tunes was quite different. Beethoven's theme is a gateway to a superior world, whereas that of Brahms is a hymn to earthly contentment: 'it is stocky, burgomaster-like, a bourgeois modification of the folk spirit' (Mellers 1957, p. 119).

Brahms' symphonic themes resemble Beethoven's mature compositions in that their changeovers gravitate towards resolution in the last movement. But whereas Beethoven, from the 'Eroica' onwards, tended to liberate his themes from harmonic tension, Brahms increases their tension. There is an undercurrent of foreboding. This basic change is much more obvious in the Third Symphony in which the first movement is constructed on a Beethovenian challenging *arpeggio* in the major key, while the final movement with themes expressing conflict and turmoil switches into minor.

This prepares us for the melancholy, poetic power of the fourth and final symphony. The opening theme leaps ambitiously up a sixth, then falls by descending thirds. The slow movement has a 'Phrygian' opening (medieval church *pre-diatonic mode* represented on the white keys of the piano from E to E) which echoes a distant, *modal* world of religious consolation. The final movement ends in the minor tonic in a spirit, not of religion but of stoicism. The music of Brahms' final years becomes both mournful and consolatory. His music is generally more mellow, but also more melancholy. The fiery *scherzos* of his youth have made way for the retrospective *allegretto*. Increasingly aware of his 'late arrival', he came to reject the 'wilfulness' of Romanticism and to hanker after the certainty he saw in the masterpieces of Beethoven, Mozart and, above all, in Bach (Einstein 1947, p. 151).

The *tone-colour* of the clarinet in the 'Clarinet Quintet', perhaps Brahms' loveliest chamber work, reveals Brahms maintaining the external form of a *sonata*, yet sharing features with the Baroque variation technique. A single elegiac tune dominates all the movements through a key scheme of Classical solemnity. 'The final sighing of the theme by the clarinet, followed by the strings' repeated minor triads are both a farewell to earthly beauty and a recognition that there is nothing else' (Mellers 1957, p. 122). Several of Brahms' final piano works invert Classical style by beginning in the major and ending in the minor. But although their mood is steadfastly mournful, nowhere else in Brahms are there so many features that anticipate the future. The irregularity of the phrases, the cross-rhythms, the counterpoints within the *figuration* often combine to create a harmonic texture which, in its linear and *tonal* relationships, is as daring as Wagner's mature work.

Brahms has been described as a man of the people because of the place occupied in his work by dances, lullabies and folk songs, all of which helped to form his Romantic musical language. But it also highlights the tragedy at the heart of Brahms' music, on the one hand, his urge to be close to the people, to unite with them, on the other, his lack of faith in and alienation from them.

Brahms has also been described as a 'Janus' figure—the Roman god who faced two ways, pointing to both past and future (Flame Tree Piano Keyboard 2015). He was steeped in the music of the past, from

Beethoven and the early Romantics back to the Renaissance and Baroque composers, both German and non-German, synthesising 'elements from their music with current Classical and folk idioms to create a unique personal style' (Burkholder et al. 2014, p. 724). His learning fused with a gift for melody and a simple, direct expression of feeling in true Romantic style so that his music appealed both to listeners who enjoyed its lyrical beauty and expressivity and to experts who admired its elegance and sophisticated craft.

There are also, however, suggestions of Modernism in his work. Schoenberg argued that 'there was as much organisational order, if not pedantry in Wagner as there was daring courage, if not even bizarre fantasy, in Brahms' (Shoenberg 1933/1947, p. 104), He identified Brahms' fondness for *motivic* saturation techniques (immersion of *motif* in a composition, keeping *motifs* below the surface or playing with their identity) his enriched harmony and exploration of remote *tonal* regions. Subsequent masters such as Mahler and Richard Strauss learned from both. Borstlap too argues that the alleged dichotomy between Brahms the 'conservative' and Wagner the 'progressive' is false, that both were 'united in the grand project of preserving, extending and personally interpreting the classical condition' (Borstlap 2014, p. 4).

The Mighty Slavophilism of Modest Mussorgsky (1839–1881)

In the nineteenth century, some composers from eastern and northern Europe were able to secure lasting places in the Classical canon (Burkholder et al. 2014, p. 744). In Russia, Tchaikovsky was the most important composer of his age, but others wrote major works. The 'Mighty Five' ('Moguchaya Kuchka')—Alexander Borodin (1833–1887), Cesar Cui (1835–1918), Mily Balakirev (1837–1910), Modest Mussorgsky (1839–1881) and Nikolay Rimski-Korsakov (1844–1908)—had in common the advancement of Russian music and opposition to Russia's musical establishment. The soil in which a national musical tradition and style embedded itself consisted of a musically gifted people and an enormously rich, regionally differentiated treasury of folk melodies and a festive liturgy emanating from Byzantine and Oriental sources.

Mussorgsky's Romantic Style

Mussorgsky is widely regarded as the most original of the Mighty Five. He saw music not as an end in itself, a subjective expression of beauty, but as a channel of communication with his fellow human beings (Hindley 1971, p. 342). His principal stage works were the operas 'Boris Godunov' (1868–1869, revised 1871–1874), based on a Pushkin play, and 'Khovanshchina' ('The Khovansky Affair', 1872–1880). The realism characteristic of nineteenth-century Russian literature is equally reflected in 'Boris Godunov', in Mussorgsky's imitation of Russian speech, in his vivid musical description of gestures, and in the stirring sound of the crowds in the choral scenes.

Mussorgsky's individual style radiates through every element of his music, as exemplified by the Coronation Scene from 'Boris Godunov'. In Boris's opening statement as the new tsar, the vocal melody closely follows the rhythm and pace of ordinary speech: nearly always syllabic, with syllables accented on strong beats, often higher and louder than the surrounding notes. 'As a result, his vocal music tends to lack lyrical melodic lines and symmetrical phrasing... He sought a melodic profile closer to Russian folk songs, which typically move in a relatively narrow range, rise at the beginning of phrases and sink to *cadences*, and often repeat one or two melodic or rhythmic motives' (Burkholder et al. 2014, p. 710).

Mussorgsky's harmony is largely *tonal*, displaying a clear sense of key, but it is nevertheless very radical with certain passages apparently more *modal* than *tonal*, and dissonances left pending or resolved in unorthodox ways. He frequently juxtaposes distantly related or coloristic harmonies, generally joined by a common tone—for example, the sequence of C minor, A flat minor and G major which include two pairings that became staples of creepy or ominous twentieth-century film music: two minor triads whose roots are a major third apart (C and A flat minor which share E flat), and a minor and major triad with a common third degree (A flat minor and G major share C flat/B). Also, the Coronation Scene's opening chords, two *dominant* seventh chords with roots a *tritone* apart (A flat and D) and two notes in common (C and G flat/F sharp), and three major *triads* related by thirds (E, C and A major) that have a common tone and are used successively to harmonise it. These kinds of chord progression reveal Mussorgsky's approach to composition, but also his familiarity with composers such as Glinka and Liszt who had used such progressions.

Another characteristic feature of both Mussorgsky and much Russian music is composition in large blocks. 'Boris Godunov' is a series of episodes held together by the central figure of the tsar. Mussorgsky condensed Pushkin's play into a series of separate tableaux in order to focus on the title character. This method is also evident in the Coronation Scene whose opening section develops the two opening 'Boris' chords, which rise up twice to a climax of intense activity. There follows a section of rapid juxtapositions in which Mussorgsky changes the *ornamentation* of *phrases* and the key every few bars. This continues until the chorus sings a folk song in C major accompanied by the first traditional harmony in the scene. He rarely uses actual folk melodies; this tune adds a realistic element, as do the bells that constantly peal, like the Moscow church bells (Burkholder et al. 2014, p. 712).

Mussorgsky also wrote two major non-operatic pieces—'Night on a Bald/Bare Mountain' (1867), a symphonic fantasy, and 'Pictures at an Exhibition' (1874), a set of piano pieces orchestrated by Ravel. 'Night on a Bare Mountain' is a tone poem inspired by Russian literary works and legend. It has also been described as a 'musical picture', 'St. John's Eve on Bald Mountain', for vocal soloists, chorus and orchestra, which Rimsky-Korsakov arranged and published five years after Mussorgsky's death. 'Pictures at an Exhibition' is a suite of ten pieces inspired by an exhibition of over four hundred works by his friend Viktor Hartmann, who shared Mussorgsky's urge to discover a new distinctively Russian artistic language. Many of the sketches seem to live up to their descriptions: the bustle of the 'Market Place in Limoges', the French-sounding style of the Tuileries music, the lumbering of the Polish oxcart in 'Bydlo' in which the *modal* construction (set in one of the old church modes rather than in a major or minor key) is 'unsettlingly similar' to that of the 'Old Castle' in 'Pictures at an Exhibition' (Plantinga 1984, p. 374).

Tchaikovsky and the 'Mighty Five' developed musical styles that were strongly personal yet also distinctly national, and at the same time suffused with Western features. They, in turn, influenced western European composers of the late nineteenth and early twentieth centuries: they were attracted to the Russian block construction, orchestral *colours*, use of *modality*, and artificial scales. In less than half a century, Russian music went from being peripheral to being a major current in Western music.

The Russian Soul of Pyotr Ilyich Tchaikovsky (1840–1893)

Tchaikovsky was the most prominent Russian composer of the nineteenth century, renowned both in his own country and throughout Europe and North America. His music synthesised his Russian heritage and Western influences: Italian opera, French ballet and German symphony and song. Apart from his symphonies, his outstanding contribution was in the field of ballet, in which he produced three masterpieces. His 'First Piano Concerto in B flat minor' (1874–1875) has perhaps become the symbol of his popularity.

Tchaikovsky was subject to bouts of depression, constantly worrying about money due to overspending. He was also troubled by the growing realisation of his homosexuality. In 1877, he attempted to escape from it through marriage to Antonina Milyukova, a financially independent woman. It proved disastrous. At the height of his fame in 1893, he conducted the premiere of his Sixth Symphony ('Pathetique') in St. Petersburg. Yet nine days later, he died of cholera, his death now thought to have been suicide as he had drunk water he knew to be contaminated.

Tchaikovsky's Romantic Style

Tchaikovsky's inclusion in the Romantic category is abundantly justified according to at least two criteria: his nationalism as evidenced by his free use of folk melodies, and secondly, his individual expressiveness. In his voluminous correspondence with his patron Nazheda von Meck, three *phrases* express his innermost character: 'I am a Russian, Russian, Russian, to the marrow of my bones'. In a second statement, he said: 'This evening I feel sad, and am shedding tears because this morning while wandering in the woods I was unable to find a single violet. What an old sniveller I am!' (Hindley 1971, p. 349).

Tchaikovsky was arguably the most Russian of the Russian composers. However, having received a Western education, he preferred Classical forms. The 'Five' composed themes in a Russian style, pouring them into a 'national mould' and giving them an exotic *colouring*. However, Tchaikovsky used authentic folk melodies but remoulded them in a Western-style. Moreover, he is the only great Russian composer to avoid all oriental influence. His aim was to synthesise the nationalist and internationalist tendencies in Russian music. He was perhaps the most genuinely Russian of all Russian composers, though having received a Western education, he preferred Classical *forms*. His main influences were Mozart whom he described as a 'musical Christ', Beethoven, Schubert, Liszt and Schumann (En-tchaikovsky-research).

Tchaikovsky is often chided for his alleged excessive post-romantic sentimentality, a charge he admitted was at times justified. He certainly opens his soul in his music, embodying one aspect of the Russian character. On the other hand, Tchaikovsky is quite capable of plumbing the depths of musical expression: the 'Trio in A Minor' (1881–1882) in memory of Anton Rubinstein is one example. The Schumanesque idea of fate constitutes the heart of Tchaikovsky's music, to the point where it becomes the narrative of his own struggle against destiny.

The forms he was instinctively drawn to were ballet and symphony, though for practical reasons he composed eight operas, two of which are masterpieces—'Eugene Onegin' (1879) and 'Queen of Spades' (1890), both based on Pushkin novels. 'Eugene Onegin' is notable for its penetration of the characters' passions and for the way many themes are generated from a germ *motive* initially announced in the orchestral prelude (Burkholder et al. 2014, p. 707).

His symphonies and concertos conform to a general pattern: a first, pessimistic movement, followed by a second—serene, gracious but sad, then a third—an *allegro* frequently in dance rhythm, finally a fourth— brimming with vitality. The 'Pathetique' is an exception insofar as the composer has written his own requiem in the guise of a peroration. His themes are expansive, decorative and distinctive, and he sometimes uses them as *Leitmotifs* in successive waves of long *crescendos* in a manner that reflects the influence of Beethoven.Tchaikovsky wrote to Nadezhda von Meck that the horn-call in the introduction to his Fourth Symphony symbolised inexorable fate. Particularly original is the cycle of keys in the first movement, based on a circle of minor thirds. Such circles of minor or major thirds were common in Russian music, reflecting the influence of Schubert and Liszt. Also expressive of Schubert's influence are the three-key *exposition* and the *recapitulation* that starts away from the *tonic* (Burkholder et al. 2014, p. 745).

Both the Fourth and Sixth symphonies triumphed after shaky starts, and they did so because Tchaikovsky met the challenge of his age, blending original ideas with traditional elements from both the Classical and national traditions to create highly individual pieces of music with broad and enduring appeal. The Sixth Symphony ('Pathetique') also contained a private programme that Tchaikovsky never spelt out but whose broad features can be gleaned from its striking sequence of movements. Beginning with a slow, sombre introduction, the ominous, impassioned first movement in B minor reveals a first theme that struggles to rise ever upwards but is then pulls down short of its goal, to be followed by a consoling, mostly *pentatonic* second theme. There follows in the development a brief quotation from the Russian Orthodox 'Requiem' which intensifies the dark, portentous mood. The second movement, in D major, is in minuet and trio form, but instead of a minuet uses a dance in 5/4 metre, one of numerous European dances from Switzerland to Russia that combine waltz rhythms with *pivot* or other *duple-metre* steps.

The dance is graceful but a B minor trio has descending gestures which suggest sorrow. The third movement in G major begins with a light *scherzando* but gradually evolves into a triumphant march as early motivic fragments blend into the main theme that achieves its definite form only on repetition towards the end. Thus far, the symphony has defined an emotional path from struggle to triumph, a pattern familiar from symphonies stretching back to Beethoven. But Tchaikovsky's 'Pathetique' recounts a different tale, ending extraordinarily with a despairing slow movement, full of sad phrases, fading away at the end over a low pulse in the strings, 'like the beating of a dying heart' (Burkholder et al. 2014, p. 745).

In the Fifth and Sixth Symphonies, Tchaikovsky reaches the height of the rhetorical expressiveness that marks much of his later music. The orchestral writing reveals an extreme dynamic range, and the building of climaxes is increased to a point bordering on hysteria. The famous 'brooding melancholy' of these works, especially the Fifth Symphony, is mainly due to his talent for exploiting darker tone *colours*.

Tchaikovsky's unexpected death nine days after the Pathetique's premiere has led some to interpret the piece biographically, linking it to his homosexuality and probable suicide, seeing it as a premonition of death, or to the recent deaths of several friends and colleagues. It is also probable that he conceived the symphony as a drama, seizing in instrumental music the 'tragic arc' of many late nineteenth-century operas in which apparent triumph ends in tragedy. In sum, Russian music owes Tchaikovsky a considerable debt for having introduced the Western musical mainstream into the Russian tradition.

The Slavonic Romanticism of Antonin Dvorak (1841–1904)

Antonin Dvorak and Bedrich Smetana (1824–1884) were the most prominent Bohemian Romantic composers whose music drew on traditions of Moravian and Bohemian folk melodies and rhythms to create a specifically Czech national idiom.

Dvorak's Romantic Style

Dvorak's earliest style, until roughly 1875, often revealed an unsophisticated dependence on classical patterns derived from Beethoven and Schubert. This appears especially true of his early chamber music, where clear, established forms are 'subject only to local disturbances' (Plantinga 1984, p. 352). For example, the 'String Quartet in A minor, Opus 16' (1874), a movement from the *tonic* to the flat *tonic* occurs through a markedly Schubertian treble *pivot tone*. Indeed, Dvorak's prolific imagination and freshness evoke Schubert, while his rustic exuberance and interest in abstract music—pure music concerned only with structure, melody, harmony and rhythm—make him Haydn's descendant. As young man, Dvorak was exposed to a new 'musical intoxicant'—Wagner. His early symphonies, especially the second in B flat (1865), reveal traces of developed orchestration clearly indebted to Wagner, but he never felt comfortable writing in this acquired idiom.

Another feature of the development of Dvorak's style was the folk music of his native Bohemia. The two sets of 'Slavonic Dances Opus 46' (1878) and Opus 72 (1886), were immediately popular and remain so. They consist of a series of contrasting sections, the first of which is a *ritornello*. They are all in 2/4 or ¾ metre; the *duple* ones characteristically move in strong even eighth-note rhythms, and those in *triple metre* often have the *hemiola* effects of the 'Furiant' (rapid and fiery Bohemian dance).

Simple *triadic* patterns (sets of three notes stacked vertically in thirds) dominate the melodies of these pieces, and these combine with their rhythmic patterns to create an appealing folk-like impression. As with Tchaikovsky, some of this music is close to actual folk songs and dances. In many other cases, only general features of folk music that Dvorak knew were assimilated into his style: their influence often appears to penetrate his music even when one cannot demonstrate specific examples. Hence, movements of symphonies or chamber works can be seen to fall into rhythmic patterns of the 'Furiant' or the melancholy 'Dumka' (originally a Slavic sung lament). And many of his melodies have a *triadic* shape, a *modal colouring* or the configurations of the 'gapped scale' (for example, the *pentatonic* scale)—all evocative of folk sources (Plantinga 1984, p. 354).

All the traditional musical forms are represented in Dvorak's abundant work. He wrote many songs, choral works and operas. His 'Stabat Mater' (1876–1877) for soloists, chorus and orchestra reveals a strong handling of these forces within a framework that is both 'international and rather conservative'. The harmonies are broadly Mendelssohnian with a considerable input of useful counterpoint, including a final fugal 'Amen'. His *cantata* 'The Spectre's Bride' (1885) and his *oratorio* 'St. Ludmila' (1886) were both written in a kind of modernised Handelian style. Beginning in the early 1870s, Dvorak worked doggedly at composing an opera. Early attempts to imitate Wagner were followed by a retrospective style of comic opera in works that were modelled on Smetana's 'Bartered Bride'. 'Dimitrij' followed in 1882, a kind of sequel to 'Boris Godunov', furnishing Dvorak with the opportunity to use his 'generalised' folk idiom in depicting the struggle between the Russian and Polish peoples. His final operas—'Kate and the Devil' (1898–1899), 'Rusalka' (1900), and 'Armida' (1902–1903)—seem to reflect again a Wagnerian ideal, with continuous music and an increasingly prominent orchestra. 'Rusalka', with a fairy-tale plot evoking E.T.A. Hoffman's 'Udine', alone made a mark outside Czechoslovakia. Its music is a fusion of folk-like melodies with full and *colourful* orchestration with a periodic nod towards Wagnerian *chromaticism* and some ornate Italianate singing, as in the second-act duet between the water spirit Rusalka and her mortal lover. But these apparently diverse elements are expertly absorbed so that they culminate in an effect of unity.

Dvorak established his reputation as a composer of the traditional large instrumental genres: the symphony, string quartet, and chamber music with piano. Interestingly, a large proportion of his most lasting works were composed during his three-year residence in New York as director of the National Conservatory of Music. Most renowned is his 'Ninth Symphony in E minor, Opus 95, 'From the New World' (1893). Its form is traditional: it has outer movements with *sonata-allegro* shapes, an episodic slow movement, and a *scherzo* and *trio*. A forceful irregularity in the first movement is the transposition of the second group of themes to G sharp/A flat major—a major third higher than expected—in the *recapitulation*. Many of the familiar melodies have a *modal* tinge, usually achieved through the use of the flat seventh in minor. (In the key of C, the flat seventh chord would be C, E, G and B flat). Sometimes, their folk-like sound is heightened with a *drone* accompaniment or a harmonisation of *root-position* sonorities.

For the Ninth Symphony, Dvorak studied Native American melodies and African-American plantation songs and spirituals, and incorporated elements of those musical idioms, including *pentatonic* melodies, syncopated rhythms, *drones* and plagal *cadences*, into his symphony. The similarity of the first theme in G major of the first movement to the spiritual 'Swing Low, Sweet Chariot' has frequently been noted.

Another acclaimed work is his 'Cello Concerto in B Minor, Opus 104', widely lauded as the finest work in its genre. It teems with beautiful melodies which, like the first one, often contain Dvorak's familiar *modal* character. The tune is especially striking when first stated by the solo cello, with its flat seventh still intact. There follows a solo part cherished by all cellists: sparkling, sonorous and instrumentally completely idiomatic. Back in Prague in 1895, Dvorak revised the last movement, substituting an extended slow *coda*, almost entirely over a *tonic* pedal, for a traditional four-bar final *cadence*. This addition gives the movement a strange shape but it constitutes an effective peroration to the whole symphony, and represents some of Dvorak's finest music (Plantinga 1984, p. 357).

Arguably, Dvorak's style was always retrospective. *Tonality* is straightforward, unburdened with *chromatic* amplification. Large-scale movements generally *modulate* to the expected keys, with surprisingly regular metric patterns which mainly fall into four-bar modules. But Dvorak's melodic inventiveness and gift for orchestral diversity, as well as his musical 'local colour', made him highly attractive to a European culture that found the daring of Wagner and disciples hard to absorb. And within Bohemia, Dvorak, like Smetana, was viewed as the authentic representative of nationalist music.

In the conflict between the Wagnerian New Germans and the Brahmsian classicals, a third group, genuine Lisztians or innovators like Smetana or Moussorgsky, wrote no more symphonies. The majority, such as Tchaikovsky and Dvorak, had a foot in both in camps. Dvorak was strongly influenced by Brahms: both attempted to marry the classical tradition, with its formal structures, to the new Romantic spirit, with its roots in folk melody and the national culture. Dvorak drew from the sources of Slavic folk dance and song just as Brahms had drawn from those of German dance and song. Dvorak was also less regionally limited than Smetana, although he still wrote *polkas, dumkas, furiants, waltzes* and *mazurkas*. And though he wrote Moravian duets and Slovak male choruses, he also wrote Slavonic Rhapsodies (Opus 45) for orchestra, which evoke the folk spirit, committed as he was to the folk songs of *all* Slavic peoples (Einstein 1947, p. 302).

PART III: SOCIAL AND POLITICAL INFLUENCES ON THE ROMANTIC STYLE

The period that forms the background to Romanticism in general was shaped by the three great revolutions of the late eighteenth and early nineteenth centuries: the American, French and industrial revolutions. The French Revolution destroyed feudalism and absolute monarchy and witnessed the seizure of political power by the wealthy but disenfranchised capitalist class. Its outbreak in 1789 inspired both the masses in France and a whole generation of European radicals to believe that the age of human liberation had arrived.

Indeed, the music of the great eighteenth-century classics Mozart, Haydn and Beethoven had charted the march of humanity to its self-emancipation. They express a universal spirit, the struggle for freedom, the aspiration to throw off the yoke of feudalism, absolute monarchy and the church—as we saw in chapter three—for example, Mozart in 'The Magic Flute', Beethoven in 'Fidelio' and his nine symphonies, most obviously the Ninth. Hence, these great Viennese classics spoke a universal musical language. Though Haydn and Mozart were Austrian, there is a sense in which they were more than Austrian composers. And Beethoven saw himself as speaking to the whole of humanity (notably in the 'Ode to Joy' in the final movement of the Ninth Symphony with its call for the 'brotherhood of man').

The bourgeois leaders of the French Revolution had led the masses to victory proclaiming on its banner 'Liberty, Equality, Fraternity'. However, when the army of the discontented petty bourgeoisie tried to put the slogan into practice, they were quickly disabused, the leaders dispelling any notion that they were ready to usher in a radical democracy. It became clear that they had mobilised the masses in order to win political power for themselves. The French bourgeoisie had flown the flag of liberty but had gone on to dash radical democratic hopes, fashioning themselves instead into the rulers of a new class society.

The rise of Napoleon, though consolidating certain progressive trends, ushered in a new despotism underpinned by the spirit of French nationalism. The autocratic monarchies and ruling classes of Europe, for example in Germany and Austria, felt threatened by Napoleon and united with Britain to defeat him. The Battle of Waterloo in 1815 heralded an era of reaction that restored or consolidated the old regimes. The policies of the post-Waterloo reaction were laid down at the Congress of Vienna in 1814–1815 dominated by the Austrian Chancellor Prince Metternich. After 1815, he did his utmost to turn the clock back and restore the old order, strengthening existing monarchies and outlawing liberal, democratic ideas, strict censorship suppressing any suggestion of a free press.

The radical hopes of a generation were destroyed. Schubert himself suffered at the hands of the Austrian political authorities: in 1820, he was arrested in the company of student rebels, held for a few days and reprimanded. He later had trouble getting his operas staged. As Einstein describes him: 'The legend of Schubert as a 'dreamer' is sheer fiction: he suffered deeply from the political oppression which prevailed in all Germany and especially in Austria after 1815...' (Einstein 1947, p. 88).

Schubert's trademark *modulation* gives powerful expression to the romantic yearning to regain the lost unity with the natural world. This is arguably the expression of a need to escape from the despotic political world of a Hapsburg-dominated Vienna, its rulers confident that they had suppressed the threatened spread of the ideals of the French revolution.

This leads us to the social background of the Romantic composer. Their training differed from that of most of their predecessors in the seventeenth or eighteenth centuries. Then, the great musicians came mostly from families of musicians, for example, the numerous members of the Bach family, Mozart and Beethoven. Handel, a surgeon's son, Gluck, a forester's, and Haydn, a wheelwright's, were exceptions. However, with the onset of the Romantic era, composers came from the wider educated middle class. Berlioz's father was a physician, Mendelssohn's family were from the enlightened Jewish circle in Berlin, Schumann's father was a bookseller, Chopin's was a private tutor, while Liszt's was an official on Prince Esterhazy's estate.

The social and political context of the new Romantic sound was the rise of individualism, the conquest over society by the bourgeoisie, a process lasting several centuries whose climax was the French Revolution. Romanticism defined itself in relation to those momentous events, the essence of which was the emancipation of the individual personality. And it was Beethoven who, announcing the new chapter in music, stood on the threshold of Romanticism.

Of course, at the start of the seventeenth century, there appeared the development of virtuosi, both vocal and instrumental, and the rise of opera, at first an extravagant decoration of princely banquets, but later, in Venice, opened to a wider public audience which appreciated music as music. If this public was at first still mainly aristocratic, there gradually emerged a bourgeois element. It was the Handel oratorio that first identified the aristocratic concert hall and the academic college as too small: new auditoriums had to be created, the clear, free secular counterparts to the dark and solemn halls of the church. In this new auditorium, the public assembled, the 'anonymous mass of people'. This was a revolution that corresponded to and reflected the great events of the time—the storming of the Bastille that sparked the profound changes that ensued—the abolition of aristocratic privilege, the political advance of the bourgeoisie, the consequent, gradual levelling of classes. 'The musical *amateur* gave way to the *citoyen* of the concert hall' (Einstein 1947, p. 14).

Mozart lived to see this development without becoming its beneficiary. 'In Austria, the traditional aristocracy on whom Mozart had depended... was severely shaken by the cataclysmic events across Europe...' (Snowman 2009, p. 100). However, he continued to compose largely for an aristocratic audience, though, as previously stressed, his music expressed the deeper social changes pervading eighteenth-century Europe. And Haydn, as we also saw, became a 'free' musician only in the final decade of his life. The real heir and beneficiary of this revolution was Beethoven who, refusing to subordinate himself to the service of his aristocratic patrons, placed them in his service. We referred in Chapter Three to the disdain with which he treated his patrons. It was unprecedented for an aristocratic circle to link up in order to guarantee a composer the freedom to compose, without obligation, and for this composer to complain if the sum of money should shrink due to inflation!

Beethoven thus set himself up as an individual facing the world, often opposing it. One example was the technical difficulty of performance. Haydn and Mozart rarely composed anything that exceeded the average technical ability of their day, but Beethoven's independent spirit created new technical problems. He didn't compose his sonatas for entertainment but as artistic documents, written not for a specific public but for an imaginary one, limited neither by social class nor national boundary. Beethoven's appeal was to humanity at large, his music possessing the power to uplift, unite and transform. In particular, works such as his late sonatas and his late quartets represent his message not to the time-bound Viennese public but to the broad swathe of humankind. Again, Beethoven drew inspiration from the democratic ideals of the French revolution.

Beethoven's antagonistic attitude towards society made him a model for the Romantic movement, one that provided a blueprint for its conception of the 'artist'. Of course, the official 'musician' who provided a service to various institutions didn't disappear—the cantor, church organist, theatre music director, operatic conductor—continued to perform official functions. But the link between such officialdom and the creative process was considerably weakened. The cantors of Leipzig's 'Thomas-Kirche' in the nineteenth century no longer wrote a cantata every week, as Bach had done. The directors of operas and concerts no longer composed their own operas and symphonies, as Handel, Gluck or Haydn had done. Berlioz was only a composer—nothing else. '…The creative musician freed himself from society; placed himself more and more in opposition to it, and he became increasingly isolated when he did not succeed in conquering it' (Einstein 1947, p. 16).

In previous centuries, the notion of misunderstood genius was unthinkable: the musician composed to order and for immediate consumption. In the eighteenth century, music was published because there was a demand for it, whereas in the nineteenth, pieces were often published in order to stimulate a desire for them. Libraries proliferate with ambitious but luckless works that gather dust as they appeal to the world. Beethoven inaugurated a period in which orchestral, instrumental and vocal music, including operas and oratorios, were written for an imaginary public or for the future. The Romantics fought against tradition, seeking originality, ascribing greater value to their work the fewer preconceptions it contained.

The Romantic era witnessed a growing split between musician and public. There is a contradiction between, on the one hand, the Romantic composer harking back enviously to the Middle Ages when music had been exalted handicraft, and, on the other, the reality of music having always been at the service of the existing ruling class—the church and the aristocracy. Before 1800, opera had been the preserve of the higher nobility, and a little later—in Venice—of the aristocracy and their guests;

but in the late eighteenth century, it was opened up to the bourgeoisie. Furthermore, certain kinds of instrumental music—the earliest
symphonies and string quartets—long remained the prerogative of the
nobility. Eventually, however, these compositions were also played in
the concert halls of Paris and London to bourgeois audiences. With
Beethoven, matters changed: his symphonies served neither the aristocracy nor the bourgeoisie nor the new petty bourgeoisie but humanity.

The Romantic composers felt painfully this gulf that separated them
from their audience. This gap first became apparent with Schubert,
who distinguished between works composed for his circle of friends and
genuine music lovers, and those he wrote for 'success' in the concert
hall. This clash, and resulting isolation, was felt by all the Romantic
composers, but most vehemently by Berlioz and Wagner. Berlioz wrote
virtually no intimate works, and the more powerful the music that he
launched, the better he felt. 'He could not wait... till the appropriate
mass of people found their way to him; he had to conquer them'. With
Wagner, artistic 'force' was needed to bridge the gap between his highly
subjective, radically new *sonority*, and a sceptical public without whom
opera is impossible.

It is a further contradiction of the Romantic era that though it placed
a premium on the emancipation of the individual artist, isolated from
his society, yet it also fostered a link with nationalism. Of course, before
1800, music had developed within national currents, but these flowed
within a common, transnational stream; for example, fifteenth-century
polyphony, generally described as Burgundian. Similarly, Gluck was born in
the Upper Palatinate, but his operatic style was both Italian and French.
As we saw, Haydn and Mozart were both Austrian but their work has a
supra-national, universal character.

Before 1800, a strong national flavour was expressed only in the
work of composers whose music failed to reach the heights of Haydn or
Mozart. Nevertheless, Austrian local *colour* is stronger in Haydn than in
Mozart, whose horizons reach out to a more cosmopolitan world. There
are some Austrian features in Mozart, but if we compare their *minuets*,
a rustic tone characterises those of Haydn while Mozart's conjure up
the world of the Hapsburg cultivated upper class (Leichtentritt 1954,
pp. 202–203).

Romanticism ushered in a much sharper national profile. The men's
choruses in Weber's 'Freischutz' (1821) have a distinctly nationalistic

colouring. Berlioz revealed more strongly than his predecessors an inclination to be descriptive—a traditional French predilection. And, of course, Verdi and Wagner, in their different ways, gave operatic voice to powerful nationalistic aspirations. Romanticism expressed the nationalist longings of many peoples—Russians, Bohemians (Czechs), Hungarians, Poles, Danes, Norwegians, Swedes, Finns—until the movement wound down either because of success through national liberation struggles or national unification, or else because of the culmination of nationalist rivalry in World War One.

An essential aspect of this turn to nationalism was the importance assumed by the folk song, not seen since the classic era of the German folk song in the sixteenth century. In Russia, Poland, Hungary, Bohemia, Norway, it became the heart of the new national art that helped to define the European Romantic movement. Composers like Chopin, Glinka, Rimsky-Korsakoff, Moussorgsky, Smetana, Dvorak, Grieg and Nielsen underline just how strong the influence of the folk song became in the nineteenth century. Previously it had been a provincial dialect, a folklore idiom of characteristic features but narrow scope; in the Romantic era, 'this nationally limited folklore expanded into a well-developed language and assumed a style, form and content that made it interesting to the musical world at large' (Leichtentritt 1954, p. 215).

The French, with their revolutionary tradition, wasted little time before launching a fresh rebellion, and the brief revolution of 1830 marks the initial wave of the powerful French Romantic movement. Arriving much later than its German counterpart, French Romanticism was from the outset enmeshed with the practical spirit of revolt, drawing inspiration from the post-1789 yearning for freedom. Interestingly, the outbreak of revolution in Belgium in 1830, which culminated in Belgian independence from Holland, was sparked by a performance of Auber's opera 'La Muette de Portici' (Leichtentritt 1954, p. 207; Einstein 1947, p. 42). Paris in the early 1830s was permeated by a Romantic aura expressed in the work of writers such as Victor Hugo, Alfred de Musset and Lamartine.

During the nineteenth century, the position and role of music changed radically as a result of the far-reaching changes in political and economic conditions and also the technical revolution. Music became a more democratic affair, mainly supported by the bourgeoisie and maintained by their commercial success. Public concerts and opera houses, symphony orchestras, quartet societies, piano and song recitals, oratorio choruses, and music festivals were achievements of the nineteenth century, which also witnessed increased ease of travel, the rise of daily journalism containing musical criticism. Moreover, a huge increase in the number of books and music printed, and the crucial rise of mass education, enabled millions of working-class people to appreciate art and music, previously impossible.

Beethoven rejected the Classical emphasis on the ancient Greek values of structural elegance and harmonious proportions. His great symphonies aspired to appeal to the heroic, to inspire the great moral deed. And in the Romantic era, bourgeois listeners demanded of music a new, arousing effect. Indeed, the bourgeois era which succeeded the Napoleonic wars looked to art as a substitute for heroic achievement. This era also witnessed the 1848 revolution which saw Wagner help defend the barricades at Dresden. His operas, however, give expression to a burgeoning German nationalism that derives its inspiration from the heroic tales of medieval folklore and ascribes to love the power to overcome the corrupt old ruling class. And in Verdi's operas, there is perhaps an even more direct link to the struggle for national liberation and unification.

The 'man' of the sixteenth, seventeenth and eighteenth centuries had looked to music for exaltation and enrichment. However, the rooms of the aristocratic families then fell silent. In the Victorian age, the new commercial and industrial bourgeoisie sought in music 'a more passionate, a more heightened reflection, to experience in art'. The music lover sought new excitement or relaxation in the concert hall or opera house following a hard day's work. By the time of the Romantic generation, listeners demanded that they be 'transported': music became for them 'a substitute for life' (Einstein 1947, pp. 43–44).

Around 1800, the relationship of the musician to society underwent a major change. Up to the end of the eighteenth century, even the greatest composers knew their place, that they were the servants of the rich and powerful. The first employer was the church, followed by the aristocracy, finally the rising bourgeoisie. 'Free' music didn't exist, any more than an architect designs a building for his or her personal satisfaction. Even music apparently arising purely from the creative well of the composer reveals itself on examination to have been commissioned work. Of course, it was musicians who created music, but within certain institutional limits, and, of course, in response to more profound social and economic processes. In the nineteenth century, music became commodified, musicians transformed into individuals dependent upon a market. But with Romanticism, music became a protest against the bourgeois transformation of society.

In France, the government of Louis Philippe, elevated to power following the July 1830 revolution, commissioned Berlioz to write a symphony for the tenth anniversary. The result was the 'Grande Symphonie Funebre et Triomphale', his last symphony and one written entirely for a large wind band, expressing perhaps strife and unrest (Zinn, online 2015). Berlioz was largely apolitical, and neither supported nor opposed the *July Revolution* of 1830. However, 'Symphonie Fantastique' was composed in 1830. Although it purports to tell the tale of an artist in despair through unrequited love, it has many turbulent passages that seem to express more than personal anguish, reflecting an era of renewed turmoil and conflict, witness of the collapse of the post-1815 Bourbon Restoration. Furthermore, the fourth movement expresses a powerful triumphalist mood, as though celebrating victory against the prevailing state power.

Berlioz's 'Requiem' was composed in 1837, commissioned by the French government 'on the day of the annual service commemorating the dead of the 1830 revolution' (Berlioz 1969, p. 229). The Restoration had restored the close ties between monarchy and clergy that had existed prior to the 1789 revolution. However, between 1815 and 1830, the great mass of the French people continued to reveal a strong antipathy towards the church. This was intensified by a newly enacted law that punished by death 'the profanation of the sacred vessels'. In addition, the government wished to honour the memory of General Damremont, killed during the capture of Constantine in Algeria. Berlioz omitted from the 'Requiem' the traditional 'Dies Irae' hymn. Now according to the Gregorian tradition, this hymn used in funerals would have represented a direct link to the clergy and, therefore, the state. However, even though Berlioz's 'Requiem' was commissioned to uphold the state, after the 1830 Revolution the state had changed and was no longer closely allied with the church as it had been under the Bourbons. 'The lack of the "Dies Irae" embodies a decision not to tie the ceremony to either the Church or state-sponsored religion' (Nemeth 2016, p. 1). Its inclusion might have been seen 'as a direct tie to the now-unfavourable Church and Monarchy' (Nemeth 2016, p. 6).

However, the Romantics' disappointment would have been magnified by the results of the 1830 revolution. It differed greatly from its 1789 forerunner: firstly, it was confined to Paris with the peasantry almost completely absent; secondly, its results were modest: they included the revision of Louis XVIII's constitution so as to abolish the hereditary element in the Chamber of Peers; the removal of the claim that sovereignty rested solely with the monarch; the abolition of the king's right to suspend or block laws; extension of the right to propose legislation to both Chambers; the abolition of censorship and the downgrading of Catholicism from the official religion of the state to 'the religion of the majority of Frenchmen'. The criteria for election candidates were lowered as were the electoral qualifications, doubling the size of the electorate, though it still included no more than 5% of the population (Evans 2017, p. 66).

Mendelssohn's light aerial music can be interpreted, like Weber's, as a kind of paean to an imagined lost world of unity with nature. It too hankers after an ideal community based on harmony, peace and goodwill. Also, his 'Symphony No. 5 in D' (in reality his second—the Reformation)—was written in 1830, in honour of the 300th anniversary of the Augsburg Confession, one of the vital documents of the Protestant Reformation which paved the way for the acceptance of non-Catholic Christian denominations. The fourth movement uses the Lutheran hymn 'Ein Feste ist unser Gott' ('A Might Fortress is Our God'). Although not a revolution in the modern sense, the Augsburg event created a novel landscape for religious expression. It resulted from the social and economic transformation—the emergence of mercantile capitalism—carried out by the rising bourgeoisie. His 'Songs Without Words' would also seem to express the longing for the historical past that preceded the arrival of industrial capitalism with its thirst for profit, its elevation of the values of success and materialism above the human values of 'Liberty, Equality, Fraternity', the heart of the Romantic vision.

Following the French revolution, ghetto walls were torn down and Jews were expected to forgo their Jewish identity in exchange for the privileges of full European citizenship. Many European Jews, including Mendelssohn's family, converted to Christianity during this time. However, the old conservative circles in Europe, beholden to the reactionary policies of the Church and the aristocracy, were hostile to the new winds of freedom extended to assimilated Jews, who had penetrated the academic and commercial life of Europe and in whom they saw the French enemy. When the converted Jews hoped to be accepted as full-fledged Christians with their Jewish pasts forgotten, they were soon shocked by the emergence of antisemitism, which made being of 'pure race', not religion, the criterion for acceptance in Christian society (GDT

2015, Felix Mendelssohn—The JewishQuestion, www.diaryofamadinva
lid.blogspot.com/2015/04/felix-mendelssohn). Again, Mendelssohn's
'String Quartet No. 1 in E Flat Major' has Jewish-sounding themes, especially in the first movement which echoes the 'Kol Nidre' prayer melody.
In the last year of his life, he composed two biblically inspired *oratorios*—'Elijah' and 'Christus'—reflecting the Old Testament of his Jewish
heritage and the New Testament of his family's adopted Protestant faith.
Was he attempting to reconcile the two parts of his identity? Was it also
a musical statement of resistance to the prevalent antisemitism? (*Felix
Mendelssohn and Jewish Identity* in Library of Congress).

After Prussia's defeat to the French at the Battle of Jena in 1806,
'reforms' were carried out. In 1807, serfdom was abolished, but since
peasants could not afford the compensation payments, formal freedom
meant little. The principal beneficiaries were actually the nobility, Prussian aristocrats retaining civil jurisdiction over their former serfs until
1848. Some political modernisation took place, but Prussia remained
without a constitution or parliament. The political impact of the French
revolution was profound, but the Napoleonic Wars in general retarded
economic development except in the Rhenish provinces under the French
administration.

Germany in 1815 was a very different place from the Germany of
1648 when the Thirty Years' War ended. Outwardly, it was not very
different: 'a still largely agricultural, a land of villages, undulating pastures
and deep forests, of medieval towns and castles, princely palaces, majestic
churches and monasteries' (Fulbrook 1992, p. 104). This is the Germany
of Weber's music, with its evocation of the sounds and moods of nature
and its dark forests.

The Romantic movement in literature, music and painting was thus a
protest against capitalism, against a society that placed profit above human
needs and values. In Britain, the movement was born in the 1790s as a
reaction against the eighteenth-century Enlightenment—the philosophy
of the bourgeois revolution. In France, Germany and Austria, it was similarly an outcry against the new harshly materialistic world but received a
boost from the disappointment after 1815 of the hopes for radical democratic change. The contradictions inherent in Romanticism found extreme
expression in the revolutionary upheaval of which the American War of
Independence was the 'prologue' and Waterloo the 'final act'. But at each
turning point, the movement split into progressive and reactionary trends

(Fischer 1963, pp. 54–55). And of course, the revolutionary upheaval continued in 1830 and 1848.

In May 1832, around 30,000 people gathered at the Hambach Festival to voice their demands for a liberal, unified Germany, for freedom of the press, for the lifting of feudal burdens, for religious tolerance and for the proclamation of a republic. But there was no consensus on a strategy purporting to implement such a political programme.

However, the predominant political tendency continued to be a reactionary conservatism. The reaction to the social unrest sparked off by the French July Revolution of 1830, and the popular political mobilisation expressed in the Hambach Festival, was Metternich's revival in 1832 of the repressive Karlsbad Decrees. Harsh censorship was imposed and a commission established at Mainz to investigate all student societies for subversives together with an additional Six Articles forbidding political rallies and associations. Measures were also taken against the excessive use of state Diets' powers.

However, important social and economic changes were creating pressures and tensions which ultimately no political repression could suppress. Changes in social relations, in patterns of production, and in the political organisation of economic life merged with rapid population expansion to amount to the onset of a radical transformation of German society. From the 1830s, capitalist relations of production were replacing feudal social relations, laying the basis of a powerful industrial society.

At the same time, the growth of pauperism alongside the complacency of 'Biedermeier' bourgeois society (a repressive, patriarchal apolitical and ascetic, sentimental work ethos) gave rise to growing concern, as expressed in the charitable activities of the churches. A huge increase in population, much of it rural, coupled with the insufficient food supply of a still pre-industrial economy led to food riots and emigration to the towns and to America. The new working class also attempted to take matters into their own hands: in 1844, the Silesian weavers, adversely affected by the competition of the more advanced British textile industry, and also the introduction of new production methods at home, rose in revolt (Fulbrook 1992, p. 115).

Romanticism thus expressed the desolation of the generation caught up in the new industrial capitalism with its ceaseless change, its individualism, anonymity and materialism. The individual had been torn from traditional village and extended family life. Atomised by the new, intensifying division of labour, he or she faced the industrial juggernaut alone, their personal, social and economic life fragmented. The Romantics all shared a hostility to capitalism, and a belief in the validity of individual passion as opposed to the well-ordered rational bourgeois world. As Fischer puts it: 'And as the relativity of all values was made increasingly clear by capitalist production methods, so passion - intensity of experience – became increasingly an absolute value' (Fischer 1963, p. 55).

We see this elevation of the individual human personality in Wagner's music drama, a 'deification of the ego' (Mellers 1957, p. 180). Opera becomes a substitute for religion in ego deification as exemplified in the Wagner cult which resulted in the construction of his own operatic temple at Bayreuth. Closely associated with the elevation of the individual was the emphasis on the expressive content of music, music as the voice of subjectivism. Again, Wagner's forged his operas as vehicles for the outpouring of his passions.

Moreover, we saw how 'Wotan's Farewell' in 'Die Walkure' (p. 45) begins and ends in E, but also how the music explores that key's possible relationships, moving tortuously through a succession of keys before ending in the *tonic*. This perhaps expresses the struggle of the individual searching for an escape route from the twin juggernauts of the developing industrial capitalist machine and the Prussian, soon to be German, state as it gathered increasing powers into its hands following the defeat of the 1848 revolution. Wagner's use of the *Leitmotif* surely also represents an affirmation of the individual squaring up to increasingly uncontrollable social, economic and political forces.

However, Bernard Shaw offered a socialist interpretation of the 'The Ring' and the struggle between the gods and the giants on the one side, and the Nibelungs on the other, as 'a poetic vision of unregulated industrial capitalism as it was made known in Germany in the middle of the nineteenth century by Engels's "Condition of the Labouring Classes in England"' (Shaw 2008, p. 13). The gods are the ruling class who must die so that the new society can be born.

The tendency of Romanticism to escape from the sober drudgery of everyday life into the fantasy world of the imagination was bolstered by political events. The liberal, democratic upsurge of the European countries against Napoleon's dictatorship didn't last. After his defeats and exile, a wave of reaction swept across Europe, extinguishing every spark of the fight for Liberty. The nationalist upturn enveloping Germany and Austria and expressed in the War of Liberation was forcibly diverted into Romantic literature. Despotic governments could suppress political movements but they were helpless in the face of the creative imagination. So, Lord Byron's practical involvement in the Greek struggle for national liberation from Turkish rule in 1821 captured the imagination of the Romantic generation. The Polish fighters for national independence against Russian oppression conjured up an aura of Romantic glamour, especially in Paris where Frederic Chopin and the poet Adam Mickiewicz led a distinguished cast of Polish exiles.

Chopin's music is full of the sadness permeating his life following the defeat of the Polish uprising in 1830. Among the numerous examples are the 'A Minor Prelude Opus 28', two 'Nocturnes, in G Minor, Opus 15, No. 3' and in 'D Flat Major, Opus 27, No. 2', and the 'Mazurka in A Minor, Opus 17, No. 4'. But also anger: it was Schumann who stressed Chopin's 'strong, original nationality' in discussing his two concertos. 'If the powerful, autocratic monarch in the north (the czar) knew how in Chopin's compositions, in the simple melodies of the *mazurkas*, a dangerous enemy threatens him, he would forbid the music. Beneath the flowers in Chopin's work there are hidden canons' (Einstein 1947, p. 217).

Paris also hosted two prominent composers, Meyerbeer and Halevy, who, along with Mendelssohn form a trio of significant Jewish musicians, a sign of the emancipatory spirit that was a product of the Enlightenment but also of Romanticism. However, on the opposite side to this tolerant cosmopolitanism, Wagner later helped to initiate a new wave of antisemitism.

But the Romantic revolt also proclaimed its support for the national liberation struggles of their people. This, in turn, as we saw, led to the glorification of their past, their folk history and traditions, with contradictory results: Wagner's immersion in medieval German folklore and iconography and Verdi's support for Italian national unification and liberation.

Wagner was swept along in the swirling current of radical revival that culminated in the European-wide 1848 revolution. As we saw, he took part in the Dresden uprising. Later, his work developed in the context of the German national movement dominated by Prussia which culminated in German unification in 1871. 'The Ring' and 'Parsifal' clearly reflect the inspiration of German medieval mythology. Writer Johann Gottfried von Herder emphasised the role of folklore in ethnic nationalism—the folklore of Germany as a nation rather the disunited German-speaking peoples.

Secondly, Verdi. In the wake of the Napoleonic wars, Italy was divided into a patchwork of kingdoms and duchies. As a radical and fervent adherent of liberal nationalism, Verdi, in the course of a fifty-year career, gave brilliant musical expression to Italian nationalist aspirations. Indeed, he was widely perceived as a figurehead for the unification movement (the 'Risorgimento') and became a member of the first national parliament in 1861. His nationalism was expressed practically—in his love of the countryside, in his commitment to the peasant community and in his work as landlord and parliamentarian; musically, it was expressed in his reverence for the musical traditions of Italy and in the fact that many of his tunes became assimilated into popular tradition.

Furthermore, in the years leading up to the 1848 revolutions, opera in Italy had become a focus of dissent, with opera houses flashpoints for political unrest. In Verdi's early phase, the late 1830s and the 1840s, many of his other operas can be interpreted as allegories for the Italian struggle against the Austrians and other foreign oppressors. Buoyed by the enormous success of 'Nabucco', Verdi wrote thirteen operas in eight years, several of which profoundly stirred popular nationalist consciousness. In 1847, a near riot was sparked off by a performance of 'I Lombardi'.

As a radical, Verdi was also staunchly anti-clerical and republican, though he compromised on the latter by conceding to those who argued that the best prospect for unification lay in accepting Vittorio Emanuele, the liberal King of Piedmont, as the monarch of a united Italy. In his lifetime, Verdi was an immensely popular figure. 'Viva Verdi' became a national rallying cry, his name being an acronym of 'Vittorio Emanuele Re d'Italia' (King of Italy). But he remained proud of his humble peasant origins. When King Vittorio Emanuele offered to ennoble him, he replied 'I am a peasant'. Verdi wanted to speak to the masses, not to an elite.

Verdi's middle period expressed his hopes that a future unified kingdom would overcome the vestiges of feudalism and usher in a new era of democracy. As we saw, the defeat of the 1848 revolutions led initially to Verdi's preoccupation with personal issues. But the 'Risorgimento' recovered. And its wider context was the growing success of the Italian movement of independence from Austria and the latter's defeat at the hands of Prussia in 1866. The 'Risorgimento' finally triumphed in 1871.

However, 'Aida', with its joint suicide of the doomed lovers, also conveys the opposite message, that our common humanity transcends our national identity. Furthermore, during the nineteenth century, Europe and North America were enthralled by all things foreign and exotic. The Suez Canal, despite being a symbol of European imperialism, linked West and East, creating a bridge potentially uniting the peoples of Europe, Africa and Asia. Verdi the radical arguably had the imagination to visualise this.

Romanticism was a gigantic leap forward, leading to 'the wild and the exotic, to limitless horizons: but... also to one's own people, one's own past...' On the positive side, Romanticism was both a means for liberating the human personality from medieval bondage and a source of political inspiration. 'The bourgeois-democratic revolution... flashed like distant lightning through the works of the Romantic artists of Russia, Hungary and Poland' (Fischer 1963, pp. 55/56).

The 1840s were a decade of growing economic hardship for the broad European masses. In 1846, a disastrous crop failure and potato blight plunged the European economy into depression. Huge numbers of desperate, starving people flocked to the towns. Artisans were rendered destitute as their incomes were slashed just as food prices soared. The crisis of the late 1840s was also a crisis of industrialisation. The centres of the 1848 upheaval were all in areas hurt by British industrial competition, which was undercutting continental manufactures. An even broader revolutionary wave, sparked off yet again in Paris, engulfed almost the whole of Europe. Capital cities in Europe were the fulcrum of revolution in 1848, but they were also major centres of industry. Here the formation of a new working class was developing apace. The spread of industry and capitalist institutions meant that economic distress affected the whole of Europe, not just isolated areas. The French revolution of 1848 was paralleled by similar upheavals elsewhere.

The 1848 revolution which first exploded in Paris (though the first rumblings occurred in Milan and Sicily) sparked off similar risings right across Europe, spreading to Poland, Germany and the Hapsburg Empire, receiving the accolade 'Springtime of the Peoples'. The uprising enjoyed initial success with French King Louis Philippe resigning and the Second Republic proclaimed. In Austria, Chancellor Metternich was forced to resign. In Mannheim, an 'Assembly of the People' from Baden demanded a bill of rights. Similar resolutions were adopted in other areas. These movements received strong popular support: 'in the face of widespread peasants' insurrections, artisans' riots and liberal pressures, rulers all over Germany rapidly made concessions...' (Fulbrook 1992, p. 118). The liberals then attempted to use the volatile situation to carry out national changes—the election of a national parliament to discuss constitutional reform and German unification.

However, the German revolutionary forces had clear weaknesses: an external spark was required to ignite the movement; forces with different objectives were exerting pressure on the regimes; and the authorities capitulated almost without defence. However, the conservative forces were able to observe the confusion and failings of the revolutionary groups, and to return later to take control of the situation with their armed forces preserved and even strengthened by conceding to peasant demands. All over Germany in 1848–1849, shaken rulers reasserted control, sometimes assisted by Prussian troops.

In Paris, rural voters, alarmed by new land taxes levied to fund National Workshops set up to assist 100,000 destitute workers, returned a Constituent Assembly dominated by conservatives and moderates. Hundreds of demonstrators, including many employees of the workshops, invaded the National Workshops in protest. The Executive Commission closed down the workshops, generating outrage amongst workers and precipitating demonstrations demanding work. Workers built barricades shouting 'Death or Liberty'. The vast majority of the National Guard refused General Cavaignac's order to mobilise, with many defecting to the insurgents. But Cavaignac turned his artillery on the barricades, with around 1500 insurgents killed, 2500 wounded and 11,727 arrested. The June events in Paris had a major resonance throughout Europe, 'emboldening moderate liberals and diehard conservatives alike and bringing them closer together in a shared fear of the masses' (Evans 2017, p. 201).

However, class anatagonisms were not the sole rock on which the ship of Revolution was wrecked. Already in the 1840s, rival nationalisms were beginning to rub up against one another. This was especially so in east-central Europe, where the revolutions in Berlin and Vienna gave a strong impetus to movements for national autonomy and unity. These movements in turn were to have a strong impact on the further development of the revolutions in Germany and Austria, opening up massive contradictions between liberalism and nationalism and giving conservatives and reactionaries the opportunity to regain the initiative. In Hungary, rival nationalisms such as that of the Croats emerged as a counterweight to Magyar nationalists seeking to impose their language as dominant.

The revolutions were essentially bourgeois-democratic and liberal, aimed at removing the old monarchical structures and creating independent nation states. Over fifty countries were affected. The central demands were for more participation in government, press freedom, workers' employment rights and national liberation demands. The uprisings were led by unstable coalitions of middle-class and working-class reformers. Many were quickly suppressed, with tens of thousands killed. But there were lasting gains, including the abolition of serfdom in the Hapsburg Empire, the end of absolute monarchy in Denmark, and the introduction of representative democracy in the Netherlands. The most significant revolutions occurred in France, the Netherlands, the states of the German confederation, forerunner of the German Empire of 1890, Italy and Austria. In France, following the defeat of the 1848 revolution, moderate liberals sought a figure who would 'maintain order while preserving the political achievements of the revolution' (Evans 2017, p. 215). They found one in Napoleon's nephew, Louis-Napoleon Bonaparte, who won a landslide victory in the elections of December 1848 against the unpopular Cavaignac, then in 1851 arrested his opponents and dissolved the Assembly. In 1851 and 1852, two plebiscites approved his actions and his inauguration as French Emperor Napoleon III.

Schumann revealed his ambivalence towards the revolution. He explained to the musician Ferdinand Hillier the strange way his creativity had been inspired by the revolutionary fighting in 1849: 'this has been my most fruitful year – as if the outer storms have driven me more into myself. Thus I've found a counterweight against the terrible things which broke in from the outside'. Without expressing support for the uprisings, he expressed a certain appreciation of them. On the other hand, in 1847, before the March revolution, he wrote three songs for the 'Liedertafel' on 'nationalist-democratic texts'. And during and after the revolutionary events in Dresden in 1849, he composed the 'Four Marches, Opus 76', writing to his publisher: 'You receive herewith some marches – not the old Dessauer type—but rather, republican… they have been written with fiery enthusiasm' (Dennis 1998, pp. 8–9).

Arguably, Schumann's eminently personal style—the deep feelings of sadness, yearning and joy—link the private and public, expressing the need both for private happiness and for public liberty. Schumann's 'Waldszenen'—'Forest Scenes', composed in 1848–1849, expresses for the first time an interest in nature or landscapes, themes in which he had not previously shown any interest (see p. 36). The piece seems to depict the forest as a place of refuge, expressing the Romantics' urge for the restoration of

a lost unity with nature. Could he have composed it as an act of consolation, moved by the loss of hope in a democratic revival engendered by
the defeat of the 1848 revolutions?

Liszt wrote his symphonic poem 'Hungaria' in 1854. One of the most
typical sections is a funeral march. Liszt evidently sought to symbolise
both the defeat of Lajos Kossuth's revolt in the Hungarian Revolution of
1848, and to express the hope that one day the Hungarian people would
liberate their country (Searle in Walker 1970, pp. 297–298).

Berlioz's *Les Troyens* was composed between 1856 and 1858. It is
often regarded as the summation of his musical career. As we saw, it
reveals to the full his talent for expressive, pictorial music. The opera
dramatises the capture and destruction of Troy by the Greeks through the
deception of the Trojan Horse, shattering Trojan celebration of apparent
deliverance from ten years of siege. The broad sweep of dramatic action,
from Cassandra's warnings to the doomed love of Dido and Aeneas
in Carthage disclose Berlioz's gift for pictorial, expressive music while
scenes such as the Royal Hunt and Storm are reminiscent of Weber's
'Wolfsschluct'—'Wolf's Glen' and 'Garden' scenes.

Cassandra's aria defiantly mocking the Greek soldiers followed by the
chorus of the Trojan women's mass suicide features music that combines
drama with Romantic tragedy. The first half of the opera has been
described as 'noble and grand', whereas the second part, set in Carthage,
is said to be lyrical and sensuous. In particular, the heartrending scene of
Aeneas's abandonment of Dido and her suicide is expressed in a ghostly
descending *chromatic* line. 'Les Troyens' arguably expresses the tragic
spirit flowing from the defeat of the 1848 revolutions, the 'Springtime
of the Peoples' having been followed by a harsh winter of dictatorship.

In 1863, the 'apolitical' Berlioz addressed a cheering crowd welcoming
him as he crossed a railway bridge into Germany on his way to a banquet
in his honour in the German town opposite Strasbourg. 'Under the influence of music... civilisation progresses and national enmities disappear.
See, today, how France and Germany are conjoined. Love of art has
united them, and that noble love will do more for their total unification than even this marvellous bridge across the Rhine...' (Bloom, Yale,
October 2003, pp. 19–38). Perhaps Berlioz was harking back, no doubt
unconsciously, to the hopes of 1848 despite the impending defeat of the
Paris Commune at the hands of Thiers' bourgeois government followed
by the Franco-Prussian war of 1870–1871.

As for Russian music, in 1861, Tsar Alexander II signed the decree emancipating the serfs. It was part of a strategy to modernise Russia and catch up with western Europe. There were two main approaches to this modernisation: the nationalists or 'slavophiles' idealised Russia's cultural distinctiveness. They believed that Russian civilisation was unique and superior to Western culture because it was based on such institutions as the Orthodox Eastern Church, the village community, or 'mir', and the ancient popular assembly, the 'zemsky sobor'. They also favoured emancipation of the serfs and freedom of speech and of the press. However, they became increasingly nationalistic, many ardently supporting Pan-Slavism after Russia's defeat in the Crimean War (1854–1856). The 'Westerners' believed that Russia's development depended on the harnessing of Western technology and the adoption of liberal government and education. Culturally, they were rationalistic and often agnostic rather than emotional and mystical. Tchaikovsky reflects this division but transcends it with his unique synthesis, combining Western Classical forms with traditional Russian music, including folksongs.

We also saw how a key feature of the Romantic musical style was the rejection of the Classical forms and the assertion of a new freedom to express the deepest states of individual feeling. This is a characteristic that unites composers such as Chopin and Schumann. In Wagner's late style, as developed in 'The Ring', Tristan, 'Meistersinger' and 'Parsifal', his 'will power is responsible for the fact that he forced this most highly personal, thoroughly subjective *tonal* language on his period as the general expression of its feeling' (Einstein 1947, p. 254).

Romanticism thus sprang from the longing for a new social unity to overcome the isolation of the individual lost in the unfamiliar cold and inhospitable world of powerful market forces. It was in part backwards-looking, idealising the community of medieval feudalism, with its imagined harmony and security, before capitalism dislocated traditional, collective social relations (Fischer 1963, pp. 54, 56–57). Again, Brahms' 'Violin Concerto' and sixteen 'Waltzes for Four Hands, Opus 39', 'show traces of nostalgia for a vanished happiness' (Einstein 1947, p. 154).

The idea of a 'stable ordered society... coloured with heraldry, surrounded by the shadowy mystery of fairy-tale forests and canopied by the unquestioned Christian heavens, was the obvious lost paradise of the conservative opponents of bourgeois society, whose tastes for piety, loyalty and a minimum of literacy among the lower orders of the French revolution had only sharpened' (Hobsbawm 1962, p. 312). Edmund Burke's philosophy first developed this anti-bourgeois conservatism. However, this idea of the 'lost harmony of primitive man' found its Classical expression in Germany, a country which in this period acquired a kind of monopoly of the medieval dream. Hobsbawm suggests this was because the 'Gemuetlichkeit' (charm) that reigned beneath those Rhine-castles and Black Forest eaves lent itself more easily to idealisation than the real cruelty and filth of genuinely medieval countries. In sum, medievalism was a stronger component of German Romanticism than of any other, radiating outwards from Germany. And in the general form of a Gothic revival, 'medievalism was the badge of the conservative and especially the religious anti-bourgeois everywhere' (Hobsbawm 1962, p. 312).

The German Romantics were thus disgusted by the figure of the bourgeois capitalist and the new society he was creating. But they couldn't yet see in an embryonic working class any alternative. Lacking hope for a better future, they harked back to the pre-capitalist past. Wagner's operas, of course, are full of German medieval mythology and the declamatory style of most of his overtures and principal arias express the epic tales, the knightly gallantry and chivalry of his heroes. However, 'despite its invocation of the Middle Ages, Romanticism was an eminently bourgeois movement...' (Fischer 1963, pp. 56–57).

This aspect of Romanticism expressed essentially the contradictory attitudes of the petty bourgeoisie, on the hand aspiring to share in the enrichment of the big bourgeoisie, on the other, fearful of being crushed in the process. They dreamt of new horizons yet clung to the old traditions, looking back nostalgically to the old certainties. This urge to recreate the old community also led to a growing preoccupation with the culture of 'the people' and the glorification of folk art. In order to overcome the widespread sense of isolation and instability, Romantic artists endowed 'the people' with an almost mystical unity. Thus, many Romantic composers cultivated the folk song, seeing it as coming from the 'womb' of the nation.

As we saw, prior to the nineteenth century, the greater the composer, the less tied they were to national musical traditions. However, the nineteenth century witnessed intensifying attempts by all European capitalist classes to create independent nation states and national markets, sparking off movements for national unification and the liberation of oppressed nations. Against this background, interest in folk music emerged. Hence, musical Romanticism witnessed the rise of national schools of music which inspired the various nationalist movements.

Brahms also became steeped in Hungarian Roma music, fascinated by its irregular rhythms. 1848 was the year of European-wide revolutions, among which was the suppressed Hungarian uprising against the Austrian and Russian armies. A flood of refugees passed through Hamburg on their way to America as a result of which Brahms developed a great love of Hungarian folk, particularly Roma, music (Bozarth 2019, pp. 168–169). This is also revealed in the 'happy endings' of several major works, where a mood of sadness is suddenly lifted and he abandons himself to 'revelry with the people'. This is again the spirit conveyed in the concluding section of both the 'Violin Concerto' and the 'Second Piano Concerto in B Flat'.

In the second half of the nineteenth century, nationalism gathered pace, becoming a powerful force in instrumental music, song, opera and choral music. National flavour was valued as evidence of a composer's authenticity and distinctive voice. Ethnicity mattered more than political boundaries; in the multinational Austrian Empire, composers increasingly identified with their ethnicity rather than with the imperial state, so that German-speaking composers such as Brahms tended to identify with an all-embracing German tradition wherever they lived.

Hence, Brahms found inspiration in Schutz, Bach, Beethoven, and other German forebears, but he also arranged German folk songs and modelled some melodies on them. And if he tended to increase his themes' harmonic tension in contrast to Beethoven who preferred to liberate them, this again perhaps reflected the deepening tension at the heart of nineteenth-century Europe. Finally, Brahms voices resignation, as expressed in the last movement of his Third Symphony, whose themes are transformed into conflict and turmoil, as though humanity is hurtling towards catastrophe while remaining helpless.

Brahms' quiescence or stasis doubtless reflects the difference between the Classical (and aspiring bourgeois) preoccupation with the possibility of changing the social and political world and the Romantic retreat into individual self-absorption and a desire to recapture an imagined lost pre-capitalist paradise. This hankering after a lost world of harmony and community morphed into disillusion at the usurpation of power by the minority who had become the beneficiaries of revolutionary change in the first half of the nineteenth century.

Moreover, Brahms' pessimism about human destiny, his scepticism about the possibilities of radical social change, was shaped by several historical factors. He came to artistic maturity in the wake of the defeat of the 1848 revolutions. The following twenty-five years were the age of capital, of liberal bourgeois supremacy with its apparently unbounded material progress. Though the great depression of 1873–1896 made a dent in bourgeois confidence, the last twenty-five years of his life remained a period of ruling class ascendancy in continental Europe following the defeat of the Paris Commune in 1871. Also, his thirty-five years of residence in Vienna were spent at the heart of a decaying Austro-Hungarian empire. We thus see an interesting contradiction at the heart of Brahms' work. While looking to the past, he also captures the essence of his age, the relentless march of bourgeois materialism with its corrosion of human solidarity. And the traces of modernism referred to earlier anticipate the upheavals, dislocation and disillusion of the twentieth century. At opposite ends of the Romantic time spectrum, Schubert and Brahms, in their different ways, express the search for love and community in a world dominated by the bourgeoisie.

Dvorak's Slavonic Dances, derived from Czech folk music, also express the Czech national spirit, aspiring to break free of Hapsburg Empire despotism. The librettos of eight out of his nine operas were similarly in Czech. During his residence in the United States, his strong affinity with Native American and African-American music, led him to believe that they should become the foundation of future American music.

So Romanticism, as Fischer argued, was a "movement of protest... passionate and contradictory... against the bourgeois, capitalist world, the world of 'lost illusions', against the harsh prose of business and profit' (Fischer 1963, p. 52). It was a musical protest that grew out of the disappointment at the failure of the successive revolutions—1789, 1830, 1848—to usher in a world based on the values that had inspired the great French Revolution. It expressed that disappointment and a yearning to return to an idealised lost world. The later Romanticism dug deep into national, folk traditions, adapting themes and idioms of the past in order to help carve out a new future for their people, one that would witness their liberation from oppression, both foreign and indigenous.

In conclusion, the bourgeoisie liberated music from its confinement within the church and the aristocratic salon but incarcerated it instead within the prison of the marketplace (Behrman 2009, pp. 121–142). The Romantic style represented a revolt against that imprisonment.

BIBLIOGRAPHY

Arblaster, Anthony. 1992. *Viva La Liberta: Politics in Opera*. London: Verso.
Behrman, Simon. 2009. From Revolution to Irrelevance: How Classical Music Lost Its Relevance. *International Socialism Journal*, 121, January 2009.
Berlioz, Hector. 1969. *Memoirs*, ed. and trans. David Cairns. New York: Alfred Knopf.
Blanning, Tim. 2010. *The Romantic Revolution*. London: Weidenfeld & Nicolson.
Bloom, Peter. 2003. *Berlioz: Reflections on a Nonpolitical Man*, vol. 78, nos. 1/2. Yale University Library Gazette (October 2003).
Borstlap, John. 2014. *Brahms the Progressive?* (30, May). http://johnborstlap.com/brahms-the-progressive.
Bozarth, George S. 2019. *Folk Music*. In *Brahms in Context*, ed. Natasha Loges. Cambridge: Cambridge University Press
Budden, Julian. 1984. *The Operas of Verdi*, vols. 1, 2, & 3, 3rd ed. London: Cassell.
Burkholder, J.P., D.J. Grout, and C.V. Palisca. 2014. *A History of Western Music*. New York and London: W. W. Norton.
Chusid, Martin. 1997. Towards an Understanding of Verdi's Middle Period. In *Verdi's Middle Period, 1849 to 1859*, ed. Chusid. Chicago: University of Chicago Press.
Conway, David. 2012. *Jewry in Music: Entry to the Profession from the Enlightenment to Richard Wagner*. Cambridge: Cambridge University Press.
Dennis, David B. 1998. *Robert Schumann and the German Revolution of 1848*, for *'Music and Revolution'* concert and lecture series. Loyola University History: Faculty Publications and Other Works, Chicago, 5-2-1998.
Einstein, Alfred. 1947. *Music in the Romantic Era: A History of Musical Thought in the 19th Century*. New York: W. W. Norton.
Evans, Richard. 2017. *The Pursuit of Power: Europe, 1815–1914*. London: Penguin Books.
Felix Mendelssohn and Jewish Identity in Library of Congress.
Fischer, Ernst. 1963. *The Necessity of Art*. London: Penguin Books.
Flame Tree Piano Keyboard. 2015. Piano and Keyboard Music. *Biography: Johannes Brahms*.
Fulbrook, Mary. 1992. *A Concise History of Germany*. Cambridge: Cambridge University Press.
G.D.T. 2015. *Critical Thinking: Felix Mendelssohn—The Jewish Question*. www.diaryofamadinvalid.blogspot.com/2015/04/felix-mendelssohn. Posted by GDT, 27/4/2015.
Glenn, Stanley. 2008. *Parsifal: Redemption and Kuntsreligion*. In *The Cambridge Companion to Wagner*, ed. Thomas Grey. Cambridge: Cambridge University Press.

Grey, Thomas S., ed. 2008. *The Cambridge Companion to Wagner*. Cambridge: Cambridge University Press.

Hauser, Arnold. 1962. *The Social History of Art, Volume Three: Rococo, Classicism and Romanticism*. London: Routledge & Kegan Paul.

Hindley, Geoffrey, ed. 1971. *The Larousse Encyclopedia of Music*. London: Hamlyn Publishing Group.

Hobsbawm, Eric. 1962. *The Age of Revolution: 1783–1815*. London and New York: World Publishing Company & George Weidenfeld & Nicolson Ltd.

Jones, J. Barrie. 1998. *Nationalism*. In *The Cambridge Companion to the Piano*, ed. David Rowland. Cambridge: Cambridge University Press.

Katz, Jacob. 1986. *The Darker Side of Genius: Wagner's Antisemitism*. Hanover and London: Brandeis University Press.

Kimbell, David R.B. 1981. *Verdi in the Age of Italian Romanticism*. Cambridge: Cambridge University Press.

Leichtentritt, Hugo. 1954. *Music, History and Ideas*. Cambridge, MA: Harvard University Press.

Mellers, Wilfred. 1957. *The Sonata Principle From C. 1750*. London: Rockliff.

Millington, Barry. Undated. *Walkure Die*. In The New Grove Dictionary of Opera, ed. Stanley Sadie. Oxford Music Online.

Musgrave, Michael. 1985. *The Music of Brahms*. London: Routledge.

Nemeth, S. 2016. *Restoration, Revolution, and Reaction* in *Berlioz's Requiem: Berlioz's Requiem as a Product of the French Outlook on Religion and Romantic Ideals*. The College of New Jersey Journal of Student Scholarship XVIII, April 2016.

Phillips-Matz, Mary Jane. 1993. *Verdi: A Biography*. Oxford: Oxford University Press.

Plantinga, Leon. 1984. *Romantic Music: A History of Musican Style in Nineteenth Century Europe*. New York: W. W. Norton.

Puffett, Derrick. 1984. *Siegfried in the Context of Wagner's Operatic Writing*, in *Siegfried: Opera Guide 28*, ed. Nicholas John. London: John Calder Ltd.

Reiss, Jozef, and Maurice Brown. 1980. *Polonaise* in *The New Grove Dictionary of Music and Musicians*, ed. Stanley Sadie, 20 vols. London: Macmillan.

RomArchive—Brahms and the Roma.

Rosen, Charles. 1996. *The Romantic Generation*. London: HarperCollins.

Sadie, Stanley, ed. 1995. *Brahms*. In *The New Grove Dictionary of Music*. Oxford: Oxford University Press.

Schultz, H. 1930. *Johann Vesque von Puttlingen*, Regensburg, p. 256, in Einstein, 1947, p. 187.

Schoenberg, Arnold. 1933/1947. *Brahms, the Progressive* (friedfoo.wordpress.com/music/brahms).

Schoenberg, Arnold. 1948. *Structural Functions of Harmony*. London: Faber.

Scholes, Percy A. 1970. *Oxford Companon to Music*. London: Oxford University Press.

Searle, Humphrey. 1970. *The Orchestral Works*. In *Franz Liszt: The Man and His Music*, ed. Alan Walker. New York: Taplinger Publishing Company.

Shaw, Bernard. 2008. *The Perfect Wagnerite*. Arc Manor (Originally published 1898).

Snowman, Daniel. 2009. *The Gilded Stage: A Social History of Opera*. London: Atlantic Books.

Taruskin, Richard. 2010. *The Oxford History of Western Music, Vol. 3. Music in the Nineteenth Century*. New York: Oxford University Press.

Temperley, Nicholas. 1980. Chopin, Fryderyk Franciszek. In *The New Grove Dictionary of Music and Musicians*, vol. 4, ed. S. Sadie. London: Macmillan.

Webster, James. 1979. Schubert's Sonata Form and Brahms' First Maturity. *19th Century Music* 3 (1): 52–63.

Weiner, Marc A. 1995. *Richard Wagner and the Antisemitic Imagination*. University of Nebraska Press. Lincoln NB and London.

Zinn, Joshua. 2015. *Revolution 10: Music About Revolution and Protest*. www.houstonpublicmedia.org/articles, 3/7/2015.

CHAPTER 5

The Modernist Styles

PART I

Twentieth century or modern Classical music refers to orchestral or solo instrumental works, chamber music, electronic music and choral music. It includes traditional forms such as operas, ballets, songs, symphonies and concertos, and also *fantasies, fugues, rhapsodies, passacaglias, chaconnes, oratorios, cantatas, suites*, improvisational and newly developed formal concepts such as variable and mobile forms that have been composed since 1900 or the late nineteenth century.

This era did not produce a dominant style and composers have created highly diverse sorts of music. Post-Romanticism, impressionism and innovatory styles such as atonality, serialism, neo-classicism, expressionism, musique concrete and minimalism, have all been important movements. Moreover, jazz was an important influence on many composers during this time. European music was transformed by three strands of Modernism in the late nineteenth and early twentieth century: Debussy's 'Impressionism', the *atonal* music developed by Schoenberg and his leading followers, Webern and Berg, and the revolutionary rhythms of Stravinsky.

The emergence of a universally popular Classical repertoire in the nineteenth century cast a powerful shadow over the composers of the late nineteenth and twentieth centuries. Concert halls and opera houses were dominated by older, established music regarded as deserving of repeated

© The Author(s) 2021
S. Sagall, *MUSIC and CAPITALISM,*
Critical Political Theory and Radical Practice,
https://doi.org/10.1057/978-1-137-52095-1_5

performance, leaving less space for new work. Modernist composers confronted the same challenge—how to guarantee a place in a crowded field through music that offered something new but which audiences, critics and musicians would accept as high-quality work justifying a place alongside the classics of the past.

A related problem facing composers from the early twentieth century on was how to preserve the traditions of the past so beloved of performers and audiences while venturing down fresh paths so as to develop styles that would give musical expression to the new, fast-changing reality. Different solutions offered themselves: applying established practices to new styles, reinterpreting customary elements, combining the features of different periods, or altering the balance of the prevailing musical conventions. Each of these strategies offered listeners something familiar to grasp while suggesting new and more challenging experiences.

Modernist composers therefore faced common problems and responded with decisively individual solutions, differing in what they valued most strongly in the Classical tradition, what they amplified, what they rejected, and what innovations they introduced. Most continued to compose *tonal* music but many wrote 'post-*tonal*' music. Some composers can be described not as Modernist but as 'avant-garde', wanting to jettison the traditions inherited from the past. We refer here to the 'avant-garde' movement that challenged the entire Classical tradition. The term, used by the French army to describe an advance group that prepared the ground for the main troops, was then adopted in the mid-nineteenth century by French artists to refer to any artist or composer who departed from tradition. The term is thus often applied to Arnold Schoenberg, but it is also usefully employed more narrowly to describe art that is 'iconoclastic, irreverent, antagonistic, and nihilistic' (Burkholder et al. 2014, pp. 779, 808). Music in the Classical tradition, therefore, became stylistically increasingly diverse, a process that intensified during the twentieth century.

So when does the modern era begin? The strongest candidate is the year 1907 when Schoenberg finally broke with the system of traditional *tonality* that had dominated European music since the late seventeenth century. For over two hundred years, a consensus had reigned about the musical language in which Western music had to be composed, the rules that composers had to follow. Suddenly, that consensus was broken, particularly striking in Schoenberg but visible in the music of all the major young composers of the first decade of the new century. After two hundred years of relative agreement about compositional issues, Western music was suddenly offered radically new possibilities.

However, traditional *tonality* didn't collapse all at once. The nineteenth century had witnessed a gradual weakening of its dominance, together with corresponding changes in the aesthetic of composition. Any attempt to understand twentieth-century music must consider its relationship to these earlier developments out of which it emerged, partly as their extension, partly as a set of fresh departures. The transition from nineteenth-century Romanticism to twentieth-century Modernism was the result of developments that unfolded gradually, and it is not entirely clear when these processes reached a critical stage at which it can be said that music had definitively entered a new era.

Wagner's revolution was basically harmonic, but it used harmony as a weapon to strike at every element of music: melody, rhythm, form and, less directly, *timbre*. Harmony is defined by key or *tonality*, and in simple melodies, there is a 'homing device' which ensures that it ends on the same note on which it began; for example, God Save the Queen. In eighteenth and nineteenth-century music, the character of harmony is derived from its relationship to the *tonic* chord of the home key; and in turn, as we saw in earlier chapters, it is harmony that enables that key to be changed through *modulation*. In Baroque music, *tonality* is fundamentally stable; the early Classical composers, up to Haydn, use *modulation* more liberally, although main sections still tend to be in one key, with *modulation* occurring at certain critical points. Later, *modulation* became more pervasive, for example, with Schubert's *development* sections, where *tonality* is most fluid. Wagner marks the climax of this development. In sections of 'Tristan und Isolde' (1859), *modulation* is so continuous as to eliminate all sense of key. Significantly, Wagner effects this in opera, where form is partly determined by extramusical factors. In sum, *tonality* is so basic to Classical form that no composer would have embraced Wagner's innovations. Brahms and Bruckner, Wagner's greatest contemporary symphonists, only did so superficially, whereas Liszt, Wagner's close disciple, used extramusical 'programmes' in his symphonic poems to fill the gap left by traditional *tonality*.

Melody, which can both shape and be shaped by harmony, became similarly more *chromatic*. Rhythm in the Classical style was largely governed by the *cadential* movement—the sequence of chords moving to a harmonic point of rest or completion through *modulation*. But it,

too, was now at risk of losing its distinct character. Wagner's successors confronted this reality with trepidation. For a while, the music
of Gustav Mahler, Richard Strauss and Alexander Scriabin created an
unstable balance between inspiration and collapse. Then at the turn of
the century, the crisis reached a climax as the embodiment of radical
innovation burst on the scene in the shape of Arnold Schoenberg.

However, if modern music can be said to have a beginning or perhaps
a prercursor, then the leading candidate is Debussy's 'Prelude a l'Apres-
Midi d'un Faune', composed in 1894. A major feature of modern music is
its lack of dependence on the *diatonic* system which had been 'composers'
compass' since the seventeenth century. Not that Debussy's 'Prelude' is
atonal or keyless, just that it gently extricates itself from music's roots in
the diatonic system, asserting that the traditional harmonic relationships
are no longer binding (Griffiths 1978, p. 7).

What is *atonality*? Its heart is the semitone—the distance between two
adjacent keys on a piano. When struck together, they create a rough
sound that irritates the ear. Similar roughness is created by the major
seventh, slightly narrower than an *octave*, and by the minor ninth, slightly
wider. These are the exact intervals between notes that Schoenberg
stresses in his music (Ross 2012, p. 61).

The work of Mahler, Strauss, Debussy and Ravel illustrate the search
by the first generation of modernist composers for a style that drew on
what was important in the past and was also faithful to their national identity. Examining the work of certain key composers from various Western
nations enables us to grasp this interaction between national culture,
Romanticism and personal style. For example, Russia is represented by
Rachmaninoff and Scriabin, Spain by Albeniz, Granados and Falla, Britain
by Vaughan Williams, Walton and Holst, Eastern and Northern Europe
by Janacek and Sibelius. Unfortunately, lack of space precludes detailed
analysis of most of these undoubtedly important figures. This study
will concentrate on those who pioneered the most significant Modernist
styles.

In sum, the word 'Modernism' has been used to signify different
approaches. Some writers confine the term to 'avant-garde' composers
who completely reject the musical traditions of the past, breaking radically
from it in order to create a new language. Other writers use the term to
refer to the complete range of composers from the late nineteenth century
including those who sought to create music that respected past traditions

while marking out fresh paths. This chapter attempts to deal with representatives of both approaches. The important, criss-crossing debates on Modernism between Theodor Adorno, Walter Benjamin, Ernst Bloch, Bertolt Brecht and Georg Lukacs, from the 1930s to the 1950s are beyond the scope of this book (see 'Aethetics and Politics', Verso 1977, and Eugene Lunn, 'Marxism and Modernism', Verso 1985).

A key but unfortunate feature of modern music has been the split between composer and audience. Increasingly in the twentieth century, 'art' music has come to be seen as the preserve of an artistic and intellectual elite, divorced from the ordinary music-loving public—in the eighteenth century the nobility or rising bourgeoisie who would have engaged the services of musicians—and in the later nineteenth and twentieth centuries, the educated middle class who increasingly attended concerts or bought records (Behrman 2009, pp. 121–142).

Two German-speaking composers born in the 1860s represent the important bridge from late Romanticism to Modernism. Although they reached maturity under the persistently powerful influence of nineteenth-century musical ideals, yet they made significant contributions to the radical stylistic changes of the early modern period. The challenge confronting them was the all-powerful Austro-Germanic musical heritage that they sought both to embrace and to transcend. As with Brahms, they needed to compose for audiences whose tastes were shaped by the Classical repertoire, to create music that combined familiarity and innovation. Mahler and Strauss were transitional figures who created new music by transforming what they inherited from the past. By the end of their lives, they were composing music that was quintessentially of the twentieth century—unlike several of their contemporaries, for example, Elgar, Rachmaninov—who remained immersed in the late Romanticism of their national traditions. Composers were expected to write music that expressed their national traditions and identity, that drew on regional traditions, but which also enabled them to develop an individual style synthesising old and new, local and international influences.

Part II

Composers

The Modernist 'Angst' of Gustav Mahler (1860–1911)

Mahler was arguably the last major link in the chain of Austro-Germanic composers that ran from Haydn and Mozart through Beethoven and Schubert to Brahms, Bruckner and Mahler himself. Mahler owed this tradition a considerable debt and he pursued and brought to a climax many of its most characteristic features.

Mahler's Modernist Style

Mahler's tendency towards ever-increasing length and ever-larger orchestral forces—features building up throughout the history of the symphony—evolved to a point in his work beyond which further development seemed both impractical and unnecessary. A lyrical quality, first introduced into the symphony by Schubert and Bruckner, pervades his work even more emphatically. Three of the first four symphonies contain a vocal element, an indication both of a strong lyrical tendency and a debt to Beethoven's Ninth Symphony. Mahler the symphonist is inseparable from Mahler the composer of songs.

Ever-larger compositions reveal a powerful new conception of the expressive potential of symphonic music. A propensity, apparent even in Mahler's earlier compositions, to constant variation, continually evolving new ideas out of old ones, was refined with ever-increasing technical assurance. Linked to this was his essentially *polyphonic* approach to *texture*, influenced by Bach whom he greatly admired. He created *textures* with truly melodic strands, creating a rich nexus of diverse, subtle correlations.

Mahler built on Beethoven's notion of the symphony as a fearless personal declaration observing that to compose a symphony was 'to construct a world' (Burkholder et al. 2014, p. 784). His symphonies often feel like a lived experience, such as in a story or pictorial scene. He created the impression of events occurring in a complex world, using different styles to create ideas, themes or natural images, for example, in the slow introduction to his first symphony when the strings softly sustain the note A in seven *octaves* to produce an effect of space, interlaced at times with ideas from other instruments—clarinets sounding hunting horns, a trumpet fanfare, a cuckoo call, a romantic horn tune in parallel thirds—the sounds of human life and nature. Here and elsewhere, he drew on the styles and rhythms of Austrian folk songs and dances, using them to respond to his urban audience's nostalgia for rural scenes and less complex times. There is a clear affinity here with the Romantic style. Apart from size, Mahler revealed considerable imagination in the manner in which he combined the instruments, achieving effects from highly delicate to gigantic. Often only a few instruments are playing as he constructs many diverse chamber-orchestra groupings from his vast reservoir of sounds. Mahler was one of the earliest composers to see music as an art not only of notes but of sound itself, an approach that became more customary during the twentieth century.

As part of Mahler's wish to depict aspects of the world, his symphonies often express a programme Romantic style. His Fifth, Sixth and Seventh symphonies (1901–1905) contain pictorial material and items borrowed from his songs, suggesting that he had extramusical ideas in mind similar to those in Beethoven's Third and Fifth Symphonies. Hence, Mahler's Fifth proceeds from a funereal opening march to triumph in the *scherzo* and an exultant *finale*. The Sixth is his 'tragic' symphony with a *finale* in which heroic struggle seems to culminate in defeat and death. The Ninth, Mahler's last completed symphony (1991), evoking a mood of resignation blended with bitter satire, is a strange and sorrowful farewell to life.

Mahler's approach can be seen in his popular Fourth Symphony in which each movement is very different from the rest, inflating the contrasts in a traditional four-movement symphony, as though reflecting the world's variety. The piece begins in G major and ends in E major, an indication that life's vicissitudes do not always bring us back home. The first movement revisits the late eighteenth-century symphony through references to Haydn and Mozart and by contrasting sonata-style forms with Romantic-style forms. The exposition has an even greater number and variety of clearly articulated themes. He introduces surprises and deceptions reminiscent of Classic-style wit such as sudden *sforzandos*, *dynamic* contrasts and harmonic twists.

The second theme recalls a Romantic song, introduced in the cellos followed by the horn, two essentially Romantic instruments. The development is fantasy-like and tonally ambitious, a romantic outburst in a classic setting, with Mahler illustrating how the two styles can be merged in a single movement. When themes are reassigned to different instruments and recombined in novel ways, they sound 'ironic and self-parodying, suggesting a feverish dream in which remembered images pop up from the subconscious in strange and distorted guises' (Burkholder et al. 2014,

p. 785). The effect is as though the rationalism of the Enlightenment had been displaced by the irrational dreams analysed by Sigmund Freud. The *recapitulation* restores rational lucidity but it is impossible to return to the opening innocence: the movement achieves balance by embracing all its possibilities as opposed to attempting to resolve all its potential conflicts. This is perhaps 'a musical metaphor for the trade-offs demanded of us by the complexities and inconsistencies of modern life. This way this movement interweaves Romantic fantasy and modern style with references to a Classical past is typical of the way Modernist music blends elements of the past and present into something new and distinctive. There is a close affinity with the paintings of Mahler's fellow Viennese, Gustav Klimt...'

In 'Kindertotenlieder' (1901–1904), an orchestral song cycle on poems by Friedrich Ruckert, Mahler's characteristic post-Wagnerian harmony intensifies the emotion and drama by bold contrasts between consonance and dissonance and between *diatonicism* and *chromaticism*. Slender *textures* create an effect of restraint, ironic for a song about the death of a child. The irony is sometimes deepened by an emotional incongruity between text and music: the opening line, 'Now will the sun shine so brightly', is sung to a sad, descending D minor melody, while the following phrase rises *chromatically* to a cheerful D major on the words 'as if no misfortune occurred during the night' (Burkholder et al. 2014, p. 786).

'Das Lied von der Erde'—'Song of the Earth' (1908) competes with the Ninth Symphony as Mahler's crowning late work. He described it as a 'symphony for a tenor voice and an alto or baritone voice and orchestra', its six movements alternating between two soloists. The texts, translated from Chinese poems, express visions of earthly beauty and transience in verses which 'alternate between frenzied grasping at the dreamlike whirl of life and sad resignation at having to part from all its joys and beauties'. Mahler here summoned the orchestra to uphold and reinforce the singers, both in accompaniment and in extensive linking interludes, just as he summoned the human voice in his symphonies to round off his musical ideas with words. The exotic atmosphere of the words is hinted at by instrumental colour and the use of the *pentatonic* scale. It is Mahler's work in which he most precisely expressed and balanced the two extremes of his personality—ecstasy and terminal foreboding.

Mahler's mature compositions express an ambivalence and ambiguity that sound modern in character, most obviously in the area of harmony and tonal relationships. Yet the music appears 'conservative' in that there is far less *chromaticism* than in contemporary works by composers such as Strauss, or even in Wagner's later operas. *Dominant* relationships continue to play a crucial structural role. There are moments of amazing audacity (such as chords built in fourths in the Seventh Symphony and dissonant *polychordal* combinations in the Sixth). While the harmonic language remains mostly unremarkable, *tonality* also seems to be approaching its final stage of dissolution: entire works, and even individual movements, no longer inevitably inhabit a single key but roam through a range of related and interlinked keys, often concluding in a different key from that in which they began.

A striking example is the 'Ninth Symphony' because of the distance of the keys: the first movement is in D major, the fourth and final in D flat major. The third movement mediates between the two: 'Such procedures alter the very meaning of tonality, which becomes a complex network of interchangeable relationships, rather than a closed system that ultimately pulls in a single, uncontested direction' (Morgan 1991, p. 22).

These *tonal* procedures flow from Mahler's innovative conception of musical form as a succession of individual episodes, bound together by these kinds of *tonal* links and by a sophisticated system of *motivic* correlations. Although he sticks to traditional forms, at least superficially, in most of his compositions, for example, sonata forms, the actual dynamics of the formal process are very different. In the traditional Classical form, there is a balance between connecting sections that have definite functional relationships to one another—whether the section is *expositional, transitional or developmental*. Mahler, however, offers a pattern of sudden oppositions between formal units that differ radically in both nature and structure. A key feature of Mahler is the high level of disjunction and juxtaposition, of fast criss-crossing back and forth between sharply contrasting and often apparently unrelated ideas. The notion of *recapitulation*, a cornerstone of the Classical form, also acquires a new meaning. Musical sections do recur but are always transformed through the process of perpetual variation that permeates all Mahler's mature compositions.

The effect of endless flux and corresponding loss of constancy, of a firm, unchanging foundation, goes far in explaining the revolutionary impact of Mahler's music on his contemporaries. Whereas Classical music was based on a closed system of musical features and relationships, able to accommodate a limited range of themes and forms, Mahler's open conception allowed him to incorporate elements whose sharp contrasts would destroy the internal coherence of more traditional music. Mahler's musical world is highly inclusive, creating space for music of a popular, even 'vulgar', type, a notable departure from the more limited content of earlier art music. Music reminiscent of popular dances and folk songs connects with bugle calls, marches and grotesque parodies to create what seems like a collage-like jumble, 'a juxtaposition of discordant qualities made possible by a more episodic approach to form' (Morgan 1991, p. 23). Mahler's epic structures display the most divergent musical material.

As one of the leading conductors of his time, Mahler acquired a unique knowledge of orchestral technique and the potential for instrumental combinations. His enlargement and use of the orchestra constitutes one of his most significant innovations. He alternates these groups skillfully, giving his However, Mahler's orchestration is never just a matter of *colour*: it also establishes the essential musical relationships. Hence, in the symphonies, interconnecting melodic patterns are differentiated through contrasts of *timbre* and a careful balancing of the instrumental powers. Mahler frequently uses 'analytic' instrumentation: 'the individual motivic units of an extended melodic line are set off from one another through the alternation of different instruments or instrumental groups, creating a sort of "melody of timbres"'. This technique would have a marked influence on later composers such as Schoenberg (Morgan 1991, p. 24).

The quality of Mahler's music emerges from the main theme of the second movement of the Seventh Symphony. At first, this music may seem too simple, even naïve in its construction and features—an ill-favoured little march tune in C major which comes in two phrases, the first *cadencing* on the *dominant*, the second on the *tonic*, a familiar harmonic trajectory. Although there are many 'accidentals', these result almost completely from the juxtaposition of major and minor elements (a characteristic feature of Mahler's style), so that the music remains substantially *diatonic* and triadic. The passage reveals certain general features of Mahler's style. There is a strange mixture of simplicity and complexity, of the ordinary and extraordinary. 'Something that on one level seems familiar and conventional has been transformed on another into something strangely compelling and intensely beautiful' (Morgan 1991, p. 27). One frequently becomes aware of Mahler's ability to take from varied sources an immense range of materials, often modest and of apparently little interest in themselves, and to synthesise them into a complex and close-knit formation that lends them fresh and unexpected significance.

It is possibly this aspect of his music that has led certain critics to describe him as the first truly modern composer. Others regard him as limited since he composed no operas or chamber music. But he fundamentally altered the face of music, at least in the Germanic world. Mahler inspired many of the younger generation, not least Schoenberg and his circle, anticipating many aspects of the music of the post-World War Two era.

The Post Wagernian Innovations of Richard Strauss (1864–1949)

Strauss shared important features with Mahler. Both were internationally renowned conductors, with an intimate understanding of the needs and resources of the modern orchestra. Both composed symphonic works of programmatic origins, needing very substantial orchestral forces. However, whereas Mahler concentrated on the symphony and orchestral song cycle, Strauss first established his reputation as the leading composer of symphonic poems after Liszt, turning then to opera. Whereas Mahler became the last symphonist the Austro-German hall of fame, Strauss became the great heir to Wagner in the operatic field, composing a body of work with a wider range of issues than his great predecessor.

Strauss's Modernist Style

'Don Juan', Strauss's, first mature work, depicts events in the roving lover's exploits though most of the work evokes moods of action, boldness and romance rather than pursuing a plot. While 'Don Juan' would seem to belong in the middle of the programmatic spectrum, 'Till Eulenspiegels Lustige Streiche'—'Till Eulenspiegel's Merry Pranks'—(1894–1895) approximates to the representational, recounting the comic tale of a prankster's exploits. 'Also Sprach Zarathustra' is a musical commentary on Nietzsche's prose-poem proclaiming that the Christian ethic should be abandoned in favour of a superman above good and evil. Although the overall course of the programme is philosophical, moments are directly representational, such as Zarathustra's address to the rising sun in the prologue which inspired the magnificent opening with a deep C in the organ pedal and contrabassoon, rising brass fanfare and triumphant orchestral climax. The passage became famous when Stanley Kubrick used it in the soundtrack of his 1968 film '2001: A Space Odyssey'.

Strauss's 1905 opera 'Salome', based on Oscar Wilde's one-act play, is a decadent version of the biblical story. With 'Elektra' (1906–1908), Strauss embarked on a long and fertile collaboration with the Viennese playwright Hugo von Hofmannstahl (1874–1929) that resulted in seven operas. Adapted from a Sophocles play, 'Elektra' focuses on feelings of insane hatred and desire for revenge. 'Der Rosenkavalier' transports us into a 'sunnier world of elegant, stylised eroticism and tender feelings in the aristocratic, powdered-wig milieu of eighteenth-century Vienna' (Burkholder et al. 2014, p. 789). Its anachronisms are magnified in 'Ariadne Auf Naxos' (1911–1912, revised 1916) which combines characters from Greek tragedy with characters from the eighteenth-century 'commedia dell'arte', and Mozartean music with Strauss's most Romantic outpourings. After four decades of opera, he turned in his final works to genres better geared to expressing his own feelings.

Strauss's early pieces emulated Mozart, Beethoven and Schubert. But his style changed radically after studying the score of 'Tristan und Isolde'. His principal models for programme music were Liszt and Berlioz, and he drew inspiration from their colourful orchestration, conversion of themes and types of programme, some derived from literary sources.

The issue of programme music is central to Strauss's musicianship. Unlike Mahler who later withdrew the programmes for his earlier symphonies, Strauss preferred programmes with detailed correlations to specific musical events in his compositions. This doesn't mean that the music can only be appreciated if one knows its extramusical basis since the pieces do have an internal musical logic. Yet, the musical possibilities suggested by his programmes were crucial in enabling Strauss to create large-scale forms quite different from those he inherited from the Classical tradition.

Strauss's principal operatic models were Mozart and Wagner, who, despite considerable differences, were both composers from the Austro-Germanic tradition. Both created different styles to capture their characters' personalities, express their emotions and communicate dramatic situations. Like Wagner, Strauss used *leitmotifs*, stylistic contrasts and the association of particular keys with certain characters to increase musical coherence and dramatic power. Most of the tone poems contain the identifiable shell of a traditional formal type: we can identify the sonata form in 'Don Juan' and 'Tod und Verklarung', the *rondo* in 'Till Eulenspiegels Lustige Streiche' theme and variations in 'Don Quixote'. But as in Mahler, the form itself feels basically innovative. In fact, in its formal features, Strauss's music has much in common with Mahler—specifically, an inclination towards episodic structures which reveal distinct and highly differentiated sections each with its own distinct character. But in Strauss, this characteristic is closely bound up with a portrayal of the various events and moods associated with the programmes. And despite its sectional diversity, Strauss's music, being more consistent, does not convey the features of stylistic contrast, of unsettled emotional ambivalence, so striking in Mahler.

Strauss introduced into his symphonic works of the 1890s technical innovations which proved of major significance in the development of twentieth-century music. He extended Wagner's practice of carrying the *leitmotif* into a purely instrumental context. He uses a series of brief, though identifiable, melodic figures, rapidly alternating and presented in changing combinations, in order to develop complex *polyphonic textures* within an intensely *chromatic* harmonic framework. The fast pace of this music discloses a novel factor: an exceptional amount of music is compressed into a short span of time, even if the new material consists largely of changes of surface details. Strauss (and Mahler) exacted a level of instrumental playing far higher than that demanded by other composers of their generation. He experimented with original effects of instrumental *colour* and atmosphere, usually suggested by programmatic factors, transforming the entire concept of orchestral sound—for example, in the effect, bordering on simple noise, of the battle scene from 'Ein Heldenleben'—'A Hero's Life' with its percussive *ostinato* sharp *pizzicato*, whirling woodwind phrases (suggesting clashing swords); or the description of bleating sheep in 'Don Quixote', created by muted brass playing *flutter-tongue* in dissonant combinations. Music could never again be the same after the introduction of such hitherto unheard elements, which by conventional standards were regarded as 'foreign' and 'unmusical'.

The two operas that Strauss composed—'Salome' (1905) and 'Elektra' (1909)—became central to the history of twentieth-century music. Labelled 'staged tone poems', they logically extend the line Strauss followed in his earlier symphonic works. Here the programme is displayed on stage as a kind of visual and vocal 'accompaniment' to the orchestral music, which reflects its emotional and expressive content. Like the tone poems, each opera is conceived as a single 'movement' in which the action unfolds in an unbroken succession. But in 'Salome' and 'Elektra', the technical advances seen in the earlier works are transported to a new and crucial stage. 'The tonal underpinnings are now strained to breaking point, and the unfolding of the musical argument achieves an almost unbearable level of intensity and complexity' (Morgan 1991, pp. 31–32).

These operas deal in lurid detail with the obsessions and murderous impulses of the protagonists. As a composer sensitive to extramusical ideas, the powerful effect of their plots become, for him, challenges to force his compositional instincts ever closer to their final consequences. The music vividly communicates the eroticism, physical horror, and psychological depravity of the stories and characters. *Tonality* is still present as an underlying governing principle but is stretched to its limits. The succession of chords increasingly assumes the character of a series of passing *colouristic* effects, rather than a logical progression through a well-established succession of keys. Dissonances are granted unprecedented freedom, and the extreme *chromaticism* often obscures the harmonic basis to the point of unrecognisability. Melodic themes freely interact with one another, breaking up the larger line into a sequence of detached *motif* fragments.

There are moments of relative calm and the overall shape of the operas is still governed by the alternation of passages of greater and lesser stability. But what impresses the listener most is the sense of an endless series of violent interruptions produced by the sudden—and, at least from a musical point of view, seemingly unmotivated—contrasts that reflect the furious pace and savage intensity of the stage action. An example of the novel harmonic structures Strauss explores is a passage from 'Elektra' where a C flat major *triad* is superimposed on an open fifth D-A, resulting in a dissonant clash of a minor ninth between D and E flat. The chord then descends *chromatically* in parallel motion until it returns to its original *pitch* level an *octave* lower. But the resolution of dissonance is delayed so long that the dissonant chordal complex becomes the temporary norm, rather than merely a departure from a *triadic* foundation, thus evolving into the 'basis for the descending progression' (Morgan 1991, p. 33).

It seems that the level of *chromatic* permeation and *tonal* instability reached in 'Salome' and, especially, 'Elektra' brought the development of music in the first decade of the twentieth century to a critical point. It became impossible to continue along the same path without totally and irrevocably undermining the foundations of the old *tonal* system. In reality, of course, the fateful step that conveyed music into a new phase of technical evolution was taken not by Strauss but by Schoenberg, at roughly the same time that Strauss was completing 'Elektra'. After this, he proceeded in the opposite direction, deciding not to pursue the same lines of technical innovation on which he'd embarked in his two great operas—a step which must be seen as historically 'backward'.

'Der Rosenkavalier' is much more traditional than either 'Salome' or 'Elektra'. To his radical contemporaries, it must have felt like a betrayal of everything that was most progressive in his earlier compositions. It represented a fundamental crossroads in Strauss's work, and he never returned to the experimental, innovative terrain of 'Salome' and 'Elektra', pursuing instead a more traditional path. Strauss composed four more operas with Hofmannsthal—'Ariadne auf Naxos' (1912, revised 1916) because of its neo-Classical features, is the most interesting.

Unlike so many of his contemporaries in the arts and sciences, Strauss remained in Germany during the Nazi era, indeed temporarily collaborated with the regime. However, he became disillusioned with Nazi racial policies and was denounced for collaborating with Jewish writer Stefan Zweig, librettist for the first post-Hofmannstahl opera in 1934. Strauss refused to remove Zweig's name from the publicity, after which the opera was banned and in 1935 Strauss was forced to resign his party position. After the war, Strauss's creative energy revived and he composed several of his most beautiful works—'Metaphorphosen' for string orchestra (1945)—a lament on the disasters inflicted on Europe by Hitler and World War Two—and the 'Four Last Songs' (1948). However, this later work has had a relatively minor influence on the subsequent development of twentieth century music.

The Impressions and Symbols of Claude Debussy (1862–1918)

While German Modernists placed themselves in the line of descent from Bach, Mozart, Beethoven and Wagner, French Modernists confronted a more complex, conflicted heritage. The German classics from Bach to Mendelssohn were well established in the French repertoire, with Wagner a dominant figure. The issue facing them at the end of the nineteenth century was escaping the all-powerful influence of their German counterparts, especially Wagner. The 'Societe National de Musique' was founded by a group of young composers including Cesar Franck (1822–1890), Camille Saint-Saens (1835–1921), Emmanuel Chabrier (1841–1894), Jules Massenet (1842–1912), and Gabriel Faure (1845–1924), aimed at inspiring a specifically French musical renaissance. Following France's defeat in the Franco-Prussian war of 1870–1871, they sought a distinctive path of their own while reviving French music of the sixteenth to eighteenth centuries as a counterweight to the German composers at the heart of the Classical repertoire. By 1900, younger French composers also faced the challenge of their own past, a tradition stretching from the Renaissance to the major figures of the late nineteenth century.

The French tradition created in the seventeenth and eighteenth centuries was very different from Wagner: apart from Berlioz, it was characterised by emotional reserve rather than effusion and loud *dynamics*, as illustrated in Lully's opera 'Armide' or Rameau's opera 'Hyppolyte et Aricie'. For them, deep emotions could be expressed through plain, direct methods rather than by overwhelming the audience with vocal gyrations, tortuous dissonance and high-pitched volume. Also, at the heart of the French tradition had been dance music suffused with the qualities of taste and restraint, the tradition of the Gregorian chant and of French Renaissance composers using *modes* rather than the goal-directed harmonic progression of modern, *tonal* music. These features were useful to French composers trying to develop a distinctive personal style but one informed by their national heritage.

In the late nineteenth century, Paris was the cultural capital of Europe, where the arts flourished and a well-established avant-garde tradition had existed for half a century, with great future influence on the development of modern art. This was especially evident in the fine arts and literature, but with music remaining curiously undeveloped. Increased *chromaticism* and intensified expressiveness—essential features of German Romanticism—were largely alien to the French tradition and temperament. In France, where the principles of functional *tonality* had never been as firmly rooted as in Germany, music was to pursue a different trajectory.

Debussy's Modernist Style

Debussy was the composer largely responsible for setting French music on a new course, maturing in the heady atmosphere of this 'renaissance'. Whereas Mahler and Strauss extended Wagnerian harmony to new levels of rhetorical intensity, Debussy pushed it in the direction of pleasure and beauty. His revulsion against 'Wagner's bombast' (despite his admiration for 'Tristan' and 'Parsifal') turned him to the French tradition from which he drew a preference for sensibility, taste and restraint. A most interesting feature of Debussy's musical development, which distinguished him both from his German contemporaries and from the composers of the 'Societe Nationale' was his interest in enlarging traditional musical resources, casting his compositional net more widely (as opposed to the 'internal' expansion of *chromaticism*) by incorporating ideas and techniques from traditions that were distant both historically, for example, the medieval *modes*, notably *parallel organum*, and geographically, as in Asian music such as Javanese gamelan music, and Chinese and Japanese melodies.

'Pagodes', the first piece in 'Estampes'—'Prints' (1903), conveys an Asian ambiance by imitating *pentatonic* melodies, low gongs and multilayered *textures* of Javanese gamelan, an orchestra comprising mainly gongs and percussion, which Debussy had heard at the 1889 Paris Universal Exposition. In 'Children's Corner', the last piece in the set, 'Golliwog's Cakewalk', imitates Scott Joplin's ragtime style, juxtaposing it with a middle section that satirically recasts the opening of Wagner's 'Tristan und Isolde' in the style of salon music, marked 'avec une grande emotion'.

Debussy's orchestral music reveals the same features as his piano works, with the additional feature of instrumental *timbre*. He often attributes a certain *theme* to a specific instrument, and different musical layers are separated through tone *colour*. His works need a large orchestra which is rarely used to make a loud sound but instead offers a great variety of tone *colours* and *textures*. 'Even more than Mahler, Debussy treated music as an art of sound and revelled in the wide range of sounds available in the orchestra' (Burkholder et al. p. 795).

His youthful works reveal the influence of Chabrier and Faure, especially the latter, who offered the young musician a model in his search for a new approach to *tonality* which, although in essence *diatonic*, would be free of the requirements of the traditional *tonal* system. Debussy's interest in Russian music, particularly Mussorgsky and Rimsky-Korsakoff, expressed a similar preoccupation.

Debussy's 'Prelude a L'Apres d'Un Faune'—'Prelude to the Afternoon of a Faun' composed in 1894 is perhaps the strongest candidate for the title of 'first modern music'. Debussy's 'Prelude' heralds the modern era as it quietly shakes loose from roots in *diatonic tonality*. It doesn't follow that it is atonal or keyless, but simply that the traditional harmonic relationships, providing coherence and impetus to Western art music since the seventeenth century, are no longer of binding significance (Griffiths 1978, p. 7).

Even when pursuing a line opposed in many ways to Wagner's principles, Debussy owed him much, especially the idea of a more naturalistic music closely linked to linguistic expression and to the surge of dramatic events and emotions. This became increasingly clear in the 1890s when Debussy abandoned his earlier predilection for abstract music in favour of a more *programmatic* approach. However, there is a difference: instead of Wagner's complex and advanced system of musical references, Debussy preferred a more 'generalised poetic evocation of moods, impressions, and atmospheric landscapes – an "emotional interpretation of what is invisible in Nature," as he once said in reference to Beethoven's "Pastoral Symphony"' (Morgan 1991, p. 43).

This approach is reflected in the first outstanding orchestral masterpieces of Debussy's maturity—the 'Prelude a l'Apres-Midi d'Un Faune', the three 'Nocturnes' (1900), and the opera 'Pelleas et Melisande' (1893–1902). Although 'Pelleas' contains a narrative, the music seems to express mainly the internal activity of its characters and the despondent atmosphere conjured up by its woodland setting. The opening of the 'Faun', with its gently billowing flute solo illustrates the kind of free, ornamental melody of 'natural curves' that Debussy came to describe as the 'arabesque'. He identified the origins of the 'arabesque' in the 'delicate tracery' of Gregorian chant which he believed could provide a model for the modern composer searching for fresh, expressive life and freedom. The traditional notion of *theme* or melody often seems inappropriate in Debussy's music, which consists of collections of brief, *thematic* fragments—mutually intertwined variations of one another rather than outcomes of a single melodic source laid down as a point of departure. '...a Debussy composition often seems not so much to "begin" as to gradually form itself out of an indistinct and atmospheric background' (Morgan 1991, p. 44).

Debussy pioneered a new *tonal* and harmonic language. Harmony assumes a new role: in earlier music, it had been a dynamic agent of musical motion, now it has become a largely static means of creating atmospheric and *colouristic* sonorous effects. In the piano prelude 'La Catedrale Engloutie'—'The Sunken Cathedral' (1910), a change of pitch occurs at bars 6–7 where E emerges as the centre for the next passage. This change isn't a *modulation* in the traditional sense of a shift from one key to another, but rather a change of *mode* from E *Phrygia*n to E *Lydian* (modern—five sharps), the note E serving as a common reference within both scales.

The presence of *pentatonic*, *Phrygian* and *Lydian scales* in this passage indicates a basic element of Debussy's style. Harmonies are selected as much as for their *colour*, resonance and general *sonority* as for their functional position within a larger harmonic sequence. He therefore feels free to use various 'exotic' *scalar* types as a basis for new kinds of vertical combinations. One kind typically associated with his name is the whole-tone *scale* in which the *octave* is divided into six equal whole steps—unlike the *diatonic* scale—so, completely *symmetrical* in structure and, therefore, *tonally* debatable. Although the *whole-tone scale* had appeared previously in the music of composers such as Liszt, and was particularly popular in Russia going back at least to Glinka, Debussy was the first to use it consistently. But even he normally used it only as one of a variety of *scalar* types (including *pentatonic*, *diatonic*, and *symmetrical*) which he combines and integrates into a larger complex of related *scalar* divisions with exemplary freedom and ingenuity.

Debussy's innovatory approach to *scale*, harmony and *tonality* represents a vital contribution to twentieth-century music, as 'far-reaching in its historical implications as the continued development of *chromaticism* in Germany and Austria'. In fact, Debussy's compositional approach changed the basic manner in which music was experienced. Traditional Western music is heard principally as a movement directed towards a *tonal* goal, and one is therefore accustomed to listen to any particular moment in terms of where it is coming from and, even more, where it is headed. But in Debussy *tonality* is approached in a more stable manner, 'defined by a series of related yet essentially stationary blocks of largely static harmony' (Morgan 1991, pp. 45–46). The listener, therefore, experiences each musical moment less in terms of what precedes and what follows it, and more in terms of its own features. This difference decisively influenced all aspects of Debussy's style. The music's 'surface'—its *texture*, *colour*, *dynamic* fluctuations—assumes a novel prominence.

The orchestration of the opening of the second of the three orchestral sketches 'La Mer—Jeux de Vagues'—breaks up the essential *sonority* into a number of individual elements, producing a musical effect comparable to dissolution of the surface in Impressionist painting through the use of many individual brush strokes. Because of these techniques of fragmentation, and also his extensive interest in atmosphere and *colour*,

Debussy is commonly described as a musical 'Impressionist'. Impressionism was a movement in which the music focused on atmosphere and mood, 'conveying the moods and emotions aroused by the subject rather than a detailed tone-picture' (Kennedy 2006). Arguably, however, Debussy is closer to symbolism, a link reinforced by his friendship with symbolist poets such as Mallarme, and his use of their texts for songs and dramatic works. One common feature is a sense of detached observation as opposed to the Romantic tradition's tendency to express emotions. Debussy's music typically evokes a mood, atmosphere or scene.

In traditional *tonal* music, harmonic progression is achieved by combining chords that are different from one another as they occupy different positions within the key system. Debussy combines chords that are similar in both quality and structure. This is exemplified in one of his most common techniques—the use of chords in parallel motion, so that a single *sonority* is moved about in melodic sequence. An example is the opening bars of 'La Cathedrale Engloutie'.

By the turn of the century, Debussy often avoided the traditional method of establishing a *tonal* centre through *dominant-tonic* harmonic relationships. He supplanted them by devising new means of creating key centres, essentially of a melodic and rhythmic rather than harmonic character. Arguably, repetition became the most significant means of creating a *tonal* focus. For example, the opening of 'Jeux de Vagues' produces a sense of *tonal* orientation through various methods of repeating the first chord, although the predominant focus is not a single *pitch* but a dissonant *chordal* complex.

Again, if we compare the *dynamic* and progressive nature of large-scale Classical and Romantic music with Debussy, his work consists of 'additive' structures in which musical sections of varying degrees of resemblance follow one another in a largely 'flat' and non-development linear order. 'The basic formal technique involves subtle variations of repeated musical units, often by means of apparently insubstantial transformations, and the mediation of contrasting units through the retention of common elements' (Morgan 1991, p. 48). Debussy's music often resembles a mosaic with apparently separate and self-enclosed units combining into larger configurations, the individual discontinuities being thus dissolved into a continuous, seamless flow. Whereas German music of the time is characterised by a *dynamic* drive towards points of climactic stress, Debussy offers a floating equilibrium between delicately interlinked musical entities, creating wavelike movements typified by fine gradations of *colour*, pace and intensity.

Debussy minimises chord progressions in traditional harmony, creating instead musical ideas or images to build a work's structure and meaning through *motives*, harmony, exotic *scales* such as *whole-tone, octatonic* and *pentatonic*, instrumental *timbre*, then composes by juxtaposing these. *Themes* do not necessarily develop but sometimes repeat with minor changes, like an object seen from different perspectives; dissonances need not resolve; *sonorities* may move along parallel lines; contrasts of *scale* type underlie the articulation of phrases and sections, and instrumental *timbres* rather than simple coloration are essential to the musical content. Debussy's mature works are fashioned more by contrasts of *timbre* and *texture* than by conventional formal devices or *tonal* function.

In all these ways, Debussy deliberately undermines the sense of urgency that underlay *tonal* music from its outset and came to the forefront in German Romanticism from late Beethoven to Wagner, and indeed among the Classicals: the need to resolve the problem posed at the start of a movement, to return to the *tonic*, to develop the potential of a *theme* until it is exhausted. In place of this urgency, Debussy fostered a modernism that focused on what he viewed as 'the traditional French values of decoration, beauty and pleasure' (Burkholder et al. 2014, p. 793). These features are apparent in the passage from the piano work 'L'Isle Joyeuse' (1903–1904). Each theme is linked to a particular *figuration*, chord or succession of chords, *scale* type, *dynamic* level, and range on the piano. This creates a sequence of images that remain separate from one another though each flows into the next. In the movement from each segment to the next, some notes remain the same and some change, creating the effect of a harmonic progression (series of chord changes forming the underlying harmony of a piece of music).

The harmonic styles of Wagner and Liszt influenced Debussy's use of *chromatic* and *whole-tone* chords: there is no urgency to resolve, rather are we content to enjoy each moment as it comes. Debussy usually maintained a *tonal* focus—a kind of key centre—as in the case of 'L'Isle Joyeuse'. However, he defied the conventional *tonal* relationships between chords by allowing each chord a degree of independence. It is this new attitude towards harmony, inviting us to enjoy each event rather than hanker for resolution, that gives his music a feeling of dispassionate observation.

Debussy's achievement consisted in imparting to these forms a strong sense of structural integrity. Yet the kind of music he composed is more loosely linked and more 'permeable' (i.e. any given section seems able to flow into or out of any other) than that of traditional *tonal* music. Yet 'the music... is held together by a tight network of melodic, rhythmic and harmonic associations' (Morgan 1991, p. 49). Debussy increasingly refined his approach in a series of revolutionary works dating from the early years of the century, for example, 'Estampes' 'Prints' (1903), 'Images'—'Pictures' Books I and II (1905), and 'Preludes For Piano' Book I (1910), Book II (1913), 'La Mer' and the third set of 'Images' (1905–1912) for orchestra. These compositions reached their most developed form in the ballet 'Jeux'—'Games' (1913).

His final years reveal a distinct change in his compositional approach: the poetic titles disappear, replaced by those of abstract music (returning him to his earliest works also marked by abstract formal designations). His music loses much of the surface voluptuousness typical of the earlier works. Already in the 'Etudes' for piano (1913), one notices a renewed tendency toward *textural* and formal economy, a trend that reaches its height in the three 'Sonatas' of 1915–1917 (for cello and piano, violin and piano, and flute, viola and harp respectively). All these are characterised by a restraint verging on austerity—a feature foreshadowing the neo-Classicism that arose a few years later.

Debussy's conception of form as 'open' was to have a major influence on later twentieth-century music. Indeed, the changes that Debussy introduced in harmonic and orchestral usage made him one of the most seminal and influential composers in the history of music. He made an impact on virtually every significant composer of the early and middle twentieth century, representing many national traditions, as well as on American jazz and popular musicians. His emphasis on sound itself as a feature of music paved the way for potential later developed by Varese, Cage, Crumb, Penderecki, and many post-war composers.

The Atonal Wanderings of Arnold Schoenberg (1874–1951)

Like other Modernists of his generation, Schoenberg started out composing *tonal* music in a late Romantic style. His early works reveal the influence of Wagner—inflated single-movement compositions in which *tonality* is present but in decline—followed by more radical works in which *tonality* disappears. Schoenberg achieves an uncertain continuity through his mastery of *counterpoint* and variation, or, with 'Pierrot Lunaire', by relinquishing large form in favour of bunches of short, related movements. His first important work—'Veklarte Nacht'—'Transfigured Night' (1899) included a *chromatic* idiom that emerged out of Wagner's 'Tristan und Isolde', while his symphonic poem 'Pelleas und Melisande' (1902–1903) reveals the influence of Mahler and Strauss.

Schoenberg's Modernist Style

In 1908, Schoenberg began composing works that avoided fixing any note as a *tonal* centre. He felt constrained to abandon *tonality* partly because the increased *chromaticism*, distant *modulations*, and prolonged dissonances of late nineteenth-century music had undermined the pull to the *tonic*, making its pronouncement at the end of a work increasingly arbitrary. Furthermore, in music with complex *chromatic* chords, it is difficult to ascertain which notes are the dissonant ones needing *resolution*. These ambiguities led Schoenberg to what he called 'the emancipation of the dissonance'—freeing dissonance from the need to resolve to consonance—so that any combination of *tones* could function as a stable chord not requiring resolution. Once this idea was accepted, atonality was inescapable. But without a *tonal* foundation, how could music be organised? Schoenberg devised three methods: developing variation, integrating harmony and melody, and *chromatic* saturation, all used before in *tonal* music, but he now drew on them more fully to give the music shape.

Firstly, 'developing variation', pioneered by Brahms, is a continuous transformation of the *thematic* material, evading literal repetition. A closely related concept—'musical prose'—is the continuous unrolling of an unbroken musical argument without resorting to the symmetrical balances produced by phrases or sections of equal length and corresponding *thematic* material (exemplified in the Classical formal unit known as a 'period'). 'With me', he wrote, 'variation almost completely takes the place of repetition' (Morgan 1991, p. 65). The result is 'a richly structured and densely *polyphonic* musical continuum in which all parts, including ostensibly "secondary" ones, are equally developmental and *motivically* derived'. Schoenberg avoids harmonic 'padding' and surface effects of 'textural *figuration*' (sound effect produced by extended *themes*), both characteristic of much late nineteenth century Romantic music.

One of Schoenberg's first completely pieces was composed in 1908— 'Saget mir, auf Welchen Pfade'—'Tell me on Which Path', the fifth song from a cycle of poems from 'Das Buch der Hangenden Garten'—'The Book of Hanging Gardens' by symbolist poet Stefan George (1908– 1909). 'The sense of floating in *tonal* space created by music that does not gravitate to a *tonic* is perfectly suited to the vague eroticism of the poetry...' (Burkholder et al. 2014, p. 816).

Secondly, Schoenberg integrated melody and harmony through a process he described as 'composing with the *tones* of a motive,' one that flows directly from developing variation. In this, he manipulated the notes and intervals of a theme to create chords and new melodies. One way this worked was to treat the notes of a theme containing three or more *pitches* just as we could a *triad* or other *tonal* chord: as a cluster of *pitches* that could be relocated, reversed and arranged in any order and register to create melodies and harmonies. Thirdly, *chromatic* saturation also shapes atonal music through the appearance of all twelve pitch classes in a segment of music.

In a two-year period of amazing creativity—1907–1909—Schoenberg finally broke with *tonality* and *triadic* harmony and 'moved into the hitherto uncharted area of free "chromaticism"', composing a series of works that fundamentally altered the course of music. Abandoning *tonality* can be interpreted simply as the next step in progressive evolution since in his work the role of *triads* and key centres had already been weakened to the point of near extinction (Morgan 1991, p. 67).

However, Schoenberg's new conception of pitch organisation revolutionised it in two ways, First, the stress on nonharmonic tones eventually reaches a point where these tones lose their predilection to resolve at all, making it difficult for the listener to spot the most latent *triadic* background. For the first time since the Renaissance, the *triad* was no longer regarded as the sole harmonic reference from which all other vertical *sonorities* emanated and to which they owed their meaning. The novelty in Schoenberg's music of this period is, therefore, not so much the dissonant chords themselves—such chords had always been used—but the fact that these chords are no longer linked to a simpler, more consonant *triadic* basis.

The second aspect, closely related to the first, is the almost complete abandonment of conventional *tonal* functions. No longer does a single *pitch*, or the major or minor *triad* based on that *pitch*, provide a functional foundation for the other *tones* and the triads built on them.

Schoenberg's music has learned to move in a 'free *chromatic* space' governed by new principles of organisation.

Despite these revolutionary predilections, it should be stressed that there is no rigid line of demarcation between Schoenberg's first *atonal* compositions and his final ones; indeed, the first 'purely' *atonal* work can't be precisely identified. The new pieces retain faint traces of *tonality*. Moreover, the chronology of these years is complicated, with Schoenberg working quickly, in bursts of inspiration, and on several pieces simultaneously. These reasons explain why the transition from *tonal* to *atonal* is so gradual that an attempt to locate a precise moment of radical change is meaningless. The 'Second String Quartet' (1908) represents a kind of bridge from the old approach to the new. In the last two movements, the sense of key is weakened to nearly complete dissolution. Also, it is hard to list the procedures for shaping the new music. 'There is no... grammar of relationships that can be assumed in advance... Musical structure has become "contextual", defined by the network of referential associations set out within each separate composition' (Morgan 1991, p. 69).

One dominant trait of this music is its resolutely linear and *contrapuntal* character. Harmony is conceived largely as a kind of vertical melody. Indeed, the distinction between harmony and melody becomes, as in Scriabin, indistinct; they are simply two ways of presenting the same underlying *pitch* content. This content consists largely of small groups of related *pitches*, described as *pitch cells* or 'sets' which are handled in different ways so as to create new material. Theoretically, any *cell* can be selected for use in a particular work; and a single composition normally uses many such *cells*, although these will generally share certain similarities, for example, related intervallic content. In the song cycle, 'Das Buch der Hangenden Garten', all fifteen songs are individually organised, each 'articulating - and in turn articulated by - its own structural context...' (Morgan 1991, p. 70).

Once developed, Schoenberg didn't use the *atonal* style systematically but intuitively, tailoring his procedure to suit the needs of specific works. The first three of the 'Five Orchestral Pieces, Opus16', demonstrate the variety of procedures adopted: the first leans heavily on *canonic* devices; the second features a recurring dissonant chord (a sort of dissonant '*tonic*'). In all these works, *pitch* cells are used as a controlling method, but with widely differing degrees of consistency and within ever-shifting compositional contexts.

As Schoenberg approached the end of this two-year period of the creative experiment, he no longer relied so much on explicit *motivic* correspondences and structural strategies such as *canon* to integrate his music. The last three works composed in 1909—the third of the Opus 11 Three Piano Pieces, the last of the Opus 16 orchestral pieces, and 'Erwartung', are not only *atonal* but *athematic* too. 'Erwartung' highlights the inner monologue of a woman waiting to meet her lover in a forest. When he fails to appear, she becomes increasingly frantic, eventually tumbling over his dead body. The text evokes a feeling of hysteria, much of it fragmentary and stream-of-consciousness memories of previous events, expressing the woman's psychological instability.

Atonality and *athematicism* represent the final evolutionary stage of Schoenberg's concepts of developing variation and musical prose: they liberated him from all previous constraints. Music no longer had recourse to external rules, and, therefore, became, he believed, more directly expressive of the composer's inner life. The period 1907 to World War One are thus often described as Schoenberg's expressionist period.

'Pierrot Lunaire', a setting of twenty-one poems by the French poet Albert Giraud, is especially interesting since it provides the first sign of a change of style that would become more apparent in later years. Several songs feature complex *contrapuntal* structures of a relatively rigid kind, marking a shift from the freer style of the earlier compositions. 'Die Nacht'—'The Night', (subtitled *Passacaglia*) is based virtually completely on manipulations of a single three-note *cell*, whereas 'Der Mondfleck'—'The 'Moonfleck' contains an elaborate double *canon* that proceeds to the song's midpoint, then moves backwards, in retrograde motion, until its opening is reached. In 'Pierrot', these techniques remain isolated but in the post-war years, Schoenberg would eventually incorporate them into a general musical system.

Schoenberg's conception of music as consisting of a free twelve-note *chromatic* field, within which any combination of *pitches* could function as a 'norm', redefined the limits of what was seen as permissible in composition. His *atonal* music laid down new markers which future composers had to follow. The notion of 'contextual music', which applies in varying degrees to all twentieth-century music no longer adhering to *triadic tonality*, can only be properly understood in relation to these new limits.

With hindsight, it seems clear that Schoenberg would eventually chart a new course given the severe limitations of his compositional approach during the *atonal* period. Without the help of 'tonal moorings' or explicit *thematic* or *motivic* correspondences, it was difficult to sustain lengthy, coherent musical structures. Interestingly, all the larger *atonal* works are vocal, relying on a text as an 'outside agent of control and comprehensibility', while the instrumental pieces are all relatively short.

Chromaticism had always provided a highly powerful expressive force in Western music, but this force had stemmed from its role as a departure from an implied *diatonic* framework. Once that structure was absent, total *chromaticism* acquired a new freedom as well as having a distinctive shock value that Schoenberg exploited with complete mastery. However, the sense of shock could not be indefinitely sustained. 'Ironically, free chromaticism, in rendering everything more or less equally chromatic and thus equally intense, tended ultimately to neutralise its own expressive basis' (Morgan 1991, p. 76).

After 1916, Schoenberg searched intensely, publishing no new music for seven years. After 1923, his pieces reflected a noticeable technical and stylistic re-orientation. His artistic crisis stemmed from his no longer trusting the largely 'intuitive' character of his pre-war music. Though experiencing a sense of creative release flowing from the freer and less systematic compositional approach of his *atonal* music, he came to view it as an insufficient foundation for extended, developmental compositions. Like Stravinsky, Schoenberg emerged from the war years bent on re-establishing stronger, more conscious links to the older Western tradition.

Schoenberg's writings suggest that his breaking of the *tonal* barrier was undertaken not so much 'in the excitement of discovery as with difficulty and a sense of loss at what was being abandoned.' He was arguably no avant-garde experimenter, seeing his venture into *atonality* as 'an inevitable consequence of what had gone before.' He felt forced to go onward, even if it should be against his conscious will (Griffiths 1978, p. 26). However, for a composer so profoundly committed to the irreversibility of music's evolution towards total *chromaticism*, this could not assume the form of a return to *diatonicism* or a new kind of *tonality*. What he needed was a system for *chromatic* music somehow analogous to the *tonal* one, a system able to incorporate the new dissonant melodic and chordal structures of distinctively twentieth-century music within a more consciously developed and systematically organised framework.

In 1921, Schoenberg confided to one of his students that he had discovered something that would 'ensure the supremacy of German music for the next hundred years.' This was the twelve-tone system according to which each work draws its basic *pitch* material from a unique sequence of the twelve *pitches* of the *chromatic* scale, known as the twelve-tone 'row' or 'series'. There is, firstly, the original or 'prime' form (conventionally designated P) of the row, with three other related forms being used. The retrograde (R) form reverses the order of *pitches* and *intervals*. In the inversion (I), each of the original intervals is inverted so that, for example, a perfect fifth upward becomes a perfect fifth downwards. The retrograde may also be inverted (the 'retrograde inversion' or RI form). Moreover, any of these four basic forms may be transposed to begin on any other pitch. Finally, the four basic forms of the row can also be multiplied by their twelve possible transpositions giving forty-eight possible versions of the original row. Normally only a selection of these will be used in an actual work, the choice governed by compositional judgements.

Twelve-tone music is often associated with a compositional style called serialism. However, the terms are not equivalent as serialism is a broad designator describing the ordering of *pitches*, durations, rhythms and *dynamics*, a method of composition using these elements. Twelve-tone music refers more precisely to music based on orderings of the twelve *pitch classes*. Schoenberg's first completely twelve-tone work is the 'Suite for Piano, Opus 25' (1924), in which he uses only eight different row forms, all related by transpositions of the *tritone* in order to exploit a significant feature of the selected row: the fact that its first and last notes are a *tritone* apart. Although the row governs the succession of pitches used in a piece, it doesn't govern their register or duration.

The role of the twelve-tone system within Schoenberg's musical development can be better grasped as a gradual outgrowth of two well-established pre-war characteristics: (i) the tendency to draw melodic material from a limited number of basic *intervallic* cells through variation procedures, and (ii) the tendency to *chromatic* saturation through the use of all twelve *pitches* in more or less perpetual rotation. Schoenberg soon stopped experimenting with other types of series and concentrated exclusively on rows containing all twelve *pitches*.

Schoenberg was establishing his own brand of 'new-classicism', a factor discernible in a renewed preoccupation with large-scale instrumental composition and a reliance on traditional formal types. 'Suite For Piano' announces this almost 'programmatically' by using standardised Baroque dance forms. The 'Woodwind Quintet' (1924), was the first twelve-tone composition to contain extended instrumental forms. Each of its four movements is based on a standardised Classical type: *sonata* form, *scherzo* with *trio*, song form (ABA) and *rondo*.

The twelve-tone works might be understood simply as 'a more systematic version of the same intensely motivic and variational conception of *thematic* development, except that here the basic material—the row— is an abstract series of intervals without any motivic content of its own' (Morgan 1991, pp. 194–195). Whereas a *motive* is a completed musical event, Schoenberg's row was a kind of pre-compositional fund for *motivic* possibilities, stressing that he regarded it in predominantly *thematic* terms. In a piece such as the 'Woodwind Quintet', everything becomes 'motivic' in that all its material is drawn from the same source, the row.

Schoenberg's discovery of a more conscious, organised method of controlling his compositions liberated his output. After a long period of silence and experimentation, a flood of new works suddenly appeared, all composed according to the new system and exploring the traditional genres renounced during the *atonal* period. After the Quintet came three further large-scale instrumental works followed by a period of operatic composition—the first two acts of his three-act biblical opera 'Moses und Aron' (1930–1932), a poignant statement of the composer's own spiritual philosophy. In the early twelve-tone works 'Variations for Orchestra', a particularly important technique was 'combinatoriality'—the 'simultaneous presentation of two different forms of a single row so constructed that new twelve-tone aggregates are created by the combination of their hexachords' (Morgan 1991, p. 195).

An unexpected but interesting development in Schoenberg's American years (1934–1951) was a renewed interest in *tonality*, which he had previously regarded as an outmoded system. He now began to view it again as a 'viable compositional method', writing several *tonal* pieces. But his main focus was on incorporating elements of *tonality* into his twelve-tone works. This return to *tonality* was perhaps consistent with Schoenberg's general inclination throughout the 1920s and 1930s 'to re-establish closer ties to the music of the past'. However, his own attitude towards it was firmly conditioned by his continuing belief in the 'progressive' nature of musical evolution. He regarded his availing himself of *tonality* less as a return than an effort to add the finishing touches to a musical development already achieved.

Two of Schoenberg's final years' works—the 'String Trio Opus 45' (1946) and the 'Phantasy for Violin Opus 47', with piano accompaniment

(1949), rank among his most original achievements. Both feature a departure from the relatively strict formal procedures of the earlier instrumental works. Schoenberg was perhaps attempting a final reconciliation between the *atonal* and twelve-tone phases of his work, and thus a synthesis of the two apparently conflicting aspects—the Romantic-expressive and Classical (or Wagnerian and Brahmsian)—that constituted his musical personality.

Regarding this conflict, a 'contradiction' in Schoenberg's twelve-tone music was frequently observed, between a progressive system of *chromatic, atonal* pitch organisation and a conventional approach to *thematic,* rhythmic and formal issues. Schoenberg believed in cultural continuity, the need to extend the older tradition. A new compositional system was required by the tradition itself, which had 'brought the old system to a point of ultimate dissolution' (Morgan 1991, p. 200).

Schoenberg's significance in the development of twentieth-century music is rivalled only by that of Stravinsky. His influence has been profound despite his music's failure to achieve wide public recognition. Even composers pursuing a different musical path have been unable to ignore his challenge.

The Modernist National Idiom of Charles Ives (1874–1954)

At the turn of the century, concert music in the United States was dominated by European standards and models while America's indigenous, vernacular features were absent. Ives composed in obscurity for most of his career, pursuing the traditional life of the ignored artist, but lived long enough to be recognised as one of the most important composers of his generation. Curiously, he never became a full-time musician, but earned his living running a successful insurance business, composing in his spare time. After vain attempts to interest performers and publishers in his music, in 1918 he was motivated by a health crisis to edit and self-publish. Ives lived in total isolation from the public and other musicians during his creative period (1895–1917), arguably important for Ives to develop a style unencumbered by the European past. Ives played a vital role in the development of American art music with a distinctive national idiom. A clear chronology is hard to trace in Ives's music, as he worked on his pieces over long periods, often abandoning a work only to pick it up again years later.

Ives's Modernist Style

At the dawn of the new century, at least one American composer was attempting to break out of the European stranglehold. Music for Ives was an expression of subjective emotion but it also had the power of transcendental revelation and held a promise of utopia. 'The instinctive and progressive interest of every man in art, he wrote, will go on and on, ever fulfilling hopes... ever opening new horizons, until the day will come when every man, while digging his potatoes will breathe his own epics, his own symphonies...' (Griffiths 1978, p. 55).

Ives' financial independence allowed him to develop his own compositional style without having to worry about how the world of professional music or the public might judge him. Maybe more than any other major composer in the history of Western music, Ives wrote purely for himself, often not even bothering to put his compositions into finished form. This was important as Ives's entire conception of music as an 'open' art form, capable of encompassing all kinds of music and fusing them into a higher synthesis, evaded the comprehension of his contemporaries. It was a path he had to pursue almost entirely in isolation. Ives had a counterpart in the field of classic literature—Franz Kafka.

Several of Ives's early works already display amazing technical innovations. 'The Song for Harvest Season' (1893), for example, contains a four-part *fugue* in which each part is in a different key; 'Psalm 54' (c.1894) contains passages written entirely in the *whole-tone* scale. The works of his Yale years seem less experimental and it is only after his graduation in 1898 that the full power and originality of his musical vision become evident. The most characteristic feature of Ives's mature style is its variety and range. Many works, for example, his songs, retain traditional *tonality*. 'The Children's Hour' (1901), 'At the River' (1916), and 'Two Little Flowers' (1921) all retain a simpler musical language long since abandoned by Ives's progressive contemporaries. But it is characteristic of Ives's approach that older techniques were not necessarily discarded after the creation of newer ones: he retained them as part of a more inclusive music, existing alongside the most radical new developments. His conception of *tonality*, as one of many possibilities available for different expressive aims, not as a 'natural' system for ordering all music, was in its way as revolutionary as Schoenberg's view of *atonality*.

But even in his simplest songs, Ives habitually arranges things slightly obliquely. The *tonality* sounds 'distanced', no longer heard entirely within

the traditional context. Thus, 'Charlie Rutlage' (1920) clearly intends to
evoke the character of a simple cowboy song of the American West, but
it also parodies that genre. There are unexpected rhythmic complexities
in the vocal line, and occasional 'wrong' notes in the harmony, which
works against the almost banal regularity of the opening piano accompaniment; and at the climax, when both Charlie and his horse fall, the
music seems to lose all control, 'breaking out in a dissonant explosion
of dense tone clusters covering the entire range of the piano' (Morgan
1991, p. 141). Similarly, in 'At the River', after each *cadence*, 'normal'
continuity is disrupted by a distorted reminiscence of an earlier segment
of the song, pulling the music away from the key centre and leaving it
suspended in a state of uncertainty.

The melody of 'At the River' (1916), derived intact from an established
hymn tune by Robert Lowry, exemplifies a characteristic Ives technique—
musical quotation. Although here Ives borrows the whole melody, usually
he only quotes fragments from well-known tunes and often combines
these in complex, multileveled textures. His sources are universal: hymn
tunes are his favourites, but popular songs, marches, and ragtime music
also feature, and less often, standard concert pieces. Invariably, Ives transforms the borrowed material, both by putting it in new, more complex
contexts and by distorting it through inner modification.

Ives often combines and reshapes musical fragments from different
sources—visible in the opening bars of 'The Things Our Fathers Loved'
(1917). The song's harmonic language, with its *triadic* construction,
expresses the composer's simpler side, although the specific *tonal* focus
of the music is somewhat inconclusive. Ives succeeds in integrating everything into a series of continuously unfolding phrases which, despite
different derivations, form a larger unity. He achieves this partly by
'techniques of rhythmic and pitch cohesion (overlapping phrases, linear
connections, etc.), and in part by a web of interrelated motivic associations encompassing all the different materials' (Morgan 1991, p. 143).

Ives's use of quotation convinced him to adopt a novel approach to
composition, one that might be described as 'combinational'. The individual components making up the music—drawn from a wide range
of sources, some borrowed, some totally original—are juxtaposed both
simultaneously and sequentially. Musical form now means balancing and
reconciling these divergent elements, and a significant aspect of the
expressive content arises from the unexpected associations called up by

their concurrence. Thus, although the materials Ives employs are generally quite 'ordinary', the manner in which he uses them gives them fresh, unanticipated life; they are transformed by their surroundings.

The unity of an Ives piece is created partly by the relationships between the materials—the various borrowed items nearly always share important musical features which Ives is keen to exploit. But this unity is also imposed on the materials from outside, by Ives's consistent attitude towards them and the way they feature within a larger all-inclusive framework. In some works, Ives uses multiple tunes, layered on top of each other in a 'musical collage' or woven together like a patchwork quilt to summon up the way experiences are remembered. He also adopts techniques developed in his experimental work, often to express certain kinds of sounds or motions, like exploding fireworks or mists over a river.

Ives commanded a wide range of styles, often mixing them—both traditional and recently invented—within a single composition. Like Mahler's references to various styles, and the juxtapositions of different blocks of material in the work of Debussy, Scriabin or Stravinsky, this heterogeneity of styles provided a method for Ives to summon a wide range of extramusical references and also to articulate the musical form by distinguishing each phrase, section or passage from the next though stylistic contrast. 'He also used style, alongside timbre, rhythm, figuration, register, and other more traditional means, to differentiate layers heard simultaneously'. An example is in 'The Unanswered Question' (Burkholder et al. 2014, p. 852).

Ives's progressive, inventive side is found in its most distilled form in his works for small chamber combinations of diverse instruments. It was during his college years that Ives began composing for 'theatre orchestras', the small bands retained by theatres to supply music for their stage performances, and he subsequently wrote for such groups, ranging in size from a few instruments to chamber orchestras for short pieces of an openly experimental kind. With these, he experimented with various new compositional techniques, often anticipating his European contemporaries (whose work he scarcely knew) by many years. Although we don't find literal quotation in these works, something of the taste of popular music is often discernible. Ives liked to use *whole-tone* and *bitonal* elements as early as the 1890s, and this predilection for experimenting with new things to challenge the ear and the mind remained with him throughout his career.

In several works, Ives experimented with *pitch* series, for example in 'Tone Roads No.1' (1911) and 'No.3' (1915), and 'Chromatimelodtune' (c.1919), anticipating Schoenberg's earliest serial and twelve-tone pieces which were not published until 1923. However, unlike his Austrian contemporary, Ives was not interested in developing a unified serial system. For example, in 'Tone Roads No. 1', there are in fact two series, neither of which is twelve-tone or strictly adhered to, with the serial element being only one among many that affect the overall *pitch* organisation. Even in 'Chromatimelodtune', where Ives uses a single series—and in this case a twelve-tone one—with unusual consistency, the music reveals a strong *tonal* orientation. 'From the Steeples and Mountains' (c.1901) even involves the serialisation of rhythmic values—a steady reduction of the durations from half notes (eight sixteenths) to dotted eighths (three sixteenths) until the midpoint of the piece, after which the process is reversed until the original half notes are reached again (Morgan 1991, p. 145).

Ives also explored dividing larger ensembles into smaller units that could be separated from one another spatially as well as musically. 'The Unanswered Question' (1906) is built around three distinct instrumental layers, each with its own specific musical character: offstage strings, playing simple sustained *triadic* music in C major continuously in the background; solo trumpet, playing a *chromatic* two-bar figure that recurs intermittently seven times during the piece, and a quartet of four flutes, which answers the first six trumpet statements (the final one remaining 'unanswered' at the end), each answer becoming longer, louder, more dissonant and *chromatic*, and rhythmically more frantic than the preceding one. This multilevelled structure, projecting an extramusical conception, was amazingly advanced for its time. The trumpet and flute parts are *atonal*, making Ives one of the earliest composers to use *atonality* (roughly contemporary with but independently of Schoenberg) and the first to combine *tonal* and *atonal* layers in the same work.

Ives most characteristic work can be found in a few extended, multi-movement compositions that he worked on during the decade 1905–1915. In these, he achieves a higher synthesis of the various techniques he used more individually in the songs and chamber-orchestra works. Here he also discloses more explicitly the underlying continuity between his own music and that of the nineteenth-century tradition. In his experimental music, Ives's characteristic approach was to preserve most of the traditional rules but to change others to see what transpired. In his teens, he composed several works that were *polytonal*, with the melody in one key, the accompaniment in another, or with four imitative voices, each in its own key. Ives can thus legitimately be described as the founder of the experimental music tradition in the United States—influencing, among others, Henry Cowell, Edgard Varese, and John Cage. Ives was a modernist who, like Bartok, Stravinsky and Berg, dipped into his nation's music to develop a unique language within the classical tradition.

During the 1960s, Ives suddenly emerged as a cult figure, appreciated as the first and foremost American composer. A major reason for this belated recognition was that many of the compositional techniques he had pioneered, such as multiple tempos, polydimensional *textures*, and *microtonal* tunings, had taken their place as part of the fundamental vocabulary of post-World War Two music. 'Ives had become a prophet and the musical world had finally caught up with him' (Morgan 1991, p. 148).

From the Heart of the Folk—Bela Bartok (1881–1945)

Bartok was a Modernist who, like Stravinsky in Russia and Charles Ives in the United States, reached into the neglected reservoir of national folk culture to discover music that enabled him to create a distinctive voice while pursuing the Classical tradition. Bartok's music synthesised elements of Hungarian and Slavic peasant music with features of the German and French Classical traditions. He reached this synthesis only after a thorough grounding in both traditions and exposure to different modern trends. Inspired by a performance of Strauss' 'Also Sprach Zarathustra' in 1902, he composed the following year the symphonic poem 'Kossuth', a work of considerable range, about a national hero, also reflecting the influence of Liszt. But his search for a distinctively Hungarian music led him in the landmark year 1904 to study peasant folk music, collaborating with fellow composer Zoltan Kodaly, with whom he founded ethnomusicology, the study of indigenous music within its social and cultural context. Bartok published almost two thousand song and dance melodies—a small proportion of the music he had collected in expeditions ranging over eastern Europe, Turkey and North Africa. He used the new technology of sound recording which preserved the unique and unfamiliar features of each folk singer and style.

Bartok's Modernist Style

For Bartok, peasant music offered modern composers a fresh start free from Romantic sentimentality. He created a new language of melodic, rhythmic, and formal elements from peasant music, arranging melodies and blending them with those of Classical and Modernist music. Most important was the potential for the enrichment of Bartok's own music that contact with folk music offered. 'The outcome of these studies was of decisive influence upon my work, because it freed me from the tyrannical rule of the major and minor keys' (Autobiography 1921, p. 410 in Morgan 1991, p. 105). It was necessary to move beyond traditional *tonality*, now regarded as an outdated system needing fresh life and energy. And the source of this new energy was folk music which used old modes no longer found in Western music. Some were similar to traditional church *modes*, but *pentatonic* and *chromatic* modes were also present. However, his music always remains rooted in classical tradition.

Folk melodies expressed great variety and suppleness. Equally important for Bartok were their harmonic foundations. Although the original folk music was *monophonic*, Bartok wanted to develop a harmonic language consistent with the intervallic characteristics of the melodies. The frequent use of seconds, fourths and sevenths suggested it might be possible to use these intervals as basic *concords*. These features resemble those of Stravinsky who also owed much to his country's folk music. The derivation of melody and harmony from a common *interval* source also recalls Debussy, Scriabin and Schoenberg, as well as Stravinsky. Bartok shared with these composers a wish to move beyond traditional *tonality* by redefining it, not rejecting it. Here again, the influence of folk music is clear as it is always *tonal*.

It took Bartok several years to integrate these elements and create a new personal style. This process can be traced to a series of compositions, mainly for piano, that he based on actual folk tunes. In the first, 'Twenty Hungarian Folk Songs' (1906, with Kodaly), the melodies are underpinned by very simple harmonisations, completely *triadic*, and, though mildly modal in ambiance, based on conventional chord progressions. But during the subsequent years, Bartok relied increasingly on harmonic features derived from the tunes themselves. Linked to this is Bartok's tendency to invent increasingly elaborate accompaniments for the melodies. In the 'Fifteen Hungarian Songs' (1917), 'one finds a wealth of pianistic variety, including *doubling* and elaborate registral layouts.' (Morgan 1991, p. 107).

Bartok first achieved a distinctive style around 1908 with works such as the 'First String Quartet' and the one-act opera 'Bluebeard's Castle' (1911), which links Hungarian folk characteristics to features from Debussy's 'Pelleas et Melisande'. His 'Allegro Barbaro' (1911) and other piano works represented a novel approach to piano music, treating it more as a percussive instrument than a spinner of melodious tunes and resonant accompaniments. 'Allegro Barbaro' has a strong affinity with Stravinsky's 'The Rite of Spring'. It indicates that Bartok had now learned to integrate his folk influences within a musical language of his own creation. Like the 'Suite for Piano, Opus 14' (1916), it represents a 'free imitation' of folk music, modified to accommodate the formal and developmental requirements of concert music. In Bartok's later music, it is generally impossible to distinguish between what is folk-based and what is not as the elements are fused into a single, harmonious vision. Convinced that the most vital traditions were those having regular contact with other cultures, his research eventually went beyond Hungarian folk music.

By 1908, before the folk influence became dominant, Bartok began using new techniques associated with progressive contemporaries such as Debussy and Schoenberg. Bartok commented that several works were written specifically as experiments. The 'Bagatelles' represent a significant landmark in Bartok's break with nineteenth-century styles. In addition to the departure from conventional *tonality*, the stern pianistic style uncovers a great reduction of the more decorative, flamboyant approach of the earlier works. The 'First String Quartet' (1908–1909) is especially significant—less experimental than the 'Bagatelles', and with little of the folk quality that permeated his later works, it is Bartok's first mature and successful fulfilment of an extended developmental form. It launched a series of six String Quartets that together form one of the major musical achievements of the first half of the century.

Bartok achieved the first persuasive synthesis of his influences with his one-act opera 'Bluebeard's Castle' (1911), with a libretto by the Hungarian nationalist poet Bela Balazs. Despite containing no folk material, the score is suffused with the character of native music. This is partly due to the close relationship between music and text: the phonetic features of the Hungarian language contribute to shaping the work's distinctive rhythmic and melodic features. The range of Bartok's sources and the skill and freedom with which he employs them are apparent throughout. Certain scenes are dominated by dissonant harmonic centres, others are mainly *triadic* and passages with *pentatonic* and *modal* scales are counterpoised to those that are largely *chromatic*. Yet, 'the score is convincingly integrated, thanks in part to the use of a characteristic "leitmotif, chromatic" in structure and closely associated with the word "blood" (the libretto's dominant symbol)...' (Morgan 1991, p. 110).

During several years of lying fallow, he studied the scores of European contemporaries, which left a distinctive mark on his music. 'The Wooden Prince' suggests the influence of Stravinsky, while the 'Second String Quartet' discloses affinities with Schoenberg. It was also a complete departure from the triadic basis underlying nearly all Bartok's previous work. Much of the harmonic and melodic material flows from a common intervallic source, a three-note basic *cell* consisting of a (perfect) fourth and a minor second. This *cell* came to play an increasingly important role in Bartok's work.

Here and in the following years, Bartok's music echoes the intensity of pre-war European expressionism, most clearly in the two 'Sonatas for Violin and Piano' (1921 and 1922), striking in their great textual density (especially the first), and rhapsodic, freely evolving formal structures. Though not yet atonal in Schoenberg's sense, their tonal focus is so ambiguous as to create a sense of unmitigated instability. The harmonic structure is inflexibly dissonant and nontriadic, and even the motivic development, usually transparent in Bartok's work, is obscured by constant, freely evolving changes. Moreover, the violin and piano parts share so little common material that they seem to have been devised independently of each other.

However, even in the most extreme works of this period, Bartok never entirely abandoned the *modal-tonal* approach acquired from his folk music studies, though it is largely hidden by the *chromatic* surface. He was concerned to attune the new post-war music to his established folk orientation, as is clear in 'Improvisations on Hungarian Peasants Songs Opus 20', the folk settings for piano composed in 1920 just before the violin and piano sonatas. *Triads* are avoided, and the underlying *modal* foundation is twisted, producing caustically dissonant *chromatic* harmonies in the accompaniment. However, since the borrowed melodic material is preserved largely intact, a distinctive *modal-tonal* focus remains. Once again, one observes Bartok's ability to reconcile apparently incompatible elements.

Yet Bartok presumably felt that the direction his music took in the early post-war years would undermine his deep roots in Eastern European *modality*. It also put him in opposition to the prevailing European tendency to neo-classicism, with which he had become familiar during his travels as a pianist. Bartok's compositions from the decade after World War One reveal him pushing towards the boundaries of dissonance and tonal ambiguity, reaching the ultimate point with the two 'Violin and Piano Sonatas' of 1921 and 1922. After 1926, following three fallow years, Bartok carved out his own brand of 'new-classical' synthesis, in which the different features of his style were integrated into a more tightly knit idiom. The works of the late 1920s and 1930s encompass a wealth of diverse *scalar* resources—*diatonic, whole-tone, octatonic*, and *chromatic*—a new, flexible style. But even when, as often, the music is wholly *chromatic*, implying the equality of all twelve *pitches*, the *chromaticism* is nearly always created by a combination of simpler but distinctive non-*chromatic* elements. By adding more basic building blocks, creating complex *pitch* configurations, Bartok could synthesise an astonishingly varied fund of *pitch* material, from simple *diatonicism* to full twelve-tone *chromaticism*.

Between 1927 and 1939, Bartok combined this orderly but flexible method of *pitch* organisation with an increasingly rigorous approach to formal structure in a series of significant instrumental compositions: the Third, Fourth, Fifth and Sixth String Quartets, the 'Second Piano Concerto', the 'Music for Strings, Percussion and Celesta', the 'Sonata for Two Pianos and Percussion', the 'Second Violin Concerto'. A particular characteristic is a new stress on tightly organised 'arch' (or bridge) forms featuring larger *symmetrical* patterns constructed with movements paired through *motivic* and formal correspondences. This is fully realised in the fourth string quartet with its five-movement structure.

All Bartok's compositions of this period have an unusual formal strictness, yet the expressive range remains extensive. The folk influence is generally close to the surface, and sometimes very much in the foreground, as in the 'Cantata Profana' of 1930. The spirits of Liszt and Debussy, so central in Bartok's early development, remain visible, especially in the slow movement written in the 'night music' style, with its impressionistic colour and fragmentary melodic effects 'within a static harmonic framework' (Morgan 1991, p. 184).

In the later 1930s, Bartok began returning to a more traditional and functional notion of *tonality* that both re-established *triadic* harmony and also encompassed *tonic-dominant* relationships. Bartok doesn't appear here to be reacting against the progressive aspects of his mature style but rather to have wanted to include as much of his musical heritage as possible within his late work. So, in the 'Violin Concerto', he often uses *triads* but also, at the other extreme, a twelve-tone row, complete with the normal serial transformations. Bartok is again, typically, intent on synthesis—the row is conceived *thematically*—providing the basis for the contrasting *themes* of the first and final movements—with a strong *tonal* orientation.

The approach of World War Two impelled Bartok, a committed anti-Nazi, to emigrate to the United States Between 1939 and 1943, he went through the third period of lying fallow. However, in 1943, following a major health problem, he produced four major works: the 'Concerto for Orchestra' (1943), the 'Sonata for Solo Violin' (1944), and two others that remained unfinished at his death, the 'Third Piano Concerto' and a 'Viola Concerto'. In these works, Bartok continued to pursue his agenda of directness, structural simplification and codification initiated in the late 1930s. The 'Concerto for Orchestra' ranks among Bartok's finest works.

Bartok re-evaluated the aesthetic and constructive features of eighteenth and nineteenth-century music in unmistakably twentieth-century terms with perhaps less sense of disruption than any of his major contemporaries, a singular achievement. He extended the *thematic*, formal and *tonal* techniques of his predecessors, and this, combined with his nationalistic outlook reinterpreted within the rationalistic orientation of a new age, combined to produce a surprisingly traditional 'tone' in his music. Unlike many of his progressive contemporaries, his music doesn't seem to play itself off 'against' traditional elements (as for example, one senses in Stravinsky) as to work directly 'with' them.

In integrating peasant and Classical music, Bartok stressed both the common elements and the distinctive characteristics of the two traditions. In both, pieces typically have a single *pitch* centre, use *diatonic* and other scales, and feature melodies created from *motives* that are repeated and diverse. From the Classical tradition, Bartok retained the elaborate *contrapuntal* and formal procedures, such as *fugue* and *sonata* form. From the peasant tradition, he drew rhythmic complexity and irregular *metres,* especially common in the Bulgarian tradition—*modal scales* and mixed *modes*; and specific kinds of melodic structure and ornamentation. Bartok intensified these qualities and thus composed music that can be simultaneously more complex in its counterpart than Bach, and more ornamented and rhythmically elaborate than his folk models.

A full illustration of Bartok's synthesis together with key features of his *neo-tonal* style is offered by 'Music for Strings, Percussion and Celesta'. Each of the four movements creates a *tonal* centre by means similar to the modal tunes of folk song and to the *chordal* motion and *tonic-dominant* polarities of Classical music while avoiding common practice harmony (i.e. of the period of the *tonal* system). Peasant melodies often start from and return to the *tonal* centre, as in the first movement theme; or else centre around a *tone* as in the second movement *theme*; or descend to the *tonal* centre from its upper octave, as in the finale. Bartok's synthesis of the two traditions to create a modernist idiom is rich in allusions to the music of both.

Bartok creates *themes* by varying small *motives*, a procedure widespread in both Classical music from Bach and Haydn to Schoenberg and Stravinsky, and in the peasant music of central and south-eastern Europe. Many Hungarian tunes use short phrases and repeat motives with slight variations as in the first movement theme while Bulgarian dance tunes typically amplify a rhythmic-melodic motive as in the finale's theme, but in the *Lydian* mode, which is used in certain peasant songs. Also, Bartok uses complex forms and *contrapuntal* methods which derive strictly from the classical tradition. Seldom does anything in this work sound folk-derived. Bartok has extrapolated elements of Hungarian and other peasant traditions and fused them with classical elements to create something truly new with a lavish connection to the past.

The Revolutionary Russian: Igor Stravinsky (1882–1971)

Stravinsky is the third giant of Modernist innovation, after Debussy and Schoenberg. The Paris premiere of his ballet, 'The Rite of Spring' in May 1913 is arguably the most famous (or notorious) opening night in the history of music, unleashing a near riot among the bourgeois audience. May 1913 also witnessed the world premiere of Debussy's ballet 'Jeux' with its innovatory freedom of form, an event occurring in turn seven months after the first performance of Schoenberg's 'Pierrot Lunaire'. Naturally, one cannot separate the elements of harmony, rhythm and form—of pitch, time and structure—in any work: all are interdependent, and Debussy, Schoenberg and Stravinsky made innovations on all fronts. However, it is Schoenberg's harmony, Stravinsky's rhythm and Debussy's form which have aroused the greatest interest and proved most important to subsequent composers. Stravinsky's career is significant for its stylistic diversity.

Stravinsky's Three Styles

Russian Period

Signs of a distinctly personal style first appeared in two short orchestral works written in 1908, the 'Scherzo Fantastique' and 'Fireworks'. The former is a study in *octatonic* pitch relationships—an interest acquired from his teacher Rimsky-Korsakov, which remained an important feature of Stravinsky's compositional method; the latter illustrates his unshifting 'preference for static, non-developmental harmonic areas' (Morgan 1991, p. 90). 'Fireworks' remains anchored in the key of E major. Stravinsky compensates for the lack of harmonic progression by manipulating small motivic units, mostly confined to the same 'pitch repertory'. He enlivens the largely motionless harmonic background through virtuosic instrumentation, foreshadowing two of the most characteristic aspects of his later style.

The music of each of the three Diaghilev ballets was conceived as part of an integrated artistic vision that also incorporated drama, dance, staging and set design. Stravinsky worked in close collaboration with the other artists on all aspects of the production. The fact that the music was designed to complement a theatrical presentation had a marked effect on its formal features and compositional planning, creating a new perception of musical structure that in its own way would prove as influential for subsequent musical development as the *atonal* works of Schoenberg, Webern and Berg.

'The Firebird' (1910), is something of a hangover from the past, reflecting the influence of Rimsky-Korsakov, particularly in the link between *chromaticism* and the supernatural features of the traditional Russian fairy tale. Much of the music remains *diatonic*, expressing nineteenth-century notions of melodic development. 'Petrushka' (1911), a love triangle involving three circus puppets, is clearly anti-Romantic and modern, the score effectively mirroring its ironic quality with a spare, tough-minded countenance in contrast to the richly sensuous *textures* still predominating in the earlier work. The opening bars illustrate a new economy. The flute melody is drawn from four pitches D-E–G-A. Moreover, this melody is knitted together from a few fixed melodic and rhythmic modules that remain unchanged in themselves and acquire variety mainly through their changing combinations. This technique remained a basic feature of Stravinsky's melodic style.

Moreover, Stravinsky adopts new formal processes: the musical shape of Petrushka's first tableau, depicting the intense activity of a pre-Lenten fair, shows the criss-crossing from flute module to cello module and back, with some overlapping, a feature which forms a basic structural model for the whole piece. Stravinsky imitates the 'popular' character of fairground music, deriving melodic material from folk and popular songs, even imitating the sound of a barrel organ and a music box. '...after being introduced separately, the music for the latter two is combined in a multilevelled texture that features striking rhythmic conflicts between the two distinct layers' (Morgan 1991, p. 94). We find, moreover, his characteristic blocks of static harmony with repetitive melodic and rhythmic patterns as well as sudden shifts from one block to another. Each group of dancers receives its distinctive music.

Petrushka's first tableau is virtually *diatonic* but it's only when Stravinsky imitates the quality of street dancers that he resorts to traditional *tonic* and *dominant* relationships. The effect resembles a colourful musical kaleidoscope. The second tableau is much more *chromatic* than the first and contains a famous dissonant chord consisting of two superimposed major *triads* with roots separated by a *tritone*—F sharp major and C major—both part of the *octatonic* scale. It is a chord of such power, it has become known as the 'Petrushka chord', referring to the puppet brought to life by a magician. For Taruskin, 'Petrushka' is where 'Stravinsky at last became Stravinsky' (Taruskin, Vol. I, 2009, p. 662).

Stravinsky's distinctive style crystallised in 'The Rite of Spring', an imaginary fertility rite set in pre-historic Russia, during which an adolescent girl is selected for sacrifice and must dance herself to death. Stravinsky again borrowed from folk melodies but the scenario, choreography and music were inspired by 'primitivism', emphasising the elemental and uncultured, and casting aside the stylishness and sophistication of modern life and artistry. This reduction of *metre* to mere pulsation is the factor that most powerfully conveys a sense of primitivism in the music. In the ballet's final dance—'Sacrificial Dance'—Stravinsky adopted two additional methods of reducing *metre* to pulse—'rapidly changing metres and unpredictable alternation of notes with rests' (Burkholder et al. 2014, p. 833).

Stravinsky vividly evokes pagan Russian rituals with a score of unprecedented rhythmic force. The music is distilled to its rhythmic core thrashed out by the orchestra with uninhibited percussive ferocity. Like Schoenberg, Stravinsky understood that *chromaticism* was loosening the power of *diatonic* harmony to sustain the musical movement. But Stravinsky's answer was quite different. For him, rhythm was a new motivating force, as 'The Rite of Spring ' demonstrated.

Stravinsky often constructs *textures* by layering two or more independent strands of music on top of each other. But the patterns within successive blocks are different, creating discontinuity. However, the collection of *pitches* used differs by only one new note, imparting a strong sense of continuity. A major contributor to the sternness of 'The Rite of Spring' is the high level of dissonance and *chromaticism*, illustrated by the repeated chord that opens the 'Augurs of Spring', the ballet's first section. Most dissonance in Stravinsky is based on the scales found in Russian Classical music, such as the *diatonic* and *octatonic* collections. Moreover, Stravinsky often identified a musical idea with a particular *timbre*. Here, the pounding chords are always in the strings with horn reinforcements, with the English horn *ostinato* recurring only in that instrument throughout the first half of the dance. In the second half, it travels through several other instruments. In music without *motivic* development, such changes of *timbre* are one means of providing variety.

A key aspect of this technique is a new conception of *tonality*: although largely independent of the traditional one, it is capable of integrating extended musical structures. While stressing that 'tonality is my discipline', Stravinsky observed: 'my chief concern is not so much with... tonality as what one might term the polar attraction of sound, of an interval, or even a complex of tones' (Stravinsky 1947, p. 36, in Morgan 1991, p. 102). This new and more broadly defined sense of *tonal* centricity transformed what had been a basically *dynamic*, and essentially *diatonic*, concept into one that was equally applicable to *diatonic* or *chromatic* contexts, recreating the tension in major and minor keys without reverting to the earlier harmonic language. For example, both *diatonic* and *chromatic* passages occur in 'Petrushka' and 'The Rite of Spring', *diatonic* ones being especially distinctive of the former work, *chromatic* ones of the latter.

Having pioneered these methods, Stravinsky continued to use them throughout his career. During World War One, the wartime economy compelled him to abandon the large orchestra of his early ballets in favour of small combinations of instruments to accompany stage works. 'Histoire du Soldat'—'Soldier's Tale' (1918) established a line of demarcation between the first two periods: a tone of economy and restraint evident in 'post-Rite' works. As ever in Stravinsky, there is a high level of rhythmic complexity and although the music is clearly *tonal*, it is often sharply dissonant and equivocal in its *tonal* focus. Cut off from Russia by World War One and then by the 1917 revolution, to which he was not sympathetic, Stravinsky began moving away from Russian topics while keeping the characteristic traits that derived largely from his Russian training.

Neo-Classical Period

In 1919, Diaghilev commissioned Stravinsky to orchestrate pieces by the eighteenth century composer Pergolesi to accompany a new ballet 'Pulcinella'. Stravinsky applied his distinctive stylistic approach to the music, reworking the piece and faithfully retaining the original music, which, however, sounded more like Stravinsky than Pergolesi. This 'discovery' of the past led Stravinsky to a reconsideration of the underlying principles of eighteenth-century classicism, reworked to establish a basis for his own music. Stravinsky's aim was not to return to the past but to re-energise some fundamental traditional compositional principles in ways consistent with contemporary harmonic and rhythmic custom. Although Stravinsky was not the first neo-Classical composer, he was the most significant. The period, lasting from 1919 to 1951, indicates a move away from Russian folk music and towards Western art music as a source of influence or allusion. But echoing and alluding to music in the classical tradition hardly differed from what he had been doing all along in using folk and popular materials, so neo-classicism actually gave him new material without requiring him to retool entirely.

Stravinsky used his distinctive idiom, forged in the Russian tradition, to establish connections to the Western Classical tradition, just as Schoenberg had used his Modernist twelve-tone system to revive the forms of the Classical past. Stravinsky's neo-Classical style expresses a predilection for balance, coolness, objectivity as opposed to Romantic programme music. In his neo-classical works, Stravinsky referred to a broad range of styles and forms. Many works conjure up the Classical era, including 'Symphony in C' (1939–1940), 'Symphony in Three Movements' (1942–1945), and 'The Rake's Progress' (1947–1951) modelled on Mozart's comic operas. 'Dumbarton Oaks Concerto' (1937–1938) looks to Bach's concertos. Eighteenth-century characteristics are mixed with modern dissonances, *octatonic* melodies, *metre* changes, and interruptions so that the music rarely sounds Classical or Baroque. Stravinsky uses the styles he evokes as benchmarks that transform his own trademark style in novel ways so that every piece has an individual personality.

The full extent of his stylistic transformation became clear in 1923 with the 'Octet for Winds' which created a sensation in the musical world. The Russian 'primitivism' of 'Rite' had disappeared, replaced by a new set of aesthetic hallmarks derived principally from the legacy of the eighteenth century: formal transparency, expressive restraint, and personal. The work's *tonal* basis is more *diatonic* than one had come to expect of Stravinsky. The 'Octet' was the first of a series of compositions, up to the early 1950s, that are founded on, but also militate against, traditional compositional models and procedures. These works became hugely influential, forming the basis for the neo-Classical movement, though the term is misleading since Stravinsky drew perhaps even more heavily on Baroque than on Classical features. However, Stravinsky's 'return to the past' embraced almost every period of Western music.

However, not every work of the middle period reveals a clear stylistic prototype. Two of the most significant, the 'Symphony of Psalms' (1930), and the 'Symphony in Three Movements' (1945) defy simple categorisation. Baroque references abound but they are accompanied by other elements that resist unambiguous ascription. Moreover, *chromatic* passages also feature in neo-Classical Stravinsky, often founded on elements drawn from the *octatonic* scale.

An excerpt from Stravinsky's 'Piano Sonata' (1924) illustrates key technical features of his neo-classicism. The opening of the first movement's main theme is based on a *diatonic* scale (C major) and is underpinned by a largely *triadic* harmonic structure. Stravinsky has rethought his long-established practice of juxtaposing two static *tonal* fields (here C and D major) into neo-classical terms.

The fact that Stravinsky came to the Western tradition as an 'outsider' doubtless explains his ability to change styles with such facility and to shape such original musical ideas despite using traditional references. 'With his own musical roots firmly planted in Russia, he could

approach Western stylistic models like "foreign objects" to be transformed... according to his own inclinations... consistent with the basic
compositional conceptions developed during his earlier years' (Morgan
1991, p. 174). Hence, his neo-classical works reveal the same structural techniques as those of his Russian period: *tonal* polarity (equality
between major and minor), static harmonic progressions, rhythmic juxtaposition and formal stratification. In 'The Wedding' (1917–1923) and
'Histoire du Soldat', the instruments are placed on the stage in full view
of the audience, while in 'Histoire', 'Oedipus Rex' and 'Persephone', a
narrator 'distances' the audience from the action, a profound rejection of
the realistic conventions of eighteenth and nineteenth-century opera and
drama.

Modern composers have been deprived of a common musical language
and have, therefore, had to construct artificial ones out of whatever
materials were available. Stravinsky was the perennial 'outsider', cut off
from his native land, who searched through the entire repertory of
Western music for a foundation for his own work. He developed a
preference for the 'impersonal formulas of a remote past'—either liter-
ally as in his neo-Classical 'reconstructions', or figuratively, as in his
serial works. This predilection provided him with a potent symbol of
the modern artist's creative isolation. Stravinsky's neo-classicism and its
continuity with his earlier style are both evident in 'Symphony of Psalms'
(1930) for mixed chorus and orchestra. Baroque features include almost
perpetual motion, *sequences*, frequent *ostinatos* (another Stravinsky trademark), and the mature *fugue* of the second movement. Again, Stravinsky
avoids a Romantic orchestral sound, stressing an 'objective' rather than
an emotional sound palette by excluding violins, violas and clarinets. In
three passages in the first movement, E is emphasized as a *tonal* centre
through assertion: the E minor *triad* as the sole harmony, E as the focus
of the melody with an E minor *triad* occurring on every downbeat, E
sustained in the bass. Such assertion of a *tonal* centre through reitera-
tion is very different from Schoenberg's *atonality*. Yet this music is not
tonal, 'since it does not follow the rules of traditional harmony'. It is
neotonal—Stravinsky is seeking new methods of creating a single pitch as
a *tonal* centre (Burkholder et al. 2014, p. 839).

In recent decades, musicians and scholars have come to appreciate how
much in common Schoenberg and Stravinsky had, especially in the music
composed in the 1920s–1940s, when both sought to revive traditional
forms, recasting them in a new, personal musical language.

Serial Period

After Schoenberg's death in 1951, the twelve-tone methods he had pioneered were as much part of the accepted musical landscape as sonata form. They were also becoming popular with younger composers, who broadened the system to series in areas other than pitch, such as rhythm. Such music based on series was no longer simply twelve-tone, and it became known as 'serial' music. Stravinsky, now 70, began using serial techniques in his music from roughly 1952. A surprising turn was noticed in 'Cantata' (1952): an interest in exact *contrapuntal* methods. It contains his first use of the exact serial technique. In fact, the series appears in only part of the piece and has a strong *tonal* orientation (not all twelve notes are used and some notes are repeated), but its use is clearly influenced by Schoenberg (all standard forms of the series appear).

Stravinsky developed his distinctive approach to serialism—in compositions such as 'Septet' (1953) and 'Three Songs from William Shakespeare' (1953) His best-known serial pieces include the song cycle 'In Memoriam Dylan Thomas' (1954), which uses a series of only five notes and its serial permutations and was his first wholly serial composition (Morgan 1991, p. 355), 'Threni' (1958) for voices and orchestra on texts from the Lamentations of Jeremiah; and 'Movements' (1960) for piano and orchestra. All these reveal his characteristic idiom of juxtaposed blocks and disrupted *metre*, although the *pitch* content is increasingly *chromatic*.

However, the 'Canticum Sacrum' (1955) contains Stravinsky's first twelve-tone music, specifically its three middle movements. 'Threni' was an entirely twelve-tone composition, a setting of the Lamentations of Jeremiah for soloists, chorus and orchestra. He followed it with a string of works in which he increasingly perfected his highly personal approach to twelve-tone serialism.In his final works, such as the biblical allegory 'The Flood' (1962), the 'Variations for Orchestra' (1964), and three sacred works for voices and orchestra, Stravinsky continued exploring this newly discovered world of *chromatic* serialism with amazing energy and youthful eagerness. These final works, which carried the composer to the distant reaches of *atonality* and of 'learned' *contrapuntal* devices, were extraordinary achievements for an octogenarian, comparable perhaps only to the operas of Verdi's last years. Stravinsky's genius lay in discovering stylistic benchmarks derived from Russian sources while imposing his distinctive personal stamp. By drawing on everything from early music to contemporary serial music, he claimed the whole tradition as his own. It is a decisive proof of serialism's centrality in the 1950s that Stravinsky adopted the twelve-tone technique, the only member of the generation of composers who shaped musical development in the first half of the century to live long enough to play a leading role in the second.

Stravinsky was one of the most influential composers of all time, whose impact equalled that of Wagner and Debussy. Through his work, elements developed in Russian music (*ostinatos*, juxtaposition of blocks, interruption, lack of development) and features he pioneered (frequent changes of *metre*, unpredictable accents and rests, and 'dry' orchestration) became the conventional wisdom of modern music, employed by composers developing many different styles. However, few could match his ability to project a single personality in any style he adopted.

Falling Foul of Socialist Realism: Sergei Prokoviev (1891–1953)

Prokofiev's life and musical styles fall into three periods: the first being his formative years in Russia, the second his years in Paris (1920–1933), and the third following his return to his homeland in 1936.

Prokoviev's Three Periods
Prokoviev's early reputation was as a radical Modernist, linking striking dissonance with motoric rhythms. Dissatisfied with his conservatory teachers, Lyadov and Rimsky-Korsakov, whom he regarded as outdated, he developed speedily. By 1909, his music was widely performed, 'attracting considerable public attention… even enjoying the distinction of denunciation by conservative critics as "ultra-modernist"' (Morgan 1991, p. 239). The music of this period is mostly of the primitive style influenced by the onslaught of Stravinsky's 'The Rite of Spring'. Prokoviev utilises driving rhythms and dissonant harmonies, and includes his first three piano concertos (1912, 1913, 1921) and the ballet, 'Ala and Lolli' or 'Scythian Suite' (1914). Prokoviev described his First Piano Concerto as his 'first more or less mature composition'. It is technically polished and also expressive of a strong personal voice. It also prefigures many features that would typify the post-war neo-Classical movement.

Prokoviev's early outlook of profound anti-Romanticism and anti-emotionalism was softened by occasional moments of 'cool lyricism'. 'Classicism' seems to have become ingrained within him. In an interview for the *New York Times* in 1930, he spoke of Classic forms as containing everything he needed. This approach is exemplified in the 'Classical

Symphony' which 'pays homage' to eighteenth-century style, most clearly that of Haydn. However, Prokoviev had already established the essential features of his style in a series of prior works: the Second Piano Concerto (1913), the Second and Third Piano Sonatas (1912, 1917), the operas 'Maddalena' (1913) and 'The Gambler' (1917), the First Violin Concerto (1917), and the ballets 'Chout' ('The Tale of the Buffoon') and the 'Scythian Suite', both composed for Diaghilev in 1915. All these works were composed within a five-year span, and display a clear predilection for pre-Romantic stylistic models. The Classical Symphony is scored for a small eighteenth-century type orchestra, and its four movements follow a Classic formal model. It has a parodistic aspect, typical of Prokoviev, poking fun affectionately at the 'conventions of a highly conventionalised style', distorting them through sudden, unexpected shifts of harmony and rhythm (Morgan 1991, p. 240).

Typical stylistic features are visible in the opening of one of the twenty short piano pieces Prokoviev wrote between 1915 and 1917 under the title 'Visions Fugitives'. The two *phrases*, each four bars long, can be subdivided into two *subphrases* of two bars each. This balanced structure is accompanied by a *texture* of Classical simplicity—a single-lined melody with a featureless *triadic* accompaniment, which, however, behaves in an unconventional manner. In the first two bars, Prokoviev typically uses non-traditional harmonic progressions, using the normal *triadic* language of *tonal* music but avoiding the operational expectations traditionally associated with it.

Middle Period:

In 1918, Prokoviev left Russia intending to return when the political situation had calmed down. But he only returned permanently eighteen years later, living in the United States until 1922, then in Paris. He toured North America and Western Europe, produced piano solo works, concertos for himself to play, for example, the Third Piano Concerto (1921), and works such as Symphonies Two, Three and Four. He fulfilled commissions for larger works—for Chicago, the satirical opera, 'The Love for Three Oranges' (1919), from which comes the famous jaunty 'March' (1921), and two ballets for Sergei Diaghilev's Ballets Russes in Paris, 'The Steel Step' (1926) and 'The Prodigal Son' (1929).

Prokoviev's contact with the West eventually influenced his style though the extent was not immediately apparent. The two main works of the American years, 'The 'Love for Three Oranges' and the 'Third

Piano Concerto', preserve the essential stylistic character of the earlier Russian pieces. After settling in Paris, Prokoviev's music assumed a more dissonant and complex character. The 'Piano Sonata No. 5, Opus 38' (1923—later simplified as opus 135), the 'Quintet for Wind and String' (1924), and the Second Symphony (1925), trace a path towards greater *textural* and formal complexity. The first movement of the symphony contains dense blocks of sound built up from *ostinato*-type layers, and a *tonal* framework much more ambiguous than before. Although *ostinato* figures were a familiar feature in earlier works such as the 'Scythian Suite' and 'Chout', here they are enmeshed with one another instead of cooperating as previously, creating complex *textural* patterns reminiscent of Stravinsky's 'The Rite of Spring'. The Diaghilev ballets, and the Third and Fourth Symphonies (1928, 1930), all express a movement towards greater clarity and simplicity. So did the only opera of the Paris years, 'The Fiery Angel' (1923, revised 1927).

Late Prokoviev:
Many of Prokofiev's most famous compositions were written after he returned to Russia. These include the children's story for orchestra and narrator, 'Peter and the Wolf' (1936), one of many works resulting from the Soviet demand for high-quality music for children, several film scores, and 'Romeo and Juliet' (1935–1936), one of the twentieth century's most popular ballets, and his greatest symphony—Symphony No. 5 (1944).

Prokoviev's later work, although lacking the energy of his youthful music, reflects, as though in compensation, a relaxed lyricism, a new expressive warmth. Works such as the 'Fifth Symphony' and Seventh Piano Sonata have definite power. But essentially Prokoviev had always been a composer with a strong traditional orientation, so 'the more conservative approach of his later scores represented not so much a negation of his earlier style as a readjustment made within its own terms' (Morgan 1991, p. 244).

In this final period, therefore, Prokoviev remained remarkably prolific despite the strained political atmosphere. He composed three symphonies (Nos. 5–7), four piano sonatas (Nos. 6–9), two concertos, one for violin and one for cello, three full-length ballets ('Romeo and Juliet', 'Cinderella', and 'The Stone Flower'); also, a number of film scores, notably two for director Sergei Eisenstein, 'Alexander Nevsky' (1938), and 'Ivan the Terrible' (1945). He also wrote several operas, most of which encountered ideological objections and were hardly heard until the 1960s. The most ambitious and musically challenging is 'War and Peace' (1943, later revised). It is cast in a traditional operatic mould and has earned a respected position among twentieth-century operatic works.

In keeping with the dictates of the Stalin regime, this later music is more *tonal*, less dissonant, conforms to Classical styles, making it accessible to the public. His orchestral suite 'Lieutenant Kije' (1934), originally film music, reflected his wish to reorient himself down the path of accommodation to the regime. Even so, Prokofiev was denounced in 1948 by the government as being 'too modern' and he composed no more music for the remainder of his life. Prokofiev had written the gigantic 'Cantata for the 20th Anniversary of the October Revolution', intended for performance during the anniversary year but blocked by the Communist Party's culture and science department, which demanded less 'incomprehensible music'. The Cantata had to wait until 5 April 1966 for a partial premiere, just over 13 years after the composer's death.

Taruskin dismissed Prokoviev as an 'ambitious, narcissistic man … never really a musical rebel, even when carefully cultivating the image of an enfant terrible at the St. Petersburg Conservatory. His "advanced" musical vocabulary… clothed a conventional musical syntax and expressive rhetoric. He was a shallow modernist who made sure that academicians… could… detect his underlying allegiance to… the traditional skills and values on which grades were based'. However, Taruskin concedes that he had a 'fabulous melodic gift' and was able to give his music a 'dazzling professional gloss, a veneer of harmonic daring, and an instant imprint (as even Stravinsky had to concede) of personality' (Taruskin 2009, p. 240).

Music for the People: Paul Hindemith (1895–1963)

Hindemith was among the most prolific composers of the twentieth century. He regarded himself principally as a practising musician, performing as violinist, violist, and conductor. The experience of performance became central to his music. In the splintered interwar world of new music, Hindemith changed his style several times.

By the late 1920s, Hindemith was disturbed by the growing gulf between modern composers and an increasingly passive public. He responded by composing 'Gebrauchmusik'—'Music For Use'—in contrast to music for its own sake. His aim was to create for young or amateur performers music of high quality, modern in style and challenging yet fulfilling to perform. An example is his musical play for children, 'Wir Bauen Eine Stadt'—'We Build a Town' (1930), in which children build their own town and govern it without adults, offering a lesson in civic virtues through singing and playing music that is both entertaining and appropriate for young amateurs.

In 1936, the Nazis outlawed Hindemith's music as 'cultural Bolshevism.' Hindemith responded by examining the role of the artist in relation to political power, the result of which was the opera 'Mathis der Maler'— 'Mathis the Painter', (1934–1935), and 'Symphony Mathis der Maler' (1933–1934), his best-known work, comprising the overture and other material for the opera. Mathis Grunewald, the painter of the famous Isenheim Altarpiece, abandons painting to join the peasants in their uprising against the nobility during the German Peasants' War of 1525. After their defeat, he realises that by abandoning his art he betrayed his vocation and his true obligation to society—painting. However, Hindemith does not see art as wholly autonomous since Mathis' moral vision is informed by his experiences. The opera can be interpreted as an allegory for Hindemith's own career. 'Mathis' was banned (in one scene Lutheran books are burned by Catholics), and had to be performed in Switzerland, Hindemith moving there in 1938. In 1940, following the outbreak of World War Two, he emigrated to the United States, remaining there until 1953, when he returned to Switzerland.

Hindemith's Modernist Style

Most of Hindemith's music is *tonal* but non-*diatonic*, centred on a *tonic* and *modulating* from one *tonal* centre to another. But it uses all twelve notes freely rather than relying on a scale. Hindemith's work is divisible into three periods: the first period, 1918–1923, was primarily a time of experimentation with Romanticism. The second period, 1924–1933, revealed synthesis of neo-Baroque and neo-classical styles, with neo-Baroque aspects prevailing. Hindemith's third period, 1933–1963, with its preponderance of neo-Classical *tonality*, appears first in his 1933–1934 symphony 'Mathis der Maler'.

During the early 1920s, the young composer broke away from his late Romantic roots, distinguished by lush *chromaticism* and mainly *triadic* harmony, marking himself out as one of the more radical members of the post-war generation, rapidly acquiring the reputation as the 'enfant terrible' of the contemporary German musical scene. His music was aggressive and volcanic. In 1920 and 1921, he composed three one-act operas of which two—'Morder, Hoffnung der Frauen'—'Murder, the Hope of Women', and 'Sancta Susanna'—dealing with highly charged sexual issues and sparking a scandal which required the police to be summoned.

The third, the puppet opera 'Das Nusch-Nuschi', is a mocking parody of Wagner's 'Tristian und Isolde'. But most remarkable is the influence of jazz and popular music. Hindemith wrote in an autobiographical sketch in 1922: 'I have 'tilled' the following fields of music: …chamber music, movies, cafes, dance halls, operetta, jazz band, military band' ('Neue Musik-Zeitung', in Morgan 1991, p. 222).

Another example of the young composer's 'nose-thumbing' post-war mindset is visible in the 'Kammermusik No. 1', (1922), which quotes a then popular foxtrot, even using a siren. The neutral title ('Chamber Music'), also expresses Hindemith's rejection of the *programmatic* titles of the recent past and his current preference for small, heterogeneous instrumental ensembles, perfectly suited to reveal the music's essentially linear and non-figurative style. It launched a series of seven pieces that were written between 1922 and 1927. Modelled on Baroque concerto forms, they reveal Bach-like *polyphonic* textures and continuously unfolding *thematic* material. These works reflect the general neo-Classical style of the period, suggesting familiarity with Stravinsky's recent work.

During the middle and later 1920s, Hindemith adopted a more disciplined approach. Although remaining very prolific throughout his career, the period from 1922 to 1927 during which he consolidated his mature style, was especially fecund, producing many of his most original and ambitious works. Apart from the 'Kammermusik' series, several large-scale chamber works appeared, also his song cycle 'Das Marienleben'—'Life of Mary', (1923), arguably the finest work of the period.

The typical features of Hindemith's style during this period are demonstrated by the opening of 'Kammermusik No. 2' (1924) for piano and twelve-piece chamber orchestra. Several traits exemplify the ' back to Bach' approach so prominent among composers at the time: 'the Baroque-like motoric rhythm, the use of brief melodic figures spun out in a continuous development, and the contrapuntal conception of the whole…' (Morgan 1991, p. 224). Hindemith's opera 'Cardillac' (1926), based on a story by E.T.A. Hoffmann, was the most comprehensive project of those years, departing conspicuously from the Wagner-Strauss tradition, in alignment with Hindemith's then anti-Romanticism. The music comprises a series of separate 'numbers', abandoning its traditional role as a conveyor of emotional content. As in Stravinsky's theatre works of the late 1910s and early 1920s, music and drama seem to run along separate paths, the rhythmically driving, *concertante* quality of the music maintaining a standoffish stance from the onstage action, responding in terms of general pacing and by providing contrasts to punctuate the main formal divisions of the stage action. 'Cardillac' established Hindemith as the leading German composer of his generation. It was followed by the twelve-minute chamber opera 'Hin und Zuruck'—'There and Back' (1927), in which the stage action moves in reverse order after the midpoint until the opening scene is reached; then came the full-length comic opera 'Neues vom Tage' 'News of the Day' (1929) dealing with contemporary people and situations.

Hindemith's outstanding productivity is directly due to his view of composition as a craft to be practised diligently, with the mastery and dedication any professional brings to their respectable occupation but without grandiose ideas of self-expression. Following from this was his emphasis on music as a social activity rather than as a 'vehicle for personal communication', an attitude reflected in the unusually high percentage of chamber works in his work. Hindemith thus devoted much time during these years composing works that could be played by non-professionals, including choral music, works for string orchestra and wind ensemble, and the children's play with music. 'Lehrstuck'—'Teaching Piece' (1929) is possibly the most significant of these works, a politically inspired stage piece for amateur performers incorporating music, acting, dance (or film), and audience participation, based on a text by playwright Bertolt Brecht, the most important innovator in German theatre of the time. Hindemith also collaborated with Brecht on 'Der Lindbergflug'—'Lindbergh's Flight' (1929), composing the music with Brecht's collaborator Kurt Weill.

Hindemith's aspiration to narrow the gap between composer and public, between musician as specialist and as amateur, had an enduring effect on his overall compositional approach, despite little of his work after the early 1930s being intended for amateurs. This radical change is apparent in Hindemith's own concert works which disclose a distinct stylistic simplification. *Tonal* areas become more clearly enunciated, *textures* are more transparent, a new lyricism appears in the music—while the sardonic and parodistic humour of the 1920s has almost completely disappeared. The first work to embody these changes was the opera 'Mathis the Painter' (1935), and the symphony based on it remains one of Hindemith's most compelling and frequently performed works. The solid craftsmanship of the earlier work survives but is now in the service of a new purposeful expressiveness weight. However, elements of the composer's youthful fire are also absent.

In 1937, Hindemith codified the principles of his new approach, establishing a solid theoretical foundation for the harmonic and melodic aspects of his music. He took the *tonal* principle as his starting point, affirming its priority as a 'natural force, like gravity' and constructed a comprehensive *pitch* system in which all the possible intervallic relationships are graded according to their 'absolute' degree of consonance and dissonance. Though searching, like Schoenberg, for a new equivalent for traditional *tonality*, Hindemith differed in continuing to accept the basic principles of the older system, seeking to extend rather than to totally replace them. He said: 'Music... will always take its departure from the major triad and return to it. The musician cannot escape it any more than the painter his primary colours, or the architect his three-dimensions' (Hindemith 1942, 1:22, in Morgan 1991, p. 227).

From the middle 1930s until his death in 1963, Hindemith's music remained surprisingly consistent in style; once his new theoretical position had been formulated, he stuck to it faithfully. His entire later work can be interpreted as a conscious effort to integrate twentieth-century compositional techniques with the music of the past, an integration reflected not only in reliance upon traditional forms and genres and the frequent appearance of such conventional procedures as *fugue, fugato,* and *passacaglia,* but also in the assimilation of actual earlier music in some of the scores. Examples include medieval chants in 'Mathis der Maler'. The differences between Hindemith and Stravinsky here are instructive: in the former, we find little of the 'distancing' effect created by the latter's elaborate manipulations; the borrowed material is wholly integrated into the total fabric as an unexceptional constituent. Hence, the 'mannered' quality of Stravinsky's music is largely absent—but also its special quality of aesthetic tension.

In his later years, Hindemith moved increasingly in the direction of large-scale compositions viewed as extensions of the eighteenth and nineteenth-century orchestral operatic traditions. The opera 'Die Harmonie der Welt'—'The Harmony of the World' (1957) is maybe his most personal statement: the protagonist, the Renaissance astronomer and speculative music theorist Johannes Kepler, incorporates Hindemith's beliefs in the mystical and cosmic implications of harmonic relationships. But the bulk of Hindemith's later output is purely instrumental. The piano piece 'Ludus Tonalis'—'Tonal Game' (1942) is particularly representative—a series of preludes and fugues modelled on Bach's 'Well-Tempered Clavier'—intended as an educational illustration of the continuing legitimacy of traditional practices within a contemporary language.

Hindemith's music and theories were most influential among younger composers during the years immediately preceding and following World War Two, since when his influence has declined. However, he remains one of the more significant figures of twentieth-century music who expresses some of its most important historical trends.

The American Idiom of Aaron Copland (1900–1990)

Copland's Jewish faith, his leftwing politics and his homosexuality made him something of an outsider. However, he became the most significant composer of his generation, his work furthering the cause of American music. Copland's socialist views, which led him to support the Communist Party ticket in the 1936 presidential election and give strong backing to Progressive Party candidate Henry Wallace in 1948, resulted in his investigation by the FBI during the McCarthyite anti-Communist witch-hunt of the 1950s. His name was included on a list of 151 artists thought to have Communist associations. He was blacklisted and 'Lincoln Portrait' (1942) was withdrawn from President Eisenhower's 1953 inaugural concert. Copland was interrogated by McCarthy and Cohn who completely neglected his music, which ironically lauded American values.

The McCarthy investigation, though a burden on his time and energy, didn't seriously affect Copland's career and international reputation. However, in 1950, he became aware of Stalin's persecution of Shostakovich and other artists and resigned from leftist groups, turning instead to support the Democrats.

Copland's Modernist Style

In 1921, he became the first of many American composers to study under Nadia Boulanger in Paris. She outlined his future path, holding him in sufficiently high esteem to commission a work she could play during a 1925 American concert tour. The result was Copland's first major composition—'Symphony No. 1 for Organ and Orchestra'. Its broad rhetorical thematic content and jazzlike features (the latter especially apparent in the Scherzo) were to remain lasting features of his style.

In the early 1920s, Copland's music reflected the Modernist notion prevailing among intellectuals that the arts needed to be accessible to only an enlightened elite and that the masses would come to appreciate their work over time. However, his work, in the mid-1920s, following his return from Paris in 1925, was heavily influenced by jazz and popular music. He became influenced by the artistic circle around photographer Alfred Stieglitz who was convinced that American artists should reflect the 'ideas of American democracy'. However, Copland found there was only the music of Carl Ruggles and Charles Ives on which to draw. It was the decade of George Gershwin and Louis Armstrong. Lacking what Copland called a 'usable past', he looked to these pioneers of jazz and popular music as sources of inspiration (Oja and Tick 2005, p. 91; Pollack 1999, pp. 101, 113, 116, 158; Smith 1953, p. 60). The jazz influences were even more apparent in his next compositions—the orchestral suite 'Music for the Theater' (1925) and the 'Piano Concerto' (1926)—where he used melodic, harmonic and rhythmic elements endemic in jazz to create an 'American' sound (Morgan 1991, p. 287; Murchison 2012, pp. 48–54).

However, by the end of the decade, he began to move in a different artistic direction, down a more abstract, less jazz-oriented path. After 'Vitebsk, Study on a Jewish Theme for Piano Trio', (1928) transitional towards a more assertively Modernist style, came the two masterpieces of this phase of Copland's development—the 'Piano Variations' (1930) and the 'Short Symphony' (1933). But growing problems with the 'Symphonic Ode' (1929) and 'Short Symphony' (1933) induced him to rethink his position. Avant-garde music had lost its 'buoyant experimental edge' and the national mood towards it had changed (Oja and Tick 2005, p. 91).

Moreover, Copland noticed two trends among composers: an attempt to 'simplify their musical language' and, secondly, a wish to reach as wide an audience as possible. This shift reflected the idea pioneered by Hindemith of 'Gebrauchsmusik'—composers creating music serving utilitarian as well as artistic purposes. There were two examples of this approach—firstly, music that students could easily learn, and secondly, music with a wider appeal such as music for films, plays and radio.

Copland also advised the Group Theatre, a company inspiring artists such as Elia Kazan and Lee Strasberg (Pollack 1999, p. 258). Moreover, the 1930s witnessed the rise in popularity of the large swing bands such as Benny Goodman and Glenn Miller: Copland's interest in the genre was revived.

He drew inspiration from 'Les Six' in France and sought out contemporaries such as Roger Sessions, Virgil Thomson, Roy Harris and others, establishing himself as the spokesperson for composers of his generation. He also helped to found the Copland-Sessions Concerts, showcasing their chamber works to new audiences. This group acquired the name 'commando unit', with Copland's relationship to them being one of both support and rivalry. He played a significant role in keeping them together until after World War Two. He was also generous with his time with young American composers, as Leonard Bernstein attested, earning the title 'Dean of American Music' (Pollack 1999, pp. 178, 215).

During the Depression, Copland travelled widely to Europe, Africa and Mexico. His musical ideas underwent further significant modification. The heightened social awareness of the 1930s, prompted him to try to reach a larger, more diverse audience, with Leftist politics permeating his works of this period. He began composing for young audiences, following the first precept of 'Gebrauchmusik'. His 'Statements for Orchestra' (1935) indicated the new direction, first fully developed in 'El Salon Mexico' (1936). This was an outstanding orchestral work evoking the spirit of Mexican popular music, the first of his trademark works, begun during his initial visit to Mexico where he befriended composer Carlos Chavez. It was followed by 'The Second Hurricane' (1936), a 'play-opera for high school students'—a sort of American version of [Hindemith's] 'Gebrauchsmusik' written in an uncomplicated style for amateur production. It teaches the Brechtian virtue of 'acquiescing in the common good'. The CBS commission 'Music for Radio: Saga of the Prairie' (1937) possibly contained a concealed programme reference to the Scottsboro Boys, nine black youths imprisoned in 1931 on unsubstantiated rape charges; and the 'Lincoln Portrait' arranges quotations from Lincoln's writings into 'a vaguely socialist narrative' (Ross 2012, p. 302). This new approach fulfilled the second objective of American 'Gebrauchmusik', composing music of broad appeal.

'Prairie Journal' (1937) was one of Copland's first works to convey the spirit of the American West, an emphasis pursued in his ballet 'Billy the Kid' (1939). This became his first broad public success, together with 'El

Salon Mexico'. His ballet music confirmed him as an authentic composer of American music, much as Stravinsky's ballet scores had identified him with Russian music. Copland helped fill a vacuum for American choreographers needing music for their dance repertory, tapping into an artistic groundswell created by the films of Busby Berkeley and Fred Astaire and the ballets of George Balanchine, Agnes de Mille and Martha Graham, helping to both democratise and Americanise dance as an art form (Oja and Tick 2005, p. 94). In 1939, Copland wrote the film score for 'Of Mice and Men' and in 1940 for 'Our Town' (Pollack 1999, p. 312; Smith 1953, p. 169).

The 1940s witnessed a major shift in musical taste, away from the populist values that infused Copland's work of the 1930s and 1940s. Intellectuals began attacking the Popular Front culture with which his music was identified, labelling it 'middlebrow, a dumbing down of art into toothless entertainment' (Dickstein, in Oja and Tick 2005, p. 91). They often associated their rejection of populist art with technology, the new mass media and mass audiences—with the world of radio, television and film—for which Copland had composed or would soon do so.

However, the 1940s were arguably Copland's most productive years, some of his music from that decade consolidating his worldwide reputation. His ballet scores for 'Rodeo' (1942) and 'Appalachian Spring' (1944) were hugely successful. 'Lincoln Portrait' and 'Fanfare for the Common Man' became patriotic standards. The significant Third Symphony', (1944–1946), became his best-known symphony. 'Clarinet Concerto' (1948), scored for solo clarinet, strings, harp and piano, was commissioned by clarinetist Benny Goodman, and complemented Copland's earlier jazz-influenced piano concerto of 1926.

During the later 1930s and 1940s, he became principally interested in the vernacular traditions of the United States, consciously adopting a more literal American orientation in the three popular ballets—'Billy the Kid' (1938), 'Rodeo' (1942), and 'Appalachian Spring' (1944)—where he sometimes used actual American folk material to create a 'homespun' musical ambience, following his use of a Mexican tune in 'El Salon Mexico'. Copland's ballet scores along with such compositions as the wartime 'Lincoln Portrait' (1942), established him as the foremost American composer of his era. But during that decade, he also composed purely abstract music such as the 'Piano Sonata' (1941), 'Sonata for Violin and Piano' (1943), and the Third Symphony. In these works, he attempted to integrate his more direct recent pieces with the large-scale symphonic aspirations of the earlier ones.

In 1949, Copland returned to Europe where he met advocates of Schoenberg-inspired twelve-tone technique, and he considered adapting serial methods to his own musical idiom. In 1950, he wrote his 'Piano Quartet' in which he adopted Schoenberg's twelve-tone technique, and also 'Old American Songs' (1950), the first set of which was premiered by Peter Pears and Benjamin Britten. After World War Two, the musical scene in the United States changed radically, a change that affected Copland. In 1950, he composed the song cycle, 'Twelve Poems of Emily Dickinson', echoing works of the 1930s, and the 'Quartet for Piano and Strings' which used the twelve-tone system. But Copland never seemed completely comfortable with this approach. His output in the following two decades was considerably reduced in volume and unfocused in style. He composed two large-scale orchestral scores—'Connotations' (1962) and 'Inscape' (1967) which explored the twelve-tone technique. Other works, such as the 'Nonet for Strings' (1960), were more *tonal* while remaining complex. However, the 'Duo for Flute and Piano' (1971) harked back to the more populist style of the period of 'Appalachian Spring'.

The stylistic uncertainty of Copland's later output expresses a common problem in twentieth century music: the difficulty of maintaining artistic consistency under the pressure of rapidly changing trends and viewpoints. In the post-war era, Copland found himself inhabiting an environment largely alien to his own musical instincts, leaving him uncertain as to his own musical voice. However, the compositions written during the second quarter of the century are permanent fixtures in the repertory, winning for Copland an assured position in the arts of the United States.

The Warm Lyricism of Michael Tippett (1905–1998)

The two most accomplished English composers to emerge during the 1930s were Britten and Tippett. Tippett's work is generally divided into three phases, though these have somewhat fluid boundaries with some internal subdivision within each period. The 1960s initiated a second phase in which Tippett's style became more experimental following his early lyricism. The mid-1970s witnessed a fresh stylistic change, less marked and sudden than that of the early 1960s, following which the 'extremes' of the experimental phase were gradually replaced by a return to the lyricism of the first period, especially noticeable in the final works. Tippett seems to grow with each work, creating increasingly differentiated and technically ambitious music, expressing ever more of the range of contemporary experience (Clarke 2013; Kemp 1987, pp. 73–84).

This evolution is visible in the first three of Tippett's four symphonies, which are evenly distributed over the later phase of his career (1945, 1957, 1972). Tippett's third Piano Sonata, (1973), returns to the more abstract conception of instrumental music visible in his earlier music. There are shifting, metrically unsettled rhythmic groupings and an equivocal malleable *tonal* language.

Since the 1950s, Tippett's output has been dominated by four full-scale operas, with music to his own librettos. The range of dramatic material reflects the diversity of his musical sources. The musical differences between the operas are equally striking. 'The Midsummer Marriage' has a largely continuous structure, based on nineteenth-century operatic models, whereas 'King Priam' contains relatively brief and sharply individualised musical segments which punctuate the larger continuity. Moreover, the latter's stark, thin *textures* are in marked contrast with the former's more luxurious ones. The following two operas—'The Knot Garden' (1969) and 'The Ice Break' (1976)—are less traditional in both musical language and form. Tippett's prolonged stylistic development, during which he has embraced an ever-expanding range of techniques and materials, reveals neither mimicry nor compromise with current fashion.

Tippett v Britten! Does the comparison make sense? The two are so different such judgments are futile. Tippett lacks Britten's fluency and technical polish; indeed, his work often appears contrived and even cumbersome. Yet Tippett's music exudes a warmth and creative imagination emulated by few other composers of his generation.

Magnificent 'Muddle': Dimitri Shostakovitch (1906–1975)

Unlike his countrymen Stravinsky and Prokofiev, Shostakovich opted to remain in Russia throughout his life. The fifteen years between the birth of Prokoviev and that of Shostakovich put the younger composer in a different relationship to the development of Soviet Russia. Whereas Prokoviev was a 'Soviet' composer in only a partial sense, always remaining something of an outsider, Shostakovich began his musical training in 1919, after the Revolution. And as a child of the Soviet state, he rarely ventured outside his native Russia; therefore, his attitudes, and indeed his whole compositional career, were closely tied to the development of musical life under the new regime (Morgan 1991, p. 244; Griffiths 1978, p. 79). Shostakovich was constantly bowing to the decrees of the Stalinist regime, stunting his natural growth in efforts to please the government. His vast output is variable in quality, especially over the four decades following the infamous 1936 'Pravda' article attacking his opera 'Lady Macbeth of the Mtsensk District' (1934). Nevertheless, he was able to compose some powerful and lasting works.

Shostakovich achieved fame in the Soviet Union under the patronage of Soviet chief of staff Mikhail Tukhachevsky, but later had a complex and difficult relationship with the government. Creative work was often difficult given his regular disagreements with the authorities over the kind of music best suited to fulfil the Soviet mission. Nevertheless, he received accolades and state awards and served as a delegate in the Supreme Soviet of the RSFSR (Russian Soviet Federative Socialist Republic) (1947–1962) and the Supreme Soviet of the Soviet Union (from 1962 until his death). His output is dominated by his cycles of symphonies and string quartets, each totalling fifteen works. These works contain much of his most original thought and expression. The symphonies are distributed fairly evenly throughout his career, while the quartets are concentrated towards the latter part. He is also known for his operas 'The Nose' (1930) and 'Lady Macbeth'.

Shostakovich's Modernist Style

Shostakovich's works are broadly *tonal* and in the Romantic tradition, but with elements of *atonality* and *chromaticism*. In some of his later works (e.g. the 'String Quartet No. 12', he made use of *tone* rows. In the experimental atmosphere of post-revolutionary Russia, the young Shostakovitch absorbed features from all the various movements into his music, forging early on his own individual, highly original style which remained with him throughout his life. This style combined rhythmic vitality, a menacing, at times violent atmosphere, and frequent satirical allusions (Behrman 2006, p. 28).

Shostakovich began experimenting early on, exploring the more progressive developments still prominent in Russian music: in two piano pieces, the 'Sonata No 1' (1926) and 'Aphorisms' (1927), we encounter an apparently new composer bent on trial and error: 'the tightly linear textures and aggressive rhythmic drive set this music off sharply from the (first) symphony' (Morgan 1991, p. 245). This evolution towards 'abstract experimentation', as Shostakovich himself described it, climaxed in the 'Symphony No. 2' (1927), a one-movement work with a final choral section setting a 'Marxist' text. Its *tonal* freedom and overall stylistic complexity are astonishing. 'The contrapuntal writing reaches levels of such density that the listener often hears only a generalised timbral effect rather than specific melodic or harmonic content' (Morgan 1991, p. 245).

Although many later works contain pages of inflated heroism and bombast, in attempts to conform to the decrees of the government, one or two stand out as perhaps the composer's finest achievements. The 'Symphony No. 5,' for example, shows what the composer could do to please Stalin, at the same time expressing the composer's true feelings about the difficulties of artistic life in Russia.

The 'Fifth Symphony' (1937) was Shostakovich's 'creative answer to just criticism', as he himself apparently put it. This work is *texturally* simpler than the earlier three symphonies and less complicated *thematically* and *tonally*, and also *formally*, representing, therefore, a 'stylistic retrenchment'. However, it would be oversimplifying matters to regard it entirely as a political concession tailored to fit in with the party's demands. It is a work of clear artistic self-confidence, expressive force and technical accomplishment. The music he composed between the Second Symphony and the 1936 attack on 'Lady Macbeth' had already revealed a partial retreat from the extremes of the former work. Both the Third and Fourth Symphonies express the older symphonic tradition, reflecting the influence of Mahler, first visible in the choral finale of the Third and the huge orchestral forces of the Fourth. The 'Fifth Symphony' encompasses, as with Mahler, a 'wide range of styles and moods, from lyricism to dynamism and from profound emotion and lofty tragedy to grandiloquence and the grotesque. It is devised as a heroic symphony in the monumental style of Beethoven and Tchaikovsky. Prokoviev and Shostakovich shared a neo-Classical predilection for eclecticism, but Shostakovich was dissuaded by official policy from casting his net too wide. He responded to state pressure by abandoning 'the zestful pickings and iconoclastic outrages of "The Nose" for the distinctive blend of Tchaikovsky and Mahler he created in his Fifth Symphony (1937)' (Griffiths 1978, pp. 79–80).

Nevertheless, Shostakovich was affected by political oppression: in the years following Zhdanov's 1948 decree, his productivity visibly declined.

The partial decline in quality was doubtless partly due to the varying degrees of control imposed by the Party but also to the changes in his own attitude towards the explicit incorporation of social and political material in his music. Several symphonies sound crudely populist in conception. The Seventh and Eighth Symphonies, written during World War Two, are ponderous, grandiose in scope, highly repetitive and overblown in articulation.

However, it seems Shostakovich was already moving in the broad direction of the Fifth Symphony before the Pravda censure; his future would doubtless have been different without it, but it doesn't follow that the path he followed, or was forced to, was incompatible with his own nature. His changing style in the middle and later 1930s, though imposed on him, was something he could accommodate within the structure of his own musical ideas. During the rest of his life, he composed much music of value, despite the unrelenting pressures of the Stalinist regime.

The later symphonies from the post-Stalin period are highly interesting works. In the later 'Symphony No. 10 in E Minor Opus 93' (1953), Shostakovich's irony and anger at the losses the Russian people suffered under Stalin during World War II is given voice in a relentless, motor-driven *scherzo*. It has a first movement that slowly builds its simple melodic materials into an extended 'climax-punctuated' statement. Equally interesting is the Thirteenth Symphony (1962), a dark, skimpily textured setting for bass, male chorus and orchestra of five poems by Yevtushenko: one of them, 'Babi Yar', recounts the execution of Russian Jews during World War Two. He asserted his individuality by musically signing the third movement of the tenth with a motive drawn from the German spelling of his name—D-E flat-C-B—in German nomenclature, D-S-C-H, from 'Dimitri Shostakovich'. He used the same theme in the Fifth and Eighth String Quartets (1952 and 1960) and in the Concertos for Violin and for Cello (Burkholder et al. 2014, p. 889).

Shostakovich's chamber music, notably his fifteen string quartets, is less burdened with the eclecticism, stylistic variability and technical imbalance of the symphonies. The final quartets are among his last works, dating from 1974. They are more intimate affirmations in which he appears to have been less burdened by external pressures and, therefore, able to develop a less diluted and more adventurous musical language. In works such as the Eighth and Twelfth String Quartets (1960, 1968), he superimposes an extremely intense *chromaticism* on largely *triadic* and *tonal* foundations. The harmonic direction is largely set by linear considerations, without conventional progressions. This continuation of the expressive and technical characteristics of the Romantic instrumental tradition using an exceedingly individual twentieth-century vocabulary is reminiscent of Berg.

There is much ambivalence in Shostakovich's music, reflecting the accommodations he had to make to survive in a state where oppressive censorship was the norm, and where, therefore, the arts, especially music, offered a safety valve for the forbidden. The comparative accessibility of his music linked to its impression of expressing inner feelings has won Shostakovich many devoted listeners not only in Russia but throughout the world. Chapter 7 'The Art of Fear' in Alex Ross's 'The Rest is Noise' (2012) provides a graphic description of the difficulties of composing under Stalin's terror regime.

The Serial Bird Singing of Olivier Messiaen (1908–1992)

Integral serialism—composition solely according to serial principles— was largely developed by composers who matured after World War Two. However, its European development begins with a member of the previous generation—Frenchman Olivier Messaien. By the end of World War Two, he was an established figure, with a major influence on younger European serialists, including his students Boulez and Stockhausen.

The Modernist Style of Olivier Messiaen

Messiaen approached individual features of composition—*pitch*, rhythm, *timbre, dynamics*—as separable elements, each possessing its own partic- ular structural attributes. The most original feature of his early music is his approach to rhythm: replacing 'bar' and 'beat' with short values (a sixteenth note) and their liberal duplication. He advances towards an 'ametrical' conception. An important notion is 'added values' whereby regular patterns become rhythmically more flexible. His early method, first apparent in his 1935 work 'La Nativite du Seigneur', adopts unprecedented flexible rhythmic successions. A typical feature is 'non- retrogradable rhythm'—a succcesion of durations that remain equal whether played forwards or backwards.

Another significant aspect of Messiaen's approach is the 'borrowing' of pre-existing material and reshaping it through the 'prism' of his own musical identity. Messiaen sought inspiration from wellsprings distant from modern Western music—Gregorian chants, Hindu, Japanese and Gamelan music. But the most important item Messiaen appropriated throughout his extensive travels was bird song. His objective was not to imitate the source but to reshape it so as to bestow upon it musical significance. In 'Reveil des Oiseaux' (1953), the structure reflects the changing sounds of birds positioned in a specific location.

Finally, Messiaen's religious nature has greatly influenced his music, contributing to the 'expressive detachment and structural rigour of his work' (Morgan 1991, p. 337). Music is the embodiment of God's universe: he therefore 'distances' himself from his music, placing its structural needs—his "prism"—between himself and his work. Despite his commitment to serial procedures, for example in 'Quartet for the End of Time', early Messiaen's *pitch* language remained largely *tonal* though coloured by 'Impressionism'.

During an important experimental phase starting in 1949. Messaien adopted even more stringent structural methods, embracing total *chromaticism*. An influential work was the 'Quatre Etudes' consisting of three twelve-element series. 'Each member of each series is assigned a pitch in a given octave, a duration, a dynamic, and an attack type' (Morgan 1991, p. 338). The pitches comprise three separate twelve-tone rows organised in descending *registral* order. These three series govern its entire content, with all four musical elements remaining fixed in relation to one another: every *pitch* keeps the duration, dynamic and attack type allocated to it in the series. The opening bars establish the general character which doesn't change. There is no sense of direction. 'The notes seem to spin themselves out freely as if in a state of suspended animation'. When the work ends, the music just stops (Morgan 1991, p. 340).

Messaien has always relied on the mosaic-type formations he developed in the 1930s, with separate portions juxtaposed and some components reappearing in static patterns. His music has an abundantly sonorous harmony and an almost rapturous expressiveness.

A People's Guide to Modernism: Benjamin Britten (1913–1976)

Britten was the most significant composer in the *tonal* or *neotonal* tradition to achieve an international reputation in the post-war era. His early period was dominated by the Classical masters. He later developed a lasting animosity towards the English pastoral school represented by Vaughan Williams and John Ireland. He was, however, devoted to the

English music of the seventeenth and early eighteenth centuries, especially Purcell. One of his closest kindred spirits was Mahler whose 'Fourth Symphony' influenced his own compositional style. And the adoption by Britten of popular tunes—as in 'Death in Venice'—is a direct legacy from the older composer (Whittall 1982, p. 203).

Throughout his career, Britten was drawn to the song cycle form. Influenced by the poet W.H. Auden, he composed 'Our Hunting Fathers' (1936), ostensibly a protest against fox-hunting but with allegorical allusions to the political state of Europe. His cycle, 'Seven Sonnets of Michelangelo' (1942), for tenor and piano, was his declaration of love for Peter Pears, who had become his partner and muse (Matthews 2013, p. 56). The 'Serenade for Tenor, Horn and Strings' (1943) sets verses by a number of poets, all on the theme of night-time. Together with 'Peter Grimes', it established him as one of the leading composers of his generation.

Among Britten's later song cycles with piano accompaniment is the 'Songs and Proverbs of William Blake', composed for baritone Dietrich Fischer-Dieskau. It presents all its poems in a continuous musical stream, painting an 'increasingly sombre picture of human existence' (Brett et al. 2013). A Pushkin cycle, 'The Poet's Echo' (1965), was composed for Galina Vishnevskaya, showing the composer's more extrovert, robust side (Brett et al. 2013). Although ostensibly written in the tradition of European song cycles, it recreates the atmosphere of the *polyphony* of south-east Asian music (Mitchell 2004/2011).

Smaller-scale works for accompanied voice include the five 'Canticles' composed between 1947 and 1974. They were written for different voices and accompaniments. The first is a setting of Francis Quarles's seventeenth-century poem 'A Divine Rapture', and, according to Britten, was modelled on Purcell's 'Divine Hymns'. Matthews described it as one of Britten's most serene works, which 'ends in a mood of untroubled happiness that would soon become rare in Britten's music' (Matthews 2013, pp. 98–99).

Britten's Modernist Style

Unlike his English predecessors like Elgar and Vaughan Williams, or the European composers whom he admired, such as Mahler or Shostakovich, Britten was not a Classical symphonist. His youthful 'Jeux d'Esprit— (Simple Symphony) (1934), has a conventional symphonic structure, adhering to the *sonata* form and the traditional four-movement pattern, but of his mature works his 'Spring Symphony' (1949) is more a song cycle than a real symphony, and the concertante 'Cello Symphony' (1963) attempts to balance the traditional concerto and symphony. During its four movements, the 'Cello Symphony' progresses from a profoundly pessimistic opening to a *finale* of radiant happiness rare for Britten by this point. The composer regarded it as "the finest thing I've written" (Powell 2013, p. 382).

Like Copland, Britten tempered Modernism with simplicity to create an accessible style having broad appeal. As a young man in the 1930s, he was profoundly influenced by humanitarian issues and public service ideals, as evidenced by his compositions for children and amateurs, his allegorical appeals for tolerance and his pacifism. One of the first of Britten's compositions to attract attention was the 'Sinfonietta Opus 1' (1932) for ten instruments, written while he was still at college. It contains structural complexities that set it apart from most English music of the period. And despite the later relative simplification of his style, he preserved his early interest in scrupulous formal systems. Britten went on to experiment with various approaches, highlighting an abiding feature—an "untroubled eclecticism that is both technically assured and expressively convincing". The style of each composition seems to be formed according to its own specific needs. What remains stable is a basically *diatonic tonal* orientation—even if sometimes strongly coloured with chromatic elements, set within a well-defined formal framework and clear, *contrapuntally* devised textures (Morgan 1991, p. 273).

In the later 1930s, several compositions marked Britten out as in the frontline of the leading composers of the younger generation. His development received a significant boost from his friendship and collaboration with W.H. Auden whom he met in 1935. Their joint works included the symphonic song cycle 'Our Hunting Fathers' (1936), 'On This Island' (1937), a cycle for voice and piano, and the later 'operetta' 'Paul Bunyan'. This work proved to be a turning-point in Britten's career as he subsequently devoted himself principally to stage works. Just before the latter, Britten had completed his first fully fledged masterpieces—'Variations on a Theme of Frank Bridge' (1937) for string orchestra, in which he uses traditional forms (Italian aria, Viennese waltz, etc.), reflecting an increasing tendency towards neo-Classicism, 'Les Illuminations' after Rimbaud, for voice and string orchestra (1939), and the 'Sinfonia da Requiem' (1940). Although the influence of Stravinsky, and perhaps also

Mahler, is audible in these works, they are shrouded by a forthrightness of expression and an easy lyricism that is both Britten's own and strangely English.

The slightly later 'Serenade, Opus 31', for tenor, horn and strings (1943), a cycle of six songs on a collection of different English texts, confirms these features. The fourth song, a setting of an anonymous fifteenth-century Scottish dirge, is based on a six-bar vocal *ostinato* which appears unaccompanied at the start of the song and then recurs eight times with minor variations while the instruments unfold a fully developed *fugue*, complete with *expositions*, episodes and climactic *stretto*. The combination of an unvarying repetitive vocal layer with an expansive and developmental instrumental one underlines the text's harsh underlying message: the inevitable transition of all humankind toward a day of final reckoning.

The music has a strong *tonal* orientation, as generally in Britten, yet much tension flows from the vocal instrumental polarity, which includes key as well as character, in a manner reminiscent of Stravinsky (compare his 1952 'Cantata' based on the same text). The vocal *ostinato* is firmly rooted in G, yet the sense of key is complicated by several *modal* elements, especially the *upper-neighbour* A flat linked to both opening and closing *tonics*, which imparts to the music a *Phrygian colour*. There are thus complex interactions between voice and 'accompaniment' characterising the whole movement, which, despite the pervasive *triadic* harmonic basis, create a distinctive quality of *tonal* tension and uncertainty. The voice ends alone, centring on G, with its final *tonic* following a low *pizzicato* E flat in the basses, the terminal note in a dissolving sequence bringing the *fugue* to a close. 'The work's true *tonal* focus is thus ultimately left unresolved' (Morgan 1991, p. 276).

One critic wrote of Britten's vocal music: 'His feeling for poetry (not only English) and the inflexions of language make him... the greatest musical realizer of English' (Davies et al. 1977, pp. 2–6). One of the best-known poetry settings is 'The War Requiem' (1962), Britten's choral masterpiece, which mixes the Latin requiem mass, sung by soprano and chorus, with settings of works by the First World War poet Wilfred Owen, sung by tenor and baritone with chamber orchestra. The two elements are combined at the end, as the last line of Owen's 'Strange Meeting' is mixed with the 'In Paradisum' of the mass. Matthews describes the work's conclusion as a 'great wave of benediction (which) recalls the end of the "Sinfonia da Requiem", and its similar ebbing away into the sea that symbolises both reconciliation and death' (Matthews 2013, pp. 125–127).

Britten's leftist and pacifist views aroused his dissatisfaction with developments in pre-war Britain and in 1939 he emigrated to the United States Returning to wartime England in 1942, he began work on his first full-scale opera, 'Peter Grimes', completed in 1945. The work has a *modal-diatonic* melodic style and solidly *triadic* harmonic basis, which illustrate Britten's fundamental conservatism. Nevertheless, its structure is highly complicated. Moreover, the opera has a dark, pessimistic subject matter, presenting a sadistic main character combining features of a romantic 'outsider' and a psychotic social misfit, giving it a distinctly modern flavour.

The theme of the individual persecuted by the crowd can be interpreted as an allegory for the situation of homosexuals in a hostile environment. Interestingly, Grimes is not a sympathetic character: we are invited to identify ourselves, not with him, but with the prejudiced crowd that persecutes outsiders on the basis of suspicion and misinformation. The opera concludes with a powerful portrayal of the uncaring sea and similarly uncaring townsfolk in a highly successful application of *bitonality*: 'strings, harp, and winds arpeggiate thirds that encompass all the notes of the C major scale, depicting the shimmering sea, as the towns citizens go about their business, singing a slow hymn to the sea in A major, each key stubbornly ignoring the other' (Burkholder et al. 2014, p. 929). The scene illustrates the eloquent dramatic effects Britten creates out of basic ingredients.

Britten's success consisted, firstly, in bringing this material to operatic life, but, secondly, in humanising the character of Grimes, eliciting sympathy as well as antagonism. It required a composer of exceptional dramatic and musical instincts to successfully bring off the range of moods demanded by the plot with diverse features such as Grimes' passionate ravings, the depiction of a powerful storm and the singing of a church congregation. English opera, so long moribund, with a subordinate role in the 'English musical renaissance', was revitalised at a stroke. 'Peter Grimes' was hailed as a masterpiece, its composer celebrated as the most significant English operatic composer since Purcell. It was the foundation stone of a flourishing of a new English operatic tradition.

Britten's operas cover a broad spectrum of musical and dramatic possibilities, notable for their variety and technical polish. They embody an important attempt to reaffirm the significance of a genre—opera created along largely traditional lines—which has generally been restricted to a secondary role in the twentieth century. The operas draw inspiration from different sources depending on the needs of each specific work, reflecting Britten's eclectic approach. Perhaps his most significant talent is his capacity to adapt 'foreign' styles, incorporating them into his own work so that they realise his aims. In 'The Turn of the Screw', where the music must convey the complex, subtle psychological ambiguities of the Henry James novella, the frequent recurrence of a 'twelve-tone row' expresses the obsessive character of the theme. Since the row consists wholly of a sequence of perfect *fifths*, it easily lends itself to *tonal* suggestion, and Britten uses it to create a score that is absolutely his own. 'The Turn of the Screw' is perhaps his most complex musico-dramatic creation. Its overall structure is unified by sixteen orchestral interludes constructed as a series of fifteen variations on an opening *theme*, organised, like all Britten's operas, following a carefully contolled progression of key changes.

In 'A Mid-Summer Nights' Dream' (1960), three clearly differentiated kinds of music interact with one another without a suggestion of stylistic discrepancy. The hard, metallic music is associated with the supernatural elements of Shakespeare's play, dominated by *ostinatos* and high voices; the more lyrical, linear flowing music suggests the lovers; and the comical, harmonically dissonant and rhythmically awkward music indicates Bottom and the rustics. Britten plays off these highly stylised figures with a flawless musical instinct, setting them in opposition to each other, but blending them within a score of extraordinary richness. Britten's abiding popularity reveals the power of music with a *tonal* centre to stir audiences, thus winning a permanent place in the repertoire.

Popular Music: Broadway and Jazz

In Chapter 1, we suggested that no sharp dividing line separated 'art music' from popular music, that attributes and conventions of the latter had always pervaded the former. Twentieth-century popular music as represented in Broadway musical theatre has a melodic richness that is reminiscent of eighteenth and early nineteenth-century Vienna. Can we not describe Jerome Kern, Cole Porter, George Gershwin, Irving Berlin, Richard Rogers, Harry Warren, Harold Arlen, Frederick Loewe, Leonard Bernstein as latter-day Schuberts? Gershwin, a composer of both jazz-influenced Classical music and of musicals, is perhaps the composer whose work clearly straddles the boundary between 'popular' and 'art music'. 'Rhapsody in Blue', 'Porgy and Bess', 'An American in Paris', display his genius in blending jazz, popular and Classical styles.

Duke Ellington was a leading composer of the Jazz Age, and one of the most influential twentieth century American composers. He was prominent in efforts to make jazz recognised not solely as entertainment, but as a form of art music, to be listened to for its own sake. Central to his style is an early tune followed by a series of choruses over the same progression. 'Cotton Tail' (1940) is a 'Contrafact', a new tune composed over a harmonic progression borrowed from a song, in this case, the chorus of Gershwin's 'I Got Rhythm'. The music at each chorus presents new ideas. 'The first two choruses feature Ben Webster soloing on tenor saxophone accompanied by the rhythm section... the music at each chorus presents new ideas... the remaining three choruses feature various combinations of instruments...' The tune returns to finish the piece (Burkholder et al. 2014, pp. 870–871). Ellington absorbed the rhythmic and harmonic features of different contributors, integrating them into music bearing his own highly original stamp.

PART III: SOCIAL AND POLITICAL INFLUENCES ON THE MODERNIST STYLES

Between 1750 and 1840, significant parts of northern Europe underwent more far-reaching economic, social and political change than at any earlier period in its history. In Britain, industrialisation had transformed the economy, creating large new urban centres of production. 'The Industrial Revolution marks the most fundamental transformation of human life in the history of the world... For a brief period, it coincided with the history of a single country' (Hobsbawm 1968, p. 1). British manufacturing, commerce and the number of wage-labourers soared, launching a development that continued into the first half of the nineteenth century.

However, in the half century after the defeated 1848 European-wide revolutions, the liberal capitalist world entered a new phase. The era of liberal triumph, having begun by defeating a revolution ended in a prolonged depression. The British boom of the early 1870s crashed into ruins but not so dramatically as in the USA and Central Europe. Nevertheless, 'amid the debris of bankrupt financiers and cooling blast-furnaces, it drifted inexorably downwards' (Hobsbawm 1968, p. 104).

The 'Panic of 1873' began as a financial crisis that triggered a depression covering Europe and North America. Its first symptoms were a financial crash of the Viennese Stock Exchange (in May) followed by the failure of several Viennese banks. By September, the crisis had spread to the USA. This followed a period of post-American Civil War over-expansion created by the railway boom. Therefore, he underlying cause of the crash was speculative over-investment, but also the demonetisation of silver in the US and Germany, the economic dislocation caused by the Franco-Prussian war of 1870–1871, and property losses in the Chicago and Boston fires (1871 and 1872). All these factors put a massive strain on bank reserves which in the autumn of 1873 in New York plummeted from $50 million to $17 million.

For maybe two generations, the Great Depression—from roughly 1873–1896—didn't destroy the world of the triumphant bourgeoisie—as far as working people were concerned, it cannot be compared with the catastrophic years of the 1830s or 1840s, or the 1920s and 1930s. But if 'depression' indicates, for the generations after 1850 a prevailing mood of unease and despondency about Britain's economic prospects, the word is accurate.

The British middle-class citizen who surveyed the economic and social scene in the early 1870s would have concluded that 'all was for the best in the best of all possible worlds'. Surely nothing very serious could go wrong with the British economy (Hobsbawm 1968, p. 103). Industrialisation and political liberalisation occurred first and fastest in Britain, France and the Low Countries, particularly Belgium, but also in Scandinavia (Britannica.com/history-of-Europe/Revolution). After 1875, the world of the triumphant bourgeoisie appeared superficially to remain solid. But it appeared less confident than before, and its assertions of self-confidence 'a little shriller, perhaps a little more worried about its future. Perhaps it became rather more puzzled by the breakdown of its old intellectual certainties, which (especially after the 1880s) thinkers, artists and scientists underlined with their ventures into new and troubling territories of the mind' (Hobsbawm 1975, p. 308). Surely, they believed, the progress of bourgeois, capitalist and liberal society would inevitably reassert itself. Surely, the Great Depression was a mere interlude. 'Was there not economic growth, technical and scientific advance, improvement and peace? Would not the twentieth century be a more glorious, more successful version of the nineteenth? We now know that it would not be' (Hobsbawm 1975, p. 308).

The most important Western ruling classes overcame the problems created by the Great Depression through imperialism, the new phase of capitalism that expressed itself in the competitive scramble for colonies— the export of capital, and the search for new markets and sources of labour in Africa, Asia and Latin America. Characteristic of this new era was the formal imperialism of the 'partition of Africa' in the 1880s, the semi-formal imperialism of national or international syndicates taking over the financial control of weak countries, the informal imperialism of foreign investment. A further crucial feature of the new period is the fusion of the state and private enterprise, the government now identifying itself as the backer, if not the saviour, of private capitalism. A new, more dangerous framework of international relations began to take shape. Following an extended period of peace, the great powers created once again an era of world wars. Of course, in Russia the Great Depression, impacting on its backward institutions, contributed to the raising of a social and economic storm that unleashed waves of growing unrest. Its early rippling effects culminated in the raging tempests of the revolutions of 1905 and 1917.

The carnage and brutality of World War One had established that the industrial and scientific progress of capitalism had not led to a world based on justice and reason, to the ideals of the Enlightenment and the French revolution, but to horror on a hitherto unimaginable scale. Rather than bringing humanity closer together, the modern world was driving people apart, not just at the level of nations fighting all-out wars but also at the level of everyday life. Industrial cities had produced, on the one hand, the greatest concentrations of human beings, yet on the other, had created conditions of poverty and alienation hitherto unknown.

Musically, the extremes of these social contradictions could no longer be adequately expressed in the closed and resolvable forms (in which dissonant notes are resolved into consonant ones) of the symphony. It is a period characterised by uncertainty, chaos, irrationality and destructiveness, which has therefore given rise to styles such as impressionism, *atonality*, *chromaticism*, dissonance, neo-Classicism, serialism, and more recently, musique concrete.

What was the social and political context of Debussy's music? France had been defeated in the Franco-Prussian War of 1870–1871, after which the Paris Commune uprising, setting a new standard of workers' democracy, was brutally suppressed by the bourgeois government. A reparations payment of £200 million was imposed on France by the Germans.

Following the defeat, French composers attempted to gain greater independence from German music (see this chapter, p. 251). The country was already reeling financially when the 1873 crash hit the world economy. France adopted a policy of deliberate deflation while paying off the reparations. In the 1880s, growth returned to the United States, but the Paris Bourse crashed in 1882, plunging France into depression, a longer-lasting and more costly downturn than any other in the nineteenth century. The Union Generale bank failed in 1882, provoking the French to withdraw three million pounds from the Bank of England, which in turn triggered a collapse in French share prices.

The financial crisis was aggravated by diseases affecting the wine and silk industries. In the latter half of the nineteenth century, French capital accumulation and foreign investment plunged to the lowest levels ever recorded. Following a boom in new investment banks following the end of the Franco-Prussian war, the collapse of the French banking industry unleashed by the crash cast a pall over the financial sector that lasted until the dawn of the twentieth century. French investments were additionally hit by investment failures abroad, especially in railways and construction. France's net national product declined over the decade from 1882 to 1892.

We saw that traditional Western music is heard as a movement towards a *tonal* goal, but that in Debussy *tonality* is approached in a more stable manner, with stationary blocks of static harmony. The listener experiences each moment in terms of its own features, the music's 'surface' assuming a new prominence. Debussy offers us a 'floating equilibrium' between lightly linked musical entities, leading to a fragmentation of sonority. This creates a sense of detachment, an escape into a dream world as opposed to the Romantic tradition of expressing profound emotion. This detachment is arguably the musical response to a fragmenting, dissolving world where the old certainties have disappeared, creating unpredictability, disorientation, bewilderment and anxiety. It is a musical style that expresses the deepening capitalist crisis of the last quarter of the nineteenth century and the early years of the twentieth, especially as it hit France.

The early years of the twentieth century saw Europe enter the era of military high-tech: World War One witnessed the first use of the machine-gun, the tank, the submarine and the fighter plane. The first aerial bombardment was recorded in 1911, during the Italian invasion of Libya, and the first concentration camps were opened in South Africa by the British and in South-West Africa (Namibia) by the Germans. 'Such developments, foreshadowing the immense violence and destructiveness of the first half of the twentieth century, stand as a warning against treating the nineteenth century... as an age of linear progress...' (Evans 2017, p. xix).

Austria was the most powerful European state until the mid-1850s, when it embarked on its long, uneven period of decline following defeat by Italy and France in the War of Italian Unification (1859), then defeat by Prussia in the war of 1866. 'Geopolitical logic dictated that rather than seeking revenge... the Dual Monarchy (ie, Austria and Hungary), had to ally itself, however reluctantly, with the new German Empire from 1871 onwards. It had to face rising nationalism on its border in the Balkans, backed by an expansionist Russia seeking to profit from the decline of the Ottoman Empire' (Evans 2017, p. 583). Each half of the dual empire contained substantial minorities—Czechs, Slovaks, Poles, Slovenes, Italians and Ukrainians in Austria, Romanians, Serbs and Croats in Hungary. Austro-Hungarian politics up to 1914 is largely the story of the 'rearguard action of the multinational empire against the rising forces of linguistic and ethnic nationalism, intertwined with growing demands for democratic participation from the emerging working classes' (Evans 2017, p. 583).

Mahler was a composer poised between two musical periods, and thus offers a mixed, even contradictory profile. On the one hand, 'his message is one of nostalgia, of great sadness at the dissolution of the world of nineteenth century Romanticism, a condition his music reflects more poignantly than that of perhaps any other twentieth century composer' (Morgan 1991, p. 28). The predominant *diatonicism* and bold melodic expressiveness conjure up a simpler and more gracious era but they are now tinged with a 'pronounced element of discordance, ambiguity, and uncertainty. For Mahler also stands at the threshold of a new age, the musical possibilities of which he had already begun to explore with great imagination and inventiveness in the early years of the century' (Morgan 1991, p. 28). Mahler expresses the trauma felt at the dawn of a new age of social and political disintegration and barbarism. Hanging over it his music is the threat of imminent havoc. Indeed, it can at times be almost frightening. As Mahler himself asked after conducting his First Symphony: 'What sort of world is it that brings forth such sounds and shapes as its representation?' (Morgan 1991, p. 24). The third movement of his Symphony No. 1 (1893) features a tune based on 'Frère Jacques'. But Mahler slows it down, transposes it from major to minor, thus evoking a funeral procession. 'The juxtaposition of a well known children's song with a funeral march evokes something highly disturbing and tragic' (Behrman 2009, p. 128).

The crucial issue in the Habsburg empire was the autonomy of its various ethno-political components. The issue of self-government of the various nationalities—Hungarians, Czechs, Germans, Italians, Serbs, Croats—represented in the empire grew in importance. The empire became over-centralised, exacerbating the conflicts among the different nationalities, and resisting the loosening that would have resulted from federalisation. For example, in the late 1890s, a wave of ethnic violence and riots swept across Bohemia over the language issue. Austrian statesman Count Badeni had attempted to reform the electoral system and language legislation, in particular allowing the Czech language to be used in communications between state officials in all parts of Bohemia, on a par with German. The problem was that whereas Czech bureaucrats spoke German fluently, German public servants were reluctant to learn Czech which they viewed as an inferior language. However, the riots and instability in the Czech territories induced Badeni to grant greater autonomy to local authorities in setting the rules governing the use of different languages (Rohac 2009, pp. 14/15).

Strauss's tone poems are masterly compositions of great technical expertise, exuding an aura of unshakeable confidence that presented a suitable musical symbol for Germany's expansionist mood and confidence at that time. Perhaps the greatest expression of Strauss's confidence (if somewhat tongue-in-cheek) can be found in the tone poem 'Ein Helden-leben'—'A Hero's Life' (1898), where the hero is depicted as a kind of 'superman' who possesses the strength and willpower to overcome all obstacles and opponents. Strauss was ideally suited to giving expression to Germany's new-found optimism following unification and victory over France in 1871.

The confident image projected by Strauss's tone poems is in striking contrast to the self-doubt and self-questioning profoundly embedded in Mahler's music. The Bohemian Jew, feeling an outsider even while occupying the most important artistic position in Vienna, fostered a far more pessimistic world-view, one that left clear traces in his music. The characteristic Mahler conclusion presents a gradual extinction, a final collapse into silence (as at the end of the Sixth and Ninth Symphonies). Strauss, in contrast, prefers endings that usher in a final realisation and glorification of the main musical substance, as in the final section of his tone poem 'Tod und Verklarung'—'Death and Transfiguration' (1889). We saw that Schoenberg rejected the Classical *triad* as the sole harmonic reference point from which all other vertical sonorities were derived. He used dissonant chords relating them to a simpler, more consonant *triadic* basis. Secondly, he abandoned conventional *tonal* functions so that a single *pitch* or a major or minor *triad* based on that *pitch* no longer provided a functional foundation for the other *tones* and the *triads* built on them. His music moved in a free *chromatic* space governed by new principles of harmonic organisation. This lack of harmonious *triadic* resolution arguably expresses the criss-crossing multiplicity of ethno-linguistic conflicts in the empire which were incapable of resolution and fatally undermined it. Its defeat in World War One was rooted in this subversion of its unity. The *atonality* of Schoenberg and the Second Viennese School, with its rejection of the Classical tradition of *tonality* and *sonata form*, flowed directly from the decay and disintegration of the Austro-Hungarian Empire in the early years of the twentieth century (Behrman 2009, p. 132).

Schoenberg's espousal of total *chromaticism*, one freed from its former roots in a *diatonic* substructure, seems to express the new anarchic order, the general European instability, the erosion and eventual collapse of the old imperial structure. However, his twelve-tone technique also ensures that all twelve notes of the *chromatic* scale are sounded as often as one another and prevents any single note being stressed thereby avoiding association with any single key. Hence twelve-tone *chromaticism*, with its rejection of resolution to the superior *tonic*, also implies 'equality' of all the *pitches*. This highlights the importance of the bourgeois-democratic principle of equality achieved through decades of mass struggles from below. Twelve-tone music would thus seem to be contradictory.

Adorno makes a general point about the *atonal* style—the lack of a *tonal* centre, a home key that acts as a central point of reference to which the piece returns. The fact that no note occupies a commanding position over the others, as occurs in the twelve-tone technique, renders the music directionless, fragmentary. It therefore expresses painful aspects of our lived experience under industrial capitalism: 'the strict division of labour, the anarchy of the market, the enslavement to the machine, the lack of control we have over our destinies...' (Behrman 2009, p. 131). Adorno argues that modern society has separated production from consumption: '...the production of art, its material, the demands and tasks that confront the artist when he works, have become divorced in principle from consumption, ie, from the presumptions, claims, and principles of comprehension that the reader, viewer or listener brings to the work of art' (Adorno 2002, p. 128). He adds: 'The shock that accompanied the new artistic movements immediately before the war is the expression of the fact that the break between production and consumption became radical; for this reason art... has the task... of revealing... the very cracks that reality would like to cover up in order to exist in safety; and that, in so doing, it repels reality' (Adorno 2002, p. 131). Crucially, Adorno argues that future economic production can no more return to primitive, pre-division of labour forms of production, in order to avoid the alienation of human beings from consumer goods, than art can. (According to Marx, workers under industrial capitalism are alienated from the products of their labour). People need bad, illusory, deceptive things because of the all-powerful propaganda apparatus; but 'the need for relaxation... is itself also a product of a circumstance that absorbs people's strength and time in such a fashion that they are no longer capable of other things' (Adorno 2002, p. 133).

Charles Ives's sympathy with the ordinary, hard-working man of the soil and his tribute to the individual's integrity and his transcendental vision came from his New England heritage. His self-reliance and lack of inhibition are generally seen as American characteristics, but his music was most intimately linked with the history, landscape, philosophy and literature of Massachusetts and Connecticut. Ives's memories of nineteenth-century New England, especially in orchestral works such as 'Three Places in New England' and the 'Holiday Symphony', depend for their evocative precision on the quotation of marches, popular songs, dance music and hymns. Dvorak would not have expected that his advice to American composers to look to their native music would be followed in such riotous celebrations of America as Ives's 'The Fourth of July' from his 'Holiday Symphony'. For Ives, the music of the American people was too diverse and too rich in reference for it to be harnessed in Dvorak's symphonic manner to the European mainstream. Instead, he demonstrated that a composer 'might forget about tradition and make of music whatever he wanted' (Griffiths 1978, p. 59).

Ives' love of and commitment to New England no doubt stems from its leading role in the historical development of the United States. New England writers and events were instrumental in launching and sustaining the American Revolution: the War of Independence began when fighting broke out between British troops and Massachusetts militia in the battles of Lexington and Concord. In the 1840s, the region was at the heart of the anti-slavery movement. It was also at the centre of the American industrial revolution, with many textile mills and machine shops functioning by 1830, remaining the US's manufacturing centre for most of the nineteenth century. It played a key role during and after the Civil War as an ardent intellectual and political promoter of abolitionism and civil rights. Clearly, the region played a pivotal role in shaping American character and identity. It is hardly surprising, therefore, that his music is infused with the spirit of traditional American folk music, albeit embedded in a Modernist idiom.

However, Ives' use of American folk songs also gives voice to broader national developments. By the late nineteenth century, the United States had become a leading global industrial power, building on new technologies (such as the telegraph and steel), an expanding railway network, and abundant natural resources such as coal, timber, oil, and farmland, to usher in the second industrial revolution (1870–1914). The enormous expansion of rail and telegraph lines after 1870 allowed unprecedented movement of people and ideas, which culminated in a new wave of globalisation. In the same time period, new technological systems were introduced, most significantly electrical power and telephones. The second Industrial Revolution continued into the twentieth century with factory electrification and the production line, ending at the beginning of World War One.

In the Spanish-American War of 1898, the United States defeated Spain, which produced a small empire, Spain ceding Cuba, the Philippines Puerto Rico and Guam. The independent Republic of Hawaii was also annexed by the United States in 1898. Alaska had been purchased from Russia in 1867. The United States tried and failed to broker a peace settlement for World War I, then entered the war after Germany launched a submarine campaign against US merchant ships that were supplying Germany's enemy countries. The publicly stated goals were to uphold American honour, crush German militarism, and reshape the post-war world. After a slow mobilisation, the United States helped bring about a decisive Allied Forces victory by supplying badly needed financing, food, and millions of fresh and eager soldiers. Ives' use of American folk songs arguably reflects its growing military power and global political influence.

The opening of Ives' Fourth Symphony consists of a threatening passage reminiscent of a horror film music, followed by a choral passage sounding like a prayer. The second movement, ironically titled 'Comedy: Allegretto' contains a complex use of 'multimetrics and temporal dysynchronies' creating a powerful dissonant effect. This Modernism arguably expresses an increasingly dysfunctional world, one in which humanity's growing scientific and technical prowess has resulted in as much destructiveness as constructiveness, in which its potential has failed to be realised, to the detriment of humanity.

Stravinsky's music remains within the tradition of modern *diatonic* harmony. But he transformed music through his revolutionary approach to rhythm and his use of dissonant harmonies. As we saw, the rhythmic innovation of 'The Rite of Spring' shocked the musical world. His individual style had matured in his second Diaghilev ballet 'Petrushka' where rhythm was becoming the most important structural and expressive element. 'Petrushka' also uses a significant number of Russian folk tunes. But it also reveals fantastic harmonies associated with the puppets which are based on traditional techniques that produced sharp dissonant combinations (e.g. the so-called *Petrushka* chord) (Taruskin 2009, p. 209). Again, these dissonances and dynamic rhythms conceivably express the intensifying contradictions and dislocation of a society in which advanced capitalist relations prevailed in the urban industrial areas—Petrograd's Putilov engineering factory boasted the most highly developed technology in Europe—alongside semi-feudal relations in the countryside and an absolute monarchy. And, of course, by the time 'Firebird' and 'Petrushka' were produced, Russia had already experienced the 1905 revolution, the 'dress-rehearsal' for the 1917 revolution.

So, while Stravinsky's music cannot strictly be described as 'music of the Russian revolution'—he himself was hostile to the revolution and, having left Russia in 1914, didn't return until 1962—nevertheless it is music that expresses the convulsions, crisis and uncertainty engendered by late capitalism that was the backdrop to World War One and the revolution.

Stravinsky's 'middle period' neo-Classical style expresses a predilection for balance, coolness, objectivity as opposed to Romantic programme music. The fashion for Russian nationalism in Western Europe was fading, partly due to the political and cultural links between France and Russia dissolving after the Bolshevik Revolution. The aim of neo-Classicism was not to return to the past but to re-energise certain traditional compositional principles in ways consistent with contemporary harmonic and rhythmic practice. It harks back to the Classical style characteristic of an earlier period, representing perhaps an attempt to recreate pre-industrial social conditions before nationalism and materialism came to dominate Europe and the western world. World War One had seen the worst barbarism ever inflicted by human beings on each other. The 1920s witnessed a consumer boom in the United States, a spending spree that culminated in the Crash of 1929 followed by the Great Depression of the 1930s. 'Histoire du Soldat -A Soldier's Tale' is arguably a cautionary tale against the amassing of material goods, the constant striving to accumulate wealth, against elevating material values above human values.

Stravinsky's third and final period sees him embrace serialism where no note occupies a commanding position over the others, rendering the music directionless and fragmentary. As we saw, it is the musical style of a society in permanent crisis, disoriented, riddled with internal contradictions, over which its capitalist ruling classes have been unable to impose harmony or rational order. The late forties and early fifties witnessed the gradual evaporation of the optimism generated by the allies' victory over Nazism, to be replaced by the cold war, the new threat of nuclear annihilation and the supremacy of the international free market. Humans proved once again that they were unable to control the forces they themselves had created.

Stravinsky, the perennial outsider, expressed in his neo-Classicism his preference for 'the impersonal formulas of a remote past', giving voice to a common plight, (Morgan 1991, p. 179), one affecting not only artists but also the ordinary people of the world alienated from their ability to prevent it pitching headlong into the chaos and destruction of the twentieth century, estranged from their power to change it.

Bartok argued that Hungarian peasant music represented the nation better than the popular urban music previously identified as 'Hungarian', a radical position at a time when Hungary was still ruled by an urban German-speaking elite. As we saw, he analysed the specimens with the new ethnomusicological techniques. This was underscored by a certain political motivation: the Austrian domination of Eastern Europe was under threat from nationalist movements in the years before the First World War, and it followed that composers should similarly strive to liberate their music from Vienna's yoke and turn instead to the national source of folk song.

In World War One, of the total army, Hungary's loss ratio was more than that of any other nation of Austria-Hungary. The collapse of the Habsburg empire may have liberated Hungary from Austrian control after World War One but it was a bittersweet moment: the Treaty of Trianon which established Hungary's borders resulted in the loss of 71% of its territory, 58% of its population, and 32% of ethnic Hungarians. The Little Entente, an alliance formed in 1920 and 1921 by Czechoslovakia, Romania and Yugoslavia with the purpose of common defence against Hungarian revanchism and the prospect of a Habsburg restoration. France supported the alliance and sensing an opportunity, invaded the country from three sides. The heated aggressiveness and morbid tone of the ballet 'The Miraculous Mandarin' (1918–1924) may well reflect the emotional stress and pessimism attendant upon life in Hungary at the time.

In 1919, during the brief period of the Hungarian Soviet Republic led by Bela Kun, the fledgling socialist state organised many theatrical performances, concerts, art exhibitions and film shows for the working people of town and country. Bartok participated in this work as did his contemporaries Dohnanyi and Kodaly (COMBAT 1919, p. 40). The Hungarian Soviet republic was brutally suppressed by the right-wing nationalist forces of Admiral Horthy who ruled Hungary with an iron fist from November 1919 (siding with Nazi Germany in World War Two) until the Germans deposed him in 1944 for secretly negotiating with the Allies.

As we saw, Bartok's 'third period' music (1926–1945), sometimes labelled a 'synthesis of East and West', featured his 'new-classical' synthesis, emphasising tightly organised arch—or 'bridge'—forms: larger symmetrical patterns constructed with movements paired through *motivic* and formal correspondences. There is a turbulence, a restlessness in the music—for example his fourth string quartet—that arguably reflects an increasingly unstable, dislocated world that is soon to plunge into the greatest political crisis in human history. The bridge form perhaps expresses Bartok's urge to oppose the growing national and ethnic divisions that intensified in Europe during the 1930s. He himself wrote: 'The wealth of folk music in eastern Europe is due to a continuous give and take of melodies, a constant crossing and recrossing that persisted for centuries .... The situation of folk music in eastern Europe may be summed up thus: as a result of uninterrupted reciprocal influence upon the folk music of these peoples there are an immense variety and wealth of melodies and melodic types. The racial impurity finally attained is definitely beneficial' (Bartok in Schneider 2011, p. 66; Bartok 1993, pp. 29–32). Bartok's music thus aspired to bridge this wealth of eastern

European folk music, to synthesise the different national folk traditions which came to the fore following the collapse of the Austro-Hungarian empire and which Bartok saw as an antidote to the prevailing nationalism.

Also important is the synthesis between the peasant culture of the countryside, represented by folk music, and the musical culture of the city. Bartok's mature style links the dissonant multi-*tonal* urban Modernism with the rural folk tradition. Now, Kroo describes the increasing unease, the profound tension, in Hungary preceding the Second World War (Kroo 1974, p. 204 in Schneider 2011, p. 21). Bartok's letters reveal him to be deeply disturbed by the rise of Nazism (Schneider 2011, p. 22). However, his Violin Concerto of 1938 contains some 'lush lyricism' that seems to clash with its 'forebodingly late date of completion on 31st December 1938' (Schneider 2011, p. 21). The first movement arguably contains a menacing undercurrent while the lyricism of the second movement seems to express a mood of sadness. Bartok is giving voice to the darkening shadow that is spreading across Europe, one which finally drove him out of his beloved Hungary.

Finally, Bartok's 'Concerto for Orchestra' (1943) contains a jaunty tune from Lehar's operatta 'The Merry Widow'. Suddenly, it is interrupted by a harsh dissonant chord. This is reminiscent of the shock experienced in the United States by the rich and the middle classes who had enjoyed boom times in the 1920s but received a rude awakening with the Crash of 1929.

Prokoviev never felt completely at home in Western Europe, and following several extended visits to Russia in the late 1920s and early 1930s, he resettled there permanently. His reentry into Soviet life coincided with the intensifying crackdown on progressive art in Russia and the proclaiming of socialist realism as the official style of the Communist Party. Those in power regarded his Parisian compositions to be 'formalist' and 'decadent',

Prokoviev turned out to be susceptible to the pressures of the Stalinist regime, and as early as 1934 began expressing views more in tune with the party. He wrote that a new kind of 'light-serious' or 'serious-light' music was required for the 'new mass audience that the modern Soviet composer must strive to reach,' and that this music must be 'primarily melodious, and the melody should be clear and simple' (Morgan 1991, p. 243). In fact, Prokoviev's music from this time discloses a more conservative and 'populist' tone.

In 1948, Zhdanov issued the notorious decree attacking all the more progressive elements in Russian art: Prokoviev's work was officially labelled 'alien to the Soviet people', a stigma not lifted until 1958, five years after his death. However, Prokoviev did not wholly compromise his musical conscience, his attitude to the political function of music remaining ambivalent. He warned against 'the danger of becoming provincial', and for the remainder of his life trod a dangerously thin line between official acceptability and the needs of his own artistic tendencies. Prokoviev had the bad judgement to die on the same day as Joseph Stalin, his passing eclipsed by the dictator whose brutal regime had so limited his freedom.

Hindemith was a composer of phenomenal talent whose career during the interwar years reflected particularly clearly some of the most important historical currents of that period. His music after World War One expressed the optimism and exuberance of the early years of the Weimar Republic (1919–1933). The autocratic Hohenzollern monarchy had fallen and Germany at last achieved democracy. Two of Hindemith's three one-act operas composed in 1920 and 1921—'Morder, Hoffnung der Frauen'—'Murder, the Hope of Women' and 'Sancta Susanna'—deal with highly charged sexual topics, while the third 'Das Nusch-Nuschi', parodies 'Tristan und Isolde'. His new anti-romantic, parodic approach is also expressed in two piano works of 1922, the 'Tanzstucke'—'Dance Piece', Opus 19, and the suite '1922, Opus 26', both consisting of dancelike movements developed in a strictly linear fashion, with sharp dissonances and an elastic, unconventional approach to *tonality*. However, most striking is the influence of jazz and popular music. The jazz style of the Roaring Twenties was the early New Orleans kind—*polyphonic*, developed through *thematic* variation and collective improvisation. 'New Orleans' remained the major stylistic feature of early jazz until the 1929 Crash. It was stamped with the aura of black liberation.

During the middle and later 1920s, Hindemith's approach became more sober and disciplined. Perhaps the most accomplished work of this period is the 1923 song cycle 'Das Marienleben'—'Life of Mary'. His style now became strongly *contrapuntal*, as in his opera 'Cardillac' (1926), with an astringent harmony based on *fourths* rather than *thirds*. The resulting absence of full harmonic relaxation, together with heavy driving rhythms imparts to Hindemith's early neo-Classical music a somewhat pugnacious character (Griffiths 1978, p. 78). And his original approach to *tonality* is illustrated in the first movement of his 'Kammer-musik No. 2' (1924), with its conclusion in E flat, a key only reached near the end. Kaslow has described Hindemith's approach here as '"tonal atonality", wherein atonality prevails amid ever-present tonality, reversing Frank Martin's (1890–1974) "atonal tonal" efforts, in which tonality prevails within atonality... A harmonic language based on movement between consonance and dissonance, rather than on Baroque and Classical "harmonic progression"' (Kaslow, online, p. 1). All this seems to indicate the evaporation of the early Weimar optimism and growing anger and despair at the deteriorating economic and political situation.

Hindemith's 1929 opera 'Neues vom Tage'—'News of the Day', a story of newspaper rivalry, reflects the 1920s fashion for operatic works on topical issues ('Zeitoper' in German, i.e. opera of the time) (Morgan 1991, p. 225). It is a satire of modern life, lampooning institutions like marriage and celebrity, involving parodies of Puccini and Berlin cabaret. Also, this new style illustrates the 'back to Bach' approach prominent at the time, as in the opening of 'Kammermusik No. 2' in 1924. This was again arguably influenced by events in Germany in the 1920s, representing a rejection by composers of the darkening clouds that were spreading over that country.

1923 was a decisive year for Germany: the country was still under a post-war obligation to pay reparations to the allies so that when it defaulted, French and Belgian troops entered the Ruhr. That year saw the defeat of the German workers' revolution; also, the hyperinflation wiped out the savings of millions of the middle classes, causing the bank rate to rise to 90 per cent. It is perhaps no wonder that at this time, the young Hindemith, adopting a version of neo-Classicism, harked back to better times in Germany, to Prussia at the heart of a Europe which was witnessing the rise of bourgeois individualism with its stress on freedom of thought and choice, economic liberty and personal ambition and responsibility.

Copland's work seems to highlight key phases in American twentieth century history. Not only did the US emerge victorious from World War One, its entry into the war in 1917 giving the decisive impetus to the previously stagnant Allied campaign. But crucially, it emerged from the war as the world's largest economy and most powerful capitalist state. But Copland's music doesn't simply highlight America great national achievements—it celebrates the role of the common man in building and developing American society. At a number of points in his long, illustrious

career, Copland testified to his profound commitment to the democratisation of both music and society, making him worthy of his Communist
Party card! His incorporation of jazz in the mid-1920s and 1930s, his
interest in Hindemith's 'Gebrauchmusik', his urge to compose music
of broad appeal such as 'El Salon Mexico' or 'Rodeo', his dance music
geared to the democratisation of American dance, as in 'Billy the Kid', all
testify to his commitment to the values of democracy and socialism.

The background to this music was the Roaring Twenties followed by
the Great Crash of 1929 which, in turn, ushered in the Great Depression
of the 1930s. The 1920s was a decade of sharp decline for the labour
movement. Union membership and activities fell steeply in the face of
economic prosperity, a lack of leadership within the movement, and anti-
union attitudes on the part of both employers and the government. The
unions were much less able to organise strikes.

The Great Depression was the worst economic downturn in US history
and did not abate until the end of the 1930s. By 1933, unemployment
reached 25 per cent with more than 5000 banks going out of business.
Roosevelt's New Deal attempted to mitigate its worst effects but it was
a period when mass strikes dominated the political landscape. Unions
lost members during this time because labourers could not afford to pay
their dues, and also numerous strikes against wage cuts left the unions
impoverished. Cities across the country witnessed local and spontaneous
marches by angry relief applicants. In March 1930, hundreds of thousands of unemployed workers marched through New York City, Detroit,
Washington, San Francisco and other cities in a mass protest organised by
the Communist Party's Unemployed Councils. In 1931, more than 400
relief protests erupted in Chicago and that number grew to 550 in 1932.
The 1936–1937 Flint sit-down strike against General Motors built the
United Automobile Workers (UAW) into a major union and led to the
unionisation of the United States car industry.

Copland's 'Rodeo' suite and his 'Billy the Kid' ballet highlight the
importance of the Wild West in American history: the domestication of
the vast prairie lands, the defeat of the rival European colonial powers
and the destruction of the Native Americans. 'El Salon Mexico', with its
use of Mexican folk music, pays tribute to the role played by the non-
Anglo-Saxon people in the building of America and expresses Copland's
'populism', his celebration of America's pioneer rural communities, his
commitment to ordinary people as opposed to the elite. 'Appalachian

Spring' expresses the innocence and optimism that the world post-1945 would usher in an era of peace and justice (Goodall 2013, p. 290).

Critics accused Copland of demeaning his art by pandering to the taste of the masses. His response was that his approach to music was his method of expressing the way the Depression had affected society. As he put it: 'The composer who is frightened of losing his artistic integrity through contact with a mass audience is no longer aware of the meaning of the word "art"' (Oja and Tick 2005, p. 338).

Tippett's oratorio 'A Child of Our Time' (1939–1941) evolves on two intersecting levels: his own solemn contemplations on the world's mid-century crisis which Ross compares to T.S. Eliot's poetic meditations, and which can perhaps be identified as Tippett's denunciation of the persecution of the Jews, while the second level uses 'redemptive selections' from Johnson's 'Book of American Negro Spirituals' (Ross 2012, pp. 472–473). This can arguably be interpreted as expressing his outrage at anti-black racism. Similarly, the 'War Requiem' combines the Latin text of the Requiem Mass with Wilfred Owen's anti-war poems, conveying a powerful message of peace.

In the 1960s, the start of Tippett's second phase, his style became more experimental, reflecting that decade's social and cultural changes. In the second of the two parts of his Third Symphony with its 'forward-directed music', there are direct references to Beethoven's Ninth Symphony. Coming just after the decade of the 'counterculture', it seems to express the hopes of personal and social liberation felt by an entire generation. Tippett's 'Third Piano Sonata' (1973), with its unstable rhythmic groupings and equivocal, pliable *tonal* vocabulary, produces a sense of flux. Perhaps this denotes the highly complex network of routes towards the other possible world that so many dreamed of in the heady days of the 1960s.

In 1934, 'socialist realism' became Soviet state policy: the First Congress of Soviet Writers met and Stalin's representative Andrei Zhdanov gave a speech strongly endorsing it as 'the official style of Soviet culture'. The purpose of socialist realism was to limit popular culture to a specific, highly regulated style of creative expression that promoted Soviet ideals. There was a prevailing sense of optimism, and socialist realism's function was to project the ideal Soviet society. Not only was the present gloried, but the future was also supposed to be portrayed in a positive light. Because the present and the future were constantly idealised, socialist realism had a sense of forced optimism. Tragedy and negativity were not permitted unless they were shown in a different time or place. Shostakovich's striking, powerful music won him widespread popularity. But his willingness to experiment was less popular with the Stalinist regime that was firmly entrenched by the 1930s. From then until his death in 1975, 'Shostakovitch's relations with the Stalinist authorities was a tense one, in which he struggled to maintain his artistic and political integrity' (Behrman 2006, p. 28).

The trigger for the great crisis in Shostakovitch's's career was his 1934 opera 'Lady Macbeth of Mtensk'. The opera was performed in Leningrad and Moscow to great critical and popular success. It tells the story of a nineteenth-century provincial woman driven to murder by the oppression and boredom of her life. It is a gripping drama, with raucous music which is audaciously modern. It was performed over a hundred times in two years, after which, in 1936, Stalin went to see it. A month later, a savage attack on 'Lady Macbeth' and Shostakovitch's music in general—'Muddle Instead of Music'—appeared in the newspaper 'Pravda': he was accused of being a 'formalist', more interested in playing with musical form and structure than in conveying a clear and simple meaning. The cultural experimentation of the previous decade had given way to the conservatism of socialist realism, according to which art had to serve the interests of the new regime (Behrman 2006, p. 28; Mikkonen in Fairclough 2010, pp. 231–248).

The 'Pravda' article concluded with an ominous warning that if Shostakovich didn't change his ways, 'things will turn out badly for him'. This was no idle threat. 1936 was the year of the first show trials when millions were purged, sent to labour camps or executed. Throughout this time, Shostakovich kept a packed suitcase by his front door, in readiness for the arrival of Stalin's secret police. Julian Barnes' short novel 'The Noise of Time' (2016) graphically conveys the atmosphere of terror pervading Stalin's Russia at the time.

After Stalin's death, the leading Soviet figure Lavrentiy Beria, head of the state security apparatus, initiated a period of relative liberalisation: destalinisation included the release of a million political prisoners, the relaxation of restrictions on private plots and halting the Russification of the republics. Moreover, in 1956 Khruschev shocked his listeners by denouncing Stalin's crimes and cult of personality. He also advocated competition rather than categorical hostility towards, the West.

Shostakovich clearly benefited artistically from destalinisation. His Tenth Symphony composed in 1953, the year Stalin died, contains a second movement which, according to 'Testimony', his alleged memoirs, purports to be a musical portrait of Stalin himself. The symphony 'evokes a sense of evil and frenzy which it would have been hard to have publicly performed in the preceding years. But the symphony is also evidence of a growing introversion in his music' (Behrman 2010, p. 86). The four-note *motif*, representing the composer's initials, seems to express the growing sense of individual freedom attendant upon Stalin's death. However, the Composers' Union condemned the work as 'pessimistic', 'gloomy' and 'modernist', indicating that the thaw following Stalin's death would take time to work its way into the arts. The Thirteenth Symphony's setting of the Yevtushenko poem (1962) dealing with the massacre of Russian Jews expresses Shostakovich's anger and despair at one of the darkest episodes of the twentieth century. His music has highlighted the irrationality and barbarism of a crisis-ridden late capitalism.

Britten's political commitment—to pacifism and against nuclear weapons, to tolerance, to the inclusion of all ages and talents in music-making—imparts to his music a quality of social engagement that has appealed to many performers and listeners as well as inspiring subsequent composers. His 'Violin Concerto' (1940) contains elements of virtuosity but these are balanced by lyrical and elegiac passages, undoubtedly expressing Britten's mounting concern with the escalation of global hostilities. The *passacaglia* in the 'gravely sorrowing finale' memorialises the anti-fascist fighters of the Spanish Civil War (Ross 2012, p. 464). In 1945, Britten witnessed the horrors of Belsen and composed 'The Holy Sonnets of John Donne', one of his bleakest works. The theme of 'Peter Grimes'—the prejudiced crowd that persecutes outsiders on the basis of suspicion and misinformation—would have put into sharp relief the oppression suffered by gay people until the 1967 law reform; but it continues to be highly relevant given its related theme of hostility to foreigners, an aspect of British cultural life highlighted by the victory of the Leave vote in the 2016 European Union referendum.

Messiaen's serialism, its lack of a sense of direction, seems to express a world of which human beings have lost control, one lurching from crisis to crisis, resulting in a profound disorientation, the world of the 1930s and 1940s, the Depression and the horrors of World War Two. And despite full employment in the 1940s and 1950s, there prevails a sense of powerlessness and anonymity, of alienation in the face of corporate and state power. Despite this, Messiaen's sonorous harmony retains hope of a better post-war world.

As we saw, twentieth-century Modernism—Debussy, Schoenberg and the Viennese *atonal* school, Stravinsky, especially his first and last periods contains many novel features including experiments in *tonality, metre,* rhythm, stress and dissonance. It expresses a historical period characterised by crisis, uncertainty and barbarism. It is the music of a century that witnessed two world wars, the Great Depression, Hiroshima and Auschwitz, the continuing threat of nuclear annihilation and, more recently, of planet destruction wrought by climate change, the Coronavirus pandemic and economic crisis.

On the other hand, there is a strong strand of resistance in modern music: its general tenor is radical and critical, with several composers expressing leftwing sympathies or identifying with popular, anti-establishment causes: Bartok, Hindemith, Copland, Tippett and Britten.

No one can predict the course of future music any more than they can foresee the future development of our society wracked as it is by increasingly severe interlocking crises. Of one thing we can be confident: composers will continue to write music, and it will express the crises of our age as well as offering resistance to a world torn apart by them, in which nevertheless the potential of human liberation has not been destroyed.

BIBLIOGRAPHY

Adorno, Theodor W. 2002. Why is the New Art so Hard to Understand? In *Essays on Music,* ed. Richard Leppert. University of California Press.

Bartok, Bela. 1993. *Essays,* ed. Benjamin Suchoff. Lincoln: University of Nebraska Press.

Behrman, Simon. 2006. The Sound of a Soviet Tragedy. *Socialist Review,* September.

Behrman, Simon. 2009. From Revolution to Irrelevance: How Classical Music Lost Its Relevance. *International Socialism Journal,* 121, January.

Brett, Philip, et al. 2001. *Britten, Benjamin.* Grove Music Online. Oxford University Press. Accessed 12 May 2013.

Burkholder, Grout, Palisca. 2014. *A History of Western Music.* New York and London: W. W. Norton & Co.

Clarke, David, Tippett, Sir Michael. 2013. www.oxfordmusiconline.com. Grove Music Online.

COMBAT—The Theoretical Journal of the Communist League, June 1978, Part 4. *The Hungarian 'Soviet Republic' of 1919.*

Davies, Peter Maxwell, Maw, Nicholas, Gruber, HK, Hollway, Robin, Hall, Martin, *Benjamin Britten, Tributes and Memories. Tempo.* New Series, No. 120, March 1977.

Evans, Richard. 2017. *The Pursuit of Power: Europe, 1815–1914.* London: Penguin Books.

Fairclough, P. (ed.) 2010. *Shostakovich Studies 2.* Cambridge: Cambridge University Press, November.

Goodall, Howard. 2013. *The Story of Music.* London: Vintage Books.

Griffiths, Paul. 1978. *A Concise History of Modern Music: From Debussy to Boulez.* London: Thames and Hudson.

Hindley, Geoffrey (ed.). 1971. *The Larousse Encyclopedia of Music.* Hamlyn Publishing Group.

Hobsbawm, Eric. 1968. *Industry and Empire.* London: Weidenfeld and Nicolson.

Hobsbawm, Eric. 1975. *The Age of Capital.* London: Weidenfeld and Nicolson.

Kaslow, David. *About This Recording—HINDEMITH: Kammermusik No 2/Concert Music for Viola/Piano Concerto.* www.naxos.com/mainsite/blurbs_reviews.asp?item_code=FECD0022&catNum=FECD-0022&filetype=Aboutt hisRecording&language=English.

Kemp, Ian. 1987. *Tippett: The Composer and His Music.* Oxford Paperbacks.

Kennedy, Michael. 2006. *Impressionism.* The Oxford Dictionary of Music, 2nd ed., ed. J. Bourne. Oxford and New York: OUP.

Kroo, Gyorgy. 1974. *A Guide to Bartok*, trans. Ruth Pataki and Maria Steiner. Budapest: Corvina Press.

Lunn, Eugene. 1985. *Marxism and Modernism.* Verso.

Morgan, Robert P. 1991. *Twentieth Century Music: A History of Musical Style in Modern Europe and America.* New York: W.W. Norton & Co.

Matthews, David. 2013. *Britten.* London: Haus Publishing.

Mikkonen, Simon in JY—'*Muddle Instead of Music*' in *1936: Cataclysm of Musical Administration.* In ed. P. Fairclough. *Shostakovich Studies 2*, November 2010, Cambridge University Press (JY—University of Jyvaskla. Electronic reprint of original article).

Mitchell, Donald. 2011. *Britten, (Edward) Benjamin, Baron Britten (1913–1976).* Oxford Dictionary of National Biography, Oxford University Press, 2004, online January 2011

Morgan, Robert, P. 1991. *Twentieth Century Music: A History of Musical Style in Modern Europe and America.* New York: W. W. Norton & Co.

Murchison, Gayle. 2012. *The American Stravinsky: The Style and Aesthetics of Copland's New American Music, The Early Works, 1921–1938.* Ann Arbor: University of Michigan Press.

Oja, Carol and Judith Tick. 2005. *Aaron Copland and His World.* Princeton: Princeton University Press.

Pollack, Howard. 1999. *Aaron Copland and His World*. New York: Henry Holt & Co.

Powell, Neil. 2013. *Britten: A Life for Music*. London: Hutchinson.

Rohac, Dalibor. 2009. Why Did the Austro-Hungarian Empire Collapse? A Public Choice Perspective. *Constitutional Political Economy*, 20 (June).

Ross, Alex. 2012. *The Rest Is Noise: Listening to the Twentieth Century*. London: Fourth Estate.

Schneider, David E. 2011. *A Context for Bela Bartok on the Eve of World War II: The Violin Concerto (1938)*. www.yumpu.com. Online magazine, 2011.

Smith, Julia. 1953. *Aaron Copland*. New York: E.P. Dutton & Co.

Taruskin, Richard. 2009. *On Russian Music*. Berkeley and Los Angeles: University of California Press.

Taylor, Ronald, translation editor. 1977. *Aesthetics and Politics*. NLB.

Whittall, Arnold. 1982. *The Music of Britten and Tippett*. Cambridge University Press.

GLOSSARY

A Cappella without instrumental accompaniment.

Adagio in an easy, slow, graceful manner.

Allegro brisk and lively movement.

Andante played moderately slowly.

Appassionato with passion.

Appoggiatura embellishing note preceding an essential melodic note.

Arabesque short, decorative composition.

Architecture (or form) the overall structure or plan of a composition.

Arch or Bridge larger symmetrical patterns constructed by using movements paired through motivic and formal correspondences.

Arioso vocal style more melodic than recitative but less formal than an aria.

Arpeggio notes of chord played successively.

Ballade composition in a narrative style, usually for piano.

Bar/measure in musical notation, a bar (or measure) is a segment of time corresponding to a specific number of beats in which each beat is represented by a particular note value and the boundaries of the bar are indicated by vertical lines.

Barcarolle Venetian boat song characterised by alternation of a strong and a weak beat in 6/8 time suggesting a rowing rhythm.

Basso Continuo part for a keyboard or stringed instrument written as a succession of bass notes with figures indicating the required chords. Also known as *thoroughbass*.

© The Editor(s) (if applicable) and The Author(s) 2021
S. Sagall, *MUSIC and CAPITALISM*,
Critical Political Theory and Radical Practice,
https://doi.org/10.1057/978-1-137-52095-1

Bel Canto Italian operatic style stressing ease, purity, evenness of tone and an agile and precise vocal technique.

Binary having two subjects or themes, or else two complementary sections or main melodic phrases.

Bitonal consisting of two musical keys played simultaneously.

Block a texture in which the pitches of the accompanying harmony move in the same rhythm as the main melody. Texture is how the melodic, harmonic and rhythmic materials are combined.

Bolero music for lively Spanish dance, characterized by sharp turns, stamping and sudden pauses.

Bravura flamboyant style.

Buffo/Buffa in the comic style; also, a singer that signs comic parts.

Cadence/Cadential a chord sequence moving to a harmonic close or point of rest, giving a sense of harmonic completion.

Cadenza a showy improvised passage or flourish in a concerto, improvised solo ornamental passage in a concerto for virtuosic display.

Canon composition for two or more voices or instruments in which the melody is repeated by successively entering performers.

Cantabile melodious, in a singing manner.

Cantata choral composition comprising choruses, solos, recitatives and orchestral accompaniment.

Canzone polyphonic setting of a medieval Italian or Provencal song or ballad; type of lyric resembling a madrigal. Short instrumental piece.

Cavatina a short, simple operatic solo; an instrumental composition in a similar style, usually with a slow tempo.

Cell small rhythmic and melodic design that can be isolated or making up one part of a thematic context, smallest indivisible unit, unlike a *motif* which might be divisible into more than one cell.

Chaconne composition typically consisting of variations on a repeated succession of chords.

Chordal relating to music characterised more by harmony than counterpoint.

Chromatic/Chromaticism frequent use of semi-tones or intervals or notes outside the diatonic scale—a feature heightening tension.

Coda concluding section formally distinct from the main structure.

Coloratura elaborate embellishment especially in vocal music.

Colour (or timbre) quality given to a sound by its overtones, i.e. quality of tone distinctive of a particular singing voice or instrument. For example, it is the difference in sound between a guitar and a piano playing the same note at the same volume.

Con fuoco with fire.

Concertante a piece of music containing one or more solo parts, typically of less prominence than in a concerto.

Concord harmonious combinations of simultaneously heard notes.

Consonance agreeable combination of notes in harmony.

Continuo part for a keyboard or stringed instrument written as a succession of bass notes with figures indicating the required chords; also, (the instruments playing) a continuo accompaniment.

Crescendo increased volume.

Da capo from the beginning.

Development the second of three parts of a movement in sonata style, in which the main theme is divided up and elaborated.

Diatonic/Diatonicism the system of keys consisting of twenty-four major and minor scales of 8 notes each without chromatic deviation. It was the basis of western art music since the seventeenth century, providing a coherent framework within which composers oriented themselves.

Diminished an interval reduced by a semitone.

Diminished Seventh Chord a seventh four-note chord composed of a root note, together with a minor third, a diminished fifth, and a diminished seventh above the root.

Diminuendo decreased volume.

Diminution the writing of a theme in shorter note values than the original.

Dolce in a sweet, soft and tender manner.

Dominant fifth note of the diatonic scale or a chord beginning on the fifth note.

Dorian mode mode represented on the white keys of the piano on a scale from D to D.

Doubling performance of melody with itself transposed at a constant interval such as an octave.

Downbeat the principally accented note (e.g. the first) of a bar.

Drone unvarying sustained bass note.

Dumka Slavic epic ballad.

Duple meter two or multiple of two beats per bar.

Dynamics variation and contrast in sound volume.

Ecossaise music for lively folk dance, originally Scottish, in duple time.

Enharmonic identical notes written differently—C sharp or D flat—i.e. notes that are very close in pitch.

Episode a digressive subdivision either derived from the main theme as in a fugue or completely new material on the plan A B A C A, where A is the principal theme and B and C the episodes.

Etude a piece written primarily for the practice of a technique; a study.

Euphony pleasantness of sound.

Exposition first part of usually three parts of a composition in sonata form in which the theme is presented in two contrasting keys.

Fantasia free instrumental composition not in strict form.

Figuration embellishment/ornamentation of a passage through using musical figures.

Figure a short phrase or group of notes forming a natural unit of melody.

Finale the last movement of an orchestral composition.

Fioritura decoration of a melody especially by vocalists and violinists.

Flutter-tongue a wind instrument tonguing technique in which performers flutter their tongue to make a characteristic "FrrrrFrrrrr" sound. The effect varies according to the instrument and at what volume it is played, ranging from cooing sounds on a recorder to an effect similar to the growls used by jazz musicians.

Form type of work, e.g. symphony, concerto, sonata, aria, chamber music; or the structure of a piece of music.

Forte/fortissimo loud, very loud.

Fourth/Fifth harmonic combination of two notes at an interval of four or five diatonic degrees.

Fugato passage in the style but not in the strict form of a fugue.

Fugue composition in which one or two themes are repeated or imitated by successive instruments or voices in a continuous interweaving of the parts.

Furiant spirited Bohemian dance tune with shifting accents.

Glissando rapid sliding up and down the scale.

Ground bass short bass passage continually repeated below constantly changing melody and harmony.

Head-motive (German: *Kopfmotiv*) musical idea at the opening of a set of movements that serves to unite those movements.

Hemiola rhythmic alteration consisting of three beats instead of two or vice versa.

Hexachord A diatonic series of six notes having a semitone between the third and fourth notes, but used more freely in the twentieth century.

Homogeneous either when something is composed of parts or elements that are all of the same kind or nature, essentially alike. Any number of instruments of the same kind performing together is essentially a homogeneous musical combination, for example, a choir or a violin quartet.

Homophony music in which all the parts move together, according to the same rhythm.

Impromptu composition usually for piano suggesting improvisation.

Intermezzo movement between major sections of an extended work; short, independent instrumental composition often for piano.

Interval difference in pitch between two notes.

Introit piece of music sung at the beginning of a church service.

Inversion changing the relative positions of the elements of an interval, chord or phrase.

Landler Austrian country dance in slow waltz time.

Larghetto composition or movement slower than andante but not as slow as largo.

Largo slow and broad.

Legato performing musical passage in smooth, connected manner.

Leitmotif a theme or musical phrase in an opera or symphonic poem denoting an idea, particular character(s), situation, places, idea or plot element.

Lied German song, especially a nineteenth-century setting of a lyrical poem for solo voice and piano.

Lydian mode scale on white keys from F to F. The modern version is a seven tone musical scale with a rising pattern of pitches comprising three whole tones, a semitone, two more whole tones, and a final semitone.

Maestoso majestic style, usually in moderate tempo.

Major/Minor A major scale is a scale in which the third scale degree (the mediant) is a major third above the tonic note. In a minor scale, the third degree is a minor third above the tonic.

Mazurka Polish folk dance in triple metre.

Mediant third note of a diatonic scale.

Melisma group of notes or tones sung on a single syllable, as found in plainsong, for display or greater expressiveness.

Metre basic recurrent rhythmical pattern of accents and beats per bar.

Microtonal intervals smaller than a semitone

Minuet a slow graceful dance in triple time.

Mode an arrangement of the eight diatonic notes of an octave in any of several fixed schemes using different patterns of whole tones and semitones between successive notes.

Modes/modal pre-diatonic (major/minor) harmonic and rhythmic systems characteristic of pre-Renaissance church music.

Modulation moving through a succession of keys, often to express sudden emotional shifts.

Monody style of accompanied solo song consisting of a vocal line, frequently embellished and with simple, often expressive, harmonies.

Monophony a single melodic line with no accompaniment.

Motif/Motive recurrent phrase, figure or theme developed through the course of a composition.

Motivic saturation deriving extended musical material from embryonic themes.

Myxolydian mode G to G on the white notes.

Neotonal twentieth century compositions in which traditional tonality is replaced by non-traditional tonal conceptions, such as tonal assertion or contrapuntal motion around a central chord.

Note value duration of a note.

Octatonic any eight-note scale, usually one in which the notes ascend in alternating intervals of whole tone and semi-tone.

Octave the chord created by the same notes at different pitches.

Oratorio choral work based on religious subject consisting of arias, recitatives and choruses.

Ornamentation art of embellishing a melody widely practised in the seventeenth and eighteenth centuries.

Ostinato figure repeated persistently at the same pitch throughout a composition.

Ostinato basso A short bass pattern repeated many times unchanged, above which melodic variations appear.

Parallel a major and minor scale sharing the same tonic are called parallel keys—e.g. G major and G minor have different modes but the same tonic.

Parallel organum a style of composition based on plainsong or plainchant (e.g. Gregorian chanting). 'Organum' is a form of polyphony developed in the Middle Ages in which at least one voice is added to the melody to enhance the harmony.

Passacaglia instrumental composition in moderately slow triple time consisting of variations usually on a *ground bass*.

Pentatonic scale consisting of five notes with the notes arranged like a major scale with the fourth and seventh notes omitted.

Period two phrases, two bars each, antecedent and consequent, each beginning with the same basic motif.

Phrase group of notes forming a natural unit of melody.

Phrygian mode scale on white keys from E to E.

Piano/pianissimo quiet, very quiet.

Pitch property of a sound, e.g. a note, determined by the frequency of waves producing it—highness or lowness of sound.

Pitch cell small groups of related pitches handled in different ways so as to create new material.

Pitch-class a set of the same pitches that are octaves apart, eg, the pitch class C consists of the Cs across all the octaves, similarly with all the notes of the scale. Pitch classes are labelled with numbers 1-12: all C notes are labelled 0, all D flats and C sharps 1, and so on.

Pitch repertory group of notes.

Pivot chords also known as 'common' chords are used when music modulates from one key to the next. The pivot chord will be a chord that both keys share. For example, modulating from C Major to G Major.

Pizzicato notes played by plucking instead of bowing a stringed instrument.

Plagal of a church mode having a keynote on the fourth note of the scale.

Plagal cadence cadence passing from a subdominant to a tonic chord.

Polka Czech dance based on half-steps.

Polonaise music in moderate time for a stately Polish processional dance popular in nineteenth century Europe.

Polyphony/polyphonic style in which two or more separate voices sound against one another, an interweaving of vocal lines.

Polytonal simultaneous use of two or more keys.

Prelude short, separate concert piece, usually for piano or orchestra.

Presto/prestissimo rapid/very rapid tempo.

Principle of variation technique where material is repeated in an altered form, involving either melody, rhythm, harmony, counterpoint, timbre, orchestration or any combination of these.

Programme-music this covers a wide spectrum, from representing particular events, as in Berlioz's *Symphonie Fantastique*, to a more general evocation of ideas and emotions, as in some of Liszt's symphonic poems.

Quadri pieces in four parts of which only one has melodic significance.

Quaver eighth note, a note with the time value of half a crotchet.

Recapitulation last of three parts of a movement written in sonata form in which the main theme is repeated with modifications.

Recitative a passage delivered in a style for singing a narrative text in which the rhythms and variations in pitch of the speaking voice are imitated.

Register/Registral layout Range of a voice or instrument, setting out a range of notes.

Relative of major and minor keys and scales, notes, chords or tonalities that have close harmonic connections.

Resolution progression of a series of voices, notes or chords to consonance or cadential rest in the tonic.

Rest period of silence.

Ricercare any of the various forms of usually contrapuntal music, especially of the sixteenth and seventeenth centuries.

Ritornello short recurrent instrumental piece in a vocal or orchestral composition.

Romanza/Romance short, lyrical piece.

Rondo form symmetrical movement in an instrumental composition, especially a concerto or sonata, with a principal theme that alternates with episodes on the plan A B A C A, where A is the principal theme, and B and C the episodes. A piece of music where the musical material stated at the beginning of the piece keeps returning.

Root-position note from whose overtones a chord is composed.

Rubato expressive fluctuation of speed within a phrase in a work.

Sarabande a composition or movement in slow triple time with the accent on the second beat—a stately court dance resembling the minuet.

Scale/Scalar graduated series of notes ascending or descending in order of pitch according to a specified scheme of their intervals.

Scena dramatic solo usually including recitative.

Scherzando played in a playful, sprightly manner.

Scherzo lively, instrumental composition or movement in quick, usually triple, time.

Secco recitative ('dry recitative') is sung with a free rhythm dictated by the accents of the words. Accompaniment, usually by *continuo* (cello and harpsichord), is simple and chordal. The melody approximates speech by using only a few pitches.

Sequence succession of repetitions of a melodic phrase or harmonic pattern, each in a new position.

Seventh chord harmonic combination of two notes at an interval of seven diatonic tones.

Sforzando accented note or chord.

Singspiele a kind of German light opera with spoken dialogue.

Sixth chord triad with an added sixth note, usually the first inversion of the triad.

Soli performance of a passage along with an entire section of an ensemble.

Solo composition/performance by a single voice or instrument with or without accompaniment.

Sonata musical form used especially for the first movement of a sonata, symphony, concerto, etc. consisting of an exposition, a development, and a recapitulation in which two themes are usually introduced, developed and then repeated.

Sonority giving out sound.

Sprechtstimme a type of vocal delivery somewhere between speech and song.

Staccato playing in a sharp, disconnected or abrupt manner.

Step a step, or conjunct motion, is the difference in pitch between two consecutive notes of a musical scale. In other words, it is the interval between two consecutive scale degrees. Any larger interval is called a skip (also called a leap), or disjunct motion. In the diatonic scale, a step is either a minor second (sometimes also called *half step*) or a major second (sometimes also called *whole step*), with all intervals of a minor third or larger being skips. For example, C–D (major second) is a step, whereas C–E (major third) is a skip.

Stretto overlapping of answer with subject in fugue or part of fugue characterised by this overlapping. In non-fugal compositions, stretto (or stretta) is accelerating coda or finale.

Strophic song using the same music for successive stanzas.

Subdominant fourth note of the diatonic scale.

Submediant sixth note of a diatonic scale.

Suite seventeenth and eighteenth-century instrumental form consisting of a series of dances; modern instrumental composition in several movements of different character.

Sul ponticello on the bridge of a bowed string instrument.

Supertonic second note of the diatonic scale.

Symmetry the quality of being made up of exactly similar parts facing each other or around an axis. The inversion of a 'figure'.

Symphonic (tone) poem extended orchestral composition, based on a legend, tale, etc. and freer than a symphony.

Tarantella music in 6/8 time alternating between major and minor keys, associated with vivacious folk dance of southern Italy.

Tempo speed of a piece or passage indicated by a series of directions, often by an exact metronome marking.

Ternary the main theme appearing three times or more, or in which the third part is a repetition of the first, with a contrasting section in the middle, and sometimes with a coda—concluding section. The second theme is played in a related key.

Texture how the tempo, melodic, and harmonic materials are combined in a composition, thus determining the overall quality of the sound: pattern of sound created by notes or lines played or sung together.

Theme/thematic melodic subject of a composition or movement.

    Monothematic having one theme.

    Bithematic having two themes.

Third harmonic combination of two notes at an interval of three diatonic degrees.

Tied note curved line joining two identical notes to denote a single sustained note with the time value of the two.

Timbre (or colour) quality given to a sound by its overtones, i.e. quality of tone distinctive of a particular singing voice or instrument. For example, it is the difference in sound between a guitar and a piano playing the same note at the same volume.

Toccata composition in a free style, with rapid runs, usually for keyboard instrument.

Tonality organisation of notes and chords of a piece in relation to the tonic. Character of a piece as determined by the key in which it is played.

Tone sound of a definite frequency with relatively weak overtones.

Tonic first note of the diatonic scale.

Transitional passage leading from one section of a piece to another.

Tremolo/Tremolando rapid repetition of notes to produce a tremulous effect.

Triad/triadic a chord consisting of a root (the first), third and fifth notes of the scale—e.g. C, E, G, with its third and fifth—constituting the harmonic basis of tonal music.

Trio composition for three instruments or voices; the contrasting secondary part of a minuet, scherzo, etc.

Triple meter marked by three beats per bar.

Tritone interval of three whole tones or six semitones.

Tutti passage to be played by the whole orchestra.

Upbeat unaccented (e.g. the last) beat in a bar, when the conductor's baton is moving upwards before the main beat.

Upper Neighbour the tone which is a step higher in pitch than the surrounding chord tones.

Verismo similarity to life and to spoken drama.

Waltz music in the tempo of ballroom dance with a strong accent on the first beat and a basic pattern of step-step-close.

Whole tone interval comprising 2 semitones (e.g. C–D or G–A).

Index

© The Editor(s) (if applicable) and The Author(s) 2021
S. Sagall, *MUSIC and CAPITALISM*,
Critical Political Theory and Radical Practice,
https://doi.org/10.1057/978-1-137-52095-1

Nocturne in G Minor, Opus 15,
No. 3, 167, 223
Piano Sonata B Flat Minor, Opus
35, 170
Polonaise in D Minor, Opus 71,
No. 1, 170
Polonaises, 167, 170
Prelude in A Minor, Opus 28, 223
Prelude in G Major, 168
Prelude No. 2 in A Minor, 169
Prelude No. 4 in E Minor, 169
Prelude No. 7 in A Major, 169
Preludes, 169
Scherzos, 168
Tarantella, 170
Waltzes, 152, 167
Chromatic/chromaticism, 153
Clementi, Muzio, 35, 93
Commedia dell'arte, 55
Concerti grossi, 32
Copland, Aaron
Appalachian Spring, 296
Billy the Kid, 295
Clarinet Concerto, 296
Connotations, 297
Duo for Flute and Piano, 297
El Salon Mexico, 295
Fanfare for the Common Man, 296
Inscape, 297
Lincoln Portrait, 293
Music for Radio: Saga of the Prairie,
295
Music for the Theater, 294
Nonet for Strings, 297
Of Mice and Men, 296
Old American Songs, 297
Our Town, 296
Piano Concerto, 294
Piano Quartet, 297
Piano Sonata, 296
Piano Variations, 294
Prairie Journal, 295

Quartet for Piano and Strings, 297
Rodeo, 296
Short Symphony, 294
Sonata for Violin and Piano, 296
Statements for Orchestra, 295
Symphonic Ode, 294
Symphony No. 1 for Organ and
Orchestra, 294
Symphony No. 3, 296
The Second Hurricane, 295
Twelve Poems of Emily Dickinson,
297
Vitebsk, Study on a Jewish Theme
for Piano Trio, 294
Corelli, Arcangelo, 23, 27
Trio Sonatas, Opus 1, 2, 3 and 4,
26, 33
Counterpoint, 21
Counter-Reformation, 64
Couperin, Francois, 24
Cowell, Henry, 271
Crumb, George, 258

D
Dante, Alighieri, 177
Darwin, Charles, 7
Debussy, Claude, 164, 251
Children's Corner, 253
Estampes, 253
Golliwog's Cakewalk, 253
Images, 258
L'Isle Joyeuse, 257
La Catedrale Engloutie, 254
La Mer—Jeux de Vagues, 255
Nocturnes, 254
Pagodes, 253
Pelleas et Melisande, 254
Prelude a l'Apres-Midi d'un Faune,
240
Preludes For Piano, 258
Sonata for Cello and Piano, 258